JESUS – BUDDHIST FACT AND CHRISTIAN FABLE
2000 YEARS OF MISINTERPRETATION

Jesus – Buddhist Fact and Christian Fable
2000 Years of Misinterpretation

PAUL FOSTER

UPFRONT PUBLISHING
CAMBRIDGESHIRE

Jesus – Buddhist Fact and Christian Fable
2000 Years of Misinterpretation
Copyright © Paul Foster 2004

ISBN 1-84426-264-2

First published 2004 by
UPFRONT PUBLISHING LTD
Cambridgeshire

Printed by CopyTECH (UK) Limited

In memory of Max Sprecher,
Jew, friend and saint who, after internment in
Sachsenhausen, Oranienburg and finally Auschwitz
bore no resentment for any man, but at the end of his life
warned us that the greatest enemy of man was his ego,
which, he said, was the true devil within us all.

CONTENTS

AUTHOR BIOGRAPHY

Cedric Paul Foster was born in Leicester in 1935 and studied at Loughborough College and the Leicester Colleges of Art and Technology before entering the army as a national serviceman in 1952. After leaving the army, he gathered experience in various walks of life before finally deciding on a career in teaching. He graduated from the University of London (BA Hons) in English Literature (1968) and shortly afterwards accepted a post teaching English at the University of Heidelberg, Germany where he later received an MA (1972) and PhD in English and East Asian Studies (1980). He also taught at the University of Tübingen and concluded his academic career at the University of Mainz, Germany. His interest in comparative religion began at fifteen with a search for truth, which was to continue for the next forty-five years. In 1958 he took up the study of Zen Buddhism and has practised both the Rinzai and Soto schools of Buddhism for many years. He is also an accomplished pianist and has played publicly. Apart from music, his hobbies are European history, especially that of France and Germany, and also the writing of fiction. He has written thirty-eight short stories and two novels to date. This is his third publication.

FOREWORD

The phenomenon of Man's emergence from his animal origins is a tragic record of mindless violence lit here and there by the sanity of creation and invention. Every civilisation which flourished in the past was blighted sooner or later by the horror of war, where, for a time, the subconscious, instinctive, irrational elements of his make-up were allowed full expression. In retrospect, the process of his development can be seen as a series of brutal convulsions followed by longer or shorter intervals of intelligent activity. The Old Testament is a graphic example of this phenomenon as it affected the Jewish people over several thousand years, and the same process of hate and violence continues today. The trade in arms is the biggest business in the world and occupies more scientific brain than any other area of research. Only sixty years ago, *homo sapiens* was embroiled in an international struggle which could well have resulted in Armageddon. During it, this same species systematically destroyed its own kind by the million, and, looking back, those who experienced it recognise it as a descent into nightmare. After the 1939–45 war was over, thinking people, whatever their religious affiliations, were forced by the appalling spectacle of horror and carnage it left in its wake to ask themselves where their God had been during this time So much, many of them said, for our Jewish dedication and our Christian conviction. Naked reality has made a mockery of our principles and a laughing stock of our faith. It was clear then as now in the light of subsequent wars and human aberration that something is seriously amiss. Either there is no God, we argue, or there has been a gross misunderstanding both of ourselves and of our religion. It was also clear that after Hiroshima and Nagasaki, Auschwitz and Treblinka, no God had taken a hand in guiding our political affairs, still less in protecting a 'chosen people'. In view of what had happened, both ideas could be seen as absurd. The sobering truth which has since dawned upon us is that, apart from the haphazard intervention of fate, we ourselves are responsible for the quality and direction of our lives.

Today, with the immense power in our hands to destroy both ourselves and our environment, we human beings face a momentous decision. Either we get to grips at last with our archaic, instinctive reactions, our egotistical, self-centred, exploitative, predatory compulsions or we go under. Either we conquer the foe within or be hoisted by our own petard.

A universal attempt to free ourselves from our sheep-like bondage to instinctive reaction by taking an unflinching look at ourselves and so discover the cause of our conditioning and the source of our reactive habits would be to herald in the greatest revolution in human history. It would be a greater discovery even than the invention of the wheel. To take this first precious step forward and away from the path of a long, horrific period of adolescence, of ignorance and bestiality and step out towards spiritual adulthood would be to create our own heaven on earth.

So far, our religions which, ideally, should be responsible for this step, have been singularly unsuccessful either in greatly improving our human lot or revolutionizing human behaviour for the better. Most of them today are so deeply identified with the particulars of their tradition that there is no desire to inquire into the nature of their origins, much less to abandon anything of that tradition for a more efficient, more rational way of bringing men and women to a state of raised consciousness where they can recognise their true nature and that which identifies them with all human beings. Notwithstanding, sooner rather than later, we will have to take measures to look inward, not outward, as has long been our habit, and so rationalise our conduct – with or without the help of a religion. The time is ripe now for that to happen.

Of all religions, only Buddhism gives explicit instructions on how to be become aware of the fatal tendency on our part to react to conditional patterns of thought and emotion and so through this awareness eventually free ourselves of their bondage. This is not to elevate Buddhism above other religions, but to state a fact. Christianity in the form we have inherited from St. Paul and in the interpretation handed down by the church has done little or nothing to universally liberate the mind of Man from his preoccupation with self and, consequently, to deliver it from all the evil which issues from this concern which is clear proof of its inefficiency. While this is true, by and large, the fact is that, hidden behind the words of Christ, as with all the great masters of the past, lie the means to that liberation. To discover what they are, however, necessitates a wholly different interpretation of his words than those current in our bibles. What this entails is explained in the following pages as an alternative interpretation.

The essay is not a plea for Buddhism, nor is it a study in comparative religion. Neither is it an exhaustive scholarly investigation. It is not a definitive argument, but rather a seminal introduction to other possibilities of thought than those to which Christians are generally used. It is an endeavour to point out that there *is* another, more tenable, provable way of reading the New Testament and, therefore, of appreciating Christian teaching than that propagated hitherto. This is its postulation.

Buddhism is used as a tool to demonstrate this thesis and Zen Buddhism in particular has been employed as a helpful source of example and illustration. The essay itself issues not from academic study alone, but from many years of practical acquaintance with both religions.

As in the accomplishment of any work, an author owes much to the assistance of others. I would like here, therefore, to acknowledge a debt of gratitude to friends, living and dead, who have accompanied me some of the way through life over the last fifty years. All of them have greatly enriched my life in one way or another. They are first of all: my loving parents, my wife, Helga for all her patience and loving kindness, A.P. Winterton, a former guide, A.A. Newman, pianist, cellist and friend, both men of exemplary character, the late Zen Master, Sochu Suzuki Roshi, formerly Abbot of Ryutaki-ji, Japan, Dae Peop Sa Nim, Zen master resident in Hawaii and Paris, Sri Bala Sai Baba the Younger of Kurnool, India, the late H.W.L. Poonja, Indian sage and teacher, formerly of Lucknow, India, from whom I learned much, and the late Gesshe Myoko Prabhasha Roshi of the International Zen Institute in Los Angeles to whom I owe a debt of gratitude and thanks, and also to the many other people of long or short acquaintance with whom I have walked and talked through life or with whom I have sat in Zen meditation. My immediate and warmest thanks are also owed to Mr Vincent Timewell for his patient reading and correction of the manuscript drafts as also to Mr Tony Pope for the same demanding and time-consuming work during the compilation of this book. I have also to thank my wife for her careful assessment of content and layout and the many helpful suggestions given both before and during its creation and preparation. Finally, my warmest thanks are due to Frau Angelika Ratzel, my former secretary, for the patient and accurate typing of the manuscript, her integrity and reliability, and the many practical suggestions she has made along the way.

Heidelberg, Germany, 2002

INTRODUCTION

The missing link between ape and man – that's us.
Konrad Lorenz

The purpose of this essay is to speak of a truth which lies at the heart of Christianity. It asserts that the Christian message as we know it has been much misunderstood and, therefore, misinterpreted from the very beginning. As a result, the organisation we recognise as 'Christianity' is something of a caricature of the intrinsic teaching put forward by Jesus 2000 years ago. This would perhaps be an impudent claim were it not for three stubborn facts which cannot be overlooked in any honest consideration of the subject today.

The first is that the 'kingdom of Heaven' has not descended to the world in any way suggested in the Bible or by the Church in its interpretation of that idea in the last two thousand years. Except for the ubiquitous presence of technological advance, which is only now beginning in some ways to modify human outlook, together with a great increase in population, and the physical modification of our environment resulting from these, human nature has not changed much. We have still not grown out of our primitive reflex to wage war as a solution to our problems, for example, and have twice witnessed war as an international phenomenon in the last 100 years, in which our native intelligence has been enlisted to produce death and destruction on an enormous scale. Weaponry, the means to kill and destroy a greater number of people more quickly and effectively in the shortest possible time is at the top of government priorities almost everywhere. So much, we might say, for the message of 'peace on earth and goodwill to all men'. In retrospect, we see that in the past, war and violence have been so much an intrinsic part of our history that we could even speak of our political history as the history of war. Looking more intently at our human record, we also see that we have enslaved each other for generations with political, economic and religious systems and that wherever we go, we murder, exploit and destroy.

Today, surrounded by the remarkable achievements of our scientific prowess, we still torture and eliminate opposition, politically 'cleanse' and murder for our convictions. We – and here one may speak generally of the nominal Christian – still have our tyrants and dictators, our secret police, our concentration camps, our pogroms and persecutions and, only a few years ago, we witnessed a maniac in our midst who at the end of his career would have cheerfully sacrificed the whole of the western civilized world to sate his own ego and who, moreover, managed during it to be responsible for scores of millions of human lives and untold suffering. As for ourselves, we plunder the earth and the sea in our greed to make money for the few under the present dispensation and are glad in this pursuit to exploit each other, animals by the hundred million, plant life on land, the fish in the sea and the world's resources in general as if all this cheap, low-minded criminal behaviour were respectable.

This, surely, is not the kingdom of God on earth envisaged by the gifted, wandering young mendicant who preached his message of love in the sun of ancient Palestine two thousand years ago. The truth is that there has been no sign of the Son of Man descending in 'clouds of glory' to redeem the world **(Mt. 13:26–30)**, and no Saviour of mankind; neither has there been detectable divine interference in our general development and no great changes in our mental horizons. Whether it is palatable to Christians or not, we are forced by the incontestable facts of our social, political and religious history over the last two millennia to admit that our mental development on the whole has not been a chapter of intelligent progression towards more happiness and humanity, but, by and large, a chronicle of crime, rapine, moral infantilism and instinctive, irrational behaviour – facts which argue well for our simian ancestry.

This is not, of course, to wilfully ignore the changes brought about by science which have made life healthier, more interesting and more comfortable for many millions of people. Neither is it to deny the benefit to humanity of art in all its forms wherever it is found, nor the good in the world, nor the undoubted good also found in the history of Christian practice. These, too, are equally incontestable facts found woven into our human history. The point here is to draw our attention to the fact that these achievements owe their origins to a capacity within us which has nothing to do with 'religion' as we normally understand that word, despite the fact that in some places and at some times 'religion' has been the source of their inspiration. Science and great art, it is suggested, both have their origins in another area of the human psyche which is to be discussed later and which is the main theme of this work.

The second fact to be considered in asserting that the Christian message has been distorted is the very large amount of research which has been undertaken on the Gospels and other biblical texts in the last 100 years, and particularly those carried out since 1950, which demonstrate that much has to be changed. This biblical research has been conducted on scientific lines by representatives of different nations and includes many different fields of study. A few of them are mentioned here to give some idea of the scope of that activity.

First of all and of great importance is textual analysis (philology, linguistics), which embraces the careful, scientific comparison of ancient languages, letter form, structure and development, and other areas of exploration as well as, for example, the chemistry of paper and leather, and other ancient writing materials and their examination at microscopic level in determining their age and composition. Archaeology has also naturally played a large role in site investigation, and in addition chemical analysis has aided these explorations with the analyses of materials which include earth, bone, wood, metals, pottery, and so forth. Other disciplines such as comparative architecture, the study of ancient political and social history, biology, physiology and anatomy (concerning the circumstances of the crucifixion for example), medicine, metallurgy, geography and, in the study of region, climatic conditions and orientation, botany (for example in determining the origin of the Turin Shroud), astronomy (in ascertaining the truth of the report of the star in the account given in **Mt. 2:1**), palaeontology and anthropology have played a part in tracing the development of man from the scientific point of view, and much more.

The conclusive facts gathered from these studies have served either to modify, supplement, correct, discredit or support the biblical accounts given in the Gospels and thus widen our knowledge of the times and events. For example, in the matter of supplementation and correction, medical experts have now made it quite clear that crucifixion did not involve piercing the hands as is so often represented on crosses in Christian places of worship and in portraits of the Passion down the ages, but has established that the nails in this process were hammered through the wrists, and that the arms were, in practically all cases, supported by rope to the crossbar. The breaking of the legs of victims alluded to in **Jn 19:31** (the victim probably died of asphyxiation in such a case) referred to in the Bible apparently took place to hasten death for some reason or other and is quite likely to have taken place as the biblical version relates, and in this particular instance to avoid the spectacle of the victim hanging from a cross during the Sabbath.

Correction has been necessary, for example, in fixing the date of Christ's birth, and also the place of his birth and thoughtful investigation has thrown considerable doubt on the story of the later Slaying of the Innocents ostensibly ordered by Herod, an enormity which, if it occurred on the scale suggested by the New Testament rendering **(Mt. 2:16)**, could not possibly have gone unrecorded in secular literature. However, the fact is that there is no report of such an event, nor even the faintest reference to it anywhere else but in the Gospels. The reference in the Bible at **Mt. 16:18** in identifying the disciple, Peter, as the future head of the Roman Church, the 'rock' on which this organisation was to be founded after the death of his master, has been exposed by scholars as a falsification added later to the original text, as has also the ostensible reference to Jesus by Josephus in a tract which describes him as 'a wise man who, through the incitement on the part of our venerable elders was condemned by Pilate to death on the cross.'

In the important matter of textual analysis, the absence of any reference to Jesus during his lifetime, other than those contained in the Gospels, is something that cannot simply be ignored. It has long been known, for example, that there is no mention of such a figure in the most important secular sources of the time. These have been collected, pinpointed and evaluated by many scholars, Christian and non-Christian. One of these, for example, Weddig Fricke, a lawyer by profession, goes into the whole matter of the Gospels with the care of a barrister preparing a case, and in his exhaustive account, *Der Fall Jesus* (The Jesus Case), he supplies compelling evidence for the need to review entrenched Christian opinion.[1]

In chapter three of this work he cites fourteen cases of the need for us to carefully consider whether the figure of Jesus ever existed. Among these, the example of Philon of Alexandria is cited. This man was a contemporary of Jesus and a man who, according to Fricke's researches, acted as a zealous intermediary between the Jews and the representatives of

Rome at exactly the time Jesus preached in Galilee. There is almost no doubt at all in view of this, therefore, that the trial of Jesus could have escaped his notice, since this fell exactly within his period of office, and yet, despite this large fact, there is no mention at all in his reports of the trial and execution of Jesus, which, according to the synoptics, caused such an uproar at the time. This is particularly conspicuous since it was precisely in the matter of unjustified executions that Philon played an eminent role, even having the courage to go so far as to take his representations before the Emperor Caligula in person.

Perhaps the most outstanding example of ignorance of Jesus' existence, however, is offered by the same author in the instance of the lawyer and historian, Flavius Josephus. Fricke writes:

> *Flavius Josephus* came from a family of Jerusalem aristocrats. His father was a priest (and, consequently, almost certainly a member of the *Sanhedrin*) which gathered to try Jesus when this ostensibly took place... That a well-known personality was tried twice in a double trial under highly sensational circumstances, first by the *Sanhedrin* and then by a Roman court in the presence of the procurator and condemned to death is something which would have certainly come to the ears of Josephus via the reports given by his father and the accounts related by his relatives, friends and parents. Further, if a man like Josephus, someone who comprehensively reported the details of every uprising, every revolt, every just or unjust execution inasmuch as this had the slightest political significance, did not mention the dramatic circumstances of the trial of one Jesus of Nazareth – and this is the case – one may safely assume that nothing of the kind took place. [2]

This last is a very serious claim, since it gravely undermines Christian belief. The other eleven claims put forward by Fricke are equally cogent and it is difficult for anyone with an open mind to dismiss them. However, despite these facts, the Roman Church in particular has managed to do just that so far. In other words, it has successfully ignored all the other evidence supplied by scientific endeavour for our perusal over the last eighty years or so, except where this might offer substantiation of its own tenets.

It is urged that we are not concerned here with the flotsam and jetsam of a past age, nor with related trivia, but with facts vitally associated with the content of the Christian message. The discovery by some freak of circumstance of the cross on which Jesus was crucified, for example, unearthed on the outskirts of Jerusalem and 'proved' by our present scientific knowledge to be genuine would not lead us very far along the path of an appraisal of his teaching. As we shall see later, what emerges as a result in recent times of all the scientific endeavour on the various levels briefly alluded to above, taken as a whole, together with its subsequent, objective, impartial evaluation, proves in fact to be something radically different from that represented to us as incontrovertible truth by the Christian Church in the last two millennia.

The third element which strongly suggests misunderstanding and misrepresentation can be derived from our present general knowledge and our knowledge of other religions. In the light of this, few thinking people would now assert that Christianity is the sole custodian of religious truth. What we can say with truth is that it has characteristics in common with other religions. Today, we are able to review our religion from a standpoint unparalleled in history. Due to the wealth of knowledge in circulation via the printed word, the internet, intercommunication made possible by travel and computer by television, many millions of people know about the iniquities of the Crusades, for example, the horrors of the Spanish Inquisition and the brutalities associated with religious and political colonisation of the Americas, among other matters. Whatever conclusions we may draw from this knowledge, a certain historical perspective has arisen in the public mind and, as a result, the Church, so to speak, has 'no cloak for its sin'. Within this perspective, we can see where this organisation failed to live up to its Christian idea s, to put the matter mildly. This failure was well shown by the present pope, John Paul, in his public plea to God in Rome in the year 2000 for forgiveness of the sins of the Church over the centuries. In addition to this realisation, he and his colleagues, past and present, have also come to understand in the last 50 years that religions other than Roman Catholicism have something of value to offer humanity and that they have the right to be acknowledged.

Apropos of this, the increased general knowledge we have acquired in the 20th century has further led to a more acute awareness of the fact that, as far as religion is concerned, Christianity is only one expression of religious truth, and that its validity may well be in an assessment of how it measures up against the findings of other religions. Until quite recently in our history, the Christian had no means of comparing his religion with any other. Indeed, at one time, such a comparison would have been considered blasphemous and any such ideas, had they been possible to express, would have been paid for in the past with torture or with one's life, and even in the last seventy years in many parts of Europe and some parts of the USA with social exile. We should not overlook the fact either that it took eighteen centuries before a man might think freely at all about his religion without being punished for it, and it is ironic to note, too, that, during the so-called Age of Enlightenment in the 18th century, it was *secular* authority which introduced the freedom to think, which we still enjoy today, not ecclesiastical.

Today, thanks to our greatly widened mental horizons – which have been variously produced by a liberal democratic government (compared, say, with the dispensations of the Middle Ages and later monarchies), an enormously increased access to knowledge brought about first by the printing press and later by general literacy, the theatre, the availability of books as well as easy access to them, journals, newspapers and magazines and in particular the introduction of the paperback in the 20th century, the establishment of institutions and clubs and associations, and, later still, the invention of radio, film, TV, and finally, today's mass communication and computer services – we are free to read, to think and to draw our own conclusions. Added to this is the individual freedom of movement over relatively large distances compared with those, say, of 100 years ago, and by international travel which allows millions of people to cover very large distances and thus experience much more of life than their grandparents could have dreamed. Very few people who enjoy the benefits of so-called Western civilization would harbour the opinion against all odds that their religion is the only one which is of any value as a purveyor of what it regards as truth. They realise that such an attitude is one which breeds conflict. This view would imply that if the one particular religion is the sole possessor of truth, then, logically, all the others cannot be, and are therefore wrong. This standpoint was perfectly illustrated in the past by the wars of the Crusades and incidentally forms a particularly abhorrent chapter in human history.

The truth, however, is the reverse; it is not that, in essence, one religion is right and all the others are wrong, but that all of them are right and none is absolutely wrong. The probable truth is that, like the blind men of John G. Saxe's poem[3] who went to see an elephant, 'all of them were partly in the right and yet all of them were wrong.' This is to say that there is something 'right' which is common to them all, while that which is 'wrong' is usually a matter of interpretation of that which is 'right'. In other words, there is that which is essential to them all and also that which is inessential. The history of most religions shows that men are generally willing to fight to the death for the inessential, that is to say, for the later elaborations which have developed from the basic teaching, while the essential understanding which links them with the rest of humanity and its religious insights is either unknown or is conveniently forgotten in the desire for power and supremacy.

The idea of oneness in diversity, however, is easily made clear with the example of a prism. A prism receives undifferentiated light on one of its surfaces and refracts it. The light issuing on the other side is multi-coloured and gives us the colours of the spectrum. We can think of these colours as the various representations of the same truth which, here, is the white light entering the first surface of the prism exposed to light.

Looking back upon the sober, immutable facts of our history with the mind of an impartial observer, and with that scientific attitude of mind which has stood us in such good stead for over 200 years, we have to admit that among the religions of our time, Buddhism stands out as a model of humanity in the best sense of the word. It has the longest record as a world religion of what we could call adult, non-egoistic behaviour. It has never resorted to war, for example, something we might define as the 'open season for murder', nor ever condoned it. It has never resorted to persecution or oppression, mental or physical or any other kind of violence in order to proliferate its ideas. It has never organised a crusade against non-believers nor instituted a pogrom, or a witch-hunt; it has never made itself rich at the expense of others' poverty; it has never destroyed animals as a ritual nor condoned that destruction in the interests of commerce, let alone industry nor given its sanction to the killing of any other form of life nor encouraged others to do so. Neither does it dictate its ideas. It has never asserted that its concepts and precepts are the best and only means of attaining religious insight, nor devised a code of punishments should these not be adhered to. If others hold different views from those of Buddhism, it does not interfere, but is tolerant, non-critical and forbearing if criticized. It does not retaliate, so that it has been said that the easiest person to kill on this earth is a Buddhist monk. However, to kill an enlightened being is to leave the world a more hellish place.

A good illustration of the Buddhist attitude was given recently by the conduct of the Dalai Lama while on a visit to Europe. After the festival was over, during which he had spoken to several thousand people, many of them non-Buddhists, about the teaching, he concluded with a smile by saying in so many words: 'Well now, it has been a real pleasure to get to know you all, but if you think all that I've said is a load of hogwash, you're quite entitled to your opinion! I bless you all.'

In stark contrast to Christianity, Buddhism has practised what it has preached over the last 2500 years and continues to do so. This is a remarkable fact and deserves a moment's consideration. It cannot, I feel, be shrugged off simply as the result of being exposed to a more fortunate political and social history. During those two and half millennia, Buddhism has been as much exposed to the vicissitudes of life and to political fluctuation as any other religion, and has several times been the object of persecution. In view of this and the peace of mind as well as understanding it has brought to countless millions during that time, we may well ask ourselves why this religious order has consistently managed to remain true to its principles throughout such a very long period.

The reason, it is suggested, lies in its primary concern with what we might call the 'mechanics of mind' and their interaction with our world, and not with legend as is the case with Christianity. For example, in response to enquiry about the nature of existence, it does not begin with nebula which concern a miraculous birth, instituted by a Father for a Son whom he plans to have killed to 'save' the world and who, in turn at some time in the distant future, but also perhaps quite soon, will return to judge us all for our 'sins', and that from that momentous point in time the good will enjoy heaven and the bad be cast into everlasting hell and, as a result, the world will be a better place for all time. None of the words used in such a formula are exposed to intense enquiry, as is the case in Buddhism, but left for the receiver to digest or 'believe'. What, for example, do the words 'save' and 'world' and 'sin' really mean? What is heaven? What hell? Who are the Father and the Son?

A typical example of this authoritative kind of language and the vague concepts inherent in it is given in **Jn 3:13–18**. In reviewing the text, however, we have to preserve an objective frame of mind. Christians have heard the words reiterated again and again and, moreover, experienced the idea in ecclesiastic ritual. They have also imbibed it from the attitudes and the convictions of others. In short, we can truthfully say that the average Christian has received these ideas at the hands of others as implacable truth and yet, when looked at coolly, honestly and with an unprejudiced mind, the whole idea presented to us is alien, incomprehensible, highly subjective (and unjustifiably authoritative) in its address. To anyone who is awake to the realities of life, its assertions are strange and unintelligible, its tone a threat. An example is quoted here in its entirety, the verses being divided by an oblique stroke:

No one has ascended to heaven but He who came down from heaven, that is, the Son of Man who is in heaven/And as Moses lifted up the serpent in the wilderness, even so must the Son of Man be lifted up,/that whoever believes in Him should not perish but have eternal life./For God so loved the world that He gave His only begotten Son, that whoever believes in Him should not perish but have everlasting life./For God did not send His Son into the world to condemn the world, but that the world through Him might be saved./He who believes in Him is not condemned; but he who does not believe is condemned already, because he has not believed in the name of the only begotten Son of God.

This is the kind of material which is presented to the would-be enquirer about the nature of existence by Christian agents who desire to enlighten him about life and death. It does not take long for the seeker after truth to realize that he is required to *believe* and not to use his own inner lights. The penalty for disbelief, he is told, is eternal damnation. In other words, it is a threat to suspend our natural, God-given intelligence, for the simple reason, we are informed, that one cannot be 'saved' by one's own efforts. But, Buddhism would ask in reply: By whose if not by one's own? It is we who must seek God, not the other way round. Although final realisation of God's immanence may indeed be an act of grace, the effort which goes into finding Him is ours and ours alone. How can there be a tree if there is no seed? And if the seed is not warmed and watered by intelligence, meditation and reflection, how can it ever grow?

The result of imposed belief unsubstantiated by reasonable foundation, in fact, is weakness. The edifice of legend might stand for a while, but in time of crisis it will fall, because it has no firm basis. If we are allowed to judge a thing by its history, in other words, what it has proved itself to be in time, then we can see that this is what has happened to Christianity. Its history is certainly not a mirror of love, tolerance and that wisdom born of enlightenment, but one generally of horror, cruelty and stupidity.

What has been recorded in St John above is highly abstruse material, almost, one might say, a code which, nevertheless, has a very profound underlying meaning when viewed from quite another viewpoint. To understand that meaning, the code has to be deciphered and rendered into concepts and language which we can understand today. Why the Supreme Teaching as we may call it was couched in these terms is something probably related to language and semantics; no one can say for sure, but the fact is that the underlying significance of St. John's words can indeed be very clearly rendered to us by interpreting them in the light of other religious experience.

The original words of the teaching as it stands in St. John's account were, however, taken at face value shortly after Jesus' demise and enthusiastically corrupted by Saul of Tarsus. From there it eventually became the legend it is today in all its complication and sophistication. Some 300 years later it was employed by a well-organised political and ecclesiastical body which was quite assured of its uniqueness in possessing the truth and which, in its early development, did in fact prove to be a very effective catalyst in welding nations and peoples together, all over Asia Minor and Europe. In the so-called Dark Ages, for example, it not only provided a foil to monarchical power, but also gave meaning to life for millions of people. The legend persisted into the Middle Ages, embodied as the Holy Roman Catholic Church, committing the crimes and outrages characteristic of unbridled power and ignorance in any age, subsequently to become an international organisation with great power and financial resources, checked to some degree by secular advance and scientific knowledge in northern Europe, and finally forced to take second place to the state in the 18th and 19th centuries.

Today, the legendary basis upon which it and its scions rest has been largely undermined, partly by the research briefly alluded to above, and partly by a knowledge of its history, ironically by the 'fruits' by which men are known and of which Jesus once spoke **(Mt. 7:20)**, but also by a metamorphosis of mind which is rapidly taking place in modern Western society. The simple truth is that this 'modern mind' is no longer willing to blindly accept a teaching without roots in fact. If the teaching is not open to rational examination and proof, it is automatically thought of as suspect in today's scientific Western society. This, and a knowledge of Church history, certainly constitute one of the reasons why so many nominal Christians in the West and elsewhere are turning their backs on Christianity in silent dissidence.

Despite this, Christians and non-believers alike appreciate that there must be a moral law in our lives, a code of conduct which acknowledges others as being equal, whether this is allied to religious belief or not. Except for a small, criminal minority, people today also know that respect for others includes not murdering them, not stealing from them, not harming them, not committing adultery, not lying or bearing false witness, not giving way to hate, and so on. At what we might describe as the lowest level, this is expedient to our lives and necessary if we are to live comfortably with each other, they say, and all this can be carried out without adherence to a Church, its impositions and demands – and they are right. Proof of this can be seen in the current Western attitude to war. Throughout Europe there is a consensus of opinion that war is undesirable. It is not that the people there have become cowardly, or too comfortable because of their increased wealth, but that, without the aid of a Church to tell them so, they have come to realise for themselves that war is not only wasteful, stupid and cruel, but also ineffective as a solution to political problems. Some will say that they have learned through experience that this is so, but in reply to this we might ask why was the lesson not learned before, since there have been wars enough in that region of the earth for centuries.

The answer lies in the increase of knowledge which in turn has resulted in a higher degree of consciousness. This demonstrates that progress in developing consciousness can take place without the aid of religion. It is at last a break with a religious tradition whose long historical record includes war and political intrigue, mass murder and genocide, large-scale persecution, robbery, terror and other forms of criminal activity, whose features are wealth, arrogance and pride, and whose infamous intent for well over 1000 years has been to curb the human spirit and rein in mental advancement. All this, we might add, in the interests of what is largely a myth. Had the teaching of Jesus been properly understood, nothing of this could have been possible.

Protagonists for the Christian Church will argue that a tradition which has lasted so long could not have been based on a fable, but this is no argument. So long as people are willing to believe in something and so long as the concept is underpinned by a firm organisational structure and drilled into the minds of children at an early age as here, the idea will continue. For centuries, millions of people believed that the world was flat. There are people today who, in spite of the huge amount of incontrovertible evidence to the contrary, obstinately believe that the world was created some 5000 years ago.

Or we might look at the matter in a slightly different way. We might say, for example, that if it could be proved that Jesus never existed, and that the whole of the New Testament story is a hoax, the Christian tradition as we know it would nevertheless continue, much in the way that we continue to see the light of a star which vanished from the heavens in Caesar's time. It will continue until it is displaced by another idea which can be recognised as more relevant to modern man and more tenable.

The probability of substantiated refutation has always been the Roman Church's greatest fear from the earliest times when it fought brutally to establish itself, the fear, that is, that another, organised view could supersede its teachings. The first objection to it came from within its own ranks over 1500 years after its establishment, as the Reformation instigated by Martin Luther. The second breach in its fortifications occurred as scientific endeavour slowly but inexorably increased human knowledge, demonstrating at the beginning of modern history that the sun and the universe did not revolve round the earth, that Jerusalem was no more at its centre than any other point on the newly discovered sphere which is our world. Later, the work of Darwin and others proved that the earth had taken countless millions of years to come into being, and that the ascent of man himself had been a very gradual development from animal origins.

With a little imagination, we can envisage the next step in man's evolution as his total emancipation from a false, outworn religious tradition, liberating him from his present, largely reactive condition to a point where he will eventually become free in the true meaning of Jesus' words. This awakening would mean a gradual, universal awareness of our true nature, which would result in more enlightened men and women, human beings who have cast off the antiquated habits of mind which have bound the spirit of man for thousands of years.

That this is possible has been proved in the lives of the many enlightened people who have appeared in the world in all ages. That it is urgently necessary in our age to produce people who can see a little further than their peers and who can offer their wisdom in dealing with the urgent, very serious problems which currently confront the world, is made abundantly clear to us in any daily newspaper. Some of these problems can be briefly alluded to, for example, in the enormous increase in world population, in the movement of populations, in the clash of cultures, in religious division, in scientific activity, especially in the fields of modern medicine whose ethics are highly questionable, in the manufacture and proliferation of arms and other means to murder which know no morals and no bounds, and, closely associated with all these, in the low-minded, exploitative commercial spirit which has become an unquestioned element of our western cultural life and which now threatens to become a global phenomenon.

None of our formal religions is in a position to deal with the genie we have created over the last seventy years or so and which is about to fully emerge from the bottle. At this point of time we are confronted with the possibility of a major catastrophe emerging from the further development of one or another of these problems or their mutual interaction which could well herald our end. The avoidance of such a calamity will require us to rapidly revise our thinking and conduct before it is too late, and to achieve that revision we need a rapid advance in consciousness. If we have any doubt about the level of our spiritual development today, we only have to review in sober detachment the antics of the Islamic Taliban regime in Afghanistan, the activities of 'God's warriors' whose desire it was to establish a 'divine state' in which its god shall surpass itself in cruelty, inhumanity and stupidity unexcelled anywhere else in the world at the moment, and, equally, the Stone Age mentality exhibited by two modern, ostensibly

Christian state governments in the bombing of ancient cities as an act of revenge for deeds perpetrated by a handful of deluded, 'divinely inspired' lunatics. And we need no great political acumen to recognize similar delusion at work elsewhere in the world where men are slaves to some hallowed belief or conviction.

It is high time we became aware of the absurd mental bondage we subscribe to which passes for religion and which has proved itself practically worthless for the last 2000 years in contributing generally to our better mental health and our human maturity.

What these terms mean precisely is presented in the light of a re-interpretation of the New Testament in the pages which follow.

---

[1] Fricke Weddig, *Der Fall Jesus –Eine Juristische Beweisführung* (The Case of Jesus –   A Judicial Presentation of Evidence), Germany, Rasch & Röhring, 1995.

[2] Ibid. p. 112

[3] Saxe, John G., *The Six Blind Men of Indostan* – see appendix

CHAPTER I

It is said that we must be born again, but before we can be reborn,
we must die; but before we can die, we must awaken to life, and
before we can awaken to life, we must realise that we are asleep.
(Buddhist saying.)

Homo sapiens: an ape that thinks – sometimes.

Clearing the way for new perspectives

Before we can proceed to the subject of consciousness and
from there interpret the words of Christ from that standpoint,
we must first know what unconsciousness is, and what 'asleep'
means in the context referred to in the quotation above.

We have known for some time now that man and animal
share the same fate of conditioning. This fact was scientifically
demonstrated by the Russian surgeon and physiologist, I.P.
Pavlov, in his experiments on dogs during the years 1925–26.
Unfortunately, his findings were later applied to human beings
in furthering the interests of Stalinism, and not more generally
to draw attention to an aspect of our human nature which is of
paramount importance. Although the phenomenon was
known to man long before Pavlov began his work, it had no
name until then. Today we refer to it as 'conditioning' or
'reflexive behaviour', and we can speak of two kinds of
conditioning: innate or basic reflexes, and acquired reflexes.

1

The basic types are those which persuade us to flinch under attack, to flee under pursuit, to weep when upset, to hold our heads when we are beset with a problem, and so on. These are natural and, so to speak, built into our mind/body system by nature.

Acquired reflexive behaviour is a pattern of behaviour adopted by us and by animals in promoting our interests. Once we have learned that a particular form of behaviour is conducive to our survival, or to our well-being, it is then adopted as a useful tool in the business of effectively dealing with life's challenges. The knowledge is then handed on to others of the species. In humans it becomes part of a communal tradition. The classical example of the chimpanzee standing on a box to reach the bananas above him was the singular result of one chimpanzee's ingenuity, later the intellectual property of the whole tribe. The same can be said of man's gradual ascent from a semi-human condition at a time when his wit first enabled him to create a bow and arrow, and later lay traps from which subsequent generations benefited and which was then endorsed generally as a means of survival. As early community life developed in those far-off days, these acquired mental patterns of behaviour increased in number and became more and more complicated.

As the brain of man developed over hundreds of thousands of years, there was a shift of emphasis from the bare need to survive as the animal does to a dimension of mental attributes not related to basic needs. Language came into being and with it the nuances of mental activity. Among many other faculties of this nature, for example, the sense of time came to be appreciated, the expressions for past and future in language and, much later, the notions expressed by such words as 'if', 'might', 'could have', and so on. By the time man was organised into tribal groups with a mutual means of verbal communication, conditioned patterns of behaviour were well established. We can see them at work from our observations of human social groups less complicated than our own, but we can also infer from these that this was also the case at the dawn of our history, since conditioned patterns of behaviour were absolutely necessary to survival. In other words, if the tribe is still intact, conditioned reflexes must have been present to facilitate its preservation. Without these patterns, the group would have long disappeared from the scene.

Today, this fact is still valid. Our societies, too, survive on highly complicated, generally accepted behaviour patterns. Without them, these societies, whatever they represent and wherever they are found, would disintegrate. Such patterns can be thought of as the matrix of our existence and for the most part they are necessary to ensure that existence. They represent the findings of generations before us, crystallized in our own behaviour. The mental patterns of thinking and conduct are either directly and deliberately imposed on us by our parents, by our teachers, by the members of our social, political, professional, racial, national or religious, group, or they are unconsciously suggested to us by the behaviour of others and later assumed by us as a *modus vivendi*. The great power of the latter influence upon young people especially, but also to some extent on adults, is only just beginning to be appreciated. In this connection, one thinks not only of the role of TV, video and the cinema, which immediately spring to mind, but also of the mutual interaction, for better or worse, of our peers at a time when we are still mentally susceptible and malleable, that is to say, in early childhood before we have built up our own viable set of conditioned processes to deal with our particular world.

The resultant of these various influences is a personality, a mosaic of conditioning, which at once identifies us with and differentiates us from the world in which we find ourselves and which, if we are mentally healthy, assists us in coping with life. In the vast majority of cases, we are quite unaware of the processes which have moulded us to what we are. Understanding this principle of adoption is so essential to what follows that it may be useful at this point to illustrate it with an example.

The bull

In a bullfight we see the spectacle of a bull lowering its horns again and again to charge the matador's cape, but never fully realising as he does so that his tormentor, the real cause of his distress, is hardly a metre away from the swingeing piece of cloth which so rivets his interest. His instinctive reactions prevent him from apprehending this fact, and yet one small twist in the focus of his mind, so to speak, could bring him to ascertain what is going on, and so allow him to make short work of his adversary. But no, he is firmly entrenched in his ancient reflexes which were laid down for him as a means of defence and attack thousands of years ago, and which have been passed on to his progeny through his genes. He goes for the cloth and not the man.

Exactly the same processes are at work in us. Man, like the bull, is also a reflexive animal for most of his waking life. He, too, albeit on a different level, is a creature immersed in the reflexes germane to his species (instinctive reaction) and those influences spoken of above which relate to his country of origin, his circumstances, social and financial, political, personal, educational, religious and the many others which constitute his being (conditioned reflexes). Adequate proof of this is to be seen in this instance by turning our attention away from the bull for a moment and directing it at the crowd. There, we can see precisely the same primordial principles in operation in the human as in the bull: we see a herd of human beings temporarily but entirely at the mercy of a vicious instinct, and not one man or woman in ten thousand to realise the fact!

Particularly disturbing evidence of the tendency for men and women to follow a particular course of action or to respond to certain stimuli in certain ways without stopping to think and thus exhibiting sub-intelligent or sub-human (conditioned) behaviour was brought to light in the experiments conducted by Stanley Milgram (1933–84) at New York City University not many years ago, and which have since become famous.[1] In determining the degree to which human beings were influenced by external authority, he set up a project which consisted of a 'learner' and a 'teacher'. The 'learner' was strapped to a chair in a room and connected to electrical shock impulse contacts fixed to the arms and head, so that he looked very much like a man due for execution in the electric chair. The two men were initially introduced to each other, the 'learner' in his chair and the 'teacher' with his pad of questions and then the two were ushered into separate, adjoining rooms. The 'teacher' was given orders to dispense shocks to the victim in the event of his not being able to answer a series of prepared questions put to him. Dr. Milgram then informed the teacher that he was acting in the interests of important medical research and that he had the task of putting questions to the learner in the next room via a microphone. If the learner answered the questions incorrectly, he was to press a button which relayed an 'electric shock' to him. The 'teacher' did not know that the shocks were simulated. The previously prepared exercises became progressively more complicated as the examination continued and the shock for incorrect answers correspondingly stronger, increasing to a final shock value of 350 volts. The teacher could hear the (simulated) cries of the victim through the two way loudspeaker system, but any hesitation on the teacher's part was discouraged and the questioner persuaded by Milgram to continue.

As the exercises became more complex, the learner began first to lose the thread and become confused at which time he would beg for a moment to reconsider the question or time to revise his answer, but instead received a shock. This only deepened his confusion until at a later stage the learner was so confused and so in fear of further pain that he could only scream. In all this the teacher was simply urged to continue to administer an increasing voltage for subsequent incorrectly answered questions. The later shocks apparently rendered the learner unconscious (there was silence) and at the end of the exercise, the teacher, after having administered the highest voltage on his panel, could assume that his opposite number in the other room was dead.

Subsequent to his experiment, Milgram had this to say:

> Just how far would a person go when ordered to administer such shocks...? I realized that this simple question was both humanly important and capable of being precisely answered...Time and again in the experiment, people disvalued what they were doing, but could not muster the inner resources to translate their values into action.

The number of people who refused to carry out the experiment beyond a certain point was dismally small compared with the number of others *'from all walks of life'* who persisted under Milgram's encouragement to the end.

Taking these considerations away from the bullring and the laboratory, we find that this same heinous condition of unawareness in the human being assumes terrifying proportions when for some reason social constraints are minimal or non-existent, or when one group of human beings becomes the permissible target of attack by another. The last century produced very clear examples of what we might call 'moral anaesthesia' in this connection, or the state of being 'asleep' in reference to the quotation, and especially with reference to that spiritual torpor induced by authority. Laurence Rees, in his documentary, *The Nazis, A Warning from History*[2], cites the case of a small town in Lithuania where, in 1943, SS troops had taken control and had, a few days later, enlisted the assistance of a number of local inhabitants to act as militia in executing the Jews of the community. Although these people were part and parcel of the community to which they belonged, the men chosen for the job apparently had no qualms about the nature of the proposed task, and only two of several dozen chose to opt out of the operation. Several decades later, when these same men, now in their fifties and sixties, were interviewed and asked why they had connived in killing innocent, defenceless people, none of them knew why they had carried out their orders. When pressed to give an answer, they could not even begin to formulate an articulate reply to the question. All of them looked foolish in their attempts to protest their innocence of felony. During the interview, there were inarticulate references to the evil spirit of the times, shrugged shoulders in trying to describe a situation which was 'unavoidable', or in some instances, it was maintained that it was a situation of 'kill or be killed', which, incidentally, was not true in this case. One of them even spoke of 'the need to do what had to be done'. Moreover, none had entertained any personal antagonism towards the Jews of their town and, therefore, had no reason to do them harm. They were men who in those hours were carried along by their emotions, in this instance by the desire to identify themselves with the order of the day through obedience to authority and, as a result, acted like so many sheep directed by a dog in a field. In the context described we could say that they were in a temporary condition of being criminally sub-human. This is the condition of not being able or willing to exercise the unique human prerogative of standing aside from our reflexive patterns of behaviour in order to act consciously. It is on occasions like these that our human is more ape than man.

The case of Adolf Eichmann

The example of Adolf Eichmann is not for a moment to concentrate in this consideration on one nation, the Germans, nor on one period of human history, as the choice of the two examples might suggest. The two – that above, and this – have been cited, first because both are still relatively fresh in our memories, and second to demonstrate that this fatal flaw in human nature, namely this blindness to our conditioning, affects us all. None of us is exempt. Every human being is the product of his or her conditioning. However, not to realise this and, as a consequence, to become attached to that conditioning, is the state of being unconscious or 'asleep', to use the Buddhist word for this condition. The 'sleep' condition in this sense becomes graphically clear to anyone who has followed the trial of Eichmann. In being entirely unaware of his conditioning, however, we must add that he was no different from countless millions of other human beings all over the world. Despite the enormity of his crime, and with this firmly in mind, we should not therefore be in too much of a hurry to condemn him out of hand.

This reluctance to condemn was made abundantly clear to me by a Jewish friend of mine who spent several years in Auschwitz and who, after Eichmann was arrested and taken to Israel, received an official invitation later from that source to attend the trial as a witness. 'Are you going to give evidence?' I asked at the time. 'No,' he said, 'I certainly will not. I want nothing to do with it.' This surprised me, since he had suffered much at the hands of the Nazis. I can still recall the expression of resolve on his face and the look he gave me in registering his determination not to go. However, it took me another twenty years to understand what that expression meant.

It must be hastily added that there is no attempt here to minimise Eichmann's role in a criminal regime. Neither is there an implied condemnation of the people who caught the man, tried him, and put him to death. Eichmann was involved in activities which he knew were cruel, criminal and totally inhuman; he had seen for himself what happened to the people on his deportation lists. Like the 'teacher' in Milgram's experiments above, he knew what he was doing, and he knew of the suffering he was causing as a vital link in an infamous chain of consequence. Again, like the 'teacher', here he recognised this fact, and during his trial even went as far as to condemn the activities of which he was a part. Thus his statement before the Israeli court, and in this it is quite possible that he was speaking the truth. But he did nothing to stop the persecution or evade what he considered to be his 'responsibility'. He felt himself to be an integral part of Hitler's diabolical machinery from which it was impossible to extract himself without being murdered sooner or later by his own colleagues. No better example could be cited for a reality situation in support of Milgram's assertion that his candidates, although they disvalued what they were doing, 'could not muster the inner resources to translate their values into action.'

It is clear from the film taken during proceedings at the time, that the court did not have to do with an unfeeling brute such as Bormann, a pervert like Mengele or a madman like Hitler, but with a man of normal sensibilities, a man who could express himself clearly and well, with insistence when necessary, but without impatience or undue emotion, a man who had been loyal to his job and his colleagues, depraved though these were. We also recognise an extremely conscientious individual in all that he did, and at the same time a man with a well-developed sense of duty and responsibility, a man, moreover, who maintained his personal dignity without a trace of arrogance while under great duress in court. He knew that he would inevitably be condemned to death, and he admitted his shortcomings and, finally, his guilt with commendable impartiality and honesty. The incongruity of these traits of character measured against the hugeness of his crime was revealed in the faces and attitudes of his prosecutors, and this perhaps at no time more than when the accused pulled himself together for the last time with great self-discipline. He rose once more to his feet to respectfully address his jurors, at the same time gathering the many papers on the small table before him into a sheaf with slightly trembling hands. He referred to day and date, time, place, memoranda, timetables, corrections, the names of superiors and inferiors alike, amendments, delays, and at one time to the correct spelling of 'Chelmno'. He spoke out clearly and objectively of his exigency in an impossible situation, his 'duty' as a loyal SS-man, his 'responsibility', his 'oath of allegiance', and further of his unambiguous requirement to carry out the orders given to him. The discrepancy between all this administrative detail and the vision of men, women and children being brutally done to death with about as much conscience as that seen at a meat factory could not be overlooked. It screamed in the minds of those listening to these accounts. Could this man be so brilliant in the one half of his mind and so blunt in the other, they asked themselves. Could it be really true that he was unable to discern that all this bureaucratic minutiae had nothing whatsoever to do with the evil that was being perpetrated at the time? It was embarrassing. Just as embarrassing was the obvious sincerity of his defence. Eichmann was completely convinced that what he had done was in the normal, conscientious performance of his duty as a soldier. More he could not add to this viewpoint when pressed to do so. In the final hours of the court proceedings, two things were clear to most people in attendance. The first was that this individual had been so firmly conditioned in the need to be loyal and conscientious that it was beyond the court in several months of interrogation to make the man aware of the fateful irony inherent in his thinking. It was clear that he was a man of integrity, but of an integrity which had been perverted to wrong ends. He was a man of an earlier generation brought up on the principles laid down for the German civil service of the time. These principles required hard, conscientious work, honesty, courtesy and uprightness, accuracy, loyalty to the state and respect for one's superiors. This must have been drilled into him very early in life, so that it remained an ineradicable part of his mental make-up.

The second fact emerging from months of cross-examination was the picture of an ordinary, self-disciplined, sincere individual under stress who, much like every human being, also had his weaknesses and was, for that reason, very much like the rest of us. Even against the background of an appalling crime against humanity in which he was directly involved, he remained one of us, whether Jew or Gentile, a man like ourselves who could err as we can also err. It is difficult to believe that anyone present during the trial could not have felt the inevitability of his position, the inexorable process of fate which had entangled him in its web and brought him thus far, like so many others in human history. His history, like so many others, is that of a man who had been deluded by the attraction of worldly power. At the end of his trial he cut a pathetic figure. As human beings in the world, we never know what challenges will be presented to us, nor how we might react to them when the crucial moment comes, so that all of us can with truth say, 'There, but for the grace of God go I!'

It was evident, too, that the court was at the end of its tether as to how to mete out fitting punishment to this individual, this balding middle-aged clerk with an incurable kink, who had become involved in a crime of such iniquity and on a scale hitherto unknown to the world. No human assizes could ever be equal to the task of judging him. For the Israeli court and the nation it represented, it was clear that he must die since, in the circumstances, there was nothing else in our human jurisprudence which could match the felony. And so Adolf Eichmann was executed and his corporeal remains totally obliterated.

Long after my Jewish friend had died, it occurred to me just why he had not wished to identify himself with condemnation in any form, not even of his persecutors during the period of successive internment in several concentration camps between 1938 and 1945. 'I don't believe in judging people,' he said after I had pressed him for an explanation for his refusal to attend the Eichmann trial, and he refused to say more.

'Judge not at all, that ye be not judged', said Jesus on one occasion (**Mt. 7:1**). It is well if we can see the wisdom of this on our own, since at first glance it sounds like a simple warning. Perhaps this superficial understanding of the remark was good enough for the people of his time. There is an implied threat in it, we feel. Put another way, we could say: 'If you don't judge others, they won't judge you', which makes good social sense. If you are tolerant of others, they will be tolerant towards you. Or was Jesus thinking of heavenly judgement? Perhaps, for this was his manner, we will say, one in keeping with the tone of the Old Testament prophets. However, in the case of passing judgement on another there is always an element of egoism present, a sense of superiority. This can be seen very clearly in the history of our human legal systems. It is only in recent times that we have come to understand the wisdom of re-education and rehabilitation which attempt to guide and assist, and where judicial ego does not play a role. Human beings everywhere will resist imposed (egoistic) authority and counter it with their own egoistic assertions and, often enough, with violence, but at the same time they can all recognise superiority without being coerced into doing so. We can see this demonstrated in children. If, for example, a teacher has inner authority born of knowledge and experience, they will immediately recognise it and inwardly discipline themselves to learn. The same is true of adults in all walks of life. Superiority without ego, like truth and quality, will finally come to the surface.

However, the deeper wisdom of the remark, 'Judge not that ye be not judged', is unfolded to us by the Buddhist concept of 'karma'. This is a much larger concept than 'fate' or 'destiny', since, as well as recognising the vital function conditioning has in our lives, it also maintains that the conditioning acquired in this life is taken with us to find expression in a subsequent one. Such a concept implies that all of us are born with certain personal attributes, good and bad, long before these are given expression. Sometimes this potential is shown at an early age as in the classical example of the young Mozart who composed and played his first musical piece at the age of six. His gifts were carefully cultivated by those around him as a child, notably by his father, Leopold and, as a result, this conditioning blossomed into the musician and composer whose music is known today all over the world. Nonetheless, there were other traits in Mozart's mental make-up which were to seal his later destiny and which were strangely at odds with his musical meticulousness: there were his utter carelessness with money, his tactlessness, frivolity and thoughtlessness in eating and drinking and his sexual conduct, elements in his life which were finally to bring him an early death.

Although we may not possess Mozart's genius, the pattern of our development is the same for us all. The propensities, tendencies, talents, attributes, energy potential and ego potential we are born with will find expression or not, according to the conditioning we are subjected to, and this in turn depends to a great extent on the circumstances into which we are born and the people with whom we come into contact. The direction our life will take is generally determined before we reach puberty, but can be modified at any time by our experience. Thus, accident or illness can radically change the career of, for example, a sportsman or woman or, for that matter, any career so that we have from then on to revise our lives. Sometimes such coincidence may be great good fortune which will act as a factor in changing the course of our lives, as in the example of the distinguished conductor, Arturo Toscanini, who began his career one evening when the current conductor of the orchestra suddenly fell ill. He stepped in to conduct and so saved the evening. It turned out that the performance became a memorable one, and Toscanini's life was abruptly changed in a direction for the better.

It is not always a matter of personal choice which may alter our lives. Apart from the phenomenon of accident and illness (for which we personally may or may not be directly or indirectly responsible), the paths of our lives frequently cross those of others. Often enough, these radically affect our own for better or worse. Clearly, marriage or a similar liaison is one of these. Other influences which immediately spring to mind are the paths of those who employ us, and those of the other human beings with whom we work and otherwise associate. Again, these are factors for good or bad in our lives. There are the paths of those who might in some cases help us to wealth, success and happiness or, conversely, maim and murder us on the road or in our own house or on some field of battle. These last are extremes and the stuff of our literature, but minor influences, good, bad and neutral, affect our lives continuously. Not the least of these are the mechanisms of the body which are operating all the time with their attendant consequences and which may or may not be a larger issue as we grow older either as illness, and other factors which shorten – or perhaps lengthen – our lives. These constellations, great and small, our innate tendencies and proclivities, together with elements still in operation from previous existences, are what make up the fabric of our existence and over which we have little or no personal control. This is the condition referred to in Vedic and Buddhist religious literature as *samsara*. Realising the full significance of this infinite network of circumstance, with ramifications, consequences and implications quite beyond our calculation, makes it impossible for us to judge others. Moreover, the act of condemning others is at once to condemn ourselves, in that any form of condemnation ultimately renders our own condition more complicated and less satisfactory. Condemnation strengthens the ego and therefore embeds us even more firmly in the fatal quicksands of self-concern. In this, to use another comparison, we find ourselves even more entangled in the net of conditioned bondage, and so begin to suffer. This, then, is the deeper, less obvious implication of Christ's remark.

A more searching consideration of the concept of *samsara* is given later.

The pharisees and others

An explicit example of conditioned behaviour in the context of this study is that of the Pharisees and others who represented Jewish religious tradition at the time of Jesus. They were what we would call 'hardliners' today, which is another word for inflexibility of mind and implies rigid conditioning over a long period. One could also think of this as a 'sclerosis of the mind', a disease of the mind which, like that afflicting the arteries, results in inhibited blood flow, infarct and sudden death. It is the hardening of attitudes and convictions which inhibit the ability to think beyond certain comfortable limitations. As far as the Pharisees of old were concerned and, incidentally, the orthodox Jews of today, practically every detail in life is regulated by a book of law, so that an attempt is made to regiment life itself to a list of observations, regulations and precepts, where there is virtually not a minute in the day which is not governed by some ordinance or other. This is the death of the mind. All our religions are to a greater or lesser extent afflicted by this inhibiting mental habit. Most of them, too, could be described as a superstructure built upon the insights of one human being. To cite a simple example, they are like the magnificent church erected not far from the site of Bernadette's vision at Lourdes. The building has nothing directly to do with her insight or with the prepared state of mind which made her vision of the Madonna possible. It is merely and only a reminder, a monument to that condition and the results arising from it.

The older a religion is, the more prone it is to resort to the written record of its existence and experience, and to the annotations of various people down the centuries who have commented upon that experience and who insist that this or that document, word, phrase, maxim, chapter, verse, sura or sutra is the embodiment of truth for a present problem. In this they are like legal systems which look back to the past for a precedent to deal with a present condition, or ageing generals who are apt to employ old strategies to a new military situation. As far as religious observance is concerned, this may be all very well, and is sometimes very fine, but it has nothing to do with the living spirit, with the 'Now' of consciousness of which Jesus was an embodiment. Scriptures are like works of art which have, in their way, captured the 'Now' of a moment long gone and crystallized it in a chosen form for posterity to appreciate. In this they are useful as reminders of those moments, but should not be confused with reality, which is the life that flows in every second and where nothing is ever exactly the same. We can liken them to changing cloud formations in the sky or the water of a river forever moving towards the sea. To be aware of this 'Now-ness' from one moment to another, on the other hand, is to be supremely conscious, but to try to live each day or even to manage the whole of life according to the caveats of a book, however beautifully wrought in words or however 'sacred', is to live in the past and so stifle the present. Ultimately, this habit renders us fools.

Generally speaking, we associate the word 'Pharisee' or 'pharisaic' with hypocrisy, with not practising what we preach, an idea developed from the New Testament, but which is not quite in keeping with the original, since the truth is that the Pharisees of Jesus' time were more liberally minded than the other party, the Sadducees. What is emphasized here is that both were thoroughly conditioned. In the New Testament they find themselves in the company of a fully awakened individual whose enlightened words and conduct exposes their bondage and their small-mindedness. In the eternal Now, their objections appear small and carping; their minds are already addled. An incident which illustrates this invalidity occurs at **Mark 7:1** To save space, the individual verse notations have been omitted, but nevertheless run on consecutively. The parentheses are mine:

Then came together unto him the Pharisees, and certain of the scribes, which came from Jerusalem. And when they saw some of his disciples eat bread with defiled, that is to say, unwashen, hands, they found fault. For the Pharisees, and all the Jews, except they wash their hands oft, eat not, holding the tradition of the elders. And when they come from the market, except they wash, they eat not. And many other things there be, which they have received to hold as the washing of cups, and pots, brazen vessels, and of tables. Then the Pharisees and scribes asked him, Why walk not thy disciples according to the tradition of the elders, but eat bread with unwashen hands? He (Jesus) answered and said unto them, Well hath Esaias prophesied of you hypocrites, as it is written, This people honoureth me with their lips, but their heart is far from me. Howbeit in vain do they worship me (i.e. God), teaching for doctrines the commandments of men. For laying aside the commandment of God, ye hold the tradition of men, as the washing of pots and cups: and many other suchlike things ye do. And he (Jesus) said unto them, Full well ye reject the commandment of God, that ye might keep your own tradition.(**Mk 7, 1–9**)

It is quite possible that the Hebrew tradition of washing and cleanliness was well ahead of other communities in the matter of hygiene at that time. Today, we can fully appreciate the need to wash our hands before eating and we are also in the advantageous position of knowing why we do so. The rules of personal hygiene were wise and probably established as the result of observation and experience. The presence of the tape-worm in pork, for example, was also a valuable item of knowledge gained through experience. Apart from the aesthetic aspect of cleanliness at the time of eating, the elders were almost certainly aware of the consequences of not washing the hands before eating. However, what Jesus wants to point out here has no connection with table manners, but with the need for them to *look at themselves*. He wants to make clear to them that they are more concerned with keeping the letter of the law than with its spirit. The spirit of the law has nothing to do with washing pots and pans and hands, but with being aware of oneself, with being conscious of the here and now, and in this matter of being aware of the presence of God. In modern English we could translate him as saying, 'You people are more aware of the pettifogging written laws of your tradition than you are of the commandments. The problem, my friends, is that you cannot see over the wall beyond your tradition to the larger issue of God's requirements.' We would say today that they cannot see the wood for the trees, so enchanted are they with their book of law. Having intimate knowledge of such a thing breeds ease and satisfaction – in a word, security. The wilful, eccentric, intransigent world of change (*samsara*) in which we live and from which we do not as a rule derive the fullest satisfaction, is presented to us for a very brief moment (our life) as a second of time in God's pageant. For the purveyors of traditional religion this is conveniently and satisfactorily explained and later congealed in a book of written record of law and precept, ostensibly for use in every imaginable situation. In this way, the life in every moment visible to the mystic, the poet or the enlightened being can be ignored as irrelevant since it cannot be written down. Everything, the pundits of the law maintain, has its reason, its place, its application, its season, its value and is reflected in the experience of generations. They say that for this reason alone it has validity. It must have validity, they argue, since so many people have subscribed to its wisdom in the past. Therefore, the traditionalist must be right. From here, its purveyors proceed to the insistence that if it is right, since so many have confirmed its rightness, then it must be the *only* form of rightness and, as a consequence, every other view is wrong. In this way, religious prejudice is established and in the worst case can result in persecution or open war, facts which can be recognised very clearly in the histories of Judaism, Christianity and Islam, and which is diligently at work in our time as in the past.

But in truth, formalised religion is a substitution; it is a book of law, a ritual and a social order in exchange for the freedom of living in every moment. This is the kind of personal freedom of which mystics in all ages and at all times have spoken. It is as though they say, 'This law and wisdom of ours is all very well, and through it one may perhaps grow in spiritual stature, but for the final step into freedom it is the last bond which must be cast off'.

A little later at **Mk 7:10**, if we accept the sequence of the gospel, Jesus goes on to give another example, presumably to the same assembly, to amplify his point. After a reference to corrupt practice among those responsible for promulgating the true spirit of the law, again suggesting that tradition has missed the point, he goes on to make quite clear to his audience that that which comes into us from the outside cannot corrupt a man, but that it is a man's thoughts which corrupt him. In other words, that which is within. It is clear from what follows **(Mk 7:18–23)** that Jesus is thinking here of the specific, traditional law of washing the hands. Attendance to such trivia is simply a matter of looking in the wrong direction. The inside is what has to be changed, and no amount of attention to external detail is going to change the inner defilement.

In the terms outlined above, we can say that attention to outward detail in this sense is to follow a pattern of conduct laid down for us as tradition stipulates, so that t becomes a habit of mind. We have become conditioned to observe it and do not think twice about our actions. We are asleep. Jesus, like all great masters, wants us to see that this kind of thing binds our minds, numbs our spirit and keeps us in a state of somnolent bondage. He wants us to realise that attachment to tradition is binding and crippling. What is of the greatest importance, he exhorts us to realise, is the awareness of what goes on inside ourselves, the evil thoughts (and here those which afflict us and which can make us into thieves, adulterers, murderers, dissemblers, blasphemers and lechers). To this, the Buddhist would only add that it is not only evil thought, but *all* uncontrolled thought which provides the impediment to true realisation.

In discussing the Pharisees and their reactions to the figure of Christ and his teaching, we should not thereby assume that this particular behaviour was only common to them and their time. In our day, too, we should note that the conditioning inherent in Christian teaching since St. Paul is still relevant in many circles, 2000 years after his death. It is a teaching which implies that 'the Jews' were responsible for Jesus' death. This foolish ecclesiastical assumption has caused unimaginable suffering among Jews for centuries, right up to modern times.[3]

Conditioning is common to all men at all times and in all places. We can see it at work today, for example, in the conditioned assumptions of the consumer society which threatens to become a global institution, in the assumptions behind the meat and pharmaceutical industries that animals are there for our exploitation, in the activities of fanatical Moslems, who imagine that their belief is the only embodiment of truth, and that suicide bombing will bring the murderer to heaven, and we can see it at work in all the armed conflicts going on in the world at the moment. We can see it in racism of all kinds, as well as in the desire to get rich, which afflicts millions of people in the West, promoted by the conviction that this is the solution to every problem arising in life, in the assumptions underlying international diplomacy and all other forms of nationalism wherever they are to be found, in all forms of propaganda, including religious propaganda, in our blind faith in science and in the values implicit in very many of the films we see and on television. At a personal level, we can see the conditioning process at work in guiding and resolving our tastes, in the way we dress, drive, walk and talk, live, judge and think. All this is the result of conditioning processes. While, as we have said, conditioning is necessary as a cohesive element in keeping society together, it must not be thought of as the final state of Man. To simply assume this is to confirm the fatal flaw in our human make-up described above. To assume that the conditioning to which we have been subjected is final is at the same time to be unaware of that conditioning. In acting without reflection and under the influences of our conditioning, we are no more free than a shoal of fish. We merely respond to outer stimuli as they do. Mentally and spiritually, we are sound asleep.

In all his encounters with the Jewish establishment of his time – the scribes, lawyers, Sadducees and Pharisees – Jesus is faced with the same, recurring problem: the conflict arising from his freedom of mind pitted against their reflexive, entrenched traditions.

> And it came to pass on a certain day, as he was teaching, that there were Pharisees and doctors of the law sitting by, which were come out of every town of Galilee and Judaea, and Jerusalem: and the power of the Lord was present to heal them. And, behold, men brought in a bed a man which was taken with the palsy: and they sought means to bring him in, and to lay him before him. And when they could not find by what way they might bring him in because of the multitude, they went upon the housetop, and let him down through the tiling with his couch into the midst before Jesus. And when he saw their faith, he said unto him, Man, thy sins are forgiven thee. And the scribes and the Pharisees began to reason, saying, Who is this which speaketh blasphemies? Who can forgive sins, but God alone? But when Jesus perceived their thoughts, he answering said unto them, What reason ye in your hearts? Whether (it) is easier, to say, Thy sins be forgiven thee; or to say, Rise up and walk? **Lk. 5:17–23**

The conditioned assumption here is that only God can forgive sins. Assuming this to be true, the onlookers belonging to the tradition are nevertheless still so fast asleep that they cannot even believe their own eyes when they see God at work through man! Thus, conditioning makes blockheads of us all.[4]

What the Rabbi meant by 'sin' in this example can only be surmised. However, it is very likely that he saw the conditions which had precipitated the disease, since this gift of understanding past causes (karma) resulting in disease of one kind or another, mental or physical, very often accompanies enlightenment. If we accept this as a possible explanation, we can then understand the apparent light-heartedness of his next remark, as he turns to his objectors and says in so many words,

'What is easier for me to say, then, "Get up and walk" or "Your sins are forgiven"?', by which latter he could have meant, 'The causes of the disease have vanished'. In short, it didn't matter what was said, the result was the same and the phrases synonymous.

A few verses further on in this same chapter, after Jesus' encounter with the tax collector, Levi, who invites the Master to his house, plies him with good things, along with 'a great company of publicans and others that sat down with them', the religious establishment begins to murmur against the disciples, saying 'Why do you eat with publicans and sinners?' **(Lk. 5:29–30)**

This at once reveals a consciousness of class, the feeling that they (the scribes and others) are in some way better than their fellow men, which is another form of conditioning to which many people are prone. Moreover, it annoys the scholars and their colleagues to think that a man so qualified by God to heal the sick should waste his time and, in their opinion, lose his dignity in feasting and drinking with the rabble of the streets. Jesus, however, is still conscious of his mission. This is clear from his reply, since he says that he is here not only to heal the sick, but to convey by example the good tidings of a knowledge of God. To their objection, he replies: 'They who are whole need not a physician, but they that are sick'. **(Lk. 5:31)** By the word 'sick' he means those who have little or no knowledge of the divine, whose minds are forever turned upon worldly pursuits. These need not necessarily be pursuits of self-interest, like making money or generally looking after oneself first and perhaps also at the expense of others, but simply a complete ignorance of divine presence. It is a matter of Wordsworth's world being 'too much with us', implying that we do not accord sufficient time to God, but are forever busy looking after our own interests.

An example in support of this suggestion occurs at **Luke 10:39–42**, where Martha asks her sister Mary for help during the work needed to make a guest welcome. It can be reasonably assumed that Martha is a trifle annoyed that she is not receiving assistance and it is also reasonable to think that her tone has a note of complaint in it. Jesus reminds her that work is not everything and that to sit with him and enjoy his company is the better 'part' of the encounter. We can be so conscientiously busy with the particulars of preparation – necessary though these undoubtedly are – that we lose the best of our guest's presence. Jesus enjoins Martha to leave the chores for a moment and come and sit with him. He knows after all that such a moment passes all too quickly.

The point is that conditioning makes us blind as well as blockheads. All of us. Jesus' intention was to open our eyes not only to other possibilities as in the example above, but also to *ourselves*. We are so sharply focussed on that which is either outside ourselves or so attached to our own inner view or our convictions that we are ignorant of all else. Millions of us pass through the cycle of our lives from birth to death and are for the most part quite unaware of our conditioning and our attachments. We think of ourselves for example, as Frenchmen or Americans, Finns or Italians, Indians or Australians, live out our lives within a society whose views and conduct we have long since embraced, speak the local dialect, walk and talk like our mothers and fathers, learn what we are told by our teachers and our parents, accept a religious view and call ourselves Christians or Hindus, Jews or Moslems, live for the most part in one country with its adopted convictions passed on to us from one uncritical generation to another, adapt ourselves to the conditions surrounding us, belong to a political party, a trade union, a club; fight our country's wars, die for another's ideal, champion our football team, marry, reproduce, identify ourselves with our work, our interests, our family, our clan, our tribe, our nation and perhaps never in seventy years or more turn round to ask, Why do I subscribe to all this? Who am I? or What is it in me which sustains the ability to see and hear, to feel, to live and love, to understand, wonder, hope and suffer? Has this brief interval in the light of life any *meaning*? Is there anyone 'out there' who can share my deepest feelings?

Never to reflect for a moment in this way, never to feel moved to ask why we accept a life compounded of conditioned reflexes as 'reality' is to live in a state which Buddhists call 'delusion'. It is to live in a dream, and accept the dream as true. The conditioned patterns which make up this illusive dream are extremely strong; they could be described as the very fabric of our earthly existence, so influential are they in our lives, and this is why we take them for real. The strength of the mental chains which bind us can be felt at the very moment we consider the possibility of throwing them over, these conditioned patterns of ours, of casting off our beliefs, or of changing our habits, and our cherished opinions or, if we find this impossible, of at least submitting them to a moment's detached and honest scrutiny.

We can freely be forgiven for finding ourselves attached to them since it is all too easy to fall prey to *samsara's* seductions, and none of us is exempt. From the moment we are born, we are automatically exposed to an illusion. On the other hand, not to recognise these acquired modes of thinking and behaviour in ourselves for what they are and so detach ourselves from the 'living dream' even for a moment during our lives is to condemn ourselves to nescience and to a slavish treadmill of uncompromising consequence both in this life and the next. This eternal round of ignorance and bondage is what Buddhists call the 'wheel of life and death'.

An ancient conditioned pattern

Sometimes it helps us to 'wake up' to the conditioning processes at work in and around us when we objectively consider the past. Jesus' own conditioning can be seen now and again in his intense Jewishness, not in the political sense as a Messiah which his contemporaries wanted him to be, but as a traditional Hebrew. This is particularly clear in one of his references to David, the ancient king of the Hebrews, and occurs in **Mk 2:23**, where disgruntled Pharisees are again on the lookout for means by which they can trap Rabbi Jeshua into treason or heresy.

> 'Look, why do they do what is not lawful on the Sabbath?' But He said to them, 'Have you never read what David did when he was in need and hungry, he and those with him: how he went into the house of God in the days of Abiathar the high priest, and ate the show-bread which is not lawful to eat except for the priests, and also gave some to those who were with him?' And He said to them, 'The Sabbath was made for man, and not man for the Sabbath. Therefore the Son of Man is also Lord of the Sabbath.'

Jesus justifies his sabbatical misdemeanour by referring to David, and perhaps this was justification enough for the Pharisees who had followed him into the cornfield. However, the incident described quite overlooks the fact that the David we read of in the Book of Samuel is anything but an example of enlightened conduct. The first we hear of him as a young man is in connection with the murder of Goliath, a swaggering giant among the Philistines who, we are given to understand, deserved to die for his provocation. David killed the man with his sling. This was his first murder. The boy David then cuts off Goliath's head as a trophy. There is a slight suggestion, too, in the account given by Samuel that this took place while the Philistine was still alive.

We might well be inclined to accept the issue today as a heroic triumph for the Bronze Age Hebrews at the time. The slaying of Goliath was the act of a hero, we will say, a deed belonging to heroic times. But David went on to murder again and again. His life is the record of a professional murderer.

> Saul has slain his thousands, And David his ten thousands. (**I Sam. 18:7 & 21:11**)

Like every hero and every tyrant, king and dictator that has plagued humanity since it could walk upright. David, from the spiritual point of view, was a moron. His case is aggravated and made the more repugnant by learning of his connivance with the Hebrew god to achieve his bloody ends. There is nothing revolutionary about this view. We have only to read the Book of Samuel with an unprejudiced mind to arrive at such a conclusion. And yet, despite this, neither Jews nor Christians in the dozens of centuries which have followed David's felony have ever questioned David's integrity as a 'great and noble king'. David's genealogy was manipulated generations later in Jesus' own genealogy so as to add to the latter's distinction.

Later **(at II Sam. 8:4–5)**, we read that this same man was responsible for killing 20,000 people.

In all this butchery he was helped again and again by his god which today, in the light of the little spiritual progress we have made since those times, we may well find repulsive.

> Then the Philistines went up once again and deployed themselves in the Valley of Rephaim. Therefore David enquired of the Lord, and He said: 'You shall not go up; circle around behind them, and come upon them in front of the Mulberry trees. And it shall be, when you hear the sound of marching in the tops of the mulberry trees, then you shall advance quickly. For then the Lord will go out before you to strike the camp of the Philistines.' **(II Sam. 5:22–25)**

Throughout the books of Samuel I and II, we read of a man not very different from others of a similar cast of mind, some of whom history likes to remember even as 'great' men: Alexander, Julius Caesar, Barbarossa, Charlemagne, Genghis Khan, Tamerlane, Oliver Cromwell and Napoleon, to name just a handful, all of them common murderers and spiritual gnomes whose business in life was human slaughter. Even today, we think of some of these people as objects of admiration. We praise their military intelligence, their daring, their tactical skill, their occasional liberality in victory (which is usually an expression of another facet of their irrepressible egos), but conveniently forget their blind, sub-human desire to destroy, their senseless cruelty and animality:

> Then Saul said: Thus you shall say to David: 'The king does not desire any dowry but one hundred foreskins of the Philistines, to take vengeance on the king's enemies.' But Saul thought to make David fall by the hand of the Philistines. So when his servants told David these words, it pleased David well to become the king's son-in-law. Now the days had not expired; therefore David arose and went, he and his men, and killed two hundred Philistines. And brought their foreskins, and they gave them in full count to the king, that he might become the king's son-in-law. **(I Sam. 18:25–27)**

For those who insist that chapters such as these somehow disclose God's word to mankind, or maintain that they are the illumined record of a 'chosen people', a little time should be taken in exercising that human faculty of ours to think and imagine. In the first place we have an example of divine collusion in the matter of war which, as we can recognise from our somewhat elevated position three thousand years later, to be a *sub*-conscious activity and one where we can see Man at his worst. Moreover, and as a matter of passing interest, it is in direct contradiction to Mosaic law which categorically declares: 'Thou shalt not kill.' In this instance, apparently, we have a god that is willing to mix with the muck of human politics, a god as general and strategist intimately involved in killing on a large scale.

In the second example, there are several elements which expose both participants, Saul and David, as ordinary rogues. In the records of human political history, their evil is identical with every criminal record wherever such historical records are to be found in the world at any time. First of all there is the emotion of vengeance akin to all men everywhere; secondly, and in addition to the vulgar practice of the times in acquiring foreskins as an article of booty, there is the dark anticipation on Saul's part that David would be killed at the hands of the Philistines. Looking back, we can see at this juncture how right Jesus was in his remark about evil coming from the heart of man. It is clear from the text that Saul did not want David as his son-in-law. How else are we to interpret the phrase 'thought to make David fall at the hands of the Philistines' than that Saul desired to bring this about in way that David himself had done with Uriah in his lust to have Bathsheba? It is a political manoeuvre which is as old as the hills. David is pleased with the idea of being raised to royalty since this enhances his prowess as a hero. This fact is something which cannot be overlooked. The language of the Bible is austere and, generally speaking, only that which has significance is mentioned. Here, the joy David feels is clearly depicted. In other words, David's ego was gratified to know that he would 'kill two birds with one stone', marry a beautiful woman and gain access to royalty. His pleasure was great at this moment, as was his anticipation to please the king. Immediately, we read, he goes forth again to kill, not the hundred men demanded by Saul, but two hundred in order to demonstrate what a great sportsman he is. The foreskins are punctiliously counted and the abhorrent tribute triumphantly presented to the king.

To conclude the issue, it does not take a great deal of effort to imagine a close-up on this filthy ritual, to picture the horror of the cold-blooded murder of two hundred men (presumably prisoners), the cries of pain, the heartless bestiality of those carrying out the killing, and the surgical operation committed on men still in their death throes, the blood and horror contrasted with the cool-headed administrative job of counting and preparing this gruesome gift in a vessel fit for the king. In our eyes today the whole procedure is revolting. Shall all this filth and horror be our religious inheritance?

The pages of the books of Samuel throughout display the antics of the typical war hero, David, the careerist murderer, the fornicator and adulterer, coming and going in his killing over Israel's dry land, communing with his god as he does so as to how he shall better gain the upper hand over his enemies.

It is also interesting to recognise as we read of his movements and conquests how similar these are to others of his kind in later history. There is nothing exceptional about them. Hatred, organised violence, brutality, horror, revenge, vulgar egoism, stupid, low-minded killing are the dominant themes in the Old Testament, as they are in the history of man elsewhere and at other times. As in any war at any time, anywhere, the depictions display the phenomenon of man-as-beast, a creature no more elevated in war than the herd of cattle he attends in peacetime. The fact that this David of the Old Testament appeals to the Almighty for help in battle does not add to his distinction and does not, for one moment, exonerate him from his crimes.

From the Buddhist point of view, all this is man in his delusion, the human animal entirely at the mercy of its emotions (like an animal), entirely deluded by what we have referred to above as the extremely subtle samsaric 'dream'. The retrospective, historical view makes this clear to us, like people in a theatre referred to above who, while involved in the performance, nevertheless *know* that it is not immediate reality. The critical commentaries of the accounts given in the Bible (above) should help us to see a little more than what conventional religion, here, Judaism and Christianity, desire to convey to us as part of our heritage.

The suggestion here is that it is an appalling mistake to identify ourselves with the history of war and murder since this is not what we were created for; our task is to grow in spiritual stature, not to descend to the state of lions and tigers. If we do identify ourselves with the doings of David and his associates and accept this record as 'divine revelation' in a 'holy book' which may not be contested, then we are conditioned. That is the point. And if, moreover, we insist that David must be revered and respected as a national hero and an agent of God, or think of him as an irrevocable part of our tradition and of ourselves as an integral part of that tradition, then we deny our ability to discriminate or to think clearly and objectively about matters. In identifying ourselves in this way, we fall short of our wonderful human heritage which is to be free from such associations, in the sense Jesus uses the word 'free'.

It is certainly not easy to leap to new insights from the comfort of a tradition. Tradition is easier to accept and practise as a way of life than objective observation. I repeat: all human beings are conditioned in one way or another and so it is not surprising that Jesus in the cornfield referred to the David of his background in this case as a model of uninhibited conduct when he and his men partook of the sanctified showbread. Jesus was a Jew and, as such, conditioned to believe certain things within the tradition to which he belonged; the Pharisees were Jews and he spoke to them in their own language, that is, in the terms of their own tradition to explain his behaviour. As much as anyone else, the conditioning process common to all human beings had moulded him, too.

In the historical perspective we enjoy today, we recognise him as a man of his time and tradition. He remained a Jew to the end, convinced of his mission to bring men nearer to God in the messianic tradition. To have broken with that tradition even if he had wanted to would have rendered him ineffective as a teacher. There is little doubt that he was aware of the tradition he represented, but – and this is the point – he was not inseparably bound to it as were the Scribes and Pharisees. He had transcended it, which is the same as saying that although he had broken the bonds of conditioned habit, he was still able to express himself within that tradition, using its language and symbols. Such is the state of enlightenment.

Attachment

Closely associated with conditioned behaviour, like smoke in fire, is the phenomenon of attachment. Attachment is a human phenomenon which can be recognised at any time among humans everywhere. As with the acquired reflexive mental structures alluded to above, it is a universal condition. The more powerful the conditioning process, the greater the attachment. Attachment can be defined as a mental or emotional bond between the experience and, say, a person, an idea or tradition (a compound of ideas), or sometimes to an animal or to things, such as money, for example, or the patterns already referred to. It can be instinctive, too, as seen in a parent's attachment to young offspring both in the animal and the human world, or it can be acquired as in an attachment to a country or a nation, the attachment to political ideas, to a wife or a husband, or a lover, attachments to our work, the house we live in or to our circumstances, perhaps to a pet, for example, or a car, to the sport we enjoy or even our state of health. Our attachments are many and can be either strong or weak, but, as the word suggests, they are a bondage. That is not to say that they are good or bad, but may be either. Smoking, for example, which, for some people can prove to be a very powerful habit, is almost certainly dangerous to health and so can be spoken of as harmful to us, whereas our affection for a pet can be seen as a harmless attachment in that it brings neither distress to ourselves nor to others. The suggestion here is not a matter of evaluation as to whether a thing is good or bad, harmful or harmless, but the need to *recognize* that the specific attachment is present within us and at work in others.

An example of what is meant here is given in the example of two distinguished Hindu spiritual teachers who were on a visit to London, where they were entertained by their English hosts one Sunday lunchtime in the late 1930s with roast beef and potatoes. One of them pointed this out to his host with the polite admonition that good Hindus do not eat beef. The other, quickly realising the delicate situation in which they found themselves and the fact that the Hindu tradition is merely a tradition and nothing more, thanked his host, ate the beef and asked for another helping. The swami was quickly able to recognise his own attachment to a traditional concept and deal with it satisfactorily in adjusting to another environment. This is enlightened behaviour.

Attachments play a huge role in our lives, and it is often very difficult indeed for us to see them as such and to detach ourselves from them in order to gain mental freedom. Should there be any doubt about this, we have only to look around the world today from the wealth of information we have to hand to find instances of religious attachments, for example, which are either cruel, pointless or even mindless, and yet their adherents insist on maintaining them even when these customs have quite lost their original purpose and are totally irrelevant to modern times.

The following example taken from an international newspaper, very clearly demonstrates the state of being conditioned and particularly that of being attached to a traditional concept. It occurred in the *Sunday Times* in 1996, entitled 'Armageddon is better the second time round'.[4] The author, Walter Ellis, is writing about the fever of anticipation which accompanies the entry into the new millennium, and here with special reference to the year 2000. In his article, Mr Ellis quotes Pope John Paul II as declaring to a congregation in Crakow, Poland, that, 'we are facing the final confrontation between church and anti-church, between Gospel and Anti-gospel.' The author says that he suspects that the Pope's words 'are rooted in revelation', and that he, the Pope, is *'looking beyond to a new Heaven and a new Earth.'* Continuing his article, the author goes on to quote the Pope as asserting that 'Mary the most Holy, the highly favoured daughter of the Father will appear before the eyes of believers as the perfect model of love towards God and neighbour... for Christians on the way to the great Jubilee of the third millennium (she will be) the star which safely guides their steps to the Lord' (my parenthesis).

In referring to the vision of the Virgin Mary beheld by the three Portuguese peasant children during the First World War, the author quotes the pope as saying that 'around the time of the millennium, God's purpose for the church will be revealed as a miraculous accommodation between the Vatican and the Russian Orthodox Church, which will establish universal recognition of the Pope as Christ's Vicar on Earth' (Ellis' words). Finally, there is reference to the 'third mystery', said to have been closely kept by the Vatican, of Mary's revelation to the children at the time which, it is suspected, will finally reveal the secret that these two branches of Christendom will reunite within the next decades.[5]

Behind the rhetorical appeal to believers, there is the hope in this century of an aggrandisement of the Church's sphere of influence. Primarily – if we are to interpret the author's assumption correctly – we have to do here with church administration, with an ostensibly divinely inspired amalgamation and consequent extension of power and influence in the eastern sphere of the European continent, a modern phenomenon with which all of us are only too well acquainted today in the commercial sector. None of this, it will be noted, has anything to do with the essential teachings of the New Testament, but only with the idea of expansion. The idea of ecclesiastical expansion is based on the missionary ideal of spreading the gospel to all the lands of the earth and this in turn is founded on the assumption that Christian teaching and that of the Roman Church in particular is the prime possessor of religious truth. This conviction is deeply ingrained in Catholic teaching so that for over nearly twenty centuries it has become an article of incontestable truth. Moreover, the conviction has become such a reflexive habit that those who subscribe to it cannot see even the most glaring incongruities inherent in Catholic teaching. For example, with reference to this text, there never was 'a most holy daughter of the Father' in the sense received by the Church. There is no such mention in any of the Gospels, of Mary (Hebrew: *Miryam*) playing a role in this sense. The idea of a 'Mother of God' is wholly alien to the text and the teaching of the New Testament. The bitter truth for many is that, apart from the poetry of the *Magnificat,* which occurs in only one of the Gospels, there are just two references to the mother of Jesus in the rest of the New Testament. Neither of them is very endearing. The first occurs at **Luke, 2:41–49** and relates the story of Jesus' parents seeking their son among the crowds in Jerusalem:

> So when they saw him they were amazed; and His mother said to him; 'Son. Why have you done this to us? Look, your father and I have sought you anxiously.' And He said to them, 'Why did you seek me? Did you not know that I must be about my Father's business?'

It is perfectly natural for a parent to be anxious when a child cuts loose without mentioning where he is going, but fairly typical of the selfish preoccupations of young people. There is probably not a parent in the world who has not experienced this. It is also perfectly reasonable to ask what had happened when, at last, the parents are reacquainted with their offspring. 'Where have you been?' we ask, or 'Whatever happened to you? We have been worried.' No less with this distinguished pair. They were worried as to what had happened to their lad. We cannot say with absolute certainty what the tone of the reply was in this case. It could have been an attitude of incredulous surprise at their ignorance or a straightforward rebuke. But whatever the tone, the result was a public affront to their parental authority. We are not informed as to what happened next nor of the closer circumstances, but what should be recognised here is that the encounter was probably not a particularly edifying one. The second encounter is recorded in **Jn 2:2–4**. It reads:

> Now both Jesus and His disciples were invited to the wedding. And when they ran out of wine, the mother of Jesus said to Him. 'They have no wine.' Jesus said to her, 'Woman, what does your concern have to do with me. My hour has not yet come.'

This can be easily interpreted as a rebuke. The word 'Woman,' used to his mother is, for our ears at least, certainly insolent, and the added, 'what does your concern have to do with me?' plainly arrogant. This is virtually all we know of the mother of Jesus. On such slender reference, this figure was later raised in title to the 'Mother of God', and elevated to the most important central figure of the Catholic religion throughout the world. Today, nobody could imagine the Church devoid of the Madonna. Millions of human beings are brought up to believe in the power of this symbol (conditioning) and find themselves deeply attached to it, despite the wisp of reference upon which it is based. Attachment to symbols is also a form of mental bondage and in this case the result of long-term conditioning.

However, of much more serious import in this papal proclamation is the fact that sentiments such as these entertained by the Pope while in Crakow are taken out of the context of individual devotion and proclaimed as future possibilities within an ostensibly factual frame of reference. Fanciful conviction, tipping dangerously over into mere superstition is illustrated, for example, by the Pope's allusions to an 'anti-Church' and 'anti-Gospel'. Looking at these two ideas factually and without prejudice, we find that there are no such entities. The Supreme Pontiff's statement suggests, however, that bodies of such a kind exist somewhere as active organisations. This is simply not true. What is true is that there is a great deal of passive rejection of the Church and its specific doctrines which have nothing to do with the teaching of the New Testament. What, for example, has the fact of the Inquisition to do with the love of one's fellow man? What have the Crusades, the persecution of non-conformists, the public burning of witches, the amassing of astronomical sums of money, the brutal murder of foreign peoples in the Americas, the wholesale corruption of the medieval Church and a thousand years of anti-Semitism to do with faith and compassion? These are the questions people today ask themselves in a free society. Added to this is the fact that there is serious doubt in the minds of many millions of nominal Christians as to the authenticity of the Gospels, not perhaps as far as their substance is concerned, although this, too, is widespread, but more in the way of doubt about their ecclesiastical interpretation.

There is no 'anti-Gospel' as such, but there is well founded doubt among those who can think for themselves, doubt which is based on a sober review of ecclesiastical history. These opinions have stemmed from the wider dissemination of knowledge already referred to above. It is probable that most of the people who could be described as 'anti-Church' or support a view which questions the validity of the Gospels or, more specifically, the Church's interpretation of them, are those who have given serious thought to the matter of religion. They may well feel today, looking back over the past, that dogma and doctrine have been substituted for a living truth. They may even feel that their religion has been an enforced conditioning process beginning in early childhood which has involved their attachment to certain ideas and concepts which they realise have no foundation in fact. This insight can be easily gained by looking again more closely at the Pope's remarks.

In the first place, his statement clearly and arbitrarily divides humanity into two opposing groups, namely, those who are for the Church (and, by implication, its interpretation of the Gospels) and those who are not. Such an assertion entirely dismisses all the Moslems in the world, not to speak of several hundred million Hindus, all Sikhs, all Jews, to say nothing either of the Buddhists, the members of all other religions, great and small, and millions of other people who entertain no opinion on religion, his or anyone else's. In this perspective, the Pope's view shrinks to parochial dimensions.

Apart from its parochialism, the view is also fundamentalist, and this is much more serious. Not far from views such as these uttered by people in authority, waiting, as it were, in the wings and ready for action, is all the apparatus of hate and oppression which, given the right explosive atmosphere, can be levelled at everything and everybody resisting the traditional, authoritative view. It functions to suppress all other opinion and finally to eliminate those who hold contrary views. So it is with us human beings, so it has always been. Any doubts about our human reflexes in this direction can be cleared up by a look at our recent history. Only a few years ago, the world was witness to a concentrated attachment to fundamentalist ideas in Khomeni's Iran. Little more than half century ago, we saw the same deluded elements at work – albeit in a different direction – in the Nazi Reich, where virtually a whole nation was conditioned to one belief and one way of thinking by one man.

Eight hundred years ago, and, incredibly, for more than 600 years after its inauguration, the Church in Spain entertained its infamous Inquisition (1233–1853), an unspeakable oppression which lasted into modern times. The horror of this long episode in Church history continuing over half a millennium and responsible for an estimated ten million deaths is so great that it can be compared with the outrages conducted against humanity between 1939–1945.

Again, we should remind ourselves that all this organised, ecclesiastical barbarity had nothing whatsoever to do with the teachings propounded by Jesus in the New Testament. When the Pope speaks of an 'anti-Church', he seems not to know that Jesus had no such organisation as a 'church' in mind, as he wandered from place to place, teaching men to be free of their conditioning and their attachments to this world. In Jesus' view, running like a golden thread through the Gospels, the only attachment admitted was an attachment to God, and this is underlined in the first commandment: 'Thou shalt love the Lord thy God with all thy heart and with all thy mind and with all thy strength' **(Mk. 12, 30).**

This, he taught, should be the awareness uppermost in men's minds. Having this, one will possess compassion for one's fellow man as a natural consequence. This is the enlightened state of mind.

His short sojourn among men and women illustrates these convictions perfectly. The 'Church', which the Pope refers to on the other hand, is the organisation history has shown it to be, a history in general of which none but the most fanatical and deluded can be proud. Moreover, it has replaced the 'free mind in God' with dogma, doctrine and law, imposition and punishment, the concept of sin and hell writ so large that there is scarcely room to notice Jesus' essential tidings of faith and love. Indeed, as many before have contended, were Jesus to return today and demonstrate the same powers of compassion and healing, coupled with the same authoritative insistence he possessed in biblical times, and were he to speak out boldly as he once did against the clergy for their shortcomings, he would be quickly taken out of circulation. In short, the Church the Pope speaks of has long since 'digested' its central figure. A Second Coming would be an acute embarrassment.

The contention, too, that there is an 'anti-gospel', to be thought of as a movement or a phalanx of feeling deliberately tilted at the Gospels themselves so as to devalue them in some way is unsubstantiated. It would be nearer the truth to say that there is a huge indifference to them shown by the majority of people in the Western world and to the traditional interpretation of them by the Church. There is nevertheless a new, widespread awakening to matters religious taking place everywhere. This new interest, however, is not confined to Christianity.

Not long ago, the late Cardinal Dyba,[6] in conversation with a journalist, remarked as many others have done in their time in defence of the Catholic Church, that it has survived major changes, such as the Reformation and the division of Church and State, and that all criticism from intellectual quarters including those levelled at it by Voltaire and Nietzsche, will not prevent it from going on triumphantly into the modern era. This suggests that the Church possesses eternal truths which are not eroded by time, and, while there may be some truth in this, it nevertheless forgets the facts that, firstly, it exists as a very well run organisation easily able to uphold its power, and that, secondly, there has never been a viable alternative to its assumptions until now. In the welter of factual information affecting everyone today, there is, and this among other considerations has thrown the Church and its doctrines into a crisis which our present pope represents here as a general movement against Catholicism.

The anticipation that its authority might one day be contested and its power overthrown has been a deep-seated fear within the Church almost since its inception as an organisation. To discourage criticism, it has invented the concept of heresy, the scourge of Western humanity for hundreds of years. Even today, it can announce with daunting presumptuousness:

> Not everyone is to be called a heretic as soon as his faith fails, but those who in underestimating the authority of the Church, stubbornly and wilfully defend their own outrageous opinions. **Catechismus Romanus 1:10.1.**

Every attempt to usurp its authority has been ruthlessly put down from the earliest times. This, too, can be attested to by historical fact.

This very need to protect its code of beliefs with such rigour is at the same time a tacit admission of weakness. Unlike Buddhism, it is unable to stand on its own feet and refer to demonstrable, reproducible fact taken from universal human experience, but must justify its existence by asking us to believe in all sorts of improbable circumstances and derivations, such as a Creator in the image of man taken from the holy texts of another race in another time, a son in that line born of an immaculate conception, destined to save the human race from sin through self-mortification, much in the manner of ancient sacrificial ritual, who dies, and who later ascends to a heaven from whence he (with God Himself) shall come to judge all manner of men for their sins, and from where, after the Second Coming, the sinful shall be condemned to an everlasting hell and the virtuous be exalted to a heaven for all time.

Added to this, all the experiences of life shall be related to this one belief, to this one, short human life, and this act of self-sacrifice. The life of Jesus shall be a model for everyone, everywhere, at all times and all other human activity, whatever it may be, rooted in this one model. Ideally, life itself, after the manner of the ancient Pharisees and those who follow in their footsteps, shall be squeezed into an armour of belief and regulation in order to obtain an eternal life conceived as a joyful but markedly nebulous experience after death. Finally, disbelief in all this shall be punished by the Church in this life and by eternal damnation after death.

This, put boldly, is the essential basis of the Christian religion as we have experienced it at the hands of the Christian Church for twenty centuries. Despite its crudity, it has constituted one of the most powerful forms of bondage (conditioning and attachment) known to man. There is little in it which appeals to common sense or reason and even less which is open to proof, but, underlying the whole emotional proposition, there is an elemental fear that unbelief will bring fateful consequences, and it is precisely upon this string which the Church has harped during its long existence. Today, however, propositions such as these are no longer palatable. The Pope's appeal to believers is very weak argument for people living in a scientific age. The perennial fear of Catholicism's possible refutation as so much superstition and its eventual decay is reflected in the Pope's choice of words and in his illustration (1997). Later, this statement can be seen substantiated by his calling some 150 cardinals together in May 2001, to discuss the crisis in which the Church finds itself. However, whatever these men might decide among themselves, the stark fact which has emerged at the end of the twentieth century is that the period of Pauline Christianity is over. If Christianity in another form is to survive at all in our age and in those to come, it will have to offer *proof* for its arguments and that is only possible if the truths of the New Testament are properly understood and presented in the light of raised consciousness. An enquiry of this kind leaves no room for emotional rhetoric and speculative claptrap.

Just how, for example, does the Pope envisage the cataclysmic event suggested in his vision of a 'new age' described above? *How* would the Virgin guide the footsteps (of millions of people) 'towards the Lord'? What does all this *mean?* Where, precisely, would this 'new heaven and new earth' exist? And why a new heaven? Has the former heaven somehow been inadequate? And does the advent of the next thousand years as calculated by our Christian calendar – itself a perfectly arbitrary measurement of time – provide any tangible evidence whatever for the belief that the world will for this reason radically change in the coming years? Viewed cosmically and set against the implacable continuum of time, the year 2000 has not the slightest significance for our planet. If our evolution is not brought to an abrupt end by asteroid collision or some other natural catastrophe of global dimensions, as has often been the case on Earth in the past, the processes of that evolution which have already been in operation for millions of years will continue against the impenetrable and inconceivable backdrop of the universe.

The idea of change as envisioned by the Pope in the article quoted above is speculative fairy tale, a fanciful bubble with no relation to fact demonstrable or imaginable. With all respect to the Pope and, without doubt, to the benign intentions behind these remarks, they must be rejected by thinking people as so much superstitious humbug.

From these few considerations, we can see now clearly what is meant by the terms 'conditioning' and 'attachment' and how strong these are in regulating our lives. For the Buddhist, these two are recognised as playing a role of paramount importance in creating and sustaining the delusion known as 'samsara' or the 'living dream', which we call life and from which it is vitally necessary for us to awaken if we are to enter upon truly adult life. At the present point in time we are not adult in the spiritual sense and our current activities, social, political, economic, scientific and religious demonstrate the fact. Indeed, from the point of view of spiritual development we have not come far in the 2000 years since Christ's appearance on earth. We have remained spiritual centaurs. We need to realize that revolutionary change of viewpoint, that awakening to the realisation of ourselves and to the nature of our world or 'enlightenment' as Buddhists call it. This is the real import of Jesus' phrase, 'to be born again'. Whether directly referred to or implied, the enlightenment experience informs the Gospels from end to end and is also the vital significance which underlies them.

---

[1] Milgram, S. *Obedience to Authority,* 1974, p. 10ff, quoted from David G. Myers 'Social Psychology', McGraw-Hill, USA, New York City University Press, 1993, p. 236.

[2] It should be noted that the perpetrators of these crimes were neither "Germans" nor "Nazis", but ordinary people working mainly in agricultural pursuits in an unimportant occupied town a thousand miles away from Hitler's hotbeds of propaganda. Rees, Laurence, *The Nazis – A Warning from History,* 'The Way to Treblinka', London, BBC Books, 1997, pp. 219-222.

[3] Just how deluded one can be in this respect is shown in the tragic reports concerning some Jews who managed to escape from Auschwitz and who were picked up by Polish farmers and others and who were later betrayed to the camp authorities on the grounds they were Jews and therefore deserved to be punished for the 'murder of Jesus Christ'!

[4] 'Armageddon is Better the Second Time Round', by Walter Ellis, appearing in The Sunday Times on 22nd December, 1996, p.7.

[5] Apparently the last closely kept secret was the attack on the Pope's life by a would-be assassin.

[6] The interview occurred in the German news magazine 'Focus', No. 14, 29th March, 1997, p.80ff (my translation and brackets).

CHAPTER II

Samsara – a new perspective

If, for a moment, we could jettison all that has been handed down to us by the ancient Hebrews, their Book and their God, their views and their morals, their interpretations of the world, actual and spiritual, and all the accumulations and accretions arising from these in the form of our religious, political and social heritage – if we could do this – we would discover certain facts which are common to all humanity. These immutable facts are summarized in the Sanskrit word, *samsara*.

In ancient Hindu and Buddhist texts, *samsara* is defined as the 'realm of birth and death'. This refers to our life which unfolds to our consciousness from the one state and closes with the other. Birth and death are borders which are also acknowledged in other civilisations as points of entry and departure in life's continuum, but with the difference that in Buddhism there is emphasis on the cyclic nature of this coming and going. It asserts that 'that which dies must be born and that which is born must die'. This, as a matter of interest, is in line with the Western scientific concept of the Law of the Conservation of Matter, where no material is ever lost and where only a change of state takes place to produce a new phenomenon. In this way, for example, a candle burns and so disappears from view, but its constituents are merely transformed to produce heat, light and smoke in which its chemical constituents eventually turn up elsewhere in another combination and, possibly, as another visible phenomenon. The same is true of our bodies; when these cease to function within life's system, they decompose to become something else (chemical combinations favourable to other forms of life), which in its turn becomes something else which then dies and decomposes and so on in a round of becoming. This phenomenon of 'becoming' is referred to as *bhava* in the ancient Sanskrit texts and Buddhism.

In a similar way, the mind also undergoes change at death. It experiences a different plane or planes of consciousness, a fact long since known to Eastern philosophy, proved by religious experience, and for which Buddhism has its own descriptive terminology. The state or successively experienced states may be sublime or otherwise, according to the degree of spiritual development or lack of it. This accords to some extent with the Christian view, except for the significant difference that the state or states after death are considered temporary in Buddhism. That is to say that after a certain 'time' – inconsistent with and independent of our worldly ideas of movement and sequence which give rise to the concept of time – the mind enters the stream of *samsara* once more and manifests itself in a body, although not always a human one. Such an assertion often appears strange to Christian westerners. This is due to our human-orientated way of thinking, a concept ultimately derived from the Old Testament, where man shall have dominion over the earth and is encouraged by Jehovah to multiply as the stars in heaven and sands on the seashore **(Gen. 22:17** and elsewhere**)**, and an opinion further promoted in our own day by a review of our mental achievements. We easily forget that we are only one of countless millions of other forms of life on the planet and that nature, as well as catering for these in the process of *bhava*, apparently does not share our convictions of superiority. Mind (life) is an entity which expresses itself in a myriad of forms, as our recently acquired biological and medical sciences tell us. Buddhism, therefore, maintains that the human mind can, in certain circumstances, be transformed after death into a mind less sophisticated than the human. In this view, it is considered a fortunate circumstance if, within the cycle of becoming, the mind can express itself in human form, since progress in the human form is most conducive to the attainment of enlightenment, whereas other forms are not.[1]

The objective nature of samsara

We know today that the objective circumstances of our biological lives are regulated by the sun and the earth's peculiar rotation, circumstances which combine to produce both day and night, summer and winter. Without the sun, all life on earth would cease. Life as we recognize it has come into being as a result of the distance between the sun and the earth. If the sun were nearer, all water would evaporate, leaving the earth an arid, inhospitable, blazing desert like the planet Mercury; if it were further away, all water would freeze to make the circumstances of the life we are familiar with equally hostile. Our human lives are played out in an acceptable area between great height and great depth – in other words, at pressures and temperatures which vary slightly, but which are amenable to our human bodies. Any large change in these results in injury to our bodies or death. The air we breathe is a mixture which we could say is finely adjusted to our needs, or, more precisely, we over many millions of years have adjusted our bodies to its chemical constitution. Any change in this constitution would also result in death sooner or later. Our bodies and their movements, and those of other creatures which share our existence under the sun, are controlled by these physical and chemical factors in varying degrees of adaptation. Thus, there are some kinds of fish which can withstand enormous underwater pressures and some plants and animals which can comfortably resist the very high surface temperatures of the desert or at other places where temperatures are scores of degrees below zero, but all of them live within a mean of pressure and temperature which supports life compared with those encountered in outer space. All these creatures and we ourselves interact chemically and physically with the world around us in that we take from our environment what is needed to sustain life and void that which is no longer needed, but which in its turn serves chemically and physically to promote the cycle of life. Every ten thousand years or so, and, largely due to the changing course of sea currents, the land masses enclosed by them experience a drop in temperature and these then undergo what we refer to as an Ice Age, which may last for several thousand years before the Earth once again yields to the sun's influence to produce the conditions we recognise today as existing between two ice caps.

This is the energy system we know simply as 'life' manifesting itself on a speck of globular, life-supporting material known as Earth, which almost certainly owes its origin to an immense solar explosion at a time in the past which may be appreciated as a number printed on paper, but which at the same time is quite inconceivable to us. Added to the transformations experienced by the Earth itself, it is also from time to time reminded, so to speak, of its interstellar relationship and the incalculably great physical forces at work in space when our planet happens to be in the track of a large meteorite, resulting in collision and total catastrophe, which devastates practically all life on the globe for several million years afterwards. After such a cataclysm, living things gradually assert themselves again under modified conditions and the cyclic, external aspect of *samsara* is re-manifested.

Meanwhile, the unimaginably great physical and chemical forces at work in the universe beyond our solar system continue to operate in their own cyclic scheme of things whose true nature will probably remain incommunicable to our human minds. Under these influences, it is possible that we, too, like the dinosaurs and other forms of life before us, will finally disappear and be replaced by a new form of life according to the eternal cyclic operation of the laws of *samsara*.

The subjective nature of samsara

For us human beings, the subjective experience of *samsara* begins with birth. From the moment we open our eyes on the world we are influenced by its characteristics. At first we experience changes in light intensity, fluctuations in temperature, contact with hardness and softness; we apprehend sound, then acquire the sense of taste and smell, become aware of our own bodies, experience pain and distress as hunger or deprivation and discomfort. Gradually, as small babies, we become aware of others, our mothers, and later, close relatives and other human beings, young and old, who share our living space. We become aware of weight and balance, movement, pleasure and pain, injury and fear, the presence and the nature of other life as animals, birds, fish and insects. Colour discernment is intensified, giving a new dimension to life, and eventually we go out into the open and become acquainted with the larger world around us. For most of us, this will be the physical environment in which we will spend the cycle of our lives. As we grow into childhood, this and the human beings who inhabit that environment will quickly mould our mental and physical habits to those vital to survival within it. Along with these characteristic developments, if not much earlier, disease and the possibility of accident will accompany us at every point on our way. Either may blight our lives at any time; one of them can cut us off from life without notice, while the other, disease, operating from without and within, can blind us, cripple us or banish us to our beds for years before we finally succumb to death. Nobody, young or old, male or female, is exempt from selection, and the diseases we are heir to as humans are legion.

This is our common heritage. Parallel with this, however, is the experience of love, the love of our parents and friends, physical well being, energy, hope, the sense of being protected, harmony and happiness and the joy of being alive, among many other nuances of pleasurable experience.

As we grow in knowledge and stature, we acquire certain attitudes of mind commensurate with our surroundings. As children, we experience the presence of others, their convictions and habits and – if we are lucky – we receive an education. The latter is a process which associates us with ideas and concepts outside our immediate experience. At the same time, all these external influences are modified by our own innate tendencies and proclivities.

According to the Buddhist view, these inclinations are what we bring with us from previous lives, and may express themselves to our advantage or disadvantage, for the good of others or to their detriment. Their presence – which, incidentally, is one implicit proof of the cyclic nature of our lives – may remain a potential or be realised in this life. Initially, their discovery and development is largely in the hands of others. As a child, an early interest in matters practical and functional, for example, may, with encouragement, produce a carpenter, a builder or an engineer. Conversely, a tendency to deceit and taking egotistical advantage may, together with a lack of love and the connivance of others, produce a cheat, a thief or even a murderer. Today, due to the spread of the general principles of psychology, we are keenly aware of these considerations, and of the fact that much depends on early influence as to whether, in later life, the good in us will flourish, or the bad. Ignatius Loyola, speaking some 500 years ago, once announced: 'Give me the child before the age of seven, and I will be responsible for the man,' thus implying the power of the conditioning process over the human mind if exercised at an early stage.

These matters, which have been known to man in a general way for thousands of years, have, over the last hundred years, been particularised and formalised in the study of psychology. In Buddhism they have always been recognised as elements playing a vital part in the general human situation known as *samsara* and are referred to generally as *karma*. Their existence is of paramount importance to the development of all human beings everywhere and in every age.

Karma

Karma is part and parcel of *samsara*, and the two are inseparably bound up with one another. Some people like to equate *karma* with fate, but this view is not quite in focus. 'Fate' or 'Destiny' might be thought of as having an author or a divine mover in the classical Greek sense where a god, for example, may determine the direction, for better or worse, of a mortal life. Its operation is very well illustrated in the Greek classic, *Oedipus Rex*. Or these two concepts are often thought of simply as 'good luck' or 'ill luck'. However, this is not the Buddhist view, which is rather more prosaic. This holds that all our actions and all our thoughts, those of the past and those of the present, have an effect on our being. What we *are* is what we have thought and done, and what we *will be* depends on what we think and do in this life. For most westerners this is acceptable enough: we are what we think, we say. But Buddhism goes further than this again and maintains that we alone are not wholly responsible for our being. Others play a large role in our lives, in supplying us with food and shelter, work, a degree of security, our bodily needs and comforts, our entertainment and something to hope for, as well as our physical, mental and spiritual progress. The thoughts and deeds of those around us vitally affect our lives and contribute to the make-up of our *karma*. And more. The experiences of others impinging on our lives in the past, before our present state of consciousness, also contribute to our *karmic* experience.

We have already touched on this, but just how detailed these connections are can be demonstrated by yet another example.

Those who reject the idea of rebirth might do well to reflect on a simple instance made known to us only recently with the setting up of the human genetic code. We know now without doubt that some genes within our make-up can be responsible for certain diseases. We know, too, that these diseases can be latent within us until such time as circumstances permit their manifestation. These 'circumstances' could, for example, be ageing, exposure to certain materials, or simply the lapse of a certain time after which the disease 'matures' or breaks out into a recognisable illness. These diseases are very often inherited.

Buddhist experience maintains that the same is true of the mental and spiritual planes and that this accounts for the fact of inequality among mankind. It explains why some have good fortune throughout their lives, almost without effort on their part, while others are plagued by ill-luck, why some die early and others live long, why some enjoy robust health for a lifetime and others are delicate and easy prey to disease, why some fall on hard times, whereas others enjoy comfort and prosperity to the end, why some are plucked off in their prime, or even in childhood, without evident reason, and others are struck down with dreadful diseases which linger on for many years, why some are gifted and others not why some make tragic mistakes or decisions in life and others do not, and so on and so forth; the list is endless. In physics one speaks of a resultant direction when many forces have been at work on moving or influencing a body, and in the Buddhist concept of *karma* it is the same. We humans are the product of many forces both past and present, and, of course, also the result of our own decisions, our will and our ego.

While this is undoubtedly the case, the Buddhist again probes further and says that what *others* have sown will also be reaped, for the simple fact is that we are not alone. A fact in support of this is the example of war where, for the decisions of a few, hundreds of thousands, or perhaps millions, of people suffer as a result.

We can see from what has been said above that *karma* is a function and is directional. That is to say, it is a force which leads the individual from one state or position to another. It is an influence not only of a fateful, negative kind as is generally believed in the West, and often used in this sense by Buddhists themselves, but also, more accurately, an operative force in our lives whose results can be both negative *and* positive. The simple fact is that *karma* can be positive, negative or neutral, using these words of course in their usual sense of bringing pleasure or distress or being neither the one nor the other. Since, from the Buddhist point of view, its operation is inexorable, it is referred to as the *Law of Karma*. We can imagine it as working in a similar way when we consider the relationship of an object to its shadow. Where there is light, an object will automatically cast a shadow. That which has been sown in the past will automatically come one day to fruition in the present. That which is sown today will also come to fruition in the future. This is perhaps what Ecclesiastes means when he says: 'Cast your bread upon the waters, For you will find it after many days' **(Eccl. 11:1).** There is no dodging the issue, Buddhists say, when it comes to doing right or wrong. It may well seem to us in our short lives that by acting anti-socially and egotistically or criminally we profit and do well in the world, but in the longer term we must pay the price for it in suffering **(Psalms 37:35–6).**

Conversely, if we act for the benefit of our fellow men and women, entertain good thoughts and curb the instinct to act selfishly, we finally benefit from the practice, even when this may not appear to be the case in our current lives. It is a matter of the cultivation of the inner being – or the lack of it. These ideas, as we can see, are reflected in the teachings both of the New and Old Testaments.

Karma is operative in this life and the next and at all times, acting like gravity as a force we cannot see, but whose influence we can feel. The refusal to grasp the concept of cyclic existence on different planes is due to the western fixation on this life as the one and only life, to be followed by an 'everlasting' (or 'eternal') existence after death, for which there is no proof.[2] The meaning of 'everlasting life', on the other hand, in the sense Jesus used the phrase is something quite different and will be treated later.

If we can adjust our viewpoint slightly and see this life as a preparation for another life on a higher (or lower) plane according to our *karmic* propensities, *samsaric* existence takes on new meaning. The path to enlightenment may oblige us to pass through several lives before we can realise ourselves, become enlightened, and so transcend the rigorous pattern of *karmic* law. Having done so, we find true freedom, liberation from the *samsaric* world of *karma* with its immutable relationships, within a dualistic world of opposites, of light and darkness, up and down, good and bad, happiness and sorrow, outer and inner, stasis and movement, and so on *ad infinitum*. Having once seen clearly for ourselves into the workings of the system, we are truly free for the first time in our lives. For the first time for perhaps aeons of time (according to Vedic and Buddhist interpretation) we find ourselves able to act spontaneously from the depths of our being, unhindered by thought associations geared to conditioned processes. In that moment we are free forever from the need to react to any other pattern of circumstances than those present in this very moment of time. We are unburdened in the sense that Jesus himself was free from the burdens of law and observation with which men encumber themselves. This is why he felt himself quite untroubled by social constraint as he mixed with the wine-bibbers, tax-collectors, publicans and prostitutes who formed part of the simple townsfolk of his day. Like all enlightened or 'reintegrated' beings in whatever era or country, and within whatever religious culture, he lived in the 'Now' of time, not, as we do, in the uncertain, hoped-for future of unfulfilled desires or the comfortable past of experience and identifiable tradition.

In enlightenment, *karma* comes to an end. This state of mind is not simply an intellectual appraisal of the situation, but what Suzuki[3] describes as a 'revolution' within the mind, where the individual is, so to speak, totally 're-polarised'. It is a profound, momentary, subjective 'in-seeing' which propels the perceiver into a new dimension of living and being.

For the moment we can think of 'enlightenment' or 'freedom' as it is often called, as a situation where the denizens of Plato's Cave stand up from the dull contemplation of their wall and look upon the light and beauty of the world lying before them at the cave's entrance, a dimension hitherto unimagined by them and indescribable in terms of the dark interior of the cave. Until that time, rebirth continues until the sufferer (the individual) finally recognises the need to realise himself and so finally comes to understand the mechanics of the System (i.e. *samsara*) described above.

The whole of the New Testament can be seen as an antithesis between Jesus in the Now of God's Enlightenment and the people around him who were awaiting a Messiah (future fulfilment) and the representatives of the religious establishment who were content with the Law and its ancient, traditional interpretations (the past).

The nature of our lives in samsara, tanha and dukkha

The word *tanha* in Sanskrit means 'thirst'. It refers in the religious sense to that thirst for fulfilment which assails us all as human beings, wherever we are found, and is the ground of our being. When we are thirsty, we seek to slake our thirst and so recover from that which distresses us. So it is in life. Thirst, *tanha*, is manifested in life as desire. Desire can take a million different objects, and find a million different expressions, but essentially there is only one desire rooted in *samsara* and this is the profound desire for personal fulfilment which, finally and paradoxically, is liberation from desire.

In our own lives we move from one desire to the next and our human world, too, is borne on the waves of desire. Proof of this is to be found by looking around us wherever we happen to be in the world. Reading newspapers with this observation in mind, for example, is to discover the sinews which drive the world we live in. As individuals, we experience desire early in life as children, and later go in pursuit of satisfaction independently as we get older. Later still, we may fulfil our desires as parents and householders, as identified members in our own particular social setting, in our jobs or careers, in the work we do, which may or may not involve either of these, in the acquisition of experience in what we do, in the attachment to certain codes of behaviour, in aspiring to some goal or other, in commitment to a cause or a movement, in personal self-sacrifice or, on the other hand, we may finally even gain authority over others, worldly power and amass a fortune. Or we may not. But desire will pursue us nevertheless, drive us on to achieve, to realise something, to gain this or that, whether the object of our desire be material or immaterial, whether it happens to be money or success, others' acknowledgement or personal, private satisfaction. Generally speaking, desire is strongest during the period of our sexual maturity and in most cases ebbs away slowly as we become older and less able to fulfil our desires.

Most of us are so preoccupied with the pursuit of our desires that we have no time or inclination to consider why we pursue them. Very few of us pause to ask ourselves why we desire this or that, since the answer appears obvious and the question silly. If one were to ask someone, for example, why he or she is busy pursuing a degree in the hope of becoming a barrister, where the chances of success are good and where, at the end of study, there is an interesting career with very good pay and much social distinction to be attained, the question might be considered not only silly, but also slightly offensive. Such an enquiry could well expose the questioner as foolish. So deeply imbued are we, and especially in these times, by the desire to be wealthy and to enjoy material well-being, desires imposed on us by the current *Zeitgeist*, that any doubts raised on the desirability of money and social distinction are immediately regarded as suspect. However, it is not that the desire to become a lawyer is undesirable in this instance, nor even the desire to earn large sums of money by rightful employment, but the wholesale commitment to an aim *without the awareness of self.*

Thoughtful Christians would think of this as putting oneself before God, that is to say, thinking primarily and exclusively of one's own advantage. Here again, the Buddhist goes further and regards concern with self as *reflexive reaction* and therefore characteristic of animal behaviour. Another illustration might assist us at this point to make this aspect of desire clearer.

In the 16th century there were two statesmen who played out their respective roles on the political stage when Henry VIII held sway over England. The one was Thomas Wolsey, cardinal of the Church of Rome and Lord Chancellor. The other was Sir Thomas More who succeeded the latter as Lord Chancellor in 1529. Both men held responsible posts in the government of the time and both were key figures in the shaping of a modern England at the close of the Middle Ages. The first, Wolsey, was a competent careerist who acquired great wealth and influence, standing in the king s favour for many years during his political life, and his power was much envied as a consequence. The other Thomas had been a successful lawyer before entering diplomatic service, served the king loyally, but kept his own counsel as far as the king's policies were concerned. The king's one overwhelming desire at the time of these two contemporaries was for a male successor, and to this end he wished to divorce his ageing queen[4] and marry a younger. He was so overwhelmed by this one great wish that he was ready to defy the power of the Roman Church which expressly forbade divorce even among its royal subjects. To achieve this end, Henry enlisted Cardinal Wolsey's diplomatic skill and influence to bring about a divorce by hook or by crook, and Wolsey for his part exerted himself mightily on the king's behalf. However, during these exertions and despite the most conscientious efforts, he fell into disfavour, was subsequently charged with treason and called to London to be executed. At the city of Leicester, halfway house on the journey south to his final ignominy, he died with the words, 'Had I but served God as diligently as I have served the king, he would not have given me over in my gray hairs.'

Thomas More, on the other hand, although just as diligent, was a much more conscious individual in that he was more acutely aware of life's priorities. He did not seek affluence and power to prop up his ego, but lived in modestly comfortable circumstances, closely integrated with his family. In 1532 he resigned from his chancellorship, ostensibly for reasons of ill-health, but probably because he could no longer agree with the king's policies. When the latter insisted that he was not only England's monarch, but also head of the Church, More refused to support him, since he could not reconcile this with his conscience. Henry and Sir Thomas had been good friends during the former's early reign, so that it was hard for the king to condemn him. He therefore threw his subject into the Tower in the hope that he would revise his opinion, but later had him beheaded on charges of treason. At his execution, More jested with his executioners, saying until the end that he had been 'the king's good servant, but God's first'.

This same theme of priority is treated in the New Testament where Jesus speaks of a certain rich man:

> The ground of a certain rich man brought forth plentifully: And he thought within himself, saying, What shall I do, because I have no room where to bestow my fruits? And he said, This I will do: I will pull down my barns, and build

greater; and there will I bestow all my fruits and my goods. And I will say to my soul, Soul, thou hast much goods laid up for many years; take thine ease, eat, drink and be merry. But God said unto him, Thou fool, this night thy soul shall be required of thee: then whose shall those things be, which thou hast provided? So is he that layeth up treasure for himself and is not rich toward God. **(Lk. 12:16–21)**

The parable of the Prodigal Son **(Lk.15:11–32)** is another example which demonstrates this principle.

Very similar anecdotes in support of the same idea appear in other religious traditions, where a son determines to go his own way and leave the love and care of his family. On his way through the world he falls on hard times during which he has to suffer privation. It is during his adventures that he thinks in misery and sadness of the happiness he once enjoyed in the bosom of his family. After many years of hardship, he returns and is welcomed by his father (God in this case), who celebrates his homecoming with great joy.

The Buddhist approach to what the Christian calls 'worldly' preoccupations is much more severe. It refers to 'worldly temptations' as implied in the examples above as *samsara's deathly ocean*, and regards involvement with them as the cause of inevitable suffering which is in the long run, the death of consciousness. By 'involvement' we mean that attachment which has already been described. It is the *attachment* to these 'sins' or 'temptations', as the Christian would term them, which is really the important thing. We know that we are obliged to live in the world, to earn our living, to do our duty, to adjust our desires and needs to those of others, and so on, but we should not become attached or too much involved with any one aspect of these associations so as to stunt our consciousness.

This is an admonition which occurs in the Bible and in the literature of other religions, but in Buddhism our attention is drawn to the underlying fact behind the symptom of *tanha,* the essential cause of our desires, and not the result of them. In short, we are asked to look into ourselves in order to discover *why* we thirst. To be aware of the presence of *tanha* at work in us is a step in the direction of raised consciousness. This looking into oneself is to eventually find the 'water' referred to by Jesus in his conversation with the woman at the well **(Jn. 4:13–14)**. This is the water, he says, which will slake our thirst for self-fulfilment for ever. He meant enlightenment. Once enlightenment has taken place, the desire for every substitute which the world could possibly offer is seen for what it is – a substitute for the real thing, a bauble and a fake. *Tanha* is present in us all to remind us that we are seeking for this, the reality which will, so to speak, finally 'fill us up' once and for all.

The truth of our lives is that we are all feverishly and unconsciously seeking that 'something' which will end our search, and on the way through life we accept many substitutes in the hope that these will help us to this end, but, sadly and often tragically, we come to discover that there is no substitute. This is the message no less of Buddhism than of Christianity.

However, we should note in passing that all this runs directly counter to the assumptions of our modern, materialistic, money-seeking, hedonistic society.

'Unease' as dukkha

The Sanskrit word *dukkha* is usually translated as 'suffering'. However, strictly speaking, the word is the antonym of *sukkha,* which means *'sweet'* and from which we derive our own word, 'sugar', for that quality. The Buddha announced in his first proposition about the essential nature of our life that it is *dukkha*, that is, 'not sweet', but sour. That is to say, it is not as we would like it to be; it is not paradise. Paradise, we could imagine, is a place or state of mind where there is no yearning, a condition of inner peace and contentment in which everything is in perfect order and deeply satisfying, and where everyone is optimally happy. Life is not like that. But then it is not a hell, which would be the contrary, although, of course, it occasionally can be for us all and, for a few unfortunates, life is more a hell than anything else. Hell is to be understood as a permanent state of suffering from which there is no relief. Life is rather a state which could be described as lying midway between heaven and hell. Its main characteristic is experienced by us as something not quite satisfactory. It is not, we feel, what it should be; it is not what it could be. It does not run smoothly. It is a struggle. Put in biological terms, from the moment we leave the comfort of the womb, we are subjected to constant stimulus. Alan Watts, in his book *The Way of Zen*, describes our human situation in this respect as that of a flea upon a hot griddle: 'The flea that jumps must fall and the flea which falls must jump'.

We human beings want things to go along smoothly and without friction, but there is always an exceptional circumstance, an obstacle, a hindrance, a blockage a setback or a turn in events to keep us on our toes and provide frustration. As a Zen adage has it, 'Spring comes and the weeds are there'. Death can be a deterrent to our plans and in any case always comes too early; sickness is ever present to thwart our hopes and aspirations or curb our activities; the processes of change in which ageing and illness are an integral part linger in our bodies and in our surroundings. The fact of change is, in itself, a frustration. Nothing ever stops, but, like a river, flows on, changing its form as it progresses, and the comfort of stillness and peace we yearn for is lost in every moment. Moreover, happiness when it comes is fleeting and quickly becomes a memory, passing like the rest of our experience rapidly down river to oblivion. That which once was is no longer here, and that which is here will soon be gone, and we with it. Meanwhile there is yearning. Deep within us we feel that there is something missing and crave inwardly for that something.

This craving or thirst (Sanskrit, *tanha)* leads to action (Sanskrit, *trishna*, grasping) and our involvement (identification) with substitutes for true happiness, as we have seen above. These substitutes may or may not lead to temporary happiness, but they will not change the basic quality of life, which is intractable, only temporarily satisfactory, and unpredictable. Moments of happiness are like the brief glimpses of light and beauty which porpoises must glimpse when they jump from their watery element, but which must return to the depths of the sea where most of their life is spent. Like them, one may emerge from the customary and the routine to experience the happy moments in life, but they will surely pass, and we are always sad when they pass so quickly.

This is what we all have to do with for the most part during life. This is the very nature, the quiddity of our life. This is *dukkha,* the state of having to deal with life, wrestle with it, manage it and put up with it, suffer it, be moulded by its exigencies, grow old with it, and finally die under its uncompromising progression.

Most Buddhists automatically translate the word *dukkha* as 'suffering' with the result that one can quickly gain the idea that all life is suffering. This is not true. Life is not to be understood as total distress. There is suffering in life, but there is also relief from suffering. Unrelieved suffering, as we have said, is hell, and we do not – most of us – live in hell. Neither do we live in a state of *sukkha* – unrelieved joy and happiness, such as we imagine happiness to be. Instead, we experience both extremes within a neutral matrix, the warp and woof of *samsara*, the Buddha's 'Middle Way', which consists of yearning for the one (happiness) and striving to avoid the other (suffering). In this we are like the rest of creation, since all life desires to survive by avoiding suffering. This desire is at the root of our being and, on the human level, gives rise to all other desire or craving. When we desire something, we hold on to the object of our desire, whether this object is mental or physical. The strength of desire for a physical object is well illustrated in the case of our sexual attachments, and this again we share with the animal kingdom. Its power can also be seen in all our emotional attachments ultimately based on desire.

We do not have to look far for confirmation of the fact that our lives are woven of desire, since all our literature, including the Bible, is its record.

This is not to say that desire is either good or bad, but to plainly point out that desire is at the core of our lives. Simply to recognise this fact in detachment is already to be partially enlightened as to our condition, since, by intellectual recognition of the fact that we are bound by desire is, for a moment at least, to remove ourselves from our involvement with it.

Further entanglement with desire, on the other hand, leads to what Buddhism refers to as 'clinging' or 'grasping', a process which contains the seeds of frustration and therefore suffering. What we cannot have leads to misery, and what we do acquire gives way sooner or later to the desire for something else. Looked at this way, our desires are seen to be endless: no sooner is one desire gratified than another takes its place. A biologist might well describe this condition as a state of 'permanent stimulus or irritation'. This, too, is the state of *dukkha*.

Summary – the chain of causation

The Buddha's Enlightenment revealed what we have described above as the 'mechanics' of our mental world in twelve points, also referred to as the 'Chain of Simultaneous Dependent Origination'. This describes how our mental world arises. One should understand it not as a sequential development, but an immediate, interdependent phenomenon. That is to say, when one of these phenomena is there, the others are also there, each depending on the other, hence the word 'chain'. Most of them have been referred to above, interacting with one another in the examples taken from human life. They are summarised here to give the reader an overall view of what we have called the 'System'.

At the head of the chain of twelve links is Ignorance *(avidya)*. This gives rise to the idea of what has been called 'separateness' or individuation. The same idea is poetically illustrated in the Old Testament as the Fall of Man, as the separation from God (Oneness) and from there to individuation as in the case of the errant angel, Lucifer.

Ignorance divides what the Christian would call the Divine Unity of the mystics into 'parts-of-a-whole' or individuated elements which create patterns or forms. These individuated forms give rise in their turn to *samsara,* from which the principle of consciousness develops. Consciousness *(vijnana)* gives rise to mind and body, which in its turn gives rise to the sense organs *(nama-rupa)*; their presence in turn gives rise to organs of sensation and perception *(shadayatana)* and thus perception and sensation *(spasha)* arise; from their presence, feeling and discrimination arise; because feelings and sensation are present *(vedana),* thirst and craving arise; thirst and craving *(trishna)* in their turn lead to grasping and clinging *(upadana),* and because of the presence of these, conception and development *(bhava)* take place, thus continuing the process of coming into being, and thus existence; because of the presence of coming into being which produces existence *(jeti)*, growth, sickness, decay and death *(jana-marana)* inevitably follow, thus producing the round of existence known to us as life, with all its characteristics.

The permanent round of desire and gratification (or lack of it), this awareness of being constantly obliged, as it were, to find satisfaction, is referred to as 'the round of becoming' (Sanskrit, *bhava*). 'Becoming' means coming into being, flourishing, decaying and dying, coming into being again, with all the accompanying phenomena this entails, and can be seen in every expression of life. To put it another way, whether we think of ourselves as Christians, Hindus, Jews or Moslems, we cannot conceive of existence as not possessing these characteristics. This is the stuff of life, and there are no exceptions to the rule. This movement *is* our existence.

This being the case, the Buddha asked, is there any way to find that permanent happiness or satisfaction for which we all so deeply yearn? Yes, there is, he added, answering his own question: paradoxically enough, happiness and fulfilment lie in the ablation of desire. By eradicating desire, the round of *bhava* and all that it implies, as explained above, is halted. This does not mean, of course, that the individual will live for ever in the body he now invests, since *bhava* or 'becoming' is part of the universal System, what the Christian would call God's Creation, or the Hindu's 'divine pageant of Shiva', but that the human being, in his personal experience of *samsara*'s burden, is now free of it, like someone cured of a disease. He or she will have put an end to the unending round of existence on the mental or spiritual plane which in turn gives rise to the physical body as set out below in the Chain of Causality. For such individuals, the round of *dukkha* is now at an end, once and for all.

Jesus knew, no less, that the way to redemption from *dukkha* lay in the putting an end to desire. To the young man who wishes to follow him he says:

> And behold, one came and said to him, Good Master, what good thing shall I do, that I may have eternal life? And he said unto him, Why callest thou me good? There is none good but one, that is, God; but if thou wilt enter into Life keep the commandments. He saith unto him, Which? Jesus said, Thou shalt not murder, Thou shalt not commit adultery, Thou shalt not steal, Thou shalt not bear false witness,

> Honour thy father and mother: and, Thou shalt love thy neighbour as thyself. The young man saith unto him: All these things have I kept from my youth up: what lack I yet? Jesus said unto him: If thou wilt be perfect, go and sell that thou hast, and give to the poor, and thou shalt have treasure in heaven: and come and follow me. But when the young man heard that saying, he went away sorrowful: for he had great possessions. **(Mt. 19:16–22)**

Proof that Jesus' words are in line with Buddhist teaching is given by the fact that the master first enquires as to the young man's moral standards. It is clear that we cannot aspire to the spiritual understanding implied here if we spend our days killing people, or animals, or are busy indulging our sexual appetites, or stealing (in all the many subtle ways there are to steal and defraud today), or if we use our time denouncing others, blaming our parents, or putting ourselves first in everything we do. All these harmful tendencies are embodied in the Buddha's 'Eightfold Path' as advice to aspirants on those things which must be strenuously avoided if one is to realise the condition of enlightenment. This is why Jesus first enquires about these things. 'If this be the case,' he then says (in so many words), 'then you are worthy of that Life I speak of; the only thing to do now is to give up your attachment to material things and then you can follow me.'

The rich young man is disappointed with this answer and turns away. Later, Jesus turns to the company with him and remarks that it is almost impossible for the rich to enter the kingdom of heaven. The disciples are 'exceedingly amazed' at this and say, in so many words, 'Well if they can't, who can?' However, the situation is very simple. If you are attached – and this is the key word – to your possessions, you have already chosen these as a substitute for the kingdom. It is simply a matter of 'For where your treasure is, there will your heart be also' **(Lk. 12:34)**.

The fact is that the two, worldly riches and pleasures, and true understanding or enlightenment, are two different things. As a modern teacher once remarked, 'If you want to buy a jewel, you have to go to the right shop; you don't go elsewhere and order a sack of potatoes!'

By being rich, one is not automatically excluded from the gift of enlightenment or from what Jesus here calls 'Life'. Neither is Jesus' injunction a plea for universal penury. Of all people, he knew well what pain and poverty were and, like every enlightened individual before and after him, realised that if people are suffering under grinding poverty, they are more likely to be concerned about their immediate material plight than what they see as the abstractions of spirituality. This is undoubtedly why the Master sought to relieve people of their physical afflictions and the pain incurred by them. If there is suffering of this kind, there cannot be proper concentration in this life on that which matters most. The opposite produces an identical result: if there is considerable material well-being, then there is little time to attend to the spiritual, since those concerned are forever entertaining themselves and so distract themselves in one way or another from the main issue in life – ultimate inward satisfaction. As far as possessions (riches) are concerned, it is plainly a matter of priorities.

> And do not seek what you should eat or what you should drink, nor have an anxious mind./ For these things the nations of the world seek after, and your Father knows that you need these things./ But seek the kingdom of God, and these things shall be added to you. **(Lk. 12:29–32)**

In Zen we read of the advice given to those who wish to meditate and so come to realisation:

> If you are poor, accept your poverty; mend your clothes and keep them clean. If you are rich, do not be attached to your riches.

It is all a question of regulating desire. Ideally, there should only be one desire, Jesus reiterates throughout the Gospels, and that is the desire for God or for what the Rabbi describes as 'eternal life'. We should not be put off our desire to seek God, he says, and develops the theme clearly:

> Therefore I say to you, do not worry about your life what you will eat; nor about the body, what you will put on. /Life is more than food, and the body is more than clothing. /Consider the ravens, for they neither sow not reap, which have neither storehouse nor barn; and God feeds them. Of how much more value are you than the birds? /And which of you by worrying can add one cubit to his stature? /If you are

then not able to do the least, why are you anxious for the rest?
(Lk. 12:22–26)

The 'rest' of our lives, earning a living, maintaining our social contacts and the friends we have, supporting our families, playing our role in the maintenance of our society, and so on, are considered above to be part of our existence, but not the most important part. Such a view is alien to us; it seems at odds with all we recognise as sensible and practical, and we reject the idea like the young man who decided to stay with his possessions, 'and he went away sorrowful'. Jesus' admonition, however, well accords with the Buddhist view, which insists that everything should be subordinated to the desire to find enlightenment, the task in this case being compared with the need to 'row' without distraction over an expanse of water to reach the 'other shore', where the 'two shores' are represented respectively as *samsara* and *nirvana*.

The need to 'see into the nature of things', as Zen puts it, is clearly proved by the Buddha's own life in his early endeavours to reach enlightenment as a young man. He leaves all the comforts of his palace, his wife and his son, gives up everything he owns, dons the rags of a beggar and goes into the woods to meditate without cessation on what Christians would be likely to call 'the meaning of life'. In this, the Buddha was living proof of the need to renounce everything in order to find the truth. His early search for liberation is also proof in action of Jesus' words 500 years later: 'Ask, and it shall be given to you; seek, and ye shall find; knock, and it shall be opened unto you'. Here, in referring to the need to 'knock', that is, to ask to be enlightened or, as the Christian mystics put it, 'to yearn to know God', he implies that there is a *need* to knock; there must be effort on Man's side. He goes on to say that those who ask, or 'knock' and seek for truth will be rewarded **(Mt. 7:7–8)**.

After his sojourn in isolation, the Buddha's eyes were opened to the truth. Returning in joy to a place where he had once been in debate with other ascetics who, from his bearing and wisdom, immediately recognised his acqured spiritual stature, he later formulated the path to enlightenment in the Four Noble Truths, three of which we have already touched upon but have not referred to directly.

In conclusion, then, the Four Noble Truths are:

- Life is suffering (in the sense described above);
- The cause of all suffering is desire;
- Deliverance from suffering is the ablation of desire;
- The way to the ablation of desire is the Eightfold Path, which we can now review.

---

[1] The attainment of enlightenment is only possible n the human form.

[2] It is likely that in the course of the next century palpable proof will be found in psychological and other research areas for the fact of pre-existence.

[3] The phrase is used by Alan W. Watts in his *The Way of Zen*, Pantheon Books, NY, 1957

[4] For a full account of enlightened reference in English literature, see R.H. Blyth, *Zen in English Literature and Oriental Classics*, Tokyo, Hokuseido Press, 1942.

CHAPTER III

Basic requirements for enlightenment

Just as everything we do, whether great or small, has its consequence, so true enlightenment is followed by compassion. After his realisation, the Buddha then considered how others could be helped to the same insight. With this in mind, we should be aware of the fact that between the first three truths expounded by the Buddha and the last truth there is a difference. The first three belong to the experience of spiritual insight and are the result of intense commitment to knowing the truth which, for him, was more important than life itself. Jesus, too, refers to the same principle **(Mt. 18:9)**:

> And if your eye causes you to sin, pluck it out and cast it from you. It is better for you to enter into life with one eye, rather than having two eyes, and to be cast into hell fire.

After rejecting all forms of self-chastisement as 'vain and unprofitable', the Buddha is said to have accepted milk from a peasant girl as refreshment and, settling himself to meditate under a tree, declared that he would not cease from that moment onwards to search for meaning in life, even if it meant his own demise in doing so. In this way he gained deep understanding of the nature of consciousness at all spiritual levels. Profound absorption and concentration of this kind is called *samadhi* in Sanskrit. It implies the total submission of self to the one desire – in this case, to know. Sometimes it can refer to the same self-effacement in submission to a divine personage.[1] This aspect of complete supplication or immersion is recognised in the East as a form of religious commitment (*bhakti*) – to which category Christianity, especially in its mystical expression, also belongs.

There is, however, another approach to religious truth which involves the intellectual faculties. This is known as *vichara* in Sanskrit. *Vichara* is guided argument towards understanding religious truth, a favourite technique used by the Buddha and his followers. Jesus, as far as we know, never used this method of instruction to enlighten his hearers in the resolute logical way the Buddha did. Instead, he inclined more to parable and anecdote as a means of convincing his listeners. The use of parable is a method whereby the mind of the hearer is coaxed by illustrative example to suddenly perceive the larger meaning of the anecdote. The story of the 'Good Samaritan' **(Lk. 10:33–7)** is a typical example. The *vichara* technique, on the other hand, is an appeal to the listener's sense of logic and his powers of deduction, much in the manner of that used a hundred years after the Buddha by Socrates and others of the Greek philosophical tradition. Its mechanics are those of the syllogism: Let this be if this is so, then that, too, must be the cause or the result or the equivalent: therefore this must be the conclusion we can draw. It throws the questioner or the listener back upon his own intellectual resources, from which position he is then forced to ask himself whether he can accept the premise or not. This, generally, was the Buddha's approach to his audience.

As has already been pointed out, he was quite ready to accept disagreement. 'If you are not in agreement with what I declare, you are quite at liberty to try out your own theories and believe what you will,' he said once. In this attitude lies the fundamental difference between the 'declarative religions' (Judaism, Christianity and Islam) and Buddhism. And the difference is of the greatest psychological importance. It implies that the individual has come to his religious convictions not by the offices of some person or body in authority above him which insists that there is no alternative to its interpretation of religious conviction, but that the individual has thought about the matter, considered alternatives, and come to understanding by himself. This is an act of conscious acceptance. Moreover, since Buddhism starts from the premise of the experience of life itself, verifiable and repeatable as in scientific analysis, and not from demanded belief in insubstantial assumptions, concepts alien to the intellect, or the example of ancient historical figures. Its tenets for this reason sit much more firmly in the mind than those fed to us on pain of eternal damnation or social ostracism if not believed. Appeals to belief are based on emotional response, not on an intellectual one. With such emotional appeals, the mind is cheated of its right to think, and in critical situations mere belief without roots in intellectual, verifiable understanding can lead to the darkening of the mind and acts of barbarism, facts well illustrated in the Crusades of the early Middle Ages.[2] In such cases we cannot speak of religion, but only of mindless bestiality.

Some will dismiss the horrors of the Christian Crusades as the demented crimes of an age gone by, as the deeds of peoples who 'knew no better'. What, then, shall we say of the last world war, or of Bosnia, Kosovo, and the recent hatred between Jews and Palestinians? What has happened to our ethical codes in all this? In review of political developments over the ages, all three religions have thrown their ethical codes to the winds when it suited them. The Old Testament is open proof of this throughout its length, despite its pious subscription to the love of God and man[3] and provides, moreover, a long and comprehensive documentation of just this incongruity.

The truth is that there cannot be true religious development without one of these two elements, *bhakti* or *vichara*. To have religious zeal alone is like the intense desire to fly without the slightest knowledge of aerodynamics, or to sail a boat without experience, or apply surgery in the wish to heal without a knowledge either of anatomy or a smattering of the consequences of bacterial infection. All these would result in catastrophe if put into practice. Religious zeal is easy to develop, as we can see in the case of fanaticism past and present. It requires little intellect, and usually results in disastrous consequences, whereas thought and investigation require discipline. On the other hand, thought alone, without zeal, is philosophy. In religious terms, thought may result in a dry canon of laws and observations that contain no life. Both elements are necessary in the individual in order to acquire true religious understanding, as we shall discover later. Here, the word 'zeal' is to be confined to work done on personal development and has no relevance to others. Zeal is to be applied in the act of enquiry, in the regular practice of meditation, and in keeping the precepts of good social behaviour, all of which is embodied in the Buddha's teaching.

The Buddha's eightfold path

The word 'Path' in this connection is significant. Unlike the Ten Commandments, for example, it is not a conclusive statement as to what should be done or not done, but implies that if the road is followed, it will end somewhere. Again, unlike the Ten Commandments, it not only embraces an ethical code, but contains the aspects both of *bhakti* and *vichara*. In other words, it not only suggests the way we should live, but also tells us how to reach that higher level of consciousness called enlightenment and so liberate ourselves from the mental bondage of conditioned attachment already described. The state of liberation is to thoroughly understand the nature of the world we live in and to understand ourselves. In this it differs from Judaism and the religions developed from it. The expansion of the 'path', the *sutras,* or enlightened commentaries written by those who have themselves attained enlightenment, form the body of the Buddha's teaching or

Dharma. These *sutras* are not 'theology' in any sense of the word, nor are they philosophical disquisitions, nor, strictly speaking, 'religion' in the sense of the word we have come to understand in the West. They are at once confirmation by others of the Buddha's personal experience and more detailed commentary upon it as assistance to those who come after.

Essentially, the *Dharma* is the description of a psychological technique which, if applied, results in mental emancipation. Within the framework of this essay, we could also describe it as a method of attaining what has been referred to as elsewhere as 'adulthood'. Adulthood suggests knowledge greater than that of the child. It also implies growth and development, and it implies potential. We know from historical fact that there are and have been men and women everywhere who have grown in spiritual stature. We know, therefore, that it is possible to transcend our lower natures and realise what Zen Buddhism refers to as 'knowing our true selves', a level of understanding possible for us all. The technique is at hand for all to use, and does not involve us in anything which taxes our credibility or involve us in commitments to an individual who lived thousands of years ago or to anything or anybody who might be thought as having an existence beyond our imagination.

The universal truth, it would seem, is that we human beings find ourselves involved in a very long, natural process of spiritual development and that the object of our lives here in this world concerns that development. Nature appears to have plenty of time to accomplish this end. Our individual lives quickly come and go like sparks falling from an anvil, but in all of them the inner drive towards this goal, weak or strong, is always present. We can, if we wish, give way to the illusion that this is not so. We can enjoy the fruits of the world and suffer the consequences of illusion, die and be reborn into the same illusion with the advantages or disadvantages of accrued experience (good or bad *karma*) and go through the round again and again until we do eventually see into the mechanics of *samsara* and our place within it, at which moment the chain of *karma* is broken once and for all. As with all chains, once one link is broken, the chain of interdependence itself is rendered useless. So it is with the chain described above. Understanding the nature of one reveals the key to understanding the nature of the other, together with the realisation that they are mutually dependent on one another, and that the one arises when the other arises. At the moment of that understanding we are free forever of its bondage. This is none other than the 'freedom' or 'eternal life' spoken of by Jesus.

Right understanding

Behind the immense superstructure which has become known as Buddhism, we discover an intensely practical mind, the mind of the Buddha. This mind is revealed in the details of the Eightfold Path which is summarised as follows:

Right Understanding is a term which suggests that anyone seeking the truth should acquaint himself with Buddha's *Dharma*, the Four Noble Truths and the Chain of Causality, so as to consider these matters carefully and critically to see if they correspond with the truth of his own experience. This is an elementary consideration, since it is no good proceeding to the rest if there is no understanding of the first premise. If the individual, man or woman, has made a thorough analysis of the *nirdanas*, (the individual elements which make up the Chain of Causality), and is led therefore to accept the first three of the Four Noble Truths as their inevitable conclusion, then the aspirant is ready spiritually to embark on a new life whose basis is now secured on these principles. The word 'Understanding' here means taking a careful look at our own personal habits of thought and conduct, our relations with others, our aspirations, our relation to life itself. It also suggests that we compare the Buddha's findings with our own to see if they are comparable and if they are acceptable. The principles lack all dogma, and there is no authority on high that dictates what is right and what is wrong. The content of the findings is its own authority.

Right resolution

Having personally recognised the truths supporting these terms, there must be the resolution to put them into action. This may seem elementary but it is nevertheless an essential step to take. Especially is this so today in a world in which we are literally bombarded with ideas and concepts all day long and from every direction. We are over-stimulated as a result. We have not the peace of mind to carefully consider matters which vitally concern our existence, and are blown like leaves in the wind from one 'new' idea to another. In this, there are newspapers with their fund of information and opinion, magazines by the thousand, radio and television twenty-four hours a day and, more recently, uninterrupted access to the Internet. On top of this medley of information we now have the mobile telephone as well as the installed telephone, general mobility for everyone either by car, rail, sea or air, and are likely to have travelled more miles by the time we are ten years old than an individual in the Middle Ages would have travelled in a lifetime. Communication has risen in our estimation to a must, and as a result the world itself has become a place of feverish, chattering activity. Although communication may be necessary to conduct the world's affairs, all this is irrelevant to our spiritual well-being. This being so, it is of particular importance to maintain a clear view of our objective and, having done that, to be determined not to be distracted by things which have nothing to do with our spiritual welfare. The situation is well summed up for us in the New Testament, where Jesus speaks in the parable of the tares which choke the sown word. He speaks here of the 'deceitfulness of riches and the desires for other things'

(Mk 4:19) which, incidentally, is so common in our modern world. This is a tragic state of affairs since, like children, we are distracted by whatever new comes within our purview, only to be betrayed later by the dissatisfaction arising from such distraction.

Right speech

In Christianity, the Ten Commandments demand that 'Thou shalt not bear false witness' **(Ex. 20:16)**, so drawing our attention to the importance of not demeaning others for any reason, but the need to practise forbearance and tolerance. Every condemnation of another is a condemnation of ourselves. In good Buddhist practice, communication should be loving, conveying information where this is necessary. It should never be a vehicle for anger or one to incite strong emotions in others, convey false information, half-truths or lies, since all these things are like seeds which eventually bear fruit. When this happens, communication becomes an instrument for the dissemination of evil. To some, this may seem to be so much straight-laced morality until we review the last hundred years of political propaganda and the suffering this has brought to countless millions of people, and how today, as a different aspect in Western society, advertising is widely employed to deceive in the interests of making money for the few.

For personal use, speech should be honest and forthright. Neither should be a means 'to hide our thoughts' which, in the last analysis is tantamount to lying. Finally, the term suggests that speech should be used sparingly, since idle chatter uses up energy which could be put to better use.

Right action or right behaviour

Right behaviour incorporates all that which is contained in the Judaic Ten Commandments and is listed under the Five Precepts. These are:

1. To abstain from killing *all* life. In Buddhism, this means showing respect for all life in killing neither human beings nor animals, birds, fish, nor even insects. It also implies showing kindness and harmlessness to other forms of life where their paths cross ours.
2. To abstain from stealing or coveting 'what is not freely given'. This involves going without when circumstances demand.
3. To abstain from adultery and to practise sexual self-control.

The other two precepts refer to lying and to abstention from the use of alcohol.

Right behaviour also means abstaining from lying and deceit, and urges us to practise honesty and sincerity in all things. We are also enjoined to avoid alcohol and drugs, which can render the individual less human in that he loses control of his mind and actions.

Right action or right behaviour require us to lead a life of simplicity. This does not suggest that we should live a life of grinding poverty, making it hard for ourselves to maintain even simplicity, as this is another form of vanity. It requires non-attachment to our possessions and suggests that the fewer possessions we have the better. If we have precious goods, then the likelihood is that we shall have to take good care of them so that they will not be lost or stolen. In such a case our minds are attached to these things. In short, expensive possessions distract our attention from what should be our main preoccupation, which is to consciously guide our minds to a knowledge of peace and understanding. Jesus, speaking of these things to his disciples, says **(Lk. 12:22–24 & 28)**:

Take no thought for your life, what ye shall eat; neither for the body, what ye shall put on. The life is more than meat, and the body is more than raiment. Consider the ravens: for they neither sow nor reap; which neither have storehouse nor barn; and God feedeth them: how much more are ye better than the fowls? If then God so clothe the grass, which is today in the field and tomorrow cast into the oven; how much more will he clothe you, O ye of little faith?

George Bernard Shaw, in the prologue to one of his plays, says that 'True virtue consists not in abstaining from sin, but not desiring it', and the same subtle truth is contained in the Buddha's Middle Way with respect to possessions. It is not that we should make a great effort to remain poor, but that we do not desire the worry and trammel entailed in being rich, and thus live simply.

The same ease is relevant to our dealings with other human beings and with other creatures. We are to treat them as we ourselves would like to be treated. This is also to follow the principle advocated by Jesus. It is not that we are to obey a frowning God in heaven for fear that he will wreak retribution upon us, but simply to observe an ethical code which is both expedient and sensible. Harm done to others inexorably obeys the law of *karma* and results sooner or later in harm done to ourselves. Conversely, good done to others (both human and animal) produces mental states which are conducive to our development. Once the karmic principle is appreciated, it amounts, in essence, to simple common sense.

Right vocation

Nearly all human beings are regularly occupied in some activity or other. According to Buddhist prescription, no aspirant to higher consciousness should spend time in activity which directly or indirectly involve the suffering of humans or other creatures. Moreover, it must be free from occupations concerned directly or indirectly with lying and deceit, cruelty, injustice, dishonesty or exploitation in any form. Especially applicable are occupations having to do with the exploitation of human beings or with war, which brings death and suffering. Activities which involve making money for selfish purposes, which is at the same time detrimental to others, are also to be avoided. It should be noted that many of the activities forbidden to the Buddhist are writ large in our modern society as being not only acceptable, but also highly desirable. The objective of making money (whether exploitative or injurious or not) has in itself been raised to a place of particular esteem in our current society.

Beyond the Ten Commandments

So much for the 'ethical content' of the Eightfold Path. We come now to the three articles of the Path which have to do with training the mind for its higher mission.

Having furnished himself with the basis of ethical conduct and attitudes towards others, the first step to be taken is that of learning to curb the ego, not by repression, as we would say today, but by sublimation. This step and the two which follow it are essential in making spiritual progress or, to put it more succinctly, to prepare the mind for the light of understanding. It is akin to tilling the soil for the planting of seed which, with water and warmth, will eventually blossom into a green plant and then a flower. Specific advice of this kind is totally lacking in the New Testament. Only occasional, oblique reference is made to the need to drill the mind towards a condition which can receive spiritual discernment. One of these is found in Matthew **(17:21)**, where Jesus upbraids his disciples for having tried unsuccessfully to rid a child of epilepsy. He then says: 'However, this kind does not go out except by prayer and fasting'. Here, he is indirectly referring to the demon in the child which caused the fits associated with this disease.

Right effort

This should be understood as strenuously preserving a correct state of mind within the spheres of thought and activity, especially that in relation to others. Dwight Goddard, in his book *A Buddhist Bible*,[4] speaking of what are referred to in Buddhism as the 'Six Paramitas', says:

> This Paramita of humility and patience will help him to bear without complaint, the acts of others without fear or malice or anger. It will help him to bear the common ills of life, the difficulties of the Path and the burden of his karma. It will keep him free from both elation and discouragement as he meets the extremes of success or failure, and will help him to maintain an equitable spirit of serenity and peacefulness ... The results of behaviour are not all outward and apparent; they also affect one's inner habits and dispositions and are surely registered in one's karma ... One should always keep his mind concentrated on the task in hand, un-distracted by thoughts of policy, or its relation to one's selfish advantage or comfort ... It will often prompt one to a course far different from the old, competitive, acquisitive, exciting habits of the worldly life ... and so long as one has no desires, he will be undisturbed by conditions. So long as the mind is free from greed, anger, fear and egoism, it rests in peace.

The next two recommendations appearing in the Eightfold Path are explicitly addressed to the practice of meditation and this was, in the main, a thing alien to our Western civilisation until quite recently. However, without some sort of mind control, even with the other factors mentioned in the Path, enlightenment is generally a rare experience.

Right mindfulness

Mindfulness means, literally, keeping the mind awake. For most of us, the state of being fully awake to our surroundings is an unusual occurrence. Practically all our lives are spent in a state of somnolence from which we are awakened only now and then by tragic misfortune, physical or mental suffering, accident, the need to adapt ourselves to rigorously changed conditions or sometimes by the contemplation of great art or the suffering of others.

For example, someone might live in a town for decades and not know the sequence of a row of shops, or the colour of the carpet on the floor of a frequently visited restaurant or café. Often enough, it is a shock to be put in mind of what we miss in life by someone else who has an eye for both mass and detail and is awake at least to the material things which surround us. Most of the time we are concerned primarily with what *interests* us and the mind as a consequence is habitually fixed on these interests. A good example of such fixation is any group of people engaged in the same work, gathered in an office or staff room, a clubroom or the local pub. The conversation turns upon the work they do or have done or will do, or the work others will do, have done or do. Or it may be talk of an interest – football, for example, or golf or family interests or cars, illness, others, work, and so on. Like the eye, the focus is on a particular object or part of an object, and the rest is relegated to peripheral vision. Since this is the case, the whole is not registered by the consciousness.

Generally speaking, if we concentrate and are awake to visual stimuli, our auditory faculties operate in the background, and the tactile sense may also be quite dormant. It is possible, for example, for someone to drive a fifty miles or more and never realise that he has done so. In this time he has negotiated curves, changed gear when necessary dozens of times, circumvented obstacles, given signals, braked, accelerated, halted, moved on uphill and down, and never for a moment during this time abandoned his private thoughts. The driver in such a case has entirely submitted his conscious mind to the semi-conscious mechanism of thought association. Only when he has arrived at his destination does the conscious mind once more take over its function. This state of 'lulled' consciousness is what passes as 'life' for most of our biological cycle. It is also a part of 'being asleep', alluded to above. Associative thinking of the kind our motorist experiences and what most of us experience for most of the time is what keeps us at the semi-conscious level. To rise to a higher, more receptive level, such a state has to be replaced by deliberate conscious awareness. This deliberation and the subsequent practice of alertness to each moment is to 'awaken up to life', as the Buddhist texts put it. Moreover, it is the only state in which we can truly say that we are *alive*.

Right meditation or concentration (dhyana)

An awareness of things outside ourselves is the precursor of an awareness of the operation of the mind inside. This is generally achieved by single-minded concentration whose object is to look dispassionately into the mind (*samadhi*) and its contents (Sanskrit, *citta*). Whatever arises there is viewed with non-attachment, and the art here is not to be seduced by its movements. These movements of mind, where one thought leads to another in never-ending succession (association), are usually connected with emotion of some kind, which may be weak or strong, positive or negative. Thoughts may be passive and have to do with nothing much of importance, or they may take us into the past or be controlled by desires affecting the future. When the thought is emotionally charged, it is especially difficult to get it under control. Beginners soon understand how strong the mind can be and how ready it is to take its owner for a ride! Vigilant, dispassionate observance of its activities is the key to its control. Zen Buddhists refer to this activity as 'looking into the mind'.

This activity is rather like someone at a theatre who, instead of being carried along by the scene in front of him, sits and watches it all with an unmoved mind. Just as this is difficult in the real situation, so, too, is it difficult in the practice of meditation. The technique of consciously focussing the attention takes time, practice and patience. With regular, daily practice, however, adept concentration mellows into contemplation, a state of stillness which the experienced meditator can achieve within a few minutes after settling himself on his cushion. From this, deeper contemplation arises until the aspirant can enter into states of mind where he gains profound insight into the nature of life, himself and others. All these stages really require the assistance of a qualified teacher who has himself experienced the realms of mind and can therefore guide the sitter to a cognition of the Supreme. Meditation does not vary much from the acquisition of other skills which have to learned by patient application and repetition. The teacher can save the learner time and energy by not allowing him or her to travel down futile paths or pursue wrong methods which might lead to disappointment and frustration. There are many pitfalls on the way which can hinder progress. For this reason, in the Japanese form of Buddhism, Zen, there are periods set aside at every intensive meditative sitting (Jap. *Sesshin*) where the meditator can ask for help and guidance from the master.

Regular meditation, that is, sitting in meditation to clear the mind of its delusions, is essential. However, of equal importance, and a measure often neglected by some meditators, is the carrying of this mind over into daily life. The two aspects work like the two wheels of a cart. Just as a cart is a useless hindrance with one wheel, so is meditation without its practical application.

To put it another way, the consciousness achieved by the practice of internal observance should be preserved when it comes to carrying out everyday jobs. This is like carrying light from one place to another, and is of the greatest importance. With time, the whole of life spent away from the meditation cushion acquires a new dimension of meaning, an experience which in itself is worth any amount of effort. Similarly, attending in this spirit to the practical matters of living in its turn reinforces the strength of our meditation.

Concluding commentary on the 'Eightfold Path'

The Path is essentially a practical guide, and is in line with what we have referred to above as the Buddha's uncompromisingly practical nature. Moreover, this so-called 'path' is to be felt and regarded as a whole, not as so many sequential steps. That it is some sort of development in stages is the first notion which might lead us astray. The Eightfold Path is a living attitude of mind. The first six steps along it are a necessary mental condition for the implementation of the last two, which are the keys to liberation.

There is nothing comparable with this in the Christian canon, since there has been no tradition of mental analysis in western religious practice or, for that matter, in western culture until quite recently. This is where the two religions diverge. In Buddhism, the ethical and the mystical elements of religion merge to form an organic unity.

One simple example of this is the concept of 'harmlessness' (Sanskrit, *ahimsa*) or non-injury. When it is personally and inwardly realised that all living things issue from one Source or, to put it in Christian terms, are the expressions of the Divine in this living moment, then it becomes impossible to do them harm. To do so would be to deny the existence of that which supports life and, therefore, our own existence. This could well be the significance of the word 'naught' (i.e. nothing, emptiness, worthlessness) in the original medieval use of the word 'naughty'. That is to say, it would be an act which renders us worthless.

In doing harm to other living things, human or animal, we immediately cut ourselves off from that Unity (Oneness) which it is our privilege both to recognise and to enjoy. We lose sight of our heritage in that moment to become a separate ego, a falsity and an illusion. The practice of non-injury in Buddhism is grounded in this intuitive knowledge. It does not issue from precept or regulation. This is certainly why the religion has enjoyed such a long period of peaceful co-existence with many different cultures.

Precept and regulation imposed upon us from without are issues far from spiritual understanding. Another example will clarify this point:

A group of people, say, have lost their way in a foreign country. There are some general, correct instructions to hand, but no indication of distance or an idea of the time needed to get from one point to another and no given landmarks. No-one speaks the language of the country and people anyway are few and far between. Finding the destination results in various experiments, disappointment and frustration. It comes on to rain. The going is hard. The worst that can happen is that one turns round in the hope at least of getting back to the starting point safely. However, if there is someone in the party who knows the way, this can give flesh and bones to the meagre instructions. He can say how long this and that route will take and confirm the distance covered by pointing out features *en route*, how much easier the whole trip is! This is because there is real, scientific, recorded knowledge at work in bringing the party to its destination. One person in the group *knows* the way. The knowledge he or she has is grounded in experience.

This is the one great difference between Christianity and Buddhism. In Christianity, a man (and sometimes a woman) may become a priest by applying to a relevant university or religious institution and then take an examination. After this, he or she may be inaugurated by ritual and can later enter the priesthood. This is largely on an intellectual level. Later, there may be spiritual maturity, or there may not, as the years pass, but in general the depth of spirituality is shallow. Unless the priest in question has been obliged to spend a long time in a monastery where, inevitably, the ego is shorn at least to some degree of its expression, there is generally only a superficial understanding of spiritual matters.

Some may find this an unjust conclusion, but a review of ecclesiastical history over the last five hundred years, as we have already noted, and the level of spiritual maturity, or lack of it, in modern society, is justification enough for such a conclusion. What passes for religious education in schools in the West, for example, has nothing to do with a serious view of ourselves as human beings, but is merely related to stories occurring two or three thousand years ago. Admittedly, ethical values are communicated to children via these stories in the hope that the point goes home, but almost everything in the case of Christianity is related to the teaching of one man, his views and his attitudes. Apart from the tradition of prayer, there is no formal training in emptying the mind or in rigorously looking into this mind in an attempt to come at the truth that lies beyond thought. 'Beyond thought' here means arriving at a state which no longer distinguishes between 'this' and 'that' at any level. It is definitively the end of all duality. To arrive at non-duality is finally to be free of this world while in the world, and to enjoy a hitherto unsuspected freedom and joy in every moment. The way to this state of mind is, for most of us, via alert, disciplined, regular meditation.

---

[1] A divine personage. In Buddhism, Avalokiteśvara. This ancient Boddhisattva plays a similar role in Buddhism to that of the Virgin Mary in Christianity. As in popular Christianity, there are a number of divine persons in Buddhism who play a similar part to the saints of Christendom.

[2] The Crusades provide a very clear depiction of man as beast and represents one of the most appalling chapters of human history at any time during man's development. For the Buddhist, such a descent into barbarity is conclusive evidence of human delusion and the consequences this can have. By implication, the need to become more conscious of ourselves in the Buddhist sense is also vindicated on such occasions.

[3] Far from being a book through which God speaks to Man as is generally assumed, well over 90% of the Old Testament is about the

worst of Man, his violence, his lowest instincts, his wars and his lust for revenge, of betrayal and intrigue, and much else which does him little credit. There is in it material to justify every crime. This is very easy to establish by simply reading any page of it from Genesis to Malachi, but the myth of its holiness continues.

[4] Goddard, Dwight, A Buddhist Bible, Boston, 1970, pp. 650-1.

CHAPTER IV

What is meditation?

There are several forms of meditation, but all of them require in the first instance a stilling of the mind's habitual activity, a letting go. Without a tranquil mind, nothing is attainable. In Buddhist meditation, the emphasis in meditation is upon not wanting anything. It is the act of giving up everything, *all* ideas, concepts, beliefs, tradition and anything else which might get in the way of establishing a clear mind. This finally even includes the object of meditation. Generally speaking, the very idea of 'giving up everything' is something we westerners resolutely resist at first. With practice, however, the prospect becomes less and less undesirable so that after a period of time it is easy to 'give up' ourselves and remain in a state of quiescence. Sitting quietly, the meditator is simply required to look into the mind with no concern about the results of the contemplation.

To contemplate or meditate, the seeker must first bring the body's desire to move under control. This means that the first step requires sitting in a position which can be maintained for some time without fatigue. In the East, the position preferred is the full (very difficult for Westerners) or the half-lotus position which, with practice, is not so difficult to attain. For those who cannot sit in either fashion, a firm, comfortable chair or stool suffices. The back must be straight and unsupported. The mind is then directed inwards, and an attempt is made to check the interminable flow of associative thought. This is the first phenomenon we encounter when we begin our meditation. This kind of 'looking' requires practice and can be difficult and frustrating at first since we are not used to being still. However, with determined, regular practice, generally the mind can be brought to heel and its force abated.

This does not for a moment suggest violence. The mind cannot be forced without serious psychological consequences. It has to be tamed with patience, and is a little like making friends with a wild animal. Patience and persistence are required, but together with these two, there must be a consciousness of mind above all which looks but which does not interfere with the mind's discursive activity. This activity has often been well compared with the fidgeting of a monkey. One can compare the practice of Buddhist meditation to someone who looks on a scene steadily and impassively. As with our theatre-goer above, the viewer looks but does not become involved with the what is going on before him. After a time, the meditator will recognise what we may well describe as the 'clutter' of its contents. In regarding the 'clutter' dispassionately in this way we encounter emotions, memories of people, their faces, their manner and something perhaps they once said, snatches of conversations, strains of music perhaps. Our immediate preoccupations come to the fore, hopes for the future and the recognition of past disappointments, desire in great abundance, flashes of mental pain often occur for many people, sometimes together with physical signals from the body, the desire to move and so in this way halt the reflection – all this and more without end, each sensation leading on to a new thought. With practice, and after an interval of time, periods of stillness intervene. At this time the meditator will also be aware of what is called 'the discriminating mind'. There is a tendency in meditation (and also in our daily lives) to find this idea 'good' and that feeling 'bad' – in other words, to identify ourselves with these ideas and feelings. The recognition of this taking place in the mind is the first step to freedom. By recognition we gradually acquire the strength to allay this fatal inclination and eventually to overcome it.

The mind's desire to discriminate is very strong. By just watching the operation of the mind in a spirit of firm detachment, its discriminative tendency and the emotions accompanying it, together with the emotional power derived from these mental movements will gradually dissipate and finally disappear altogether. A state of quiescence (contemplation) remains. Once this has been recognised, the next stage is that the sitter tries to exercise more control over this chaotic mental turmoil. One effective way of doing this is to count the breaths as they arise naturally in the body. This can usually be done by counting from one to ten and then beginning again with 'one'. If the numbers can actually be seen in the mind's eye, so much the better. It is important to stay awake and not drowse off into sleep, since this is the first pitfall beginners encounter. Eventually, after days, weeks or even months of regular practice, the mind will calm to a point where the beginner can acquire calmness with relative ease shortly after composing himself to sit. We could describe this as the end of the first stage and the beginning of the second. Whether this takes a long time to arrive at or a relatively short time to achieve depends very much on the habitual mental state of the meditator. In general, in very active people it takes longer to attain.

The second phase is the deepening of this calmness. Deepening proceeds at a speed which is beyond our control. The tempo at which we make progress in our meditation depends to a large degree on our sincerity of effort, our desire, in other words, to be free of all bondage.

It also depends on those aspects of our personality, positive and negative, which we have brought with us into this life. There are people who reach a degree of enlightenment within a few days or weeks and others who require years or even decades to do so. Some schools of thought believe that several lifetimes are needed for enlightenment. This may well be so for full enlightenment, but is certainly not true for a degree of enlightenment.

Japanese Zen Buddhism (Chin. *Ch'an*), distinguishes between *kensho* (a sudden flash of understanding) and *satori*, enlightenment proper. Even after enlightenment has been achieved, there are from that point on deeper and deeper levels to be discovered. Chinese Buddhism maintains that there are big Buddhas and little Buddhas. Although this is undoubtedly true, no one should be dismayed by the fact. Every advance in self-knowledge and self-mastery, every step taken along the path of heightened consciousness (awareness) is to be equated with striking gold. Anyone who meditates regularly grows in spiritual stature.

It has been said, too, that every degree of enlightenment can be likened to a dark cave where candles are lit. Even the first candle dispels darkness, bringing a new phenomenon to the cave. As more candles are lit, more and more darkness recedes before the light until at last we can find our way out of the cave into the light of day. It is then that we can speak of liberation. Through our own efforts to control the mind, we begin to 'light candles' and so are eventually enabled first to understand the situation in which we find ourselves and later to do something about it. This is the significance of what Jesus meant in his reference to 'those who walk in darkness'. His personalised answer to the situation was to 'believe on him'. In this case he offers his help to those who yearn for light as every Bodhisattva has done in the world up to now and those who still do. Because Jesus knows the answer to the dilemma in which man finds himself, he announces that he is the 'light of the world'.

> Then spake Jesus again unto them, saying, I am the light of world: he that followeth me shall not walk in darkness, but shall have the light of life. **(Jn. 8, 12)**

The idea of 'sitting' in darkness is also included in the Bible; an example occurs at Matthew, **4. 16**. *The people which sat in darkness saw great light;* and *to them which sat in the region and the shadow of death, light is sprung up.*

In Luke, too, we find an example using the concept of light which is similar to the Buddhist illustration above:

> If thy whole body therefore be full of light, having no part dark, the whole shall be full of light, as when the bright shining of a candle doth give thee light. **(Lk. 11, 36)**

A moment before, at verse **33**, Jesus had spoken of putting one's light upon a candlestick, so that 'they that come may see the light'.

The idea which persists through these references is that there must be light so that an individual may perceive and understand, whereas darkness is felt to be a state of ignorance or unknowing, a Godless situation in which there is hopelessness and misery.

After meditating for some time – and here again, one cannot be specific, for the reasons already noted – the regular meditator will finally realise that he is of the 'same substance as others,' that is to say, the same spiritual substance. This means, simply, that all of us proceed from the same Mind. This is not just a matter of the flesh and blood and bones of physical existence, but is something which refers to the mental properties, too, which we all share, so that the meditator begins to discover that the differences are only superficial, just as, on the physical plane, we may be tall and thin, or short and fat, have various complexions, be muscular or flaccid, be mentally agile or require time to understand, be kind and generous or mean and cautious, thoughtful or selfish and so on – all these things are acquired attributes of our personality, but are not our essential, spiritual selves. From this point, he or she will see the people encountered in life with new eyes, the eyes of clarity and will not be led into making those distinctions common to the 'sleeping mind'.

There are many examples of this throughout the New Testament, but three may be enough here to make the matter clear. Apart from the officers of the religious establishment who come to him with their trick questions seeking to ensnare him into treasonable declaration, there are also other points in the gospels where Jesus does not allow himself to be deflected by the attitudes of others. Even in the matter of kinship when he is informed that his mother and his brothers were outside, desiring to see him, he declares that the only people who are his kin are those that 'hear the word of God and do it'. **(Lk. 8, 19–21).**

Neither does he give way to emotional reaction in others where, on the occasion when the disciples, James and John, feel rebuffed by the indifference to their master by the inhabitants of a Samaritan village (in the class system of the times, the Jews regarded Samaritans with distaste), they suggest that they be empowered to rain fire 'to come down and consume them' as in the time of Elijah. Jesus rebukes them for this outrageous suggestion with the reminder that we are all of the 'same substance' as Buddhism would say, and announces, 'You do not know what manner of spirit you are of.' And adds: 'For the Son of Man did not come to destroy men's lives, but to save them.'

And finally, at **Jn. 7, 24,** he urges others to see as he himself sees (proving thereby that he sees life differently than those around him) when he defends himself against pharasaical objection to having healed a man on the Sabbath: 'Do not judge according to appearance, but judge with righteous judgement'. **(Jn. 7, 24)**

As time passes and meditation is kept up in the manner described, the meditator may or may not acquire certain mental powers. As well as the control of the mind, he or she may experience in the first place weightlessness, the 'vanishing' of the breath, heat in the lower abdomen, relief from disease (whether of long-standing or of short duration), mental freedom of an unsuspected kind, profound inspiration, the solution to persistent problems, great happiness or experience unusual quantities of energy. Whether some or many or all of these appear in the course of time, there will be a general loosening of the habit of clinging to worldly things and a decrease in the activity of the ego. This, in turn, will produce more regard for others and their problems and prompt the need to help if asked or if the situation demands such assistance.

This phase can, before final enlightenment, then deepen into other spontaneously-bestowed attributes in some people, such as the ability to heal serious diseases, either directly or indirectly, via direct physical contact or at a distance, the ability to see straight into the character of people and circumstances, the ability in some to see into the immediate future with accuracy, extraordinary ability in some skill or technique, the manipulation of circumstances, the performance of wonders, unusual control of the body beyond that recognised as normal even with training, and a host more. Such remarkable abilities occasionally occur without apparent preparation in this life as in the case of the ability to speak another language without prior study, for example, and in these cases they can be regarded as the products of an earlier spiritual existence, phenomena which also support the case for rebirth.[1]

These abilities are not exploited by the true aspirant, except in certain urgent circumstances where either the imminent death or serious injury of another person are at stake. In a situation such as this, an adept may intervene out of reasons of compassion.

The phenomena which have been alluded to here are merely the consequences of a mind which is now freed from the normal, restrictive laws controlling our everyday world, and should simply be regarded as proof of the aspirant's advancement.

Much of this will sound very unlikely to the western reader confirmed in the view that 'nothing can exist which has not been proved to exist', until one reads of well established cases of their occurrence. When they do occur, such happenings are great scoops for some newspapers and for sensation seekers in general. These 'parapsychological phenomena' as they are called today are now being looked into by scientists with the greatest interest, industry and intensity in some parts of the globe, no doubt with a view to making them function in the familiar world of relativity. For the meditator they are a powerful temptation, since, theoretically, every wish can be fulfilled by implementing the power which has become accessible to him. To succumb to such temptation, however, would be to land the meditator back in the usual world of dualistic relationships and with appalling consequences.[2] Jesus himself alludes to this state at **Lk. 11,26.**

Diversion from the Path in this way, which may also involve the possibility of grave mental illness or perversion, is something which requires considerable strength to avert. In the higher realms of enlightened meditation we have the examples both of the temptation of the Buddha in secluded meditation, and that of Jesus in the wilderness.[3] These ethereal realms of meditation are not everybody's experience and certainly not all of them occur at the same time. However, as progress is made towards this stage, it is good to have a teacher at hand to save the meditator from possible psychological hazard.

Once this stage has been safely navigated, the meditator moves on to full enlightenment.

What is enlightenment?

Enlightenment is a state of mind which embraces the realisation that all things, including oneself, the 'me' of everyday existence, are One. It is what psychologists refer to as mental integration. As a result, it is a state of total freedom from the world of relativity, that is to say, from the world of dualism. For the aspirant, it is a state where he is no longer ensnared by worldly temptation of any kind or any desire whatever to aggrandise the ego. All desires are seen as part of an illusion with the consequence that the ego vanishes completely. What is left is supreme clarity of mind, psychological equanimity and, above all, compassion. This last is not simply the 'goodwill to all men' of Christianity, but, a love born of knowledge. It is the result of a deep, inward realisation that love or compassion is the matrix which holds our human world together, and that, conversely, egocentricity is that which is at the heart of all anti-social behaviour in all its forms from full-scale war to shop-lifting, from the egoism of political despotism to the arrogance of putting out the life of a fly on a window-pane. In enlightenment, the true devil which is in us all, our ego, has now been banished forever.

From this moment on, the aspirant is free from all fear, free above all from the fear of death. He experiences every day and every minute of every day as an infinitely precious experience. He or she is not concerned with fears of the future and knows that when the time comes to die that death, too, has been overcome. Those who have had the experience of enlightenment, however shallow, will know that they have entered into a realm for which they and everyone else were created, and that this is the goal of every life.

Someone once described the experience of enlightenment as similar to pulling out the third segment of a telescope. The first segment we can imagine is that which has formed our bodies over millions of years to the miracle of complexity it is today. The second is the mental development we have experienced which has been responsible for our survival against great odds through millions of years, all the way from the conception and manufacture of a bow and arrow to the creation of means to catapult us into space. The third segment, which is the fully integrated individual, is one which will be pulled out either by nature or by ourselves. If left to nature, the task of our becoming truly human as a species may take another million years. On the other hand, we can tackle the job ourselves and rise to those heights for which we were created within a lifetime. Many examples exist of men and women who have reached these realms in the past in all ages and places. These are those who have done work upon themselves, so to speak, and who have reached higher spiritual planes. Both the Buddha and Jesus[4] promised every seeker for truth who has perseverance that he would eventually succeed in gaining higher cognition, but never has the matter been so urgent than it is at the moment in view of an exploding global population, the means we have of waging war, and our potential for destroying the environment.

Below are some examples of men and women who have experienced mental states very similar to that of enlightenment, beginning with fleeting admission into a new, meaningful dimension of mind, and ending with descriptions of the effects of great enlightenment. What true enlightenment is for those who experience it, however, can never be described. The reason for this is that it does not belong in our dualistic system of understanding, and cannot therefore be understood by using its terms. One can say what it is not, and one can say to what it approximates as here, but the cognition and illumination of the mind itself remains an experience which neither 'is' nor 'is not'.

Experiences of enlightenment in our time

A tip-of-the-tongue yet genuine experience of the Buddhist's 'other shore' which many people have had in the course of a lifetime is given here by John Buchan, in his book *Memory-hold-the-Door*[5] published in 1940. It is a case of drawing the curtains apart for a brief moment to reveal unsuspected beauty. One could call it the experience of *kensho*.

> I had been ploughing all day in the black dust of the Lichtenburg roads, and had come very late to a place called the Eye of Malmani – Malmani Oog – the spring of a river which

presently loses itself in the Kalahari. We watered our horses and went supperless to bed. Next morning I bathed in one of the Malmani pools – and icy cold it was – and then basked in the early sunshine while breakfast was cooking. The water made a pleasant music, and nearby was a covert of willows filled with singing birds. Then and there came on me the hour of revelation, when, though savagely hungry, I forgot about breakfast. Scents, sights and sounds blended into a harmony so perfect that it transcended human expression, even human thought. It was like a glimpse of the peace of eternity.

Slightly deeper than this is the experience of someone who fulfilled the requirements for understanding to enter the nirvanic aspect of mind in that, for a moment or two, he forgets himself and the world around him. The example is taken from Raynor C. Johnson's *The Imprisoned Splendour*[6]

I was sitting on the seashore, half-listening to a friend arguing violently about a matter which merely bored me. Unconsciously to myself, I looked at a film of sand I had picked up on my hand, when I suddenly saw the exquisite beauty of every little grain of it: instead of being dull, I saw that each particle was made up on a perfect geometrical pattern, with sharp angles, from each of which a brilliant shaft of light was reflected, while each tiny crystal shone like a rainbow. The rays crossed and recrossed, making exquisite patterns, of such beauty that they left me breathless.

I was used at odd intervals to seeing the invisible counterpart of minute objects, but this was quite unexpected and fascinating. Then, suddenly, my consciousness was lighted up from within and I saw in a vivid way how the whole universe was made up of particles of material which, no matter how dull and lifeless they might seem at first sight, were nevertheless filled with this intense and vital beauty.

For a second or two, the whole world appeared as a blaze of glory. When it died down, it left me with something I have never forgotten and which constantly reminds me of the beauty locked up in every minute speck of material around me.

At line thirteen the author says that suddenly his consciousness 'was lighted up from within' and from that moment there was a deepening of his understanding. This is the portal to true enlightenment, this and the fact that the ordinary world surrounding him appeared as 'a blaze of glory.' True insight is always an unforgettable experience, and the deeper the insight the more likely it is to permanently change our attitude to life in general.

The next stage in the spiritual experience of *Samadhi* is the recognition of Oneness.

The person cited here was suffering from rheumatoid spondylitis at the time, a condition which had left him with the feeling that life was meaningless. During this illness, presumably during convalescence, he wanders out into meadowland one warm, summer day and seats himself against a pine. The following example is cited by the same author in his book *Watcher on the Hills*[7]:

> I do not know how long I sat, but after a period of 'empty' enjoyment, I became intensely aware of many of the objects which were in the area. The rocks, the trees, the birds, the stream, the clouds, the flowers, became extremely meaningful to me. I realised the rocks, trees etc. were I; I they; all brothers. And I was exceedingly joyful in realising this kinship.
>
> From this awareness, we flowed into, became, the great Golden Light – the rocks, trees, etc. and this 'I' were no longer just kindred separatenesses. We disappeared. We became the Light which is Love, Consciousness, Eternity, It. No name was given, nothing was heard. Nor did this 'I' then or after experience frenzy or any sort of fitful or emotional upheaval. Rather Peace, Certainty was known.
>
> Because of the experience, I know that everything involved in this process is God, is Love, Light, Bliss...that everything is in migration, movement, towards the Great Awakening to That which, in essence, everything is. Nothing, nothing is excluded from the redemptive process. Not only all men, but men and rocks and stars and trees are brothers, are

divine, and carry within them the splendour awakening to Itself.

> After this event I somehow knew that this was the last time (of incarnate existence), that there would be no more I's for this soul's development…that it 'had crossed the line into the land of no to-morrows'. Yet I also realised that we cannot really go Home until everything goes Home again.

Here we have a case of true enlightenment. It is interesting for us since the experience begins with a more acute awareness of the things around him, in other words, with heightened consciousness. This then flows into a mental state where the subject feels himself at one with the rest of creation. There is, he says, no 'separateness.' On the contrary, there is a strong sense of union with all he sees. Remarkably, too, the experiencer realises that everything is in movement toward awakening to what it essentially *is*. The experiencer has awakened to the realisation of 'non-ego' or the 'no-I' of Zen Buddhist terminology. There is the realisation of 'All is One' common to mystical Christianity and Buddhism, and lastly, there is the certain knowledge that the author would not be reborn on this spiritual plane.

The last line especially reveals a depth of insight unusual in western mystical experience, but which is a central issue in all the Buddhist *sutras*. It embodies the vow 'to enlighten all living creatures'. This is deep insight indeed. What is of particular interest, too, is the fact that the experience had developed spontaneously in this case and not, presumably, at the end of long, intensive religious training, and almost certainly not in any Buddhist institution. The facts surrounding the case are sparse.

The phenomenon quoted above does not for that reason invalidate the Buddhist position. On the contrary, it only confirms it. In this case, illness had reduced the demands of the ego in the previous months. There is a note of resignation in the (unquoted) introduction to the passage, suggesting that the patient had given up resistance to the disease, and had accepted the fate allocated to him. In the passage quoted above, there is dispassionate detachment, and there is peace. The mind had come to a halt as the patient settled himself under the tree. This was the moment at which insight could enter consciousness, and the rest of his experience followed like water flowing from a higher to a lower level.

The next and deepest stage of enlightenment is not recorded in Christian tradition as far as I am aware, but remains the last stage of human insight into what the Christian believer would call the Divine. It is the realisation of 'Emptiness' (*Śunyata*), or 'Absolute Absence', 'No Mind', or Void, the Unmanifested – all of which terms rendered into modern English may appear very strange to us. Perhaps the nearest we can get to such an idea (an idea which is not an idea or a concept) is to resort for the moment to the concepts of 'Phenomenal' and 'Noumenal', seen as opposites. This is to suggest that everything we can comprehend, see, feel, touch, hear or cognise in any way belongs to the *phenomenal*, whereas that which cannot be so cognised must nevertheless 'be' or in some sense, 'not be'. It is, if we wish, a frame of reference, at least for our minds, in order for the phenomenal to exist at all. This 'Not-ness' is quite beyond description. The author of *Ask the Awakened,* Wei Wu Wei,[8] approaches the matter obliquely so as to shed more light in the area:

> The essential understanding surely is just this: as that which we think we are, we are nothing, we are not. But as Nothing (nothing we can know as anything), as that which 'we' are not, we are everything that is or could ever be. Not, of course, of as 'individuals', as objects – which we never were and never could be – but as human-beings – which are figments only – but as the unmanifested which is the subject of manifestation.

This may take some digesting at first, but it nevertheless hits the nail on the head. A moment later, realising that digestion here may be a problem, the author tries again:

> How does this process work? In the first place the metaphysical aspect of the mind has to be sufficiently developed to take over control of the psychosomatic

apparatus. In all ordinary cases this is a matter of many years, not of learning but of experience, for our system of 'education' is exclusively devoted to developing the samsaric ego-ridden mentality. Consequently it requires a metanoesis or paravritti (turning over) to awaken the nirvanic aspect of mind, which can occur without its being recognised as such; but, recognised or not, the process of bringing it to maturity is long and only depends indirectly on thought. This gradual development is phenomenal and subject to time.

The intemporal awakening, Bodhi or Sambodhi of which Anuttara-samyak-sambodhi, the complete, unexcelled Enlightenment of the Buddha is a further development, may be regarded as a final transfer of control of the psychosomatic apparatus from the samsaric to the nirvanic aspect of mind. The Chinese termed the latter the original or self-mind, 'self' mind meaning not personal but subjective. The phenomenon is then said to be 'liberated', which does not mean that the apparent individual can do whatever he likes for the rest of his life, for his phenomenal aspect remains subject to a pattern according to which he is being 'lived', but that he has recognised himself as subjectivity and, as such, is perfectly free from the illusions of the living dream **(pp. 179–80).**

If this still appears to be too much to understand at one go, we can for a moment get away from all conceptual thought and language and do something for ourselves.

When we look at an object, for example, we say that 'we' look. We (subject) look at a bottle(object). Here, there is, we suppose, a subject which looks and an object which is looked at. But – and this is the point – we can also be aware of ourselves as we look at the bottle. Who or what is it then that looks at us as we look at the bottle? What, precisely, is it that is aware? One thing is clear: there cannot be *two* subjects. Or are there two objects? If there are two objects, myself and the bottle, where and what is the subject that sees these? *What* sees? Or, to change the focus only slightly: *Who,* then, am I?

Sometimes this question alone is enough to propel a ready mind into the realisation that 'I-as-ego' cannot be, and that the full reality of our existence is a 'Not-I' (pure Subjectivity) of which 'I-as-ego' is a by-product of that Subjectivity. This 'Not-I' cannot in any way be regarded as our object. It IS, and this is all we can say about it if we wish to say anything at all. Given a name for the convenience of being able to refer to it at all, we can speak of it as Void or Plenitude, Non-duality, *Prajna* or No-Mind. Just what IT is defeats every attempt at definition, since this would render it an object. It is Subject from which all else, including ourselves, arises. Understanding this inwardly (subjectively) and completely is full enlightenment.

A few modern examples follow in illustration of enlightenment in practice. This is necessary in order to obviate the impression, firstly, that enlightenment is beyond the reach of 'ordinary mortals', a view which is entertained by many practising Buddhists of all persuasions today, and secondly, that it is the attainment anyway of the very few, and thirdly, that most enlightened beings lived hundreds and hundreds of years ago. Some organisations even go so far as to assert that enlightenment is not where the emphasis should be in meditative practice, but that the practice of non-attachment alone is important. In this, they purport to follow the instructions of an ancient master whose teaching, rightly, frowned upon 'goal-seeking', that is, the idea of 'attaining' enlightenment as one would grasp anything else. However, practice without the will to understand, uninformed by the one permitted desire to know the truth of our human condition, is like spring without green or a lion without teeth. Buddhism without enlightenment would be of exactly the same order.

The first example is taken from modern Japan and occurred about thirty years ago. The experience was told in private to a group of Zen students under the direction of Sochu Suzuki Roshi who had visited London for a week or two.

The Roshi was travelling by plane over the Pacific to the United States where he was to hold formal meditation sittings for students interested in Zen. During the journey he met an elderly lady who told him she was on her way to visit her soldier son's grave situated at a military cemetery on one of the ocean's small islands. Her only son had been killed in an attack on the island during World War II. She was making this long and difficult trip by plane and boat because, she said, she had nothing to lose. 'You see, I am riddled with cancer', she added, 'and this is the last thing I'll do before I die'. The woman was 64 years of age at the time, and apparently the doctors had given her up as a hopeless case. Sochu commended her courage in undertaking the journey and the two of them talked of this and that for the rest of the journey until the plane touched down in Guam. At the airport they wished each other well and said goodbye. Roshi was moved by her courage.

One hot afternoon about three years after this event, Ryutaki Monastery, near Mishima in Japan received a visitor. It was the same woman who had flown over the Pacific with Sochu to Guam. On that occasion, the two had exchanged visiting cards as is the custom in Japan and so she knew of the address in Mishima. The old lady was warmly welcomed by Sochu at the entrance and asked if she would like to withdraw to his shaded quarters in order to take tea with him and the head monk. After introductory courtesies and respects on both sides, the three of them settled on cushions and sipped the hot tea in the cool of the annexe next to the meditation hall. Roshi then naturally asked his elderly acquaintance how she was and how she had fared in the meantime. 'Was she in pain?' he asked sympathetically. 'Only occasionally', she replied, the master being relieved to hear this, then continued, 'And did you discover your son's grave?' he asked gently after a moment or two. 'Oh yes!' the lady replied and smiled happily. 'After I had found his grave, nothing mattered anymore, do you see? For me, that was the happy end,' she added. 'Oh really?' our master replied with that air of innocent, childlike surprise he always adopted when he had something else in mind, a characteristic we all knew very well. He nodded several times at this as a sign of understanding and sympathy. The three of them continued to drink the bitter tea without saying more for quite some time while a bird twittered excitedly outside. The master at last broke the long silence by politely enquiring, 'And...er... what are your plans for the future?' At this, the old lady burst out laughing. She laughed and laughed until the tears rolled down her cheeks so that the head monk was hurriedly obliged to relieve her of the teacup she still held in her hand. The laughter bubbled up into the wooden beams of the room and out into sun-filled courtyard beyond. At this, our master bowed deeply in silence.

Although there was not the slightest intention on anybody's part in this interview for it to resemble an ancient Zen *mondo*[9] or formal conversation with a master in the heyday of Chinese Ch'an (Zen) Buddhism, it turned out to be just that. In those times, an encounter with the master was always, or nearly always, an opportunity for him to test the level of a monk's spiritual development and sometimes an occasion for the monk to test the master. In this case, however, there was no such formal relation, the lady simply being a visitor to the place. Her suffering and the progressive course of the disease had forced her to give up all hope of living for much longer. The only thing she had wanted to do as a last act was to see her son's grave. From that moment onwards, she said to herself, she would be free to die. She was, if we might use an applicable phrase here, 'dead to this world'. Since all the parties to this episode have now departed this life, it has been impossible to enquire just why the old lady unexpectedly arrived at Ryuataki-ji on that hot summer day. Almost certainly, however, it was one of those turns of fate (karma) which are sometimes responsible for bringing people together for some purpose. Again, almost certainly, either shortly before her visit or at that the very moment while sipping tea with Roshi she gained enlightenment in the sense of the examples above. In other words, she was catapulted into the Now of Jesus' 'everlasting life', that ineffable realisation that 'all is always now' and that in truth we have never left the 'Now' of our true home, the real selves we carry about with us, but only imagine ourselves to have done so. In that moment of realisation, the woman could see this truth very clearly for herself. Ideas such as 'past' and 'future' lose their meaning. Reality is before one's very eyes in this very moment and, moreover, we see that it has never ever been anywhere else! This was probably so overwhelming for her during the interview that all she could do in reply to Sochu's sincere, apparently harmless, but well-timed question was to give way to a perfectly spontaneous, utterly sincere reaction. Seeing this, the master knew that she had understood the point.

The next case took place quite recently, probably about 1996 or a year or so later. The master here is H.W.L. Poonja whose teacher was the distinguished guru and Indian saint, Sri Ramana Maharshi. He is in interview here with a young but spiritually advanced American devotee. One should not be put off by Poonjaji's rough-hewn style of expression and bear in mind that he is speaking to modern youth. Other young people were no doubt present and listening to this encounter.

The student finds himself (or herself) in something of a mental knot. This is a common phenomenon prior to breaking out into realisation. It is probable that just before the interview recorded here that the student had asked how it is possible to gain enlightenment. He or she might have asked (in view of what is said and the sequence of what is said) how to go on. Like many others who have put their hand to the plough, after a time they lose their way and are not sure how to progress or whether to move on at all. At this point a teacher or another enlightened person is of the greatest assistance. He will say:

'Get rid of all notions, intentions, and desires. Give up distinctions between this and that, between the past and the future, inquire and you will fulfil your promise that "If I get a human form, I will get enlightened."

'This incarnation as a human being is blessed. The only purpose of this life will be fulfilled if you are free. Otherwise this miserable suffering will not end. This human form, this temporary 'apparel' is meant only for freedom. Eight point four million species you have passed through to sit in front of me.[10] It is not difficult to be free. Freedom is within you. Love is within you and you are searching at the supermarket! This samsara is a supermarket dealing in commodities. Turn your back on it and you are free. Return home.

'The sun is so big, much bigger than the earth, yet a single cloud can hide the sun. Clouds are thoughts. Likewise, the I-thought is hiding the Self. The I-thought is hiding peace, beauty and love. How to remove the cloud? Enquire, and it will vanish when you enquire, because it is not real.'

It is interesting to realise that the man who walked the stony paths of Galilee 2000 years ago as a forward-looking representation of Jewish culture, and the other cited here who began life as a Hindu have much in common. The injunction above to get rid of all intentions and desires, (distinctions) between this and that, past and future and so on – how similar this is to Jesus' appeals to his disciples and those around him to give up their worldly concerns **(Lk. 12,16–21; 12, 22–31; 12, 22–31;12, 33–34; Mk. 10,24.)** and 'follow him'; the need to be free **(Jn. 8,32–3)**, to turn to God within **(Lk. 17, 20–21)** for where else could God be, he asks, but in our hearts? **(Mk. 9, 23; 11, 22– 24; 12, 27; Lk. 11,10)** He was at pains to point this out to us on many occasions, and the path to Him, Jesus says, is through humility **(Mt. 5,3; 19, 3–4; 19,14; Mk. 10, 15; Lk. 6,33ff.)**.

This is then to return 'home' like the Prodigal Son, or the need to 'enquire' within our hearts (minds)**(Mt. 7,7)**.

The principal difference between the Christian view and that of the Eastern is the preoccupation in Hindu and Buddhist culture with the psychological aspect of our being, our minds. It is concerned not with one very small group of people in the world waiting for salvation by a saviour, but with the mental condition of all men everywhere, regardless of their race of their tradition. The stage, therefore, is on a much larger scale than that ever conceived by the Hebrews, and latterly

Buddhist analyses of the human mind in interaction with its environment have been seen to conform with the findings of modern science in the last twenty years.[11]

By 'eight point four million species' Poonjaji is referring at this juncture to the very long evolution needed to become human and also the long time it takes for man to be weaned from his selfish preoccupations before he can say, 'I've had enough and need to know the truth for myself!' and then go out and find someone who can help him to this realisation. As with Poonjaji, Christ's whole objective was to bring his contemporaries back to a knowledge of God.

The next example from the same source and around the same time appears to be a very simple means to enlightenment, but we should recall that the questioner has spent some time, perhaps years, struggling with the basic problem of human unfulfilment.

Poonjaji[12], can you help me?

Well, let's see. You have been in Poona for fifteen years. Did you get what you want?

Well, I grew a lot.

Let us say that you went to a restaurant for a big meal. As you come out a friend says, 'Let's go to that other restaurant.' Will you go?

No, I am already full.

So I ask you, 'Are you full? Did you get what you want in Poona?'

No.

So what do you want?

Pure consciousness.

Very good. So how to get there? If you are at the office and you receive a phone call that your house is burning down, what would you do?

I would drive home right away.

Good. Along the way a friend says, 'Let's go to a restaurant.' What will you do?

I will go home.

Go home. Yes. Why? Because your house is on fire. You have to take care of the house first, right? You may not even eat that day, right? You might forget about lunch. You will forget about friends along the way. Like this, you come to me to see consciousness. Okay?

Good. Don't think of past or future. The past is a graveyard. It is the office and you are rushing towards your house. If you don't think of the past, you can't think of the future either. To think of the future, you must stand in the past. So the past and the future are not in your mind. Mind itself is only past and future, so don't think now. Okay?

Just a few seconds. I want just a few seconds out of your life. Okay?

No thought, no past, no future. Now tell me: 'Who are you?' In this no-thinking you are facing consciousness and consciousness is facing you. So tell me: 'Who are you?'

I am consciousness.

Yes, very good. Now look around you and what do you see?

I see emptiness everywhere.

Yes, emptiness everywhere. Now in emptiness, give rise to a thought. Any thought will do. From where does it come?

It comes from emptiness.

Very good. And what is it?

It is empty!

Yes, Now let it sink back into emptiness and what happens?

It is like a bubble that starts to form and sinks back.

Yes, and what do you see?

Emptiness everywhere. Even thoughts, people; the world is empty.

Very good. And this realization?

Also empty!

Jesus is reported to have said **(Lk. 17,21)** that the kingdom of heaven is within us. How relevant that remark is in this context! When the young man uses the word 'emptiness', here he is not thinking of a vacuum. He is not 'thinking' at all. All thought has been abandoned. He *sees* the kingdom of heaven and knows that he and it are one. And more. He sees, too, that the world and the universe beyond it are also 'empty', that is, he is experiencing 'pure consciousness' or Subjectivity. This is our substance and the substance of everything else in the world and beyond it. Seen in this relationship, all the other sayings Rabbi Jesus utters in this connection make greater sense than the usual ecclesiastical interpretations and once again also immediately acquire an unsuspected profundity. When, for example, Jesus says that the 'kingdom of heaven is at hand', he could have meant as many have believed that the 'end of the world is at hand'. This idea, however, has proved quite wrong. The idea that Jesus is to ascend into heaven there to enjoy God's eternal happiness has enjoyed popularity for centuries. However, if 'the kingdom of heaven is at hand' is understood as the ubiquitous presence of Subjectivity *now and forever*, the phrase then assumes absolute clarity.

Holistic seeing (enlightenment) as a religious common denominator

The idea of wholeness is edging its way more and more into our modern consciousness. Developments in physics, chemistry, biology and medicine together with all their associated disciplines have produced a world in the last hundred years which could not have been dreamed of in 1900. At the same time, all of them interact with one another to produce that world. The development of the modern motor car, for example, is a case in point where all four major disciplines, together with mathematics and a host of subsidiaries, are incorporated into its final production. Older ideas of a mechanistic study of physics, chemistry or medicine have ceded to completely new visions of interdependence. The communications sciences, which might also broadly include transport and aviation have managed, metaphorically at least, to 'shrink' the globe, and the process will no doubt continue as communication techniques improve and the speed and capacity of aircraft increase.

Commensurate with these developments, a process of growth and inclusion is taking place in our mental horizons. For those interested in developments in the Stock Market, for example, the latest details on market closure in Japan the day before can be reviewed by the New York stockbroker over breakfast the next day. No self-respecting US banker, for example, would dream of ignoring developments on that and other markets merely to concentrate on those of his own. Although he may be culturally far removed from the thinking of the men who manage financial matters in Tokyo and Frankfurt, those men will be an ineradicable part of his working world, and his well-being will depend to some extent on theirs. The same principle applies more and more to our economic interdependence, and there may well come a time in the near future when 'cooperation' and not 'competition' will be the theme of peaceful economic existence.

However that may be, this enormous, modifying, accelerating, expanding, liberating worldwide phenomenon of what is usually called 'development' with its attendant inclusiveness has been going on around us for the last fifty years with no significant change taking place at all in the strongholds of religious tradition. Orthodox Jews still believe that the world was created by the God of a 'chosen people' some five-and-a-half thousand years ago and waits as they did 2000 years ago for a Messiah to relieve them of they know not what. Christian Catholicism talks of an Ecumenical Council, which hopes to bring both the Protestants and perhaps the Greek Orthodox Church under its iron wing, but would not, for one moment, seriously consider modifying its own orthodoxy beyond a mild apology for the crimes it committed long ago. All this despite the considerable wave of scientific research into Christian beliefs already referred to earlier. Islam, too, is still for the most part so firmly entrenched in its views that serious discussion which might entail criticism or a modification of its beliefs and tradition is quite out of the question. Buddhism today flounders in the complexity of 2500 years of tradition and its various scions produce, internationally, only few people of illumined vision despite the richness in this regard of its written tradition. Hinduism, while regularly producing a few remarkable people of high spirituality and capacity, remains encapsulated in India, so that the influence of these few is generally limited to one geographical area. All these religions today are principally concerned not with the holistic vision which underlies them all, but with the superstructure of religious observance, ritual, tradition and belief which has developed over thousands of years from this one basic understanding. Under the huge weight of all these differing views, the 'colours' of the prism alluded to above, the vision of Oneness is almost totally obliterated. Proof of this religious involvement with inessentials is demonstrated from time to time by the appearance of enlightened masters who draw men's attention again to the priorities of religious commitment and to the holistic vision as the true meaning of our lives. Jesus was such a man and there have been many others in various cultures since his time.[13]

The vision of Oneness needs no specific religious tradition. It is the heritage of all men everywhere, and the spiritual common denominator which includes us all whatever our religious background. The only prerequisite is that we possess a determined desire to know its nature and that we lead a life which does not bring distress to other living beings. These two.

If the desire in us is strong enough, the 'doors of perception' will be opened in good time and illumination will enter in, a process exactly like that of planting a seed which, in its natural season, will eventually sprout and bear fruit in the manner of the parable of the mustard seed **(Mt. 17. 21)**. As the one thing common to all religion, it is that which is left when all the paraphernalia of tradition has been abandoned. All the rest can disappear completely, but the possibility of what Christians call the 'vision of God' will remain since it is part of the programme laid down by nature and inherent in us all for our further development into human beings proper.

It is our potential, almost, we might say, our obligation to realise this.

Since it is a human potential which, strictly speaking, has nothing essentially to do with our formalised religions, the holistic insight, as I prefer to call it, occurs in our poetry and literature. It appears when an author has, via other means than the religious, come to exactly the same spiritual understanding as the contemplative or the truly conscious individual. Just two or three examples are set down here as illustrations from English literature.[14]

> To see a world in a Grain of Sand
> And a Heaven in a Wild Flower,
> Hold Infinity in the palm of your hand
> And Eternity in an hour.[15]

Seeing into the nature of things for the first time, Thomas Traherne, a 17th century clergyman, records his experience:

> The Corn was Orient and Immortal Wheat which never should be reaped, nor was Ever sown. I thought that it has stood from everlasting to everlasting. The Dust and Stones of the Street were as precious as GOLD... The Green Trees... transported and ravished me; their Sweetness and Beauty made my heart to leap, and almost mad with Ecstasy, they were such strange and Wonderful Thing...
> **From The 'Third Century', 3**

And Wordsworth in his time:

> There was a time when meadow, grove and stream,
> The earth and every common sight,
> To me did seem
> Apparelled in celestial light.
> **William Wordsworth**

These quotations are not to suggest either that the subject is the exclusive property of literature and poetry. The suggestion here is that the insight we speak of can be acquired outside a formal religious framework. Neither does it only and wholly concern the subject of light and beauty in natural surroundings as illustrated in the examples. Nor does it belong to the realm of mysticism. Formal Christianity, not recognising that the holistic vision is every man's birthright, has always relegated mysticism to the domain of the contemplative's cell, bringing forth the realisations gathered there from time to time as evidence for its particular interpretation of Jesus' mission or the presence of God on earth.

However, the inner vision, the 'no me' or 'No Mind' (Jap. *Mu-shi*), as it was called in ancient China and later in Japan, no more belongs to the visionary's cell than a bird to an aviary. It is ours to find, and we can find it in whatever we put our hand to, even, apparently, in the art swordsmanship.[16] Primarily, and at its highest, the experience concerns looking into ourselves and recognising that we are not lacking anything (in other words, the very opposite to that dictated by the Church), that we share with every other thing a perfect, unadulterated Oneness and that we are therefore united with everything else, animate and inanimate, and finally, that when we look for a 'me' there isn't one, but only the 'Emptiness of Oneness'.

This experience is the 'revolution of mind' which Daisetz Suzuki refers to in his essays on the subject.[17] In the light of this realisation we are no longer the puny little selves we once were, but the giants of the Pentecostal intuition, free and compassionate, liberated for ever from that narrow self which is principally concerned with its own well-being, and which is prepared to annihilate anything which stands in its way. We are free of it once and for all.

It is not easy to eradicate self. It may even take a lifetime to corner the beast and slay it, or it may take a much shorter time than that, but this is not the point. Mere time in our sense has nothing to do with the issue. What is important is that every step taken to erode the dominance of our lower selves will be a step taken towards that goal for which we were created, full adulthood.

The alternative

Since, we believe, nature has programmed us for a higher development, a fact which can be safely assumed from the many mortals who have made the 'last step' to spiritual maturity, to enlightenment or to full personal 'integration', as we have come to know from the considerations above, there is in the long run no real alternative open to us. Nature will take her time to fashion the final model of man where the last 'segment' alluded to a moment ago is drawn out to its fullest extent. As human beings and unlike other species, we are in a position to delay that plan or to subvert its enfoldment. Looked at this way, the biblical idea of 'free will' takes on a modern, more meaningful aspect. We are free, of course on the one hand, to reject the way nature has laid down for us, but in reality there is no free choice. Failure to conform with nature's demands only results in suffering, at best, on a personal level, in the continued, unabated thirst for fulfilment, and at the worst, on a general level, in our own possible destruction as a species.

The other, true aspect of so-called 'free will' is the wisdom of seeing that both liberation and fulfilment lie in rising above our lower selves to attain enlightenment. In this way, we combine will and energy to greatly accelerate the process of a natural development. That this can be done is proved in every decade by those who have come to enlightenment themselves. This thought is also at the centre of Jesus' teaching. 'I have come,' he said, 'that they may have life, and may have it more abundantly' **(Jn. 10, 10).** It is quite certain that he wasn't thinking at that moment of worldly possessions, riches, dominance over others, fame and fun, or even personal success in using the word 'abundantly', but of that abundance of freedom and happiness which comes from choosing nature's (or God's) alternative to these.

---

[1] It is not to be assumed, of course, from this list that one person can accomplish all these things, but there are people who can perform any one, or a number, of these remarkable feats. Some of these have submitted their powers to scientific examination to the astonishment of those conducting the experiments; others may live unassuming lives and yet be able to perform cures where professional medicine has resigned all interest. On a smaller scale, there are others who are able to discern the truth of a matter without being furnished beforehand with relevant material in order to come to an essential understanding of the matter in hand. This corresponds to a large extent with some people's ability to do a thing without having had previous training and is not a seldom phenomenon in the musical world where individuals have the grasp of an instrument within a week or even less. Of other phenomena, the author once had the experience in India of being told what he had (specifically) been doing hours before and hundreds of miles away by someone whom he did not know and could not in the circumstances have possibly got to know from others. It was, to say the least, an unnerving experience.

[2] Every advanced meditator will experience for himself, sooner or later, what the "gifts of contemplation are. Apart from an easy, relaxed state of mind, which is among the first of such endowments, followed by a sharpened feeling of being wide awake which is often accompanied by an immediate, acute perception of other's motives and character, there may also be an improvement in general health where excellent health is lacking. These acquirements are all very well and an enrichment to life. The danger comes when the adept finds himself in possession of power without having the will or mature perspective or depth of character to deal with it. He (or she) is

then very much in the position of the 'Sorcerer's Apprentice', and the results can lead to catastrophe. This is the reason why the ancient sages in India always provided a long test of character for the aspirant (chela) after careful selection before allowing him access to power. We do much the same in the choice and training of personnel in the Civil Service and other responsible areas of service.

³ The temptation of Jesus by the devil in the wilderness finds an exact counterpart in the life of the Buddha. In Gruber and Kersten's book, *Der Ur-Jesus, Die buddhistichen Quellen des Christentums* (The Original Jesus) which is also available in English, the authors present a direct, two-column comparison of the story of this sojourn in the desert, occurring in the gospels on p.214. The parallels occur respectively at **Lk. 4, 3-8,** and in the **Samyuttanikaya 22, Verse 47.** In other respects, too, the book gives conclusive proof of the similarity of the two religions. See bibliography.

⁴ See **Jn. 11, 26** and **Majjhimanikaya 22, verse 47** which read respectively: 'And whoever lives and believes in Me shall never die...' and 'Those who have enough faith and love for me ascend to heaven.'

⁵ Buchan, John, *Memory Hold the Door,* Hodder & Stoughton, 1940, pp. 120-1.

⁶ Payne and Bendit, (ed.), *The Psychic Sense,* London, Faber & Faber, 1943, pp. 183-4.

⁷ Johnson, Raynor, 'The case of J.P.W.', *Watcher on the Hills* , Hodder & Stoughton, London, 1959, p. 65,

⁸ Wei Wu Wei, *Ask the Awakened,* London, Routledge & Kegon Paul, 1963, p. 106.

⁹ The "*mondo*" was usually an exchange between the master and monk in which the line of communication was on two levels. Outwardly, it seemed to be a perfectly mundane observation of this or that, but in fact was a test of the other's depth of realisation. It preceded the *koan* in this assessment. In one way one could describe the *mondo* as a spiritual 'clash of arms' where, if each were satisfied with the other's understanding (that is, both spoke the same spiritual language revealing that understanding) then they 'retired', but often enough, one of the parties was 'injured', that is, one of them had still something to learn.

¹⁰ The term '8.4 million species' was a favourite among the ancient Chinese to give the impression of a large number. They often spoke,

for example of the '80,000 pores of the body' and here Poonjaji is using the same expression of dimension to emphasize hugeness.

[11] For a consideration of this aspect, see the works of Fritjof Capra, notably *The Turning Point ,The Tao of Physics,* USA, Simon & Shuster, 1982.

[12] The '-ji' of 'Poonja' is a title of respect and endearment.

[13] Among these are Dae Poep Sa Nim, who is mentioned in the work, Harada Roshi, working in Switzerland, France and Austria, Joshu Sasaki Roshi, Genso Sasaki Roshi, working in Europe and elsewhere in the West, Natagawa Roshi, Japanese master visting Europe and elsewhere; Thich Nhat Hanh, a Buddhist master from Southeast Asia who spends much of his time in Europe and the USA. Gensho Viun Hogen Roshi in Germany and elsewhere in Europe, and many more qualified teachers practising in the USA.

[14] For a full account of enlightened reference in English literature, see R.H. Blyth, *Zen in English Literature and Oriental Classics,* Tokyo, Hokuseido Press, 1942.

[15] William Blake, 'Auguries of Innocence', in Nicholson & Lee, eds. *The Oxford Book of English Mystical Verse.* 1917.

[16] A short but pregnant account of the mental attitude towards an opponent in swordsmanship is given in D.T. Suzuki's book, *Zen and Japanese Culture,* Bollingen Series LXIV, New York, Pantheon Books, 1959, which quotes from an essay on the subject written by Takano Shigeyoshi.

[17] The term 'revolution of mind' is often quoted by Suzuki in his reference to the phenomenon of enlightenment in the series (2 vols) *Essays in Zen Buddhism,* Rider, London, 1958.

CHAPTER V

When I mention religion, I mean the Christian religion; and not only the Christian religion, but the Protestant religion; and not only the Protestant religion, but the Church of England.
Henry Fielding, The History of Tom Jones

However, for those who are neither cowardly nor stupid enough to swallow lies and absurdities and who are prepared to take the consequences in order to clean up their thinking, to make it freer and more upright, I recommend them to investigate the history of their belief with the eye of the critic
Karlheinz Deschner, *The Falsified Belief*

One day the devil and a friend stopped to listen to a man preaching the truth to a group of people in the market place. 'That looks bad for us, doesn't it?' the friend observed. 'Not really,' the devil replied, 'give them time and they'll make an organisation out of it.'
Anon.

An approach to understanding the New Testament and a new interpretation

Faced with the difficult intellectual problems which have come to light recently regarding the New Testament, John Bunyan might well have put the matter in his own way by declaring that 'anyone approaching the City of God but by the Door of Faith will find his way barred by a deep Moat of Doubt and Insecurity, by Thickets infested with Snares of Self-Deception and Self-Justification, by Fogs of Contradiction and Irregularity, by enticing Paths which lead into the Desert of Ignorance, and by great high Walls of Tradition and Prejudice.'

In this situation, we can do one of two things: we can accept the New Testament with all its glaring irregularities and incongruities, just as it is, lock, stock and barrel as the fundamentalists among us do, and have done for centuries in both denominations, believing it to be divinely inspired and therefore unassailable, or we can avail ourselves of our greatest biological prerogative and begin to think about the matter.

In the analysis which follows, an attempt has been made to incorporate all the independent, relevant, scholarly research conducted so far into the interpretation of the New Testament. It assumes that the conclusions drawn by patient investigation and observation are objective, scientific conclusions and that they are offered as facts in order to promote better understanding of the material under consideration. No theological material of any kind, either ancient or modern, Catholic or other, plays a role in the development of the arguments involved here so as to avoid all entanglement with established Christian views and beliefs. This attitude is not, of course to diminish their value, but for the moment to remain as independent of them as possible and thus, it is hoped, preserve an open mind on the issues under discussion.

Only the four Gospels will be considered in this essay. The study assumes moreover that these provide the quintessence of a teaching. The rest, Christianity as we know it, is largely developed from a Pauline interpretation of this quintessence. In other words, it suggests that an interpretation other than that handed down to us through the ages is both possible and plausible, if not desirable.

Finally, it should be noted that there is no intention during this examination to antagonize Christian readers. On the contrary, the intention is rather to present the message of the so-called New Testament in a new, positive and stimulating light. If, to do that, it is necessary to excise a great deal of accumulated untruth, distortion, superstition and humbug, so much the better.

A historical perspective with some linguistic considerations

The first record in Aramaic of Jesus' words was made some 70 or 80 years after his death, that is to say, just within living memory of those who were with him during his ministry, and therefore on the borderline at that time between reported fact and legend. Comparing this interval with a similar span in modern times, we could say that it corresponds with the reports, say, of First World War veterans and their personal experiences of that war in their time. However, the many points of similarity as also the sequence of events reported in each gospel supply indication that there was a consensus of opinion existing between the authors of the Gospels with regard to the principal events of Jesus' ministry. The books which bear the titles Matthew, Mark, Luke and John may not have been written by the apostles themselves, but by people who had heard these accounts from them or from other men and women who actually accompanied Jesus on his walks through Galilee. Scholars agree that it is highly probable that an older text once existed which perhaps consisted of notes and reports recorded nearer the time. The contemporaries of

Jesus, even the youngest, the lad Thaddeus, would have reached an advanced age by the time the Gospels were finally set down, and people living to the age of eighty or over were, we may safely assume, a fairly rare phenomenon in those days. Despite variations in length, style and content, and also the fact that some collation, comparison and agreement between the authors almost certainly took place as to what was to be included and what excluded, the Gospels nevertheless appear to be an honest and conscientious attempt to set forth the life and teachings of the Master. These works were first translated into Greek and later, with the establishment of the Church, from the original Aramaic into Latin. Approximately 1500 years after the death of Christ, the New Testament was then translated under great duress into several European languages and, by the end of the 19th century, into practically every language known to man.

Professor Lapide's[1] observation that the New Testament is a 'translation of a translation of a translation' in reference to the first two translations, namely, Greek and Latin, is a valid one. In the course of these translations and despite the undoubted goodwill and conscientiousness of the translators, appalling errors were made. This is something which can be reasonably expected since, even today and with all the means of cross-reference we have at our disposal of checking for accuracy, and the addition of computerized lexigraphical technology available to us into the bargain, mistakes are still made in translation even where competence, integrity and conscientiousness are all unimpeachable.

The results of linguistic research into translations of the New Testament over the last few decades have revealed scores of errors, some of which very seriously distort the utterances of Jesus. Of these only two are mentioned here by way of illustration since our main preoccupation is not linguistic, but more semantic and psychological in character. They nevertheless make clear how important this aspect alone is in considering the basis upon which Christianity has developed.

Both are taken from a recent publication, *The Castrated Gospel*, by Johannes Dietl-Zeiner.[2] In his book, the author demonstrates with great care and attention to detail how an error was made in translation from Hebrew or Aramaic, and how this error has persisted into the later Latin and in all subsequent translations from that language into all modern languages. The reference here is to **John, 12–25,** where we read:

He that loveth his life shall lose it; and he that hateth his life in this world shall keep it unto life eternal.

The author explains that the mistaken concept given by the word 'life' arises in this case from a wrong choice of meaning for the Greek words, respectively, *Philon, apollüei* and *mison.* The first of these words, he points out, is not translated by *'to be greedy for'* as it should be, but by the infinitive *'to love'*. The second word in this case 'lose' is not translated using *'pass out of sight, vanish, pass away'*, but simply with *lose,* and the third word, *mison,* is normally translated in our bibles (wrongly) with the verb *'to hate'*. The complete and correct translation, he suggests, should read:

He who hangs on to (his) life (i.e. fearfully) the same will find life escaping him; but he who is not anxious about his life, or those who are not anxious about their lives in this world will preserve them unto (i.e. right into) eternal life.

The esoteric aspect of this quotation will be dealt with later. Suffice it to say here that, as a result of the revised translation, Jesus' remark assumes a more positive character than hitherto. The translation given here, it is suggested, is much more in line with the joyful message of the Rabbi's teaching than the traditional rendering.

The other example concerns Jesus' preceding words in this connection at **Mark, 8, 34–35.**

Whoever desires to come after me, let him deny himself, and take up his cross, and follow me. For whoever desires to save his life will lose it, but whoever loses his life for my sake and the gospel's will save it.

With the same meticulousness as above, Dietl-Zeiner explores the translations of Hebrew, through the Greek and Latin and later modern translations and demonstrates in subsequent translations that all of them slavishly follow the primary errors of the Greek model. Here again, it is a case of wrong choice in selecting a word to fit the Greek word *stauron* which, he urges, has been given the meaning 'cross', instead of the translation *palisade* which latter means the same as it does in contemporary English. At this point, he says, the word could in context mean *protection and security* or *shield*. The author then goes on to explain that the Greek word *arato* in the Bible has been translated as *'to carry'* in all cases, thereby ignoring the verb which belongs to it which is *'to pray'* or *'ask for something'*. Moreover, the Greek word *apolesei* occurring as it should at verse 35 of the same quotation is, he feels, insufficiently considered and raises the issue of whether the word 'to lose' is appropriate at all, suggesting that *'sadly'* or *'to make unhappy'* would be much more fitting choices. With these considerations in mind, we are asked in conclusion whether the following might not be a better alternative to that which we have been presented with for so long:

'When one of you desires to follow me, he should rather not do so, but instead pray for protection ('palisade' as a wall of protection and in another sense: a divine shield) and so become my disciple. For those who seek to preserve their lives of their own volition will find sorrow (in so doing). For he who gives up his life will be freed by looking to me and the joyful message' **Mk. 8. 34–5**.[3]

The Rabbi's remark now assumes quite a different complexion. It immediately does away with the problem which has haunted many scholars and others for centuries, that is, the horrific prospect imminent for those who want to follow Christ being obliged to 'take up a cross' in order to do so. Surely, they asked themselves, Christ was not suggesting that anyone wishing to emulate him or come into the kingdom of heaven should submit himself to crucifixion. The idea is absurd. Could it be, they pursued, that the idea of 'taking up a cross' was to assume some burden or other, suffering perhaps, or to accept the 'sins of the world' upon their shoulders? Whichever way it could be turned, the idea was objectionable and unhealthy, but eventually ended up in English as an idiom meaning to endure a burden, to put up with some more or less heavy grievance over a long period. 'To pray for a divine shield' against the vicissitudes of this life is much more easily digestible and quite free from the perversity of the original translation.

This much, then, as brief illustration of one of the lexical errors with which the New Testament is strewn and which is a subject of serious enquiry in its own right. There are, however, other errors of a semantic nature lying in wait for the translator among the subtleties of language often at places where he anticipates not the slightest danger of misunderstanding. Quite often, as in the case following, they are very simple, but nevertheless crucial.

English speakers travelling on the European continent may have come across heavy vehicles bearing the slogan, *Just in time...*' broadly advertised at the rear of the truck. The haulage contractors have heard the phrase somewhere, appraised it as coinciding with their ideal of punctuality and, in keeping with the tendency in Germany today to adopt English words and phrases as a sign of being abreast of the times, have proclaimed their logo to the world. However, those who are thoroughly familiar with English will recognize that the slogan is not the positive thing it is meant to be. To them it does not suggest unerring punctuality, but, on the contrary, that there were difficulties on the way which, either by luck or initiative, were overcome and have allowed the vehicle to reach its destination 'just' (i.e. barely) on time. Further, the implication behind the phrase for the native speaker is that punctuality suggested here is more a thing of chance than intention. The three dots after the word 'time' in the logo only serve to strengthen this impression. It can be safely assumed that this is certainly not what the road transport firms in question wish to convey!

Mistakes of the same kind have occurred in translating the New Testament as Lapide elsewhere points out in his book. In it he lists five other sources of error apart from lexical ones. They include errors in grammar and syntax where, he notes in the gospel of Mathew alone, 120 mistakes occur in connection with what he calls 'violent' attempts to bring the Greek into line with the Hebrew original. From the semantic point of view, for example, he says, the ideas of the *kingdom of heaven, salvation, grace, reconciliation* which, in the Hebrew are part and parcel of an ancient living tradition, and thus also an integral part of the language, are, in the Greek tradition, completely alien, and so have no place in the language. The same is true, the author goes on to say, for what he refers to as the 'theosophical level', the 'infrastructure' of the Hebrew religious spirit inherent in such concepts as *messiah* and its associations, in the words *resurrection, the will of God, doomsday* and many others.[4] This should not surprise us. As an illustration we could well imagine scholars two thousand years hence, for example, deliberating upon the meaning (and implication) of the word, 'redbrick' in modern English used in connection with British universities at one time. We might assume that they would trace the word 'brick' to a building element and rightly associate it with reddish coloured bricks found on excavation at various sites which, they would say, was typical building material at the time and a material used for house construction. Here, they would make the first mistake since the brick used for university construction is, although it is reddish, of quite a different kind. It is darker, denser and the face side is glazed. We could reasonably expect these investigators to cease their enquiries at this point, having satisfied themselves that this was all there was to the matter. But this is only half the story. It would not touch upon the essential point of the issue embodied in the word 'redbrick university'. Their findings, although correct as far they go, would nevertheless miss the point entirely. The conclusion would quite overlook the class consciousness inherent in

British society at the time, and so ignore the covert comparison between the newly established universities in their rawness and newness, and, primarily, their absence of tradition, their pure functionality in some cases. These facts are at odds with the monumental, medieval, decorative universities, for example, of Oxford and Cambridge, with their 'dreaming spires' and cloistered privacy, their extensive lawns and quadrangles, some of which have stood the tests of time for 800 years, politically, geographically and intellectually. At the subconscious level there is also the insinuation that those who attend the modern universities could only be of lower calibre than those studying at the older ones with their long established tradition of learning and academic excellence. Such are the nuances which would be lost on the later scholar and researcher.

In the same way, we could imagine other recondite problems being studied in 2000 years time evoked by such phrases in English as 'a stiff upper lip' and 'cloth cap' with their social nuances, by 'Eton and Harrow' and the term 'Official Birthday', by the term 'fish and chips', and a 'Welsh Sunday'. In the literary, social and historical spheres, phrases such as 'Humpty Dumpty', 'Heath Robinson', 'the light fantastik', 'to know the ropes' 'Tea for Two', 'the cup that cheers…' and many, many others, especially those idioms which have relevance to English life would make it very difficult for scholars to arrive at the truth behind the word or phrase.

Added to the problem of textual inaccuracy is the deliberate inclusion of what today we could refer to as either legendary or 'propaganda' material in the Gospels. Among the legendary is the account of Jesus' miraculous conception and his royal lineage, the visit of the Three Kings of Orient occurring in Matthew and Luke, as well as all that we know of the Christmas story and, in all probability, the Slaying of the Innocents. The temptation of Jesus by Satan in the desert occurs in other religious traditions and for this reason might be suspect if it relates to something which actually occurred, despite the fact that its inclusion has a profound religious significance.

Parallels and propaganda

Among the accounts of miraculous happenings, as Peter de Rosa[5] and Siegfried Obermeier[6] point out respectively, very similar, almost parallel narratives are encountered in texts relating to the birth of the Buddha and to that of Mohammed the Prophet, in the teaching of Zoroaster, in the Gnostic myth of Apollo and in the cult of Mithras – all of them far too analogous to dismiss as mere coincidence.

In the matter of ulterior misinformation, on the other hand, recent scholastic research has also established with considerable certainty that the famous quotation occurring in **Matthew 16, 18** where Jesus is supposed to have said,

> And I say unto you that you are Peter, and on this rock I will build my Church, and the gates of Hades shall not prevail against it.

is also a later propagandistic insertion into the Gospels. No less partisan are the references to 'the Jews' to be found in John and felt by some scholars to be explicitly anti-Semitic. At **John 6, 41,** for example, we read that:

> The Jews then complained about Him because He said, 'I am the bread which came down from heaven

where the word 'Jews' is not qualified by 'some' or 'a number' or where another word like 'Pharisees', 'scribes or 'elders', 'people' could have been equally well and more accurately employed. The word 'Jews' in this generalised sense is used in the same way a little later at verse 52:

> The Jews therefore quarrelled among themselves saying…

and so throughout this particular gospel. Much more propagandist (not to say obnoxious) are threats such as those to be found in **John** at **15,6,** apparently proceeding from the mouth of Jesus:

If anyone does not abide in me, he is cast out as a branch and is withered; and they gather them and throw them into the fire, and they are burned.

As has been pointed out by critics of the New Testament, among them philosophers and even some theologians, the caveat is abhorrent because it has aided and abetted fanatics, lunatics and murderers who have at various times in our history committed atrocities against Jews in the service of either church or state for two millennia.[7]

The problems touched upon here are clear. It cannot always be said with certainty on the one hand what is truth and what is untruth, what was actually uttered by Rabbi Jesus and what served after his death as a private motive for his successors in proclaiming their political, power-motivated interpretations or, on the other, what has simply been misunderstood for generations by a succession of translators. Indeed, one can go so far as to say that perhaps the only satisfactory way of getting at the truths contained in the New Testament or, let us say, to substantiate them, is not so much to tackle them from the 'outside so to speak, as from the 'inside'. It is a more reliable method to find parallels in the wisdom and experience of other religions which in their turn confirm the truths of Christianity than to rely solely on the statements found in the New Testament for validation of universal truth.

This may strike fundamentalists and their associates as sheer heresy, but heresy or no, the facts of time and experience are rapidly outdating much of what in the past we have taken for divinely proclaimed truth. Here, too, scientific endeavour has caught up with us to expose ancient superstition, myth and untruth.

Beginnings

Among the 'Fogs' referred to a moment ago is the actual year in which Jesus was born which is still a matter of debate. Obermeier among others (p.17) draws his reader's attention to the fact that the authors of the Gospels give Jesus' birth as occurring some time during the reign of Herod the Great, whereas historical fact gives the date of this Herod's death as the spring of the year 4 BC. The matter remains unresolved.

The next ruler, Herod Antipas, is stated by the apostle Matthew to have decreed the slaying of all the babies born at the time of Jesus, so as to refute the prophecy that another could possibly compete with him for the throne, and yet nothing of this appears in reliable accounts of the time. One of these chroniclers whose reports are testified by other contemporaries is Flavius Josephus (born AD 37) and author of a meticulous report, *The Jewish War* who makes no mention of this appalling crime, an enormity which would have been provocation enough for open rebellion, especially at this time. However, this event is not mentioned by any other contemporary.

The circumstances of Jesus' childhood and early manhood are shrouded in mystery. Of his father, Joseph, only the bleakest detail. Of his mother not much more. It seems to be a fairly well substantiated fact that Jesus had one or more brothers while sisters are not accounted for, and whether he was married or not has been an oft debated question without final resolution.

There is, then, an unaccountable gap in the life of Jesus until, as the evangelist tells us, he had reached the age of thirty (**Lk. 3,23**) or thereabouts when, Luke says, he began his teaching. All kinds of conjectures have been made by numerous authors to fill this vacuum from speculations on his having spent a long sojourn in Egypt to his having visited India and Asia, while others account for this large lapse of time by suggesting that Jesus spent much of this period either with the

Essenes or was attached for a time and in one way or another to the Gnostic movement. The best work in this direction is based on plausible suppositions drawn from the painstaking work of archaeologists, historians and scholars in Middle Eastern Studies who have put together a mosaic which, although still far from being complete, nevertheless provides the reviewer with a very good idea of the life and times of Christ's contemporaries.

'Jesus would be easier for us to understand if we knew everything about the world and its history in which he lived, including the ideas and ideals of the people of those times. We need more knowledge of the relationships than is offered to us by the introductory chapters' (i.e. of the Gospels). Thus, E.P. Sanders in his book, *Son of God, A historical Biography of Jesus* (my brackets). He goes on to add that it would, for example, have been a great help if we knew in what situation the Gospels were written down. My response to this is that it would certainly be interesting, but would it really help us to understand Jesus' teaching? After two thousand years, perhaps the best we can hope for is a slow augmentation of our knowledge in this respect as the decades creep by to an even greater distance in time, while realising that our knowledge will never be quite complete. It is a situation similar to counting grains in Zeno's parallel of the heap of rice.[8] Despite the abundance of detail modern research has supplied, the figure of Christ himself nevertheless shimmers uncertainly in the desert heat. We can see the man's face, so to speak, but his features elude us despite the fact that we have strained our eyes in the last few years to see more clearly. We hail the figure, but it slips away at our approach. The question remains as to what we can do to bring the figure more sharply into focus.

Practically all the books which have been published over the last twenty to thirty years on the subject of Jesus, his teaching and his life and which have merited a large readership have been based on scientific lines of enquiry. That is to say, they have concerned themselves with historical interrelationships, linguistic enquiry, archaeological excavation and bibliographical comparison among others. This kind of enquiry is felt to be the most reliable because it is objective, deals with provable material, tangible ideas, and therefore falls into line with our modern ideas of scientific truth. The tacit assumption underlying study of this nature is that 'If it can proved scientifically, then it must be true.' While this kind of thinking most certainly has its place in such an investigation, it must nevertheless be present only as background. We should not run away with the idea that scientific demonstration of this sort is the end of the matter. Wisdom and the facts of human experience are as important to correct assessment in this regard as are tangible, demonstrable fact. As well, therefore, as the external evidence associated with Jesus' appearance in the world, there is also the alternative which makes enquiries into the substance of New Testament teaching, an approach which employs internal reference and the reasonable inferences one can draw from these. This does not mean, on the other hand, a swing towards subjective opinion. Internal facts such as, for example, our current psychological knowledge of mob behaviour as in that occurring in the trial of Jesus before Pilate are also facts which are quite as cogent as historical testimony relating to place, time and participants. The important thing here is the need to be keenly aware at all times of the danger of deluding ourselves. Apart from the ease with which we can align ancient thinking with our own modern assumptions, we can also delude ourselves, for example, with what we regard as 'scientific fact'.

In illustration of this we can see that it would be naïve to assume that the discovery of the actual chalice from which Jesus drank at the Last Supper or, as we have already noted, the unearthing of the cross on which he was crucified could add a grain to the moral validity of the New Testament teaching. They would not. Similarly, it would be just as naïve to imagine that the establishment of the authenticity of the Turin Shroud as that in which Jesus was wrapped after his crucifixion could really do much to promote Christian belief. As in the days of Christ, this is to 'seek a sign', to seek outward confirmation for an inner truth. In this way, a symbol becomes a substitute for relying on our own intrinsic, spiritual potential.

The other side of the coin is subjective interpretation, and perhaps the most notorious example occurs with the first of Jesus' interpreters, namely, Saul of Tarsus, who, we know, founded a community allegedly based on the words of Jesus, but which the Master himself would never have recognised. Moreover, from what we glean as external evidence, those who knew Jesus personally flatly rejected the later Paul's claims at the time.[9] It is a highly dubious assumption, for example, that Jesus ever intended to break with Jewish tradition. From the evidence we have in the Gospels it is much more likely that he wished to reinterpret or perhaps extend that tradition rather than overthrow it. Paul, however, developed a 'Christian' movement which was finally to depart from Jewry altogether and eventually become the glorification of a man he proclaimed as the Son of God and who died on the cross for our sins, for everyone now on earth and for those to come and for all time. As essentially a devout Jew, he interpreted Jesus' life and his death in particular as the redemption of Jewry through the sacrificial blood of one man dying for the people. This was not a new idea even at that time. Subconsciously, it was for him the realisation of a dream harboured in those days by every pious Hebrew. For generations before, the ancient Jewish population had awaited a messiah, and the idea of placing Jesus in that role, albeit as an un-political one, was extremely convenient.

Looking back over the centuries and from the vantage point of our knowledge of nature and of the universe and, much more recently, the realisation that there are millions of other planets similar to our own, some of which may well be populated by mortals like ourselves at perhaps varying levels of development, the idea of a universal saviour as envisaged by St Paul becomes not only ludicrously parochial, but preposterous.

The movement he founded on these ideas was to go from strength to strength. It even adopted all the ornaments of Judaism, adding to a Son and a Holy Ghost and later a 'Mother of God' to the original Father (Abbas).

After the Romans disappeared from the political and cultural stage, Christianity gathered force to become a substitute for the social and political vacuum they left behind them. A thousand years later, in the early Middle Ages the Church provided the people of Europe with a meaningful existence and was later to become a multi-national institution with a strictly all-male administration from pope to priest, riddled for centuries from top to bottom with the primary Hebrew idea of sin and redemption, and was finally to develop into a political force with its own state within a state.

In the nineteenth century, the pope became the 'infallible' leader of a huge concern with immense financial resources, great political influence and tightly organised means of dominating millions of people.

Whether we subscribe to this organisation or not, or to one of its scions, it must be honestly admitted that all this is a far cry from the admonitions and wisdom uttered by a wandering preacher in Galilee two thousand years ago. Indeed, most of it, in fact, stands in the way of an appreciation of the teaching. However, because so much of this Christian superstructure is almost as old as the sayings of Christ, it has been sanctified by two millennia of history to become a practically unassailable bastion of legend and misinterpretation.

The only way to discover the heart of Jesus' teaching, it is suggested, is to turn our backs on this superstructure which has developed in the wake of his crucifixion, and confine our attention exclusively to the four Gospels, which we may reasonably accept, despite their many shortcomings, as reliable accounts of what was actually said and what actually happened. In this we can take into account the results of recent research on the subject so as to sidestep misinterpretation and linguistic error wherever possible

As we have seen, even this is not easy, since the Gospels fall a long way short of the standards of biographical accuracy required by twentieth century scientific investigation. They could in any case never be anything of the kind. The method here, then, must be a little like that employed by those skilful operators working in the silent, backstage ateliers of the Louvre in Paris, inaccessible to the public where layer after layer of superimposed paintings and other 'improvements' in conformity with the taste of subsequent generations have been obtruded upon the Old Masters, and where all of this is carefully removed to reveal the original in all its beauty and uniqueness. Following their example, the greatest care, then, must be exercised in the undertaking. In throwing off all the accretions of Christian mythology amassed over such a long time, it is all too easy in that new freedom to succumb to the fantasies of our own persuasions.[10]

Today, however, there is an antidote to this tendency. We are now in a position to compare the words of Christ with the utterances of other spiritual masters in the course of human history. Where such coincidences occur, we can accept them as universal truths applicable to all men in all ages, and as also relevant to our conclusions. These universally applicable truths would concern not only the ethical truths of religion where there is already close agreement between them all, but also include the mystical elements common to human experience, whether these stem from religious sources or not.

The comparison focuses for the most part on the findings of Buddhism and, to a lesser extent, on ancient Vedic tradition. As well as broadening the scope of comparison, such a focus obviates the likelihood of accidental internal comparison by reference to religions having their roots in Judaism. In this way, it is hoped that the bogus exclusiveness of Christianity as the only true teaching which has been proclaimed by the Church for so long can be exposed for what it is – an illusion.

The Gospels

The Gospels are represented to us in about 170 pages, where a 'page' here is defined as containing approximately 500 words.[11] The New Testament as a whole, including the four synoptical reports, occupies roughly 380 pages. According to this assessment, the four Gospels represent about 44% per cent of the whole.

The address made to the Gospels here is carried out in the spirit of one who reads them for the first time and from the point of view of an enquirer concerned to understand their truth, without deference either to an assumed divinity or to long established attitudes of belief. It will consider both content and tone of the four evangelists' reports as well as the Hebrew background to them in the light of our modern understanding of the world, and also in the light of other religious knowledge outside the Christian tradition. In this it seeks a common denominator which links Christianity to other paths leading to God and is in this sense interdisciplinary. An approach of this sort is necessary at a time when the people of the world are rapidly coming together, and when, on the one hand, we have great power and have made great material progress, but where, on the other, there are signs everywhere of our descent from the human to something less than human.[12] Before the fundamentalists can oppress us again with their medieval fare in a time of moral decay[13] we should have opportunity to awaken to our humanity by understanding the deeper meaning of the texts we have at hand.

Finally, it is not intended to approach the New Testament with an analytical tool which is too fine. While it is true that there is at present too little scientific sense in our religion, too much rationality on the other hand produces a dissection which leaves us guessing at the unity. Ultimately, 'religion', that which 're-binds' us to our origins, is a non-rationalistic experience and, ideally, requires a mixture of wisdom and common sense to interpret.

Before commencing with the analysis of the Gospels themselves, it is advisable to take a look first at the social and political background from which they arose, since these are inextricably woven into the events related by the synoptics. It was precisely these currents of socio-political unrest which, we recall, were ultimately responsible for the brutal amputation of Christ's ministry. The Bible refers to them only darkly here and there, and as a consequence we have always considered them as peripheral. This is not the case at all. At least two men in Jesus' following were committed partisans[14] in a 'local political situation' which was extremely volatile. A brief sketch is therefore necessary to light up the background against which the teaching was preached.

Social and political background to the events recorded in the New Testament

Palestine had been a bone of contention for many years before Jesus appeared on the scene. Three hundred years before his time, Alexander had conquered the country and was followed some thirty years later by Ptolemy I. After him, Antiochus III, the Seleukide, subdued the country in 198 B.C., an event which finally gave rise to the Maccabean Revolt in 167. Later, the country was ruled by the Hasmonaer, among them Alexander Jannai (ca. 103–76), who proved to be a despotic leader like his father, Johannes Hyrkan, a man bent on a policy of expansion. The Pharisees resisted him as a usurper to the crown, a keeper of whores and a man who sullied his office as high priest by marrying a widow, thus committing a grave offence against Mosaic law. The ensuing revolt which was the result of this transgression accounted for 50,000 lives. Among these were 800 prisoners who, while being crucified, were obliged to watch their wives and children cut to pieces.

This atrocity led to political division and confusion between the religious and political powers in the land which was to rankle on into Christ's time.

After Jannai's death, his widow, Alexandra, ruled the country (76–67 B.C.) and for a short time there was peace in the land, but within ten years this was torn to shreds once more by a merciless struggle between Alexandra's two sons, Hyrkan II and Aristobal II. The civil strife was exacerbated by the intervention of Bedouins in the south and by Arab forces in the east, incursions which threw the country into an appalling state of confusion and bloodshed. Those Jews who were allowed to think clearly in all this horror formed a delegation and sought an arbitrator. They approached Pompey, then resident in Damascus, and asked him to come to their assistance. However, the irony of the situation was such that the quarrelling brothers also sought support for their respective causes from the same quarter. Pompey decided to support Hyrkan II in this fraternal dispute and accordingly marched on Jerusalem to settle matters – as he hoped – once and for all. Aristobal ensconced himself in the temple at Jerusalem for three months until, in utter exasperation, a small Roman force broke open its doors, seized Aristobal and took him prisoner to Rome. Henri Daniel-Rops sums up the political situation and the feelings of the Jewish people at this point:

> Thus it was that the Romans came to Palestine almost as saviours and this explains why there were Jews who, 75 years later, were in favour of their rule or at least felt that they could accept it as the lesser evil. Anything, indeed, rather than civil war! However, the Romans were not successful in maintaining their favoured role of arbitrator without some embarrassment. Their Palestine policy proved itself to be a confused affair if not plainly contradictory. One gains the impression that their much vaunted understanding of human nature capitulated before the unlimited reserves of cunning ingenuity among the Jewish people as it did before the

astonishing ease with which its leaders changed their allegiance. (p. 87)

It is possible that the Romans were not at all aware of the undercurrents of Jewish political, social and religious life any more than the British Raj was either of the subtle range of religious and social differences existing among its Indian subjects at the time of the British Empire. It is very likely indeed that the sturdy practicality of Roman administration in dealing with its Jewish subjects was similar to that of the British in dealing with theirs. It was, if you will, an 'empirical approach' with no pun intended. In other words, there was little interest in the national culture of conquered nations.

Aristobal, together with his two sons, returned to Palestine after escaping from prison in Rome and immediately set about mobilising an army against his brother Hyrkan with the result that bloody civil strife broke out once more. At this juncture, Rome was too busy with its own civil strife to divert its attention to the Middle East, and so it was that Herod Antipas, a desert prince from Idumea in the extreme south of the country, saw his chance to exploit the situation. He suppressed an uprising in Galilee, later ingratiated himself firstly with one Roman party and then with another and so succeeded in climbing the steps to power finally to become a force to be reckoned with in the land.

Added to all this travail, Roman taxes were high and not easy to circumvent, and as a result of these factors, protests and revolts were the order of the day. Herod put these down with fanatical energy. While this was going on, another character entered the political arena, Antigonos, one of the sons of Aristobal under the favourable influence of a Parthian invasion, and after negotiations had failed to remove Herod from his office as Tetrarch to which position the Romans had raised him, now gathered a small force of dissatisfied Jews and attacked Jerusalem. Once again, the city was drenched in blood. Herod fled to the fortress of Masada on the Dead Sea and later took a ship to Rome in order to re-open negotiations with its new leaders there. The Roman senate decided to appoint the young man – then only 23 years old – King of Judea. His opponents vehemently resisted the imposition of a monarchy, and bitter fighting was resumed, continuing for another three years. Finally, Rome intervened to end the strife and so, with eleven legions and 6000 cavalry, took the capital. Herod emerged as victor while Palestine was taken over by Rome as a protectorate thirty-seven years before the point from which we reckon our time.

Although a young, competent, if ruthless ruler, Herod did not enjoy the popular support of the people and by far the greater part of the Jewish population was against him. Despite the good terms he enjoyed with Rome, terms on which he could depend at any time for backing, he knew that the throne he occupied as Tetrarch was a slippery one. Like all tyrants before his time and after, his principal aim was not to cede the authority he had gained to anyone and to this end he brutally suppressed all opposition in whatever form it arose. To maintain and consolidate his hold on power, he had his secret police and his informants everywhere. In this way, an uneasy peace was thrust upon a politically explosive situation, and a substantial degree of law and order was restored to the social and political chaos of a few years before. We can easily appreciate the fact that this was paid for by the populace at the price of total despotism. Repressive rule, however, did not prevent plots from being hatched to assassinate Herod and overturn his government even, apparently, by members of his own family. He replied to these conspiracies with the utmost ferocity, murdering his formerly beloved wife, Mariamne and his sons by her, along with five others begat from the nine other wives he entertained in his retinue. Lynchings and executions of men and women took place all over the country throughout the thirty-five years of his reign of terror. After ordering that all the influential people in his kingdom be summarily executed after his demise, he died in agony, but in his own bed in the year 4 BC.

Thus, the life and death of this Herod the 'Great', so-called perhaps because of his successful expansionist policies and also perhaps because of the architectural legacy he left behind him, although there was nothing 'great' about him at all in the moral sense. After his death, the Romans partitioned the country into three areas under the rule of Tetrarchs, Herod Antipas, the man spoken of in the Gospels held Galilee in the north, Philip, his step brother, was accorded the hilly territory to the east, and Archelaus, who was to rule over the southern lands of Samaria and Judea. This last began his rule by false strategies with the result that uproar broke out among the people once more. Henri Daniel-Rops describes the situation:

> The temple courtyard was stormed with the result that at least three thousand people died during the clash...When the new ruler (Archelaus) set off for Rome, further upheavals took place...Roman legions were twice unsuccessful in an attempt to quell the uprising. Gangs of partisans banded together all over Palestine. The royal palace in Jericho was burned to the ground. Two thousand deserters from Herod's army attacked royal troops...while in Judea the son of one, Ezechias, (a pretender to the throne) whom Herod had had executed, now came forward to claim his rights. Varus, Roman governor in Syria, personally intervened (with the result that) two thousand Jews were crucified. (P. 92, my brackets).

Archelaus, however, continued to blunder. Opposition against him seethed until finally a group of independent representatives took the initiative into their own hands and sailed for Rome in the year 6 AD to request Augustus to intercede in the Jewish interest. The latter responded by banishing Archelaus to Gaul and by seizing his territory, which then became a Roman protectorate. The governor of this province with his headquarters in Jerusalem was to be Pontius Pilate.

It was against this background that Jesus first opened his eyes on the world in Galilee. This violent, unstable socio-political climate was the setting to Jesus' enlightened teaching of tolerance, goodwill to all men, and his own infinite compassion. It was directly responsible for his murder, but ultimately and indirectly, too, for the subsequent shift of primary emphasis from Jesus' teaching to that of his death which, in its turn, was later to involve hundreds of millions of people in a serious error. As we have already pointed out, the important thing was that Jesus *lived*. He was an example to the end of what enlightened understanding and conduct is and, moreover, an example to which all of us can aspire if ever so humbly by comparison. That he died in the way he did and why is irrelevant to his teaching of freedom and enlightenment.

After Jesus' death, the seething turmoil of political unrest was to continue for the next seventy years, finally to boil over into open revolt and end once more in Roman military intervention and, on this occasion, the destruction of the temple in the year 70 AD. Whereas the Bible gives only a hint here and there of the rumbling volcano underfoot, modern historical research has been able to reveal not only the details and extent of this uncomfortable political atmosphere, but also the psychology and motivations of a people under great restraint.

New lamps for old?

So much for the principal historical events accompanying Jesus' life. In what now follows, considerable care has been taken to distinguish what is fact and what is not. In this connection, however, two types of fact must be taken into consideration: that of historical fact and the facts of human experience. The first is clear enough; the second needs clarification.

As an illustration we might take the Hebrew idea of the Jews as a 'chosen people', that is to say, a people chosen by God to be 'saved'. Whatever the Jews might think of themselves, it is nevertheless a fact that other races and religions have aspired to and succeeded in acquiring what this word might suggest, that is, a 'knowledge of God'. Other cultures have produced saintly men and women both before the ancient Jews and after the appearance of Jesus. This is a fact proven by their similar elevation of mind, their conduct and their teaching. These are people who have derived their spiritual greatness from other convictions than biblical ones. This is a fact of human experience. It therefore suggests that religious aspiration and spirituality is not something confined to ancient Israel. In our wider, and in many respects more liberal, scientifically informed world today, such a provincial idea runs counter to our intelligence. It can be compared with the medieval belief which imagined Jerusalem to be the centre of the world, and the world the centre of the universe. We know now that such an idea is fanciful and that a globe or a sphere has no centre on its surface, and that any and every point on it could be an imaginary 'centre'.

We know, too, that the so-called 'Holy Land' is no more holy than any other part of the world. Indeed, viewed from the perspectives of historical fact, this particular geographical area has been and still is far from anything we could describe as 'holy'. The Old Testament as a whole offers substantial proof of this fact. Looked at proportionally, analytically, and with a cool head, that is to say, with our own brains and unaided by the views and conclusions of others, the Old Testament readily evinces itself as a socio-historical record of the Children of Israel and their tense relationship with their God over many generations. The concept of a strict, father-like God is woven into their doings, and it is this element only which distinguishes it from any other recorded racial history. Despite the fact that this history has ostensibly to do with a higher being, we should not automatically assume that it is specifically religious. Compared with other sacred texts, it does not, for example, like them, concentrate wholly on the means of acquiring religious insight, but is, taken generally, an extended account of the development of one human society.

A candid appraisal of it reveals all the horror of man as subconscious animal (in the sense outlined above), all the violence of hatred associated with this state, of war, of savagery and brutality, constituting a long tale compounded of some greatness and much wickedness, lit here and there by poetic beauty and wisdom. In this it is a mirror unto ourselves, whoever we may be and wherever we may be in the world. Its high-minded religious fervour and its passionate God-centred ethics have not contributed greatly to making either Jews or the Christians following this tradition into more civilised human beings. This we might also regard as a fact of human experience. The Bible remains, essentially, the Book of the Jews, and as such is a monumental contribution to the complex mosaic of a human culture which includes religious aspiration. It therefore has its place in the world of socio-religious literature. However, the idea that the Bible is the 'Book of Books' (i.e. *the* definitive book on religion) and that the Jews are God's elect are ideas which cannot be substantiated as fact. They are assumptions adopted from Hebrew mythology.

The loud assumptions of the Old Testament which are echoed in the New will not therefore be accepted in the interpretation which follows. Instead, emphasis will be placed on the objectifiable facts of human religious experience. These may have nothing to do either with Judaism or with Christianity, but may also apply at times to these two in order to demonstrate that they are common to all religion.

In other words, the interpretation does not assume that Christianity is the sole representation of religious truth. The means to our psychological integration and thus our maturity can, in any case lie outside all reference to the Bible or, for that matter, outside any kind of formal, religious organisation or teaching.

Interpretation

Peter de Rosa, in section II of his book, *The Great Myth,*
observes, speaking of the four Gospels, that they read much
like a novel by Kafka in that the majority of chapters can be
read in any kind of random sequence and that this would make
no difference to their content, and that, moreover, the things
done and said in them allow of the most varied
interpretation.[15]

We must also be on our guard against unconscious
interpretation. That is to say, either we interpret a text
according to well established assumptions such as those
suggested above or it is interpreted according to personal,
subjective convictions. With these dangers in the forefront of
our minds, then, we can attempt an interpretation which, it is
hoped, will present a totally new approach to a long debated
subject.

The historical Jesus

The first question which unbiased scholars have asked
themselves is whether there ever was such a remarkable person
as the Jesus recorded in the Gospels. The question can by no
means be dismissed as ridiculous or blasphemous. It is justified
by a row of unusual historical facts, some of which have
already been referred to above, but in addition to these, and
astonishingly enough, no mention is made either of Jesus
himself nor his ignominious trial and death on the cross by
Justus of Tiberius, who was Jesus' contemporary and a
historian of things Jewish who lived only few miles away from
the scenes depicted in the New Testament. This man was the
author of an extensive history of the Jews at this period and
afterwards.

No mention either is made of Jesus (Rabbi Jeshua) by
Suetonius 150 years after Jesus' death, nor by Pliny the

Younger who was an avid recorder of the social and political details of the times. Publius Cornelius Tacitus who, in describing the term 'Christian' merely mentions that it is derived from the word 'Christ' (a man), who was condemned to death by Pilate during the reign of Tiberius.' But this is at second hand and at a time when early Christianity was already an established organisation.

There is, however, reference in the Babylonian Talmud in that section referring to Jesus and his disciples. It refers to his having been given a chance to save his life and runs:

> On the eve of the Passover they hanged Jesus. Forty days before this event, a herald went forth and proclaimed [his guilt] saying: 'Jesus is to be stoned because he has performed magic, led Israel into temptation and caused its people to fall away from their religion. Those that know anything in his favour should come forward and bear testimony in his favour.' But nothing could be found in his favour and they hanged him on the eve of the Passover.[16]

By the word 'hanged', here it is presumed that 'hanged from the cross' is meant, although this, too, is strange, since the Jews were not permitted to crucify. No mention is made of Roman intervention in the extract which could have justified an execution of this kind. Nothing, moreover, is mentioned in the Gospels at all of Jesus being submitted to a plebiscite of the kind mentioned in the extract. Sometimes in Hebrew texts, the word 'hanging' refers to the barbarous practice of hanging up the corpse of one who had been killed by stoning. It is not therefore absolutely clear what or who is meant in the context. 'Jesus', a corruption of 'Joshua', was a common name in those days, and those who went about speaking of doomsday and the coming of the Lord were many.

A line later, the Talmud (**XX**) speaks of Jesus as a 'tempter', and in the next paragraph there is reference to disciples who, apart from one, Matai (Matthew), are not otherwise mentioned anywhere in the Gospels. This again is a remarkable situation. We naturally ask ourselves whether the text is referring to the Jesus of the Gospels or to another? We know with a pretty fair degree of accuracy that a certain Jesus was crucified during Pontius Pilate's administration. We know, too, that such an execution was carried out by Romans with, admittedly, the support of the Jewish mob. Although the Talmud's report is nearer in time to the actual event of Jesus' death, there is doubt as to whether it is speaking of the same person, since it is wholly different in character and reference from that of the Synoptics. Which is correct? Which can be dismissed and which accepted? In both there is also the yawning question as to what had happened to Rabbi Jeshua's friends and devotees. Where were the people who had been healed and were grateful for sight and freedom of limb? If there were ever forty days in which to submit a petition in favour of his release or at least a repeal of the death penalty, what had happened to them? Where were these men and women in the New Testament record of his trial? Was there no one of a larger group of disciples admitted to the trial, to plead for mercy or mitigating circumstances?

There are other oddities in the Talmudic reference above which need not concern us here, but which nevertheless cry out for clarification. The text constitutes one of those 'thickets of ignorance' mentioned earlier, in which one can quickly lose orientation. As far as we are aware at the moment, there is no other commentary on the life and work of Jesus which is independent of the Gospels. Many years after the death of Jesus, Pliny and Suetonius referred to above merely remark on the Christian movement as an already established body and in terms that are on the whole condemnative. A movement indicates a founder, although it is fairly sure that Christ himself had no intention of setting up an international organisation. This was the later work of Paul, about whom much more is known than about his Master.

Given that Jesus was born at some time during the reign of Herod Antipas somewhere in the province of Galilee, although exactly where is also uncertain in recent scholarship, the enquirer is then immediately faced with the question, What happened after this? Where there is no reliable information, there can only be conjecture. On these quicksands of supposition and in order to fill the gap in our knowledge.[17] While some of these arguments are certainly interesting as plausible possibilities even if the evidence on which they are based is slender, the long hiatus of about thirty years (if we are to believe the evangelist's report) is too great not to have permitted some substantial evidence of his existence before taking up teaching. It is as though Jesus the man has no personal history, no social matrix from which his talents as a healer and teacher of men could have developed. Suddenly, he is there, receives baptism from John and begins his ministry. Either the Synoptics did not know anything themselves of a possible background, or they chose to ignore it. Some sort of background there must have been if Jesus ever existed as a human entity. The fact of background cannot therefore be overlooked unless, of course, it was deliberately ignored by the Synoptics to heighten the impression of Jesus' divinity. It could also well be that the writers of the New Testament considered background either as irrelevant or too banal for inclusion in their text. The only 'background,' if one can call it that, is the genealogy given in the first pages of the Gospel according to Matthew which is probably untrue,[18] and for the modern researcher of no use at all. Indeed, its very inclusion might suggest the dilemma of a lack of background! This innuendo is not meant to discredit the committee which once sat to deliberate how the Gospels should be written or to suggest either that it was guilty of manipulation. It is only to indicate that we should not impose our modern norms and literary evaluations on a group of people who were not writing the kind of meticulously detailed history we are familiar with today. The historical facts from non-Christian sources are that there was no one at the time who could confirm the evangelists' reports. On the other hand, the suggestion that Jesus' former life was omitted either because it was considered

147

irrelevant or to enhance his divinity fit in well both with the messianic and also the with elements which are an integral part of the Gospels. For us today, the historical gap in Jesus' life is strange and unaccountable. The question uppermost in our modern minds is: where did Jesus come from prior to his appearance as a candidate for baptism?

We can be fairly sure about two things. The first is that a man called Jesus (Jeshe) went about preaching in Galilee, and that what he said and did was not only a blessing to the multitudes, but also a rebuke to the religious establishment of the day, an attitude which cost him his life.[19] The other fact is that the four officially accepted reports of these events, the Gospels, also very strongly suggest an earlier text. If this is not the case, then there was a general consensus of agreement, subsequent cooperation and coordination between the writers in collating these renderings of that original under the titles, Matthew, Mark, Luke and John.

---

[1] See Lapide, P., *Has the Bible Been Properly Translated?(Ist die Bibel richtig übersetzt)* Gütersloher Verlagshaus, 1992, in which he uses this phrase and where at p. 79ff in particular he speaks of the essential 'Hebrewness' of the Gospels and in which '…every translation of the [Hebrew text] leads to a partial rape of its Semitic mental environment, tears the form from the content and severs the whole which can only be fully understood in its totality.' (My translation and brackets. See also pp. 80 and 81ff).

[2] Dietl-Zeiner, *Das Kastrierte Evangelium, Die Falsch Übersetzte Bibel und die Wiederentdeckung der Lust* (The Castrated Gospel, The Wrongly Translated Bible and the Re-discovery of Lust), Ariston Verlag, 1996

[3] Ibid. P. 130.

[4] Lapide, Ibid. p. 40ff in which the author clearly points out the impossibility of translating from the original Hebrew into other languages, namely and in the first place: Greek and from thence to Latin, and from there to virtually every language in the world.

[5] De Rosa, Peter, *The Great Myth,* London, 1990.

[6] Obermeier, Siegfried, *Starb Jesus in Kaschmir?* (Did Jesus die in Kashmir?) Volker Hennig Verlag, Holzminden, 1994.

[7] The need to burn dissenters, 'heretics' and Jews is a very clear piece of evidence of depraved misinterpretation of the Gospels. It also demonstrates the aberration of mind from which men suffer when they follow their unconscious drives. At no other time than these is this two-legged creature more ape than man. The persecutions taking place all over Europe in the 15th, 16th, 17th and 18th and in Spain even in the early part of the 19th century manifest religious insanity and are facts which are hard to dismiss by the Roman church, from which this nonsense and horror originally stems.

[8] Zeno of Elea (c. 490-430 BC) and his example of a heap of rice averred that a whole is divisible at *ad infinitum* and that there is a contradiction involved in the assumption that 'an infinite number of parts can be added up to a final total,' see 3rd ed., 1963, p. 238.

[9] The rejection of St. Paul's claims to leadership of the Christian movement as well as his interpretation of Jesus' message by the small group of original followers of Jesus in Jerusalem subsequent to Jesus' death is clearly outlined in Baigent, Michael and Leigh, Richard, *The Dead Sea Scrolls Deception,* Jonathan Cape, London, 1991, especially in chapters III, sections, 'The Accounts of the Apostles' and 'Paul – Roman Agent or Informant?' The book as a whole offers material which has met with varying critical assessment, but which at the same time poses the need to take a second look at the way Christianity has been translated by the church.

[10] Among these are that Christ did not die on the cross but was taken down, resuscitated and later fled the country after recovering from his injuries to turn up in Asia Minor (Obermeier). The evidence for this possibility is slim. There were examples of men crucified in error (as Roman citizens, for example, or through a miscarriage of justice) and in some cases these were then actually taken from the cross, although the injuries sustained after this treatment were usually so serious that it is unlikely that the sufferer would survive for more than a few hours.

[11] There have been suggestions that Jesus' childhood was spent in a Buddhist country, but there is no substantial proof for this, apart from the remarkable correspondences between the New Testament and the Buddhist canon, demonstrated by Gruber and Kersten in their work, *Der Ur-Jesus – Die buddhistischen Quellen des Christentums,* Langen/Müller Verlag, München, 1994 (also exists in English translation). Apart from these two sources which offer what they can

as palpable evidence for their theses, the others can be dismissed as fiction.

[12] If this simple statistical representation is accepted, it follows that the rest is Paul's interpretation of the Gospels and the message of Jesus. The ultimate material on which Christianity stands is in fact, then, this 44%.

[13] We do not have to look very far for confirmation of this even in our own century. Since the end of World War II, 'man-as-beast' (subconscious man) has been at work in Columbia, Cuba, Uruguay, Bolivia, Brazil (massacre of the indigenous population, Nova Fazenda, 1957), Peru (massacre and extermination of the Coćama Indians, 1964), Guatamala and the introduction of murdering Tupamaros, Chile under Pinochet and others, 1970, Ireland, north and south, from 1968 to the present day, the senseless murder of one another in a social and religious war; South Africa, Cambodia, Korea and Vietnam, the appalling scenes of horror issuing from almost every area of Africa, but notably from the Congo, Kenia, Nigeria, Chad, Burundi, Algeria, Biafra, Somalia and Eritrea, to mention just a few since this time; China, its oppression, its Red Guards and its so-called 'Cultural Revolution'; Russia, between (1917-1953), the Middle East, a chapter for itself, involving two religious groups, equally convinced of their ideals, and finally, Europe's Croatia, Kosovo and Bosnia to mention the major areas of conflict which do not only include open war, but the torture and execution of the civilian population in every instance. If this is not sufficient proof of the inefficacy of our religious beliefs (mere belief without knowledge and self-cultivation), then what is?

[14] Moral decay has very little to do with a lack of sexual inhibition as it is sometimes made out to be. True decay stems from a lack of regard for the 'other', man or animal. What this means can be seen from that which passes for entertainment on our TV screens: the savage with a revolver or a knife or an automatic machine gun; the big-business entrepreneur who will exploit without discrimination to make money and the fact that this form of immorality is widely accepted; the erosion of values to be seen now to an ever increasing degree in the capitulation of local and national governmental bodies to the interests of 'business', a phenomenon which can be seen in Europe especially, in almost every township and city where the surrounding countryside is raped and deformed by commercial building and activity. The

150

same immorality in this sense of the word can be extended to the deforestation of large parts of the South American jungle and the attendant direct and indirect murder of the Indios there. Moral decay is writ large in our medical laboratories, in the heinous activities of pharmaceutical firms, in the meat industry and generally in the feeding and maintenance of animals meant for human consumption. Here, especially moral government, reason and humanity is eclipsed by a primary interest in profit.

[15] The zealots (Simon Zelotes) and the 'Sons of Thunder' **Lk. 6, 15** were probably interested in political issues. With some imagination we could also suppose that Judas Iscariot was more interested in a political messiah than his friend's peaceable teaching and for this reason betrayed him, but this is mere conjecture.

[16] See Peter de Rosa above.

[17] See The Babylonian Talmud (Babylonische Talmud ed. Reinhold Mayer, W. Goldmann Verlag, München). Section 'From Israel's History', subsection 'Of Heretics and their Bible', p. 207-8 where we read: 'A herald went forth for 40 days: This [man] goes forth to be stoned, because he had performed sorcery, tempted Israel and brought about division [among the people]. Anyone who can say anything in his favour should come forward and make a plea for [his life]. But they found nothing and hanged him on the eve of the Passover (my brackets). The notes to this and the rest of the text is of the highest interest to those wishing to know more about the circumstances of Jesus' death.

[18] See note 6 above.

[19] Two notable scholars have summed up this unlikelihood: Weddig Fricke, (see Prologue above, note 1) who says at p. 59f in the same book, 'In this, the Gospel of Matthew is no different than the (notations) of some modern fundamentalist Jews who know, for example, precisely in what verse of the Bible the Balfour Declaration was predicted, (as well as) the founding of the State of Israel and Israel's Six-Day War (1967)' (my translation brackets). This observation follows another quoted from the biblical scholar,Uta Ranke-Heinemann who observes: 'He (i.e. Mathew) exerts himself to the utmost to make sure that these prophecies are fufilled, even if this means breaking his back from time to time!' (From *Nein und Amen, Anleitung zum Glaubenszweifel* (No and Amen: Instruction to Doubt the Faith) Hamburg, 1992, p. 37 (my translation and bracket).

CHAPTER VI

On opening the gospels for the first time. Mission and the philosophy of inevitability

What do the Gospels say and how do they say it? These should be the questions of an independent observer. The first thing which is impossible to ignore as we read them is the sense of mission. The messianic element characterises all the Gospels and is sustained from beginning to end. It is to be met with practically on every page, accounts for about forty per cent of the content and roughly ninety per cent of the tone. Without these elements, the New Testament would be greatly impoverished. At work in creating the tone there are two voices of authority, that of the Old Testament, heard through the words of Jesus who often quotes from this source, and his own very strong, personalized voice which speaks with unwavering authority:

> Though I bear record of myself, yet my record is true; for I know whence I came, and whither I go, but Ye cannot tell whence I come, and whither I go. **(Jn. 8,14)**

> I am the light of the world: he that followeth me shall not walk in darkness, but shall have the light of life. **(Jn.8. 12)**

The Old Testament is represented, for example, in the first four chapters of the gospel according to Mathew where one finds allusion to the prophecies of Isaiah, hear the caveats and long-term forecasts of Micah, Hosea, Jeremiah, Daniel,

Leviticus, Samuel, and discover references to the Book of Numbers, Ezekiel and Deuteronomy among others. The Gospel according to Mark, too, begins with,

> As it is written in the Prophets: 'Behold, I send my messenger before your face, who will prepare your way before you.' The voice of one crying in the wilderness: Prepare the way of the Lord; make his paths straight. (**Mk. 1. 1–3**)

There is withal an atmosphere of time immanent, that the time has come for man to turn to God.

> The time is fulfilled, and the kingdom of God is at hand. Repent, and believe in the gospel. (**Mk. 1, 15**)

The prefatory material of the Gospel according to Luke is similar in content to that of Matthew in that he, too, quoting Isaiah, draws the reader's attention to the fact that John the Baptist will… 'be called the prophet of the Highest; for you will go before the face of the Lord to prepare his ways. To give salvation to his people by the remission of their sins…' (**Lk. 176**) and in addition there are many other references to the Old Testament here.

Jesus' first words in Luke occurring in the second chapter are in answer to those who seek him when he declares: 'Why did you seek me? Did you not know that I must be about my father's business? (**Lk. 2,49**) Other examples of the fulfilment of prophecy occur at **Mt. 17,22–23,** and at **17, 9; Lk. 9,22; Jn.3,14; 8,28,10,35** to mention just a few, and the course of Jesus' passage through life shall be in line with prophecy (**Mt. 5,17–19**).

From the start there is an inevitability about the course of events. Jesus has been appointed by God as the bringer of good tidings to man, and his way has been decided upon. The Dove of the Lord has descended upon his head and he himself has declared that he must be 'lifted up' (**Jn. 2, 14**) on the cross when his mission on earth has been fulfilled. All references to the past and to the immediate future are woven into a web of fate from which there is no extraction, a fact which is confirmed at intervals as the Gospels proceed.

In the Gospel of St. John, which differs in some ways from the other Gospels, there is more emphasis in the beginning, for example, on John the Baptist recognising Jesus as the Messiah: 'Again, the next day, John stood with two of his disciples. And looking at Jesus as He walked, he said, "Behold, the Lamb of God!"' **(Jn.1,35–6)**

Even in using the word 'Lamb', there is that insinuation of a sacrificial lamb implied in Jesus' destiny. That there was expectancy among the people of a messiah is clearly given by one of the disciples-to-be who says,

> One of the two who heard John speak, and followed Him, was Andrew, Simon Peter's brother. He first found his own brother Simon and said to him, 'We have found the Messiah' (which is translated, the Christ).

Added to this all-pervasive element of destiny where the Hand of God guides the expectancy of generations through the centuries and which is eventually to seal Jesus' fate on the cross is Jesus' own very strong leaning towards the predictive. As early as the second chapter of the Gospel, we hear him speaking to Nathaniel in oracular tones about the young man's later perceptions, a man whom, apparently, he has just met.

> Most assuredly, I say to you, hereafter you shall see heaven open, and the angels of God ascending and descending upon the Son of Man. **(Jn.1,51)**

Later, in Jn, 2,14, there is explicit reference to his fate when he says, 'And as Moses lifted up the serpent in the wilderness, even so must the Son of Man be lifted up...' referring quite clearly here to the process of positioning the cross into its socket from the horizontal to the vertical.[1] The comparison is a strange and unpalatable one. We might be forgiven for feeling that Jesus is either looking forward to the prospect of his execution or that he wishes others to commiserate with him. A sense of mission is in the air. In another place, while addressing those congregated in the temple, he proclaims,

> You both know me, and you know where I am from; and I have not come of myself, but He who sent me is true, who you do not know. But I know Him and He sent me. **(Jn. 7,28)**

It would be difficult to imagine a bible indeed without this ubiquitous element of predetermination recognisable both in the Old and New Testament. The whole of Christ's ministry is underlined by the inevitability of his mission to men, his ultimate death on the cross, and his inevitable collision with authority. He refers to these things repeatedly. His tragic path has been set by those who foretold his fate many hundreds of years before his birth, and he must needs tread that path. This, apparently, is the way the God of Love had chosen for him.

Nevertheless, those who reserve the right to think in all this may well find the plan both repulsive and incongruous. Although the concept of one man dying for the rest of the world until the end of time has been later taken up by hundreds of millions of people and adopted by them as an essential part of their religion, it is, as we have seen, something completely irrelevant to religious development and religious maturity. This is proved by other religions which are just as advanced as the Christian and where this element is absent. What actually happened in this jungle of hallowed scriptural reference, this rigid adherence to predestination and the 'fulfilment of the law' which unerringly led to Jesus' ignominious death was that he was prevented from that moment on from teaching us anything more about the ways of God. If at all as a messiah – in the religious sense, not the political – he was in the world to reveal God to men, the Emmanuel, 'God with us', and that as fully as possible. Without the ballast of the Jewish historical imperative, he may well have gone on to do more good and brought more light into the world, but this was not to be so. His ministry was brutally and needlessly interrupted by an ingrained obsession with prediction of whose validity he himself was thoroughly convinced. At least this is true up to the point where death was at hand in the garden of Gethsemane. Here, understandably, he asks God to take the cup of death from his lips and perhaps it is at this moment that he begins to doubt the authenticity of the legend which had led up to this event.

Later, one of the gospellers reports **(Mk.15,34)** that when Jesus was on the cross he cried out in a loud voice asking why God had forsaken him. This is perhaps the saddest moment of all in the whole New Testament narration. Right to the bitter end, the soothsayers are there in the background to confirm their vision:

> With Him they also crucified two robbers, one on His right, and the other on His left. So the scripture was fulfilled which says, 'And he was numbered with the transgressors.' **(Mk. 15, 27–8)**

The heartlessness of inevitability

The heartlessness of this inevitability and the cold-blooded commentary at this point in the Gospels easily remind us of those pitiless clerics who took notes during inquisitorial procedure while another human being was tortured. Those among us whose lives have enabled them to gain emotional detachment from the scene of the crucifixion and the Gospel in general will ask:

'What has this shameless brutality to do with the God Jesus represented to men by his acts of kindness and understanding?' Are we not at liberty to view the crucifixion as a hideous extension of the primitive ritual of god-appeasement current among the Jews, from Abraham's time to that of Jesus? Even while Jesus suffered on Golgotha, the irrepressible stench of roasted animal sacrifice outside the temple still hung everywhere over the town. In this aspect of their religious observance, the Jews of the time were not very far removed from the barbarity of primitive peoples, ancient and modern, who slay animals and birds as part of a religious act of god-propitiation.

There are other abhorrent hints and inferences which give us a good idea of the hidebound society in which Jesus lived. In their modest way they support the larger issue of prophecy. One of these occurs in **Jn. 19, 31–33.**

> Therefore because it was preparation Day, that the bodies should not remain on the cross on the Sabbath (for the Sabbath was a high day), the Jews asked Pilate that their legs might be broken, and that they might be taken away. Then the soldiers came and broke the legs of the first and of the others who were crucified with Him. But when they came to Jesus and saw that He was already dead, they did not break His legs. But one of the soldiers pierced His side with a spear, and immediately blood and water came out... For these things were done that the Scripture should be fulfilled 'Not one of His bones shall be broken.[2]'

We can see from this that Jewish custom was influential enough to impose its will on Roman authority. The spectacle of men (and occasionally women) dying outside the town was felt to be an offence to public propriety and religious sensibility on a holy day, and so the bodies were removed.

As is often the case with us human beings, we often fail to see the glaring incongruities of our actions. Here was a community at pains to honour a festival of thanksgiving (the Passover) to the god who had, by their own account, led them out of Egypt almost 1300 years earlier and who, after loving their god with all their being, were obliged by their religion to love their neighbour as themselves and who, a few hours before, had screamed like savages in chorus for the agonising death of another human being.

Exactly the same murderous incongruity can be seen at work in the persecution of the Jews (and others) in the history of Christianity. Within a tradition of professed love, tolerance and understanding, there is the long, evil chapter of the systematic burning and torture of heretics as well as non-believers in an extended season of ecclesiastical insanity. And not only they. We can see the same subconscious energy at work in all kinds of fanaticism, whatever its persuasion. Once fanaticism has entered the heart and brain there is madness, and as madmen we have, for so long as the fit takes us, lost the ability to judge matters consciously and independently of our emotions. We then take our place among the wild dogs, tigers and sharks and other merciless predators in the animal world. In these moments we have forfeited our birthright as true human beings and become something less than human and, on occasion, less than beast.[3]

The elements of past and future

In the New Testament, the operation of what is here referred to as a 'sense of mission' assumes two modes of expression, that of looking backward to the prophecies of old, and that of looking forward to that which is to come. Sometimes even, the recollection of the past and the vision of the future are combined in one utterance as here in **Matthew (23, 34ff)** where Jesus speaks of the city of Jerusalem:

> Therefore indeed, I send you prophets, wise men, and scribes; some of them you will kill and crucify, and some of them you will scourge in your synagogues and persecute from city to city, that on you may come all the righteous blood on earth, from the blood of the righteous Abel to the blood of Zechariah, son of Berechiach, who you murdered between the temple and the altar... See! Your house is left to you desolate; for I say to you, you shall see me no more till you say 'Blessed is He who comes in the name of the Lord.'

In another place he says, speaking of the admonitions of the past with reference to those before him:

> Well did Isaiah prophesy of you hypocrites, as it is written: This people honours me with their lips, but their heart is far

from me. And in vain they worship me. Teaching as doctrines the doctrines of men. **(Mk. 7,6)**

In this connection and just prior to the corresponding verses which bewail Jerusalem, the apostle Luke reports Jesus as saying in reply to those who warn him of Herod's spies out to kill him:

> Go, tell that fox, 'Behold, I cast out demons and perform cures today and tomorrow, and the third day I shall be perfected.' Nevertheless I must journey today, tomorrow and the day following; for it cannot be that a prophet should perish outside Jerusalem. **(Mk. 9,12)**

Thoughtful people in our day find this very strange fare. It smacks of that predeterminism which would rob us of our ability to think, plan and create, and so enjoy a freedom of mind which we know is our right. It is a system which renders us mere pawns in an inflexible pattern of fate whose structure and unfolding has long been determined by some kind of divinity. The flaw in this idea is that this god cannot then presume to judge us for that which we are not responsible. Our own lives are not run by prophecy of any kind today, and we are glad of it, but for the Jews of the time and before Christ's coming, prophecy was among those elements which held the Jewish community very tightly together.

Prophecies right and wrong

From this remark alone, quoted from the evangelist Mark above, we can see how thoroughly imbued Jesus was with the idea of his role as Messiah, even to the last detail. It is at points like these that the modern reader of the Bible begins to ask himself with all due respect whether all this anticipation of failure and martyrdom is not a little exaggerated, if not artificial.

> And how is it written concerning the Son of Man that, He must suffer many things and be treated with contempt. **(Mk.9,12)**

Now and again, this bleak outlook is warmed for those around him with the promise of the kingdom of heaven, and a little before the remark above, Jesus says, addressing the few who had gathered to hear him, which included some of his disciples:

> Assuredly, I say unto you that there are some standing here who will not taste death till they see the kingdom of God present with power. **(Mk.9,1)**

What he means precisely by 'present with power' is not clear, but if he meant the glory of God descending in power and presence to redeem his people in the time he and they were alive, or shortly after this, then he was most assuredly wrong. Nothing of the kind came to pass either in those days or later.

Sometimes prophecy gets in the way of logic as at **Luke, 8,10** where Jesus informs his disciples that they are privileged in being the select few who can hear the 'mysteries of the kingdom of God' at first hand, whereas 'the rest' must hear them through the parable and still not be able to understand.

> To you it has been given to know the mysteries of the kingdom of God, but to the rest it is given in parables, that...

And at this point we go into the past again:

> Seeing they may not see, And hearing they may not understand.

This sentiment is derived from **Isaiah, 6,9.** If they (the people) are not to understand, where is the point in talking to them?

On the other hand, there are moments where Jesus sees the future clearly, as when he prophesies the destruction of the temple 70 years after his death **(Lk.21,5–6)**:

> Then as some spoke of the temple, how it was adorned with beautiful stones and donations, He said, 'These things which

you see – the days will come in which not one stone shall be left upon another that shall not be thrown down[4].

It is a historical fact that the temple was utterly destroyed by Titus in the course of Roman suppression of Jewish uprisings. On other occasions, we can be left to make up our own minds as to whether the prophecies Jesus made are correct or not. For example, to quote from the same gospel and the same chapter, twenty-eight verses **(8–36)** are occupied in expounding a dismal future to his hearers. The view of the world to come is full of fearful cataclysms.

And there will be great earthquakes in various places and famines and pestilences and there will be fearful sights and great signs from heaven. **(Lk.21,11)**

You will be betrayed even by parents and brothers, relatives and friends; and they will put some of you to death. **(Lk. 21,16)**

And there will be signs in the sun, in the moon, and in the stars; and on earth distress of nations, with perplexity, the sea and the waves roaring. **(Lk. 21,25)**

All this, Jesus tells his hearers, will come to pass when 'you see Jerusalem surrounded by armies, then know that its desolation is near.' **(Lk. 21,20)**

In verse 32 of the same chapter we are told that this generation will not pass until all these things have taken place and that the kingdom of God at this time is near as these signs shall bear witness.

For these are the days of vengeance, that all things which are written may be fulfilled. **(Lk.21,22)**

In all this, the simple truth is that Jesus was wrong. And if we are honest with ourselves, we will note that these false prognostications, their tone, their insinuations (such as that at 'vengeance' above) and their dramatic delivery do not add to his distinction, but rather detract from it. They reveal on this occasion a slavish dependence on a tradition of 'that which must be fulfilled', a naivety which places Jerusalem and, therefore, Jewry at the centre of world events, an ignorance of the nature of the sun and the stars, and, withal, a bombastic delivery which is apparently out to impress. He was not only imbued with the idea of his own fate, but extended this to include the apocalypse. 'And this gospel of the kingdom will be preached in all the world as a witness to all the nations, and then the end will come.' **(Mt. 24,14).**

Two thousand years have passed since Jesus' prophecies were made and, although the horrors of war and famine as well as the natural phenomenon of earthquakes continue for other reasons than those which fulfil a prophecy, none of the events forecast, except for the fall of the temple, has actually taken place. To wait for them to come to pass would be to place ourselves absurdly in the same position of mental subservience and to a programme of inevitability as the Jews of his time.

What is not generally appreciated and which at the same time is a product of the biblical research alluded to earlier is the historical fact that the Messianic Jesus was not a revolutionary figure come once and for all to redeem a sinful world as the Church would have us believe, but that he was very much a product of his time. The political background to this has already been touched upon, but what is not fully realised is that Jesus firmly belonged to a much larger tradition of messiahs and redeemers, 'sons of God' who, prior to him, had had their day in antiquity. Among these were the Gnostics who believed in a first-born son of God, a saviour of souls for a heaven of light. The Egyptians, the Babylonians, the Persians who, later in the worship of Mithras and Dionysus, were all peoples who at some time in their history had also awaited the end of the world and the coming of a new period of light and peace. This situation would be brought about by a 'saviour', that is, one man born of a deity. In this connection, Hans Schwabe, in his book *What is truth? The Historical Jesus*[5], reminds us that in Indian mythology one comes across the legend of a saviour's (Krishna) birth by the virgin Yasoda who is the incarnation of the god Vishnu, and at this occasion, moreover, shepherds in the neighbourhood sang the praises at the birth. Later, the tyrant Radsha decreed that all those born in that night should be slain.

In addition, Professor Lapide writes, in his book, *Child Refugee*, that:

It is unlikely to be a matter of blind coincidence that Mithras, for example, the 'saint' and sun-god of the Romans from which the first day of the Christian week is still named, was born of a virgin in a manger on precisely 25th December and was paid homage to by shepherds who promised freedom on earth, that he was later crucified, rose again at Easter and finally was lifted up into heaven – this to mention the most striking likenesses to the Greek evangelists.[6]

Much later than these, the Essenes of Jesus' time constituted another group of men who piously awaited the end of time in the hope of a better life to come. The idea, therefore, of a redeeming Christ, a saviour who would bring men to a better world was not at all a new idea at the time of Jesus, nor even a Jewish one.

In the first place, we have grown out of an age when we look for signs in the heavens which might convey a message relevant to imminent natural catastrophe (unless scientifically based) or with a view to our political and social future.

The average twelve-year-old in western Europe, the USA and elsewhere in the world has more knowledge of the sun, the moon and the solar system, not to mention the constitution of the earth and its relation to the universe than adults in Jesus' day who in no way could have imagined these things, much less the future of Man.

Today, looking back over a century to two world wars, to Auschwitz, Treblinka, Hiroshima, Nagasaki, Dresden and seventy years of Stalinism, we know that there is no divine intervention in our political affairs. The last thing we would want today, for example, is a god that would seek his 'vengeance' among us for things committed and omitted so that ancient prophecies might be fulfilled. The concept of a vengeful god is an obnoxious one. No one in his right mind yearns for the return of a god like this, for even in our minuteness we mortals may judge our gods in these times as dog may judge its master.

The old Hebrew god of revenge and chastisement, power and partisanship died with the last clouds of smoke over Auschwitz-Birkenau. All the hapless human beings from all over Europe who lost their lives there and elsewhere in such places, whether Jew or Gentile, are testimony to this fact, and their awful silence broods upon our religious convictions. At no time in the history of man was God's intervention in these places more needful than at this time barely sixty years ago, but there was no God at hand and no aid, but only further horror. There is no doubt either that the horror of mass persecution would have continued had Hitler gained the upper hand in his war. Finally, we are forced to admit that it was only the sheer force of arms which brought the whole infamous business to an end. Since 1945 and in view of what had happened over the previous twelve years of terror, thinking humanity has been compelled to revise its ideas of the god of the Bible. With the end of this war, a page in the history of Man had been turned for ever.

The tone of the New Testament and the Messianic imperative

Just as it is impossible to overhear the Messianic element in the New Testament, so it is also impossible to overhear the tone of its message. Just how tone and the message are woven together can be seen, for example, in Jesus' encounter with the Samaritan woman at the well. It is also one of the very few places in the Bible where there is a trace of humour.

In reply to the woman's remark that she has no husband, Jesus says wryly:

> 'You have well said "I have no husband" for you have had five husbands and the one whom you now have is not your husband; in that you spoke truly.' In the course of their conversation, she goes on to say that 'Jerusalem is the place where one ought to worship' and is told: 'Woman, believe me, the hour is coming when you will neither on this mountain nor in Jerusalem, worship the Father. You worship what you do not know; we know what we worship, for salvation is of the Jews. But the hour is coming and now is, when the true worshippers will worship the Father in spirit and truth; for the Father is seeking such to worship Him…' **(Jn. 4, 17–23)**

In this passage we find all the ingredients of tone to be found in the New Testament as a whole. First of all, there is the element of forecast and, in this case, the authoritative and perhaps slightly arrogant attitude Rabbi Jeshua takes in speaking to a woman common to many Semitic males, even today. This can be felt particularly in verse 21 of the quotation. It is also contained in the next verse in language which suggests a 'collective arrogance' when Jeshua remarks, 'for salvation is of the Jews.' Added to this, there is an undertone of intimidation which could be expressed as: '…the hour is upon you and therefore look to yourselves before it is too late.'

This is the Messianic imperative which vibrates throughout all the four Gospels, sometimes as a gentle inference, as above, but sometimes as a direct threat, as on another occasion when Jesus addresses the Pharisees:

> You are from beneath; I am from above. You are of this world; I am not of this world. Therefore I said to you that you will die in your sins; for if you do not believe that I am He, you will die in your sins. **(Jn. 8,23–24)**

And again:

> Woe to you, Chorazin! Woe to you, Bethsaida…But I say unto you it will be more tolerable for Tyre and Sidon in the day of judgement than for you.

> And you Capernaum, who are exalted to heaven, will be brought down to Hades...But I say unto you that it shall be more tolerable for the land of Sodom in the day of judgement than for you. **(Mt. 11,22–24)**

> Likewise it was also in the days of Lot: they ate, they drank, they married wives, they bought, they sold, they planted, they built; but on the day Lot went out of Sodom it rained fire and brimstone from heaven and destroyed them all. **(Lk. 17, 28–29)**

It is true to say that the tone throughout the Gospels is authoritative and declamatory as in many other parts of the Bible; it is the imposition of the will of God on Man and could be summarised as: 'Departure from the way of God will result in death and judgement, for this is sin which brings eternal damnation. On the other hand, to return to God is to find the kingdom of heaven and partake of everlasting joy. To accomplish this return is to believe in Jesus as God's representative. This is the only way to salvation. Time is short: believe and be saved.'

It is the language of warning. Whenever Jesus turns from his work of healing or in speaking to the people in parables, he resorts to this kind of authoritative address. If, in order to clarify a matter, he asks a question at all in order to clear the mind of his counterpart, the clinch is always in the third line.

Illustrative of this is when Jesus is asked whether it is lawful for Jews to pay Roman taxes or not in order to lead him into committing himself on a political issue. In reply, Jesus asks:

> Whose image and inscription is this? They said to Him, 'Caesar's.' And he said to them, 'Render unto Caesar the things that are Caesar's, and to God the things that are God's. **Mt. 22, 17–21)**.

In another exchange with the religious representatives of the day, this time in the temple, Jesus is asked by them on what authority he teaches what he does as he does. As usual, Rabbi Jeshua finds himself on a confrontation course, the outcome of which will certainly not lead to better relations. Jesus replies with a counter question:

> 'I will ask you one thing and answer me: "The baptism of John – was it from heaven or from men?"'
>
> And they reasoned among themselves, saying. 'If we say, "From heaven," He will say, "Why then did you not believe him?" But if we say "From men," all the people will stone us, for they are persuaded that John was a prophet.'

So they answered that they did not know where it was from and therefore would not say. Jesus then retorts: 'Neither will I tell you by what authority I do these things.' **(Lk.20,1–8)**

If we are at all able after so many centuries of partisanship to take an impartial stance in this, we will have to say that a remark of this kind is a fine way to make enemies. Even though the scribes, we are told, were angling to catch Jesus in his words and so publicly condemn him, his own attitude is highly provocative on this occasion. Even the dullest among us are not inclined to publicly expose our superiors. No one, not even today, may do that with impunity. The objection to this, the committed Christian will insist, is that Jesus was their superior and not the other way round. Be that as it may, he had not risen to a position of superiority by general acknowledgement, but by self-appointment. He had the people behind him, a fact hinted at in the text, and there is little doubt that his teaching was informed by inspired authority, something which the crowd and some Pharisees could certainly comprehend, but for the religious establishment generally he was an upstart with a sharp tongue, ready at any moment to strike at the very heart of their social and religious justification.

Whether some of them were hypocrites or not, direct, public condemnation and exposure is always a shameful thing for those who suffer from it, a shame that leads to the desire to eradicate its cause

It is not suggested that Jesus should have accepted hypocrisy, but there would have been better ways of dealing with it on occasion. A smile and an innocuous question pointing in the direction of the truth, for example, is a very effective technique used by Indian sages when, someone is deliberately provocative. This elevates the questioner instead of shaming him, and at the same time guides him towards the truth. Is this not a question of 'turning the other cheek'?

The fact that Jesus in his directness and tactlessness as here and sometimes downright rudeness in many other places (**Lk. 11, 37–54 & 12, 1–2**) strongly suggests that he had deliberately chosen the way of martyrdom. He wanted to play the part of the 'sacrificial lamb' which, in our relatively enlightened times, appears to be both mentally unhealthy and also futile for the reasons already suggested. The Pauline idea which has come to dominate the Christian Church, that of the concept of one man's blood washing away humanity's sins is as difficult for the rational man to accept as that which follows. On this occasion it is a warning from the Rabbi which is strongly reminiscent of the tone of the Old Testament:

> Therefore as the tares are gathered and burned in the fire, so it will be at the end of this age: The Son of Man will send his angels, and they will gather out of his kingdom all things that offend, and those who practise lawlessness, and will cast them into the furnace of fire. There will be wailing and gnashing of teeth. Then the righteous will shine forth as the sun in the kingdom of their Father. He who has ears to hear, let him hear! (**Mt. 13, 40–43**).

Now this is all very well, but the fact is that it does not mean much. We have come to accept this form of address as part and parcel of our religious education as Christians, but we need not do so. Reviewed by the kind of mind we possess today, we realise that there is much more 'sound and fury' in such utterances than sense. Not even the rendering here into modern English has done much to make the meaning clear.[7] The representation of inner values via allegory at this point interferes with understanding. *What* does it mean? we ask. It may well have been helpful to the local Jews and others who encountered Jesus on his walks through Galilee, and perhaps even welcome to a people awaiting a Messiah, people, moreover, who were amenable to a teaching supported by parable and biblical allusion, and who were used to this kind of imperious address. Both the tone as illustrated in the example above, and the Jewish historical content were an integral part of their culture. However, the modern mind resists the tone and cannot deal with the content. It asks: 'What tares?' and 'What fire? Where? What kingdom? And what is meant specifically by 'practising lawlessness'? Who will cast out whom? *How* do the righteous 'shine forth'? and 'Who is the Father?' Finally, the reader asks, 'What, precisely does all this *mean* and to what end is it directed?' And because the tone is offensive to our ears today since it carries a threat and the content is incomprehensible, and because nothing of the kind suggested in the passage has ever occurred in the last two thousand years since it was uttered, it is dismissed as something in common with the fairy tale. Such biblical injunctions are judged today certainly by the great majority of people has having no relevance to life as we know it. In short, they do not fulfil our spiritual needs.

Looking through a religious text today, we require something more than a grim-faced god, looking down at us from on high and telling us in military terms what we have to do or not do, together with the immediate assumption that there are two kinds of people (as asserted in the first pages of the Koran, for example), viz. those who believe and those who do not (the Believer and the Infidel). All this is quite unpalatable and does not satisfy the intelligent Westerner for one moment. High-minded humbug is just not on his timetable.

Religious form and content

Every religion has assumed a form to express its content. Whatever 'religion' is, and it is difficult to define, we can nevertheless assert that those religions which at the moment we recognise as highly developed possess three principal attributes. These are: a form of worship, a system of ethics and an inner kernel of truth common to them all. Although the outward expression, the form, varies in Judaism, Christianity, Islam and Buddhism, to take four prominent examples, the ethical code is virtually the same in all four. All of them also proceed from the same core of understanding and must do since the 'core', spiritual awakening, is an experience common to all human beings.

The difference between Buddhism and the other three is that Buddhism has always placed the awakening experience at the centre of its concerns, and still does, while the others have largely eclipsed that essential experience by a concentration on form. In Christianity, the content has lain deeply buried in a form which has only been pierced by mystical experience from time to time in every age, so that those seeing through the outward form to the essential content are few. The mystics who have, at various times over the last 2000 years, plumbed to the bottom of religious content are thought of by the Church as marginal to Christian worship instead of being central to it. Essentially however, these few are the real purveyors of Jesus' message. It is they who have seen beyond the personality worship of Christ and his martyrdom to that mental elevation he himself experienced at some time in his life and which later moved him to walk among men.

The content of religion is what Aldous Huxley once referred to as the 'perennial philosophy' in the book bearing that title. It is that which has initially inspired all formalised religion and which we now recognise in their varied, manifold expressions. One can compare them with a hand thrust, say, through a paper wall where a child might see the different fingers and not suspect that each of them can be traced to one wrist and one arm. From this point of view we can define religion as the art or skill of discerning within ourselves and for ourselves the Source from which we and Creation arise. The actual discernment may have nothing to do with a formal tradition, as we have said or, for that matter with any form of mystical ritual, not even a form of meditation.

The realisation of what Zen Buddhism in particular refers to as the 'All' or the 'Source' or 'One Mind' may arise spontaneously in some people. The all-embracing insight into the nature of our world and ourselves within it has found many expressions.

There are people for example who, like Wordsworth, 'inadvertently' slip into a realisation of mystical wholeness without the slightest 'religious' preparation for the experience and then are left in a state of total bafflement and wonder. Still others, on the other hand, may experience it after several decades of an intense desire for it. Others may find this Unity in diversity through artistic activity, and others yet again through the attrition of ego which their circumstances impose upon them. In this case we might think of poverty and simplicity coupled with a deep awareness of the significance of this life as in the case of Jakob Boehme[8] or Hui Neng[9], or a recognition of the tragic poverty and helplessness of other human beings which induces a desire to help. The self-sacrifice of Mother Teresa is a modern example of this last. Another, conscious way to enlightenment can be the total submission of self to a higher being as in the example of the Hindu saint, Sri Ramakrishna[10], and many, many others.

Whatever the defenders of the Christian view may have to say on this, it remains an attested fact of mystical experience that the object of such worship is, in the last analysis, immaterial. God takes on many forms and is present everywhere. The transcendence of the object (that which is worshipped) and the transcendence of the subject (the worshipper) which results at a higher level of understanding is of importance, not the ritual and tradition surrounding them.

This realisation is always identical with that of other mystical insights experienced in other religious traditions. Once this is realised, we can see that there are not the slightest grounds for conflict; conflict can only arise from ignorance of the true nature of the content informing all our religion. Proof of the omnipresence of God or the Source is once more supplied by R.C. Johnson in his book, *The Imprisoned Splendour,* from which I take the liberty of quoting a passage in full here since it is a remarkable illustration of spiritual un-preparedness, or apparently such. I say 'apparently', since Buddhists believe that there is no such thing as accident or coincidence in such matters. They would maintain that the manifestation of spiritual understanding must have a precursor, in such a case the desire for enlightenment in a former life.

That quoted here is the experience of an apparently indifferent churchgoer standing in a village church in England sometime in the late 19th century listening to the recitation of the 'Te Deum'.

My thought began to contrast the modest praises uttered in this humble place in the outward world, by its crippled organ, the puny voices of this juvenile choir and handful of villagers with the stupendous unimaginable pæans which must needs be heard above when 'all angels cry aloud, the heavens and all the powers therein'. While thus reflecting I caught sight, in the aisle at my side, of what resembled bluish smoke issuing from the chinks of the stone floor, as though from fire smouldering beneath. Looking more intently, I saw that it was not smoke, but something finer, more tenuous – a soft, impalpable self-luminous haze of violet colour, unlike any physical vapour, and for which there was nothing to suggest a cause. Thinking I experienced some momentary optical defect or delusion, I turned my gaze farther along the aisle, but there too the same delicate haze was present...I perceived the wonderful fact that it extended farther than the walls and roof of the building and was not confined by them. Through these I now could look and could see the landscape beyond. ...At a single visual act, and without need of glancing from one point to another or from this object to that, the building I stood within and the whole landscape were in view...I saw from all parts of my being simultaneously, not from my eyes only...Yet for all this intensified perceptive power there was as yet no loss of touch with my physical surroundings, no suspension of my faculties of sense. A momentary doubt as to whether I was experiencing faintness or passing out of the body was solved by a grasp at the pew-back before me and nudging, as if in inadvertently, the arm of the person at my side. Thus satisfied of my physical bearings, I gave myself up with a pleasurable curiosity, to await developments. I felt happiness and peace – beyond words.

Upon the instant the luminous blue haze engulfing me and all around me became transformed into golden glory. into light untellable...The golden light of which the violet haze seemed now to have been as the veil or outer fringe, welled forth from a central immense globe of brilliancy...But the most wonderful thing was that these shafts and waves of light, that vast expanse of photosphere, and even the great central globe itself were crowded to solidarity with the forms of living creatures...a single coherent organism filling all space and place, yet composed of an infinitude of individuated existences...I saw moreover that these beings were present in teeming myriads in the church I stood in; that they were intermingled with and were passing unobstructedly through both myself and all my fellow worshippers.

The heavenly hosts drifted through the human congregation as wind passes through a grove of trees; beings of radiant beauty and clothed in shimmering raiment...

But this vast spectacle of mingled heaven and earth was succeeded by an even richer experience; one in which everything of time and place and form vanished from my consciousness and only the ineffable eternal things remained...And as the point of a candle flame leaps suddenly upward when an object is held just above it, so the flame of my consciousness leapt to its utmost limit and passed into the region of the formless and uncreated to tell of which all words fail...For a few moments of mortal time, which are no measure of the intensity of the spirit's experience in the world immortal, all consciousness of my physical surroundings was withdrawn…

Eventually, while thus rapt, the remembrance of the outer world from which my consciousness had been transported returned to me, like an old half-forgotten memory. This world and my recent surroundings were exhibited to me, but at a most remote distance, as when one looks out upon a scene through a reversed telescope…Without shock or violence the consciousness which had been so highly exalted relapsed and sank to its normal limits and became readjusted to physical conditions; the spirit was returned to its fleshly sheath as a jewel is replaced in its casket after use and locked away. Once more I was standing in the church, perfectly well and unmoved. I feared lest some physical collapse had occurred and created a scene. Happily no external sign of this terrific visitation had occurred; no one was aware that anything had happened. Only a few moments could have been occupied by an experience in the spirit, of which the incidents were so vivid and the details so numerous that my memory still fails to exhaust them. The singing of the 'Te Deum' had not concluded. The words that first fell upon my re-awakened ears were those of the moving cry raised for all here exiled in the flesh, 'O Lord, save Thy people and bless Thy heritage. Govern them and lift them up for ever. Make them to be numbered with Thy saints in glory everlasting.' Had those around me who sang those words been lifted up with me, they too would have known that, although a veil was before their face, they were already numbered with the saints in the Eternal Eye: they would have seen that the everlasting glory was about them at that moment and continually. **(p. 102)**

This, truly, is a stupendous vision. It is interesting to note that at the second paragraph his consciousness is deepened 'as a candle flame leaps up suddenly' to understand what he calls the 'formless and uncreated' which is the goal of Buddhist meditation and the ineffable 'No Mind' of Zen Buddhism.

The attendant perception of a higher octave of understanding variously alluded to as 'Reality' or 'Higher Being', 'God', 'Transcendence' or the 'All', 'Cosmic

Consciousness' and so on, is the direct result of this transcendence. This cosmic principle is alluded to in both the Old and the New Testaments, but there is a huge difference between them and its description in Buddhism. In the former, the vision, the direct knowledge of God is immanent for example in many of the psalms, in the writings of some of the prophets, but nowhere are the prerequisites set out clearly and logically with a view to enlighten. Instead, for much of the time the reader of the Old Testament is beguiled with the incidents of ancient Jewish history and the declamatory tone to which we have already alluded. Its tone of threat and horror is something apparently which Jesus himself warmly condoned. An example of style and content is taken at random from the Book of Malachi, here at chapter 4, which is typical of well over eighty per cent of biblical expression:

'For behold, the day is coming, Burning like an oven, and all the proud, yes, all who do wickedly will be stubble. And the day which is coming shall burn them up', says the Lord of Hosts, 'That shall leave them neither root nor branch. But you who fear my name The Sun of Righteousness shall arise With healing wings; And you shall go out and grow like stall-fed calves. You shall trample the wicked, For they shall be ashes under the soles of your feet On the day that I do this', says the Lord of Hosts.

Here we have the old song of vengeance and vindictiveness, and the quotation is little more than an expression of the desire to do harm. Today, we wonder indeed whether this was the God Jesus spoke of in his healing compassion. Where, we ask, is the God of Love in this diatribe? We will wonder, too, at the naiveté of subsequent generations throughout Europe up to the 18th century finally to appear in the USA, Canada, Australia, New Zealand, South America, even India, and elsewhere in the world where people have accepted this violent, impassioned, intimidating, nonsensical brew as divine instruction and the Word of God for so long. Small wonder that, after its inception among Christians everywhere as the authoritative 'Book of Books', appeals to the Bible could justify every crime.

Throughout the whole of the Old Testament there is not one single place where there is a calm, logically argued treatment of the nature of the human mind, about the role of desire as a determining factor of that mind, about the freedom which is attained when life is seen for what it is, nor the merest practical advice which anyone could follow with benefit to his character and, ultimately, by pursuing a clearly detailed path so as to find enlightenment at the end. Practically all of the Old Testament is highly emotional in tone and often enough of little import as in the example above. As anyone can prove for himself by opening the Bible at almost any page and by viewing it with an open, unprejudiced mind, we find, as here, tone and content in over-heated combination to produce mere cant.

In the Gospels we find little practical instruction and none in terms of a description of the mind's mechanism as to *how* Jesus' kingdom may be found or how the freedom he speaks of from his own experience might be discovered. There is, however, some personal address which is almost wholly absent in the Old Testament and some advice on that level. An example of this is his counsel to Nicodemus, we will remember, who visits him after sundown **(Jn. 3, 1)**.

The New Testament, taken as a whole reveals a man moving forward on an inevitable path towards ultimate barbarity, purportedly under divine coercion. We can imagine him still to be firmly under the all-pervading influence of the Old. Along this path Jesus nevertheless demonstrates the Great Principle inasmuch as he embodies humanity, compassion, wisdom and an understanding of the Great Way. In accepting this, however, we must also be aware of the fact that these qualities are the *result* of divine insight, not a *path* towards the insight itself. Only once does Jesus gives us an inkling of consistent training which might lead to the understanding we have alluded to as Transcendence.

This is indicated in the Gospel according to **Mark**, at chapter **9**, verse **29**, where the disciples ask Jesus 'privately' why they were unable a little before to cast out the 'unclean spirit' (verse 25). To this, Jesus replies: 'This kind can come out by nothing but prayer and fasting.'

We read, too, that from time to time he drew aside from his disciples 'to pray', as in this brief example from Mark, chapter 6, verse 46: 'And when he had sent them away, He departed to the mountain to pray.' In this he sought the peace to find communion with God, recollect himself or, as we should say today, to meditate. We can safely assume that he did this to replenish the spiritual energy dispensed in healing others. It was to return in prayer to the Source of that energy.

From this we may deduce that he was in possession of knowledge and method by which he could do what he did. In our time, this aspect, his ability to achieve what he achieved, is of the greatest interest, not the prophecies of old and those of the future, not caveats and warnings of a life hereafter in hell or elsewhere, nor the traditions and beliefs of an alien people, still less the schoolmasterly, largely condemnative tone which informs so much of that tradition, but the 'how'. It is this which interests all greatly.

What did this man know which we do not know? To answer this question we must delve into the Essential behind the form. To do this is at the same time to expose that which is irrelevant, cut it away and so find the very heart of the good tidings of the Christian message. The heart of the Christian message, it is averred, is none other than to find your own mind (the 'Father' of Christian tradition) or your 'Original Face' in the Zen Buddhist.

Yasutani Roshi, speaking in the 1950's, tells us that a very good way to discover the 'Essential' is to look into oneself.

If you want to realize your own Mind, you must first of all look into the source from which thoughts flow. Sleeping and working, standing and sitting, profoundly ask yourself, 'What is my own Mind?' with intense yearning to solve this question. This is called 'training' or 'practice' or 'desire for truth' or 'thirst for realization'. What is termed zazen (formal meditation) is no more than looking into one's own mind. It is better to search in your own mind devotedly than to read and recite sutras and dharani (Buddha's sermons and their commentaries; mantras or religious recitation) every day for countless years.[11] (My brackets)

The result of 'looking into oneself' in this manner is recorded in the same book as the experience of a fifty-one-year-old American woman artist. She had progressed very slowly from a Christian background, which she rejected, had married, had borne children, passed through a stage of addiction to alcohol, of dissatisfaction with life, feeling all the time that there must be *something* in life which could make more sense of her life and then set-off to search for this. Her odyssey began with reading religious literature and philosophy, as she explains in the book which, in turn, brought her to the practice of meditation. She went to Japan and sat at various monasteries very intensively under a number of masters. Back in the USA, she continued with her practice and came under the direction of Yasutani Roshi where, during a *sesshin* at Pendle Hill, after great personal effort, she attained enlightenment. She explains this in the following words:

The third day my eyes would not stay open – with each breath they closed. When I fought this off, my mind was immediately filled with problems of my family and marriage. It was a terrible struggle against both sleep and mental torment. With each breath I was determined to get hold of Mu (a non-conceptual word on which her concentration was fixed), but it went down and down and disappeared in nothingness.

'Go deeper,' the roshi said. 'Question "What is this Mu?" to the very bottom'.

Deeper and deeper I went...

My hold was torn loose and I went spinning...

To the centre of the earth!

To the centre of the cosmos!

To the *Centre*.
I was there.
With the sound of the little *kinhin* bell (a small hand bell used
to initiate a new phase in meditative procedure)
I suddenly *knew*.
Too late to see the roshi that night. I rushed to the first
dokusan (interview with the master) in the morning.
Questions…
Sharp voices…
Laughter…
Movement…
The roshi said: 'Now you understand that seeing Mu is seeing
God.'
I understood.
After further meditation at another location, this time in the
state of New York, she announces several weeks later:
I feel clean.
I feel free.
I feel ready to live every day with zest, by *choice!*
I am delighted by the adventure of each moment.
I feel as though I have just awakened from a restless,
disjointed dream. Everything looks different!
The world no longer rides heavily on my back. It is under my
belt.
I am no longer restless.
At last I have what I want. (Ibid. p. 253–4; my brackets)

Here we have a modern declaration of the Kingdom of God,
the awakening to our True Nature. This is what psychology
calls personal integration, and Buddhism 'the end of samsara'.
It is end of our endeavours to find happiness and the end of
desire. It is the realisation of a new world and a new
dimension.

The experiencer would certainly not have described herself
as over religious and neither someone committed to any
formal expression of Christianity or Buddhism. Her final
understanding arose from an intense desire to know the
meaning of life and a desire to find peace of mind. This
intensity led her to work hard to get rid of the mental obstacles

that blocked her way to that understanding. The understanding in turn led to freedom, to overcoming the world and to a new dimension of life, just as Jesus assured his followers over two thousand years ago:

'Ye shall know the truth and the truth shall make you free.'

The 'seed' and the real point of living

During his ministry, Jesus saw himself as the Son of Man, the servant of all (a parallel he uses in several places in the Gospels) who sows the seed: 'He who sows the seed is the Son of Man' **(Mk. 13,37)** but he does not say explicitly *what* the seed is. Instead, he goes on in his commentary at this point to relate to the disciples what happens to the seed when it falls to the ground. The 'seed', it is suggested, is the content of the First Commandment: 'Thou shalt love the Lord thy God with all thy heart and with all thy mind and with all thy strength...'

This is the main burden of Christ's message. He is so adamant about the need for this that he says elsewhere in this connection that, in so many words, 'if your hand or your foot is a cause which may hinder you from coming into closer communion with God, then it is better to cut off the offending limb' **(Mk. 5, 30)**.

This radical piece of advice shows how important it is for a man or woman not to lose sight of their relation to God. A little later **(Ml. 9, 43 and 45)**, he uses the word 'sin', which has been defined as 'an absence of God' or a 'life without God'. The Hindu or Buddhist would speak of a man or a woman in this connection as 'taking the wrong path', or of an action which is 'unfruitful' and 'vain'. The implication here is that of substituting something worldly for a recognition of God within ourselves as, for instance, in the case of someone devoted exclusively to the pursuit of money, sex, or entertainment or to the act of subduing others to his will or indeed deriving pleasure from whatever source without a thought of God. All this is a poor substitute for a knowledge of ourselves, and in the end is realised as merely transient and insubstantial. The realisation is bitter for those of such persuasion when they discover – if they discover – that such pursuits do not bring the ultimate satisfaction for which we yearn.[12]

This is the state of coming to 'naught', and reflects the older, much weightier sense of the word 'naughty' used in the Middle Ages, that of proceeding to nothing and ending in nothing, a state of zero worth which has since been equated with sinfulness.

The last quotation in the Gospel according to Mark above uses the word 'sin' in this sense. This state of affairs, that of 'coming to naught', is not only well illustrated in the parable of Lazarus **(Lk. 16, 19),** and the parables of Rich Fool **(Lk. 12, 16),** but can also be clearly seen in historical retrospect when we review the lives, say, of the world's dictators. Deflection from what is the main issue in life, an awareness of ourselves and the essential life behind all things which keeps us alive, was as much an error in Christ's day as it is in our own. Rabbi Jeshua in his encounters with the men and women of his time did not condemn our human desires, knowing that these are naturally a part of our being, but it is quite clear that he recognised the motives of our behaviour as lacking orientation to what we refer to here as the Source of Being. Among many other illustrations of tolerant understanding of our human weakness, there is the famous anecdote of the Woman Taken in Adultery where a crowd had gathered to stone her.

'Has no one condemned you'? He asks her at **Jn. 8, 10–11** after he had enjoined those in the mob who had no sin to come forward to throw the first stone, and when she says 'No' to this, he answers 'Neither do I condemn you; go and sin no more.' **(12)**

What he was insistent upon was that we human beings put the horse before the cart and not the other way round as we are all to prone to do. Today, we would speak of 'recognising priorities'. 'Seek ye first the kingdom of heaven, and the rest shall be added unto you' **(Mt. 6, 33)**.

Jesus addressed his message to those who were ignorant of the nature of God (the multitude) and those who had turned away from Him (the sinners), but his scorn and anger were reserved for those who deliberately perverted religious truth into a hidebound system of observances and lifeless ritual, together with punishments for non-compliance. He reviled those priests who sought personal advantage in society and as a means of making money in the garb of religious advisors. These three strands of his ministry are specifically illustrated in the three examples below, but occur in many other places throughout the gospels. Of hidebound tradition we read:

> The scribes and Pharisees came to Jesus, saying, Why do your disciples transgress the tradition of the elders? For they do not wash their hands when they eat bread.

And after reprimanding them for transgression of the law themselves, he turned to the crowd and said: 'Hear and understand. Not what goes into the mouth defiles a man, but what comes out of the mouth, this defiles a man' **(Mt. 15, 17ff)**.

The same theme also occurs at **Mt. 12,3–12; 19. 3ff; at Lk. 5,30ff and at 6,2ff and 7,39–42 and at 15,2.**

Of personal advantage he says: 'Beware of the scribes who desire to go around in long robes, love greetings in the market places, the best seats in the synagogues and best places at feast, who devour widows' houses and for a pretence make long prayers...' **Mk. 12, 38ff; and also at 11, 42; 16, 14, and at Jn. 12, 43)**.

> Now the Pharisees who were lovers of money also heard all these things and they derided him.
>
> And he said unto them: 'You are those who justify yourselves before men but God knows your hearts. For what is highly esteemed among men is an abomination in the sight of God.' **(Lk. 16, 14–15)**

And of making money in the temple precincts we are told that he actually resorted to physical violence in driving the small-time traders from their stalls with a hastily contrived whipcord **(Mt. 21, 12).**

The most tragic example in the gospels of misplaced values is Iscariot's betrayal of his friend for thirty pieces if silver.

All the Gospels relate that Jesus is at pains to demonstrate at every turn that man's first task is to put himself in touch with God, implying all along as he does so that the major problem with us is distraction from this goal.

Of this, Thomas Traherne (1637–74), English cleric, writer, poet and mystic, puts this matter of 'distraction' or 'unawareness of our origin' very simply: 'Pigs eat acorns, but neither consider the sun that gave them life, nor the influence of the heavens by which they are nourished, nor the very root from whence they came.' This, then, sums the matter up for us, too.

The content of the Gospels

The content of the Gospels can be summarized in the two great commandments:

> Thou shalt love the Lord thy God with all thy heart and with all thy mind and with all thy strength: this is the first and great commandment, and the second is like unto it: thou shalt love thy neighbour as thyself. **(Mt. 22,38–39)**

The whole of Christ's ministry was to demonstrate these two great principles. All his doings and utterances were aligned to these two central issues. Remove these two themes and there is no New Testament.

The second commandment is not dealt with here except in passing, since it is plainly manifested in his cure of the sick and in the other miracles he performed for the benefit of human understanding. As he says himself: 'The blind receive their sight and the lame walk, the lepers are cleansed, and the deaf hear, the dead are raised up, and the poor have the gospel preached to them'(Mt. 11,5) which is tantamount to saying, 'See here, I am the embodiment of the principle I teach: if you understand the love of man which I show to you, you can see the origin of my power, the Father.' His main concern, therefore, in walking among men was to show them how they themselves could attain to a knowledge of God. This was his principal objective. To this end he spoke in parables, but also on many occasions spoke outright about the nature of the dimension of mind which he referred to as the 'Kingdom of heaven'. Like many before and after him, Jesus lived in this dimension and spoke directly from that understanding. As far as we can gather from reading the Gospels, he, like a good Zen master, never overlooked an opportunity to bring those around him to a new understanding of themselves and their relation to the world. In this he was tireless. The 'dimension' we speak of here was for him more real or just as real as the daily, familiar world in which we live and which we think we know so well. Hence his intensity, his passionate, personal engagement with the people he came into contact and his categorical refusal to accept any form of self-deceit, lying, or misrepresentation of religious understanding **(Mt. 3,7; Mt. 22,13–16)**. This uncompromising spirit, virtuous though it was, earned him the enmity of many people, especially those in power at the time **(Jn. 5,18; Mk. 14,1)**. Since he was the living embodiment of the understanding we have already alluded to by reference and illustration above, and because he could justify his understanding by exercising the powers which issue from such knowledge, he intensely personalized the teaching **(Mk. 14,7; Jn. 17,5–12)**. Moreover, he saw himself in the historical role of the Christ, the Messiah, or the 'Anointed One.' This personalized approach, which is sometimes referred to in Buddhism as 'Subjectivity speaking', led in his own day to confusion and objection among his hearers, and since his time to a personalized 'saviour' cult. This latter is perhaps understandable, but it has led to enormous error. As the distinguished Oxford scholar, Geza Vermes, in his book, *The Religion of Jesus, the Jew*, has rightly noted, Jesus himself would have agreed to the first three lines of the Christian 'Credo' of both denominations: 'I believe in God the Father Almighty,/ Maker of heaven and Earth,/ and of all things visible and invisible…' and to the last two: 'We confess one baptism for the remission of sins./ And we look for the resurrection of the dead and the life of the world to come. Amen,' but the rest, he says, would have mystified him since they 'appear to have nothing to do with the religion preached and practised by him.'

What, then, is the essential teaching behind the words, 'Thou shalt love the Lord thy God with all thy heart and with all thy mind and with all thy strength?' What do the words 'heart', 'mind' and 'strength' imply in the context of the commandment? Clearly, the words and phrases are emphatic; they leave no room for compromise. This is what we are *commanded* to do, so we may assume from this fact that the matter is important.

In Zen Buddhism this is made abundantly clear. To gain enlightenment, a great deal of work has to be done in clearing the mind of its initial clutter. This takes time and energy and very often is accompanied, too, by a degree of suffering. The aspirant to enlightenment is required to sit formally for many hours a day at a *sesshin,* for example, and will almost always have pain in the knees, legs and back as a result. Added to this, all kinds of thoughts enter his heart to disturb its equanimity, and keeping these out of the mind by intense concentration and at the same time keeping the back straight amounts to a veritable battle with oneself. The master, usually a man, but sometimes a woman, will urge us to 'to throw ourselves into the solution of Mu unremittingly.'

This 'Mu' is a sound meaning 'No' and was uttered by the great Zen master, Chao-chou (778–897) as a retort in the 9th century to a monk who, apparently after much reflection, asked the master whether the 'Buddha nature' (in Christian terms, 'God') was in a dog. In the normal way of things we can assume that God or the Buddha nature is at work in all things, even in the atoms of inanimate things, so that we could reasonably expect the master to have said 'Yes' in reply to his question. The monk no doubt wanted this confirmed. 'Does a dog have this nature, and if so, could it then know what enlightenment is?' is another way of phrasing this existential question. However, the master said 'No!' with emphasis which immediately overturned the monk's mental world and threw him into confusion. The object of his saying 'No' to the monk's earnest question was to catapult him into even more self-reflection. In other words, he was not quite at the point where he could be enlightened, since there were still thoughts and concepts in his mind. What the master wanted to know from him was that which proceeds from a mind which is empty of these considerations. Other examples of what this 'No-mind' is will follow. For the moment, our meditator is concerned with emptying his mind. To do this generally requires maximum effort on his or her part. It is to throw out every conceivable image and thought from the mind and to concentrate on what is left. That which is left is referred to by Bankei, another Zen master of the 17th century, as 'the Unborn'. In other words, it is That which has not manifested itself as either a thing or a concept in our dualistic world of relationships and opposites. It is, to use a biblical phrase, 'not of this world.'

To pit one's mind against what appears to be the unsolvable, the *koan*, is to do just what is required of us in the first commandment; it is to commit one's heart, mind and all one's strength to finding out what or where God is. To enable a man or a woman to do this, the later expression of Buddhism in China and Japan made use of the *koan* method as a means to fix concentration. The idea behind this application is to bring the mind to a state where it can no longer 'think' at all; it gives up thinking, which is the same thing as saying that the discursive mind is exhausted. From this point – that is to say when the mind no longer functions along its natural course of associative and inductive activity - a new dimension of mind is open to its cognition. This is the 'No-mind' of Zen Buddhism, or 'That-which-Is' of Christian mysticism, or what Jesus describes as 'Everlasting life' or the 'Kingdom'.

A *koan* is a riddle, therefore, which will not allow itself to be solved by ratiocination. *Koans* range in difficulty and have been graded by Zen masters of the past into categories of suitable for judging the varying stages of spiritual perception. Their solution will reveal the degree of penetration the student has reached into what Christians might well call the 'Sublime', but which Buddhists refer to as the 'Buddha nature' or 'Bodhi'. All the terms refer to 'THAT which comes before a thought' or the Essential which is incapable of description, but which is behind everything we know in the phenomenal world. It is, to use Poonjaji's examples, 'That which lifts the wave', 'That which persuades the flower to grow, the heart to beat, and the sun and moon to shine' and without which there would be nothing of phenomena, but only 'darkness on the face of the earth.'

From this it will be clear what sort of effort s implied in the First Commandment.

Once having achieved enlightenment, this priority of putting God first is then automatic. The reason for this is that the mind has undergone a total overhaul. It is no longer the small mind of desire and yearning, but, as the woman in the last illustration makes clear in her own way: 'I am no longer restless / At last I have what I want.'

---

[1] The usual form of crucifixion was to lay the victim on the cross while he (or sometimes she) was still on the ground and then lift him up while the base of the cross was fixed into an already prepared socket. The arms were generally bound to support the weight of the sufferer and the nails driven not into the palms of the hand as is so often misrepresented in painting and sculpture, but through the wrists. See also under 'Crux' in *Harper's Dictionary of Classical Literature*

and Antiquities, ed. H.T. Peck, New York, Cooper Square, 1965, p. 432ff.

[2] Death by crucifixion was generally a lingering one and suffering could last for several days. If for some reason as here the authorities wished to precipitate death, the legs of the victim were broken using a heavy metal mallet. This produced shock and the victim usually died within a few minutes of this treatment.

[3] See above at Chapter I, footnote 3.

[4] In this case, Jesus' prophecy was 100% correct. Seventy years after his death, the city of Jerusalem was razed to the ground by the Romans.

[5] See Schwabe, H., *Was ist Wahrheit? Der Historische Jesus* Frankfurt/M, 1989.

[6] Lapide, P. *Flüchtlingskind* (Child Refugee), Munich, 1981, p. 69ff (my translation).

[7] It may well be, of course, that we have to do here with the difficulties hinted at by Professor Lapide when he speaks of that inner meaning conveyed to Jesus' listeners by the original Hebrew. Examples of this 'inner meaning' are given elsewhere in this text on the linguistic aspects of translation. Here, we could mention the 'old school tie' as an example, which, for Englishmen, is full of meaning, but for others has very little or none at all – and 2000 years hence would be completely meaningless!

[8] It is said that Jacob Böhme (1575-1624), the Silesian mystic, (elsewhere spelled as Behmen and Beyme) had the ability to speak other languages in this way.

[9] Sixth patriarch of Zen, flourished AD 638-713.

[10] Sri Ramakrishna (1836-1886), Indian saint and mystic.

[11] Quoted in Kapleau, Philip, *The Three Pillars of Zen*, New York, Harper & Row, 1966, p. 161 (my brackets).

[12] This does not *necessarily* mean an explicitly 'sinful' preoccupation, but *any* occupation to which one is entirely dedicated without consideration for the Source from which the appreciation of these occupations arise. A positive illustration of the right attitude to life is perhaps that of Johann Sebastian Bach who, as far as we can judge from the sparse material left to posterity about his person, was a man who put God first in his life and then his music.

CHAPTER VII

On being born again

In the Gospel according to St John, we read at chapter **3, 1–8** of the Pharisee, Nicodemus, who, we recall, comes to Jesus by night. We might reasonably assume that he does so for fear of being discovered by his colleagues talking to Jesus. However this may be, he is convinced of the Rabbi's authenticity and says: 'Rabbi, we know that you are a teacher come from God; for no one can do these signs that you do unless God is with him.' **(Verse 2)**

In reply to this Jesus says, 'Most assuredly, I say unto you, unless one is born again, he cannot see the kingdom of God.' Not knowing what to make of this, Nicodemus thinks of physical birth and objects with the question: 'Can he enter a second time into his mother's womb and be born?' The answer to this strikes at the bedrock of all religion.

> Most assuredly, I say unto you, unless one is born of water and the Spirit, he cannot enter the kingdom of God. / That which is born of the flesh is flesh, and that which is born of the Spirit is Spirit. Do not marvel that I said to you You must be born again.'

We are not told of Nicodemus' reaction to this, but later, in verses 15 and 16 respectively, and apparently sequentially in this connection, Jesus goes on to speak of 'eternal' and 'everlasting' life. It is well worth examining these two phrases since they represent the core of Jesus' teaching, the underlying reason, that is, why we should render those things to God first, which are the 'things that are God's.'

In the remarks above, Jesus uses one of his favourite phrases when he wishes to underline the importance of a thing; in this case it is 'most assuredly'. It is a tribute to the apostle or whoever took down the words of the Master here that the insistence implied in the phrase has been maintained. Another testimony of his fastidiousness is given by the use of the word 'see' in the first quotation, as well as the principal idea of being 'born again'.

Putting the last observation used by Jesus into modern English we might say: 'And don't be surprised that I use the expression "You must be born again"; the body's one thing and the spirit is another. I'm talking about the spirit, not the body.'

Later in this context he speaks of the wind which we cannot see, but which is nevertheless there, and its action and its effects can be recognized. It is not that the wind can be 'seen' in the usual way of seeing things in the phenomenal world around us, but that there is another way of seeing, a 'seeing into' which is much more akin to 'seeing' the solution to a problem, or suddenly realising the truth of a situation, for example. The word 'seeing' in this sense is much used in Buddhism where it refers to the inspirational way of seeing, that is, having immediate insight into the true nature of a thing and, in particular in this case, of 'seeing into one's true nature.' This is to realize the 'Spirit' which invests everything and of which we are also an inseparable part. This is to be 'born again'.

To be 'born of the Spirit' is the same experience; it is precisely this 'in-seeing', that which the Christian would call 'communion with the divine' and which the Buddhist and Vedic scriptures refer to variously as 'Atman', 'Bodhi', 'Buddhakaya', 'Non-Duality', 'No-Mind' and 'Buddha nature' as we have seen. Other terms for this insight are 'Whole' or 'Wholeness', 'Oneness' the 'One' or 'Dao' (Tao).

Below are a few examples of this phenomenon. The first is taken from the Buddhist Lankavatara Sutra, where the Buddha replies to a disciple, Mahamati, who asks: 'Pray, tell us, O Blessed One, what are the fruits which self-realisation brings?'

> First there will be a strikingly clear insight into the meaning and the significance of things (i.e. for the recipient of the insight into his relation to the world he lives in and to other human beings). After experiencing this 'revolution within his mind' taking place in his deepest consciousness, he will experience other states of samadhis (deeper states of meditative insight), even to the deepest of these. He will be able to enter the realm of consciousness which is beyond the human mind-system, even indeed the consciousness of the Buddha Himself. Accordingly they will acquire all power such as psychic powers, self-mastery, loving compassion and other attributes which will enable them to enter other Buddha-lands. (My brackets)

Later in the same sutra the Buddha mentions again that the seeker after truth, in this case a Bodhisattva, experiences a 'turning point' in his consciousness. It is as though a kind of 'death' of the old mind followed by a 'rebirth', which, he says, has nothing to do with the death of the body in the ordinary sense, which Nicodemus suspects in his conversation with Christ. It is a disruption, so to speak, of the 'old mind', and the reconstruction of a new, all-embracing consciousness which is liberated from the control of the former mental structure with its habit-orientated, reflexive, reactive responses to life. This 'revolution of mind' is called *acintya-parinama-cyuti* in Sanskrit and can be translated as 'transformation-death'.

To put the matter 'upside down', so to speak, in order to understand this phenomenon from a different point of view, we can say that the 'real' world we see around us becomes, at the moment of insight, 'unreal'. We suddenly see the truth behind duality and, as a result, duality is realised by us as a deception, a trick of the senses. This new understanding is referred to in the Ashtavakra Gita, a Vedic scripture less well

191

known than the Bhagavad Gita with which the West has now been familiar for some time. It asserts:

> Ignorance of Atman (Godhead, One Mind, Cosmic Consciousness) makes the phenomenal world around us appear real. This illusion is dissolved in the realisation of our true nature (the ineffable insight). Just as the illusion of a piece of rope can be mistaken for a snake, so it is dissolved by knowledge of its real nature[1] (My brackets).

A similar view is also expressed in the Bhagavad Gita. For those who may still be unfamiliar with its figures, we are concerned here with an interview between the divine incarnation of Krishna and a noble archer, Arjuna, on the field of battle. Before the battle begins, a discussion arises between them on religious issues where, among many other matters, Krishna declares:

> All living beings are led astray as soon as they are born by the delusion that this world is real. This delusion arises from their own desire and hatred. But the doers of good deeds, whose bad karma is exhausted, are freed from the delusion about the relative world.[2]

After this in-seeing experience, the person having acquired the perception then sees the world from an entirely new perspective. To illustrate this changeover from one 'wavelength of mind' to another very simply, we can take the example of the hologram or stereogram which has become quite popular with us today. According to the Dictionary of Contemporary English, a hologram is 'a kind of photograph made with a laser that looks as if it is not flat when you look at it from an angle' **(p. 683)**. We could, however, add that it is more than this, since modern holographic photography today can produce a photographic surface which appears as, say, a sandy beach or a blue sky or herbaceous border or a hedge and when we look at such a surface we see *only* this pattern and take this for granted as that which the artist wants to convey. However, when we acquire a certain attitude of mind, a certain viewpoint by looking at the surface for some time, we may come across something entirely different from that presented to the eye. We suddenly discover that within this surface or behind the object superficially portrayed is another, deeper (apparently three-dimensional) figure which, say, in this simple case, could be the picture of an animal or a number or a face which takes us entirely by surprise and delights us on discovery. At that moment we understand that the ability to see differently is a latent capacity within ourselves.

'The kingdom does not come with observation; nor will they say, "See here!" and "'See there", for indeed the kingdom of heaven is within you', says Jesus. (**Lk. 17:20–21**)

In September, 1894, a woman living in England took leave of her friend, a farmer's wife who had given her roses on her departure. Of these she said that they were of exquisite colour and scent and she deeply appreciated the gesture and the gift. She says that they 'appealed to me with quite exceptional force and vividness.' For weeks prior to this incident she had been reading much of the work of the poet Walt Whitman, and had been discussing the matters he expresses with her husband. Her mind, we can take it, had been sharpened to the point where it was ready to receive the intuition which was shortly to follow:

I left my friend and was walking slowly homeward, enjoying the calm beauty of the evening, when I became conscious of an unutterable stillness, and simultaneously every object about me became bathed in a soft light, clearer and more ethereal than I had ever before seen. Then a voice whispered in my soul: 'God is all. He is not far away in the heaven; He is here. This grass under your feet is He; this bountiful harvest, that blue sky, those roses in your hand – you yourself are all one with Him. All is well for ever and ever, for there is no place or time where God is not.' Then the earth and air and sky thrilled and vibrated to one song, and the burden of it was 'Glory to God in the highest and on earth, peace and good will toward men'.

On my return home both my husband and his sister remarked a change in my face. An infinite peace and joy filled my heart, worldly ambitions and cares died in the light of the glorious truth that was revealed to me – all anxiety and trouble about the future had utterly left me, and my life is one long song of love and peace...at all hours of the day and night – the song is ever with me...[3]

This is an example of someone brought up strictly in the Christian tradition from childhood onwards and so the vision takes on its particular interpretation. With time, and if the 'rebirth', in Jesus' sense of 'being born again' is deep enough, the experiencer will gradually gear the whole of his or her subsequent life to this one great intuition. In this way, life itself is then of a different order. It is a matter of the intuited life quality taking over the former patterns of reactive habit and early conditioning. If the experience is deep enough as in this example, the human psyche undergoes a permanent change.

The next three illustrations of the same process of 'being born again' come from the other side of the globe. The first concerns a short interview between a monk and the Chinese Zen master, Chao-chou, whom we have encountered above. The monk, Fo-chien, asks him, 'What is your way of teaching?' We would say today, 'What is it that you teach?' or 'What is your essential teaching?' We can safely assume that the question was a serious one uttered in sincerity. Zen masters in those days were not to be trifled with or treated familiarly. We can also assume that Fo-chien's mind had been wrestling for a long time with just what it was that he was supposed to learn at the hands of the master. To this earnest enquiry, Chao-chou retorted: 'You ask me about my way of teaching and I have already found out yours!' It is said that this tart reply opened Fo-chien's mind. Why this apparently happened so quickly is that Zen students then as now are mentally prepared by being given a *koan* (an intellectually unanswerable question) precisely in order to bring about the change of 'wavelength' referred to above. This man's mind was ready to receive the full impact of *satori*, or mind-opening as it is called in Japanese, simply as a result of this brief but pungent exchange. Zen literature is full of these mental clashes between monks and masters. In the midst of his new apprehension, Fo-chien nevertheless had the temerity to approach the master again in order to probe a little further and so assure himself that he was now seeing everything in the other perspective. He pursued: 'What, then, is the ultimate truth of Zen, pray?' This time the master helps him to final, perfect realisation and says, like the woman's inner voice above a thousand years later: 'A world of multiplicities is all stamped with the One.'

The shift from the samsaric to the 'nirvanic wavelength'

From these two experiences and from the other examples of insight given above we can see that in each instance a shift takes place in order to tune our minds in, as it were, to another 'wavelength'. In Zen, this shift could be brought about suddenly in several ways, provided the student was in the right frame of mind to receive it from a master. The master was always in a position to know just how far the pupil had travelled on the spiritual road. This is as true today as it was in ancient times.

In the annals of Zen, for instance, we discover examples where this shift of mind was sometimes facilitated by a quite unexpected thump or a clout from the master, sometimes by a loud cry or an unsuspected act of (apparent) aggression, downright offensiveness or an act or a word which appears to be completely unreasonable or, on some occasions, by an apparently unrelated quotation from the scriptures or from other literature.

An example of physical violence is given in the record of a young man new to the monastery who came to pay his introductory respects to the abbot. On meeting him, the master suddenly struck the boy so forcefully that he fell to the ground. No sooner had the lad risen to his feet than he was given another blow. 'Why do you strike me?' the young man cried in consternation and confusion. The master then turned his back on him. The young man was himself about to turn away from this embarrassing encounter when a monk nearby admonished him, 'Make your bows, brother!' he said as the master was taking his leave. The lad did so and at that very moment his mind was opened.

What happened here was that the young fellow was forced by this highly irregular situation to adapt himself rapidly to another attitude of mind. The unpleasantness of the introduction literally propelled him from his usual frame of mind to another. His mind was probably a mixture of the need to defend himself and total surprise. He had expected the few formal pleasantries of welcome and encouragement customary at such interviews, but was given a mighty thwack instead. In the next second he was stunned, and on getting to his feet again was perhaps still ready to recover his normal equilibrium, though this was already somewhat shattered by the welcoming blow. The second attack left him quite speechless and at a complete loss as to what to make of the situation. The other monk (probably the head monk on this occasion) then saw opportunity to catch him in this state of momentary mental confusion, the third phase here, and 'shift' him onto another plane of consciousness. As it happened, the device worked perfectly.

The second example is of an encounter between master and monk, where the two had been in each other's company for years. This fact was not to indicate, however, that they were on the same spiritual wavelength. The one knew the truth, the other was still seeking it. The master, in other words, lived in that dimension of truth so far described, while the monk did no yet suspect its nature. One evening they were together when the candle the monk was holding blew out in a gentle gust of air. There was total darkness for a moment or two while the monk sought means to re-light the wick. When, finally, the candle was relit, the master immediately blew it out again. This brought full realisation (*satori*) to his companion.

Jesus, who enjoyed the state of full realisation or 'Bodhi', was also fully aware in every moment of life and ready therefore to turn any situation into one where another could realise his own true nature. He was ready to bring men to the 'rebirth' of his own analogy, or what elsewhere is called inner illumination. Although apparently 'in this world' he was not, as we say, 'of this world' and yet quite able to enjoy the company of others without being insincere in this. He was nevertheless 'about his Father's business.'

The difference, we suggest, between 'in' and 'of' here is that Jesus was not totally and utterly immersed *in* and identified *with* the world as all of us experience it, but that he stood apart from the world of illusion like every other conscious, 'awakened' individual.

> But the scribes and Pharisees murmured against his disciples saying; Why do you eat with publicans and sinners? And Jesus answered unto them, They that are whole need not a physician, but they that are sick. **(Lk. 5, 30–31)**

The word 'sick' here is interesting. If we accept the evangelist's choice of word, we must also recognise it as a strong one. Here, it certainly means 'sick in mind'. It does not infer a recognisable mental illness; that is certain, but refers to our habitual, concentrated preoccupation with matters peripheral to the central issue of personal liberation. Diversions such as the indulgence in alcohol and good company coupled here in the biblical quotation are not wrong in themselves when they do us and others no harm, but the point is that these things, pleasant as they are, should not distract us from being aware of ourselves. They should not, in other words be *substituted* for what Jesus regards as the main issue in life. To do this is to be 'sick'. In Buddhist terminology this human habit is referred to as *avidya,* or ignorance.

'For what will it profit a man if he gains the whole world, and loses his own soul?' Jesus says in this connection at **Mk. 8, 36.**

In an encounter with a scribe, the Rabbi is praised by the scholar for his declaration that there is one God **(Mk.12,32 ff)** The scribe says:

> 'Well, Master, thou hast said the truth: for there is one God and there is none other but he: and to love him with all the heart, and with all the understanding, and with all the soul, and with all the strength and to love (his) neighbour as himself, is more than all whole burnt offerings and sacrifices.'

To this Jesus replies that he is 'not far' from the kingdom of God. By the phrase 'not far' we might reasonably assume that the scribe was aware of the path to realisation, but had not yet followed its whole length and gained illumination.

On 'being born again', the 'kingdom' and the enlightenment experience

Once a Zen master was asked by a samurai what the words 'heaven' and 'hell' meant. The question was a well-considered one, the warrior having thought deeply about its implications. To his surprise and anger, the master, instead of answering his question, turned upon him to ask what kind of a noble family would employ such a useless coward as him in its house. In fury, the samurai seized the hilt of his sword and began to draw when the master in the same second held up his hand for him to stop. 'That is hell,' he said. The samurai, seeing the point, sheathed his sword once more. 'That is heaven,' the master added with a smile. The samurai smiled, too, in understanding. This moment of insight is the moment of 'being born again', of seeing into the world of 'No-mind' as the Chinese call it (Wu-shin), or of recognizing a state where the 'I' of the ordinary mind, of everyday living is suddenly obliterated and in its place there is what Aldous Huxley calls 'unitive knowledge', where the small 'self' and the Self are then realised as one. 'Being born again' is to receive that push which propels us into another dimension of realization which we would not have believed exists.

Yet another example taken from the literature of Zen. This time it is a conversation between either a monk or a visitor to the temple and the Chinese Zen master, Huang Po (d. ca. 850). The point at issue once more is the meaning of 'being born again'. The questioner asks:

Q: What is implied by 'seeing into the real nature'?

A: That nature and your perception of it are one. You cannot use it to see something over and above yourself…If you form a concept of the true nature of anything as being visible or audible, you allow a dharma (teaching) of distinction to arise.[4] (My brackets)

We can see from this that the master throws the question back at the inquirer by suggesting that he look at where this 'real nature' comes from. This is another of the techniques used by masters past and present to awaken the student to his or her own higher consciousness. There is no acquisition in the sense of reaching out and grasping or of *seeing* this 'kingdom' in the sense of a subject, 'I', 'seeing' an object called the 'real Self', but, as the mystics have declared during the whole of Christianity's existence, it is a union, one where the awareness of an 'I' and an object (either thing or concept) disappear altogether. The master concludes:

The Absolute is Thus-ness – how can it be discussed? You people still conceive of Mind as existing or not existing…as something to be studied in the way one studies a piece of categorical knowledge, or as a concept – any one of these definitions is enough to throw you back into the endless round of birth and death. The man who PERCEIVES things always wants to identify them, to get hold of them. Those who use their minds like eyes in this way are sure to suppose that progress (i.e. towards enlightenment) is a matter of stages.

If you are that kind of person, you are as far from the truth as earth is far from heaven. Why this talk of seeing into your own nature?[5]

Here, we discover that enlightenment arrives when the mind is ready to receive it or, we might say, when the time to be 'reborn' is ripe. Since the experience is within, it cannot be 'something-out-there' for the probing ego to grasp with its intellect. There must be that giving up we have spoken of so that the other kind of vision can take place. And further, since it is a realization of 'that which neither exists nor does not exist' as Zen Buddhism puts it, it cannot possibly be talked about as if it were a concept. It cannot be talked about at all. If it is not a concept, we cannot talk, therefore, of 'progress towards enlightenment' as if it were something to be understood in stages. It is either there or it is not there. Either the door is open or it is closed; either it is raining or it is not raining; either one understands or one does not understand.

Of course, this is not to say that enlightenment cannot be prepared for by acquiring the right frame of mind for the experience to take place. The occurrence of satori or the enlightening vision is not very likely for those who spend their time torturing animals in a laboratory, for example, or for people who indulge their selfish egos in gaining power over others which results in their harm, or even for those who are intent on satisfying their desires without much regard for others around them. Thus, a certain consistent level of good moral conduct (Sanskrit: *sila*) is necessary before the liberating vision can be experienced. The word 'moral' here is used to mean all behaviour which has the good of others as its inspiration. Put another way, it means non-egotistical behaviour. Every endeavour which leads away from the acquisitive, self-loving ego with its insistent demand for security provides a helpful path towards self-realisation.

Ego, we can say, is content with substitutes for the liberating vision and among these substitutes are also concepts. Concepts tend to harden with time like uneaten bread and need constant review in order to keep pace with that change of circumstance which is the very nature of samsara. Jesus for his part found himself confronted by an orthodoxy which was completely blinded by its own conceptual view of life. Its representatives came to him in the hope that their traditional opinions would be confirmed, but frequently they went away, stung by the words and example of someone who had transcended every kind of concept.

> Woe to you scribes and Pharisees, hypocrites! For you cleanse the outside of the cup and dish, but inside they are full of extortion and self-indulgence. **(Mt. 23.25)**

Habit and ritual are the straitjacket of the living spirit. These people had lost touch with the living principles which had once invested the first inspired idea and which later gave way to a vacant ritual. They placed more value on the exercise of the ritual and their proud custody of it than on the spirit of the original which had caused it to come into being. In short, they had lost contact with inspirational knowledge and seized upon the second-hand representation which seemed more real to them; the living idea, since it was no longer understood, was abandoned for a dead symbol. This process of decay is, unfortunately, true of all religions and many secular organisations, too. Realizing this, Jesus sends the young man away who had come to him as a prospective disciple, but who first asks him whether he may first leave the group around Jesus in order to bury his deceased father with the astonishing but explicit, 'Let the dead bury their own dead.' **(Lk. 9.60).** The use of the word 'dead' has given offence to many and no doubt the young man in question also went his way feeling bruised by this remark. On the other hand, it clearly illustrates the Rabbi's priorities. It states quite categorically that those who cannot discover the living truth within themselves might just as well be dead or as the beasts of the field, which also eat, copulate, age and die in ignorance like Traherne's pigs.

On the other hand, waking up to life by ridding oneself of deadening habit and ritual is well exemplified by an ancient

Zen master renowned for his plain speaking, Lin Chi (Jap. Rinzai). Several times a week he would round upon the monks gathered together to hear him 'blaspheme' against their most treasured religious opinions, explode all their learning, rip away all their egotistical pride in knowing the sutras by heart, joust at their piety, make fun of their ritual, undermine their carefully cultivated traditional Buddhist ideas and upset their sheep-like conformity. In doing this, he would use the plainest language, not even shirking direct, personal abuse or what we would call the four-letter word comparison today. For all that, he was one of the greatest Zen teachers who ever lived. In this excerpt he is telling his assembly not to cling to name and form (he was never tired of doing so) and to get at the basic reality behind things and concepts. His uncompromising attitude as far as this is concerned is similar to that of Christ's.

Seekers generally cling tightly to names and terms, letting themselves be impressed by preached words such as 'sinful' and 'holy'. In this way they only succeed in clouding their understanding, and there is a total lack of living clarity. There's no understanding reality like this. The twelvefold teaching is nothing but superficial talk. Since you who seek cannot see through it all you seek (instead) support in the bandying of words or seize upon revelations and add a theological meaning to them as well. All this leads to nothing else than the undermining of your own independence. As a consequence you are subject to the law of cause and effect and are unable to escape birth and death in the threefold world. If you do want to free yourselves from these two and from the compulsion of coming and going, dressing and undressing, then take notice of 'That' and hold on to 'It' which is here and now listening to the Dharma. It has neither form nor appearance, neither roots nor stem, nor (does it dwell) in one place. It is free like a jumping fish in water and adjusts itself to a given situation. The way it works is unaccountable; if you look for it, it escapes you. The harder you seek, the further off it is. This is why it is referred to as 'mystical'. (Reality appears to be 'mystical' as long as the seeker imagines it to be instead of just 'letting it happen'. Then he will recognize the truth and belief will disappear of its own accord.) (My brackets except for the last).[6]

Lin Chi died in the second half of the ninth century, but his words still cogently apply as much to our minds and our religious systems today as they did more than a thousand years ago.

In the first four lines, he urges us to give up the accretions we have learned from our orthodox teachings, radically and once and for all. All of it, he says, is mere words, a mere shadow of the real thing. At best, he suggests, you lose your independence, the ability to think for yourselves. At the worst, as we have seen in the history of Christianity, are the perversities of an Inquisition, a crusade or a pogrom. And, he warns, you (the monks) will be bound to what he later refers to as 'coming and going', here meaning birth and death. In Buddhist terms, this means being bound to the wheel of rebirth, and in Christian, living in ignorance of what Jesus was pleased to call a 'kingdom', by which he meant that unsuspected dimension to the world of which we are unaware.

One of the qualities of this kingdom (which as we have seen, is an inner realisation, not a place), is that it cannot be laid hold of in the usual sense of grasping something any more than one can 'grasp' inspiration. It is either there or it is not there. For this reason, Lin Chi suggests in the closing lines that his monks let go of everything in order to allow what he calls 'It' to happen. If 'It' is sought by grasping, by seeking to attain, Lin Chi adds, the experience will elude us. Seeking in this sense is an activity of the ego, the 'I', whereas the experience of suddenly finding, of realising is ego-less; it includes neither a subject which seeks nor an object which is to be found, but a Whole which is immediately and marvellously 'known'.

When Jesus urges his followers to 'seek' the kingdom of heaven, he knows full well that it cannot be grasped like a cup or a spade. This kind of grasping is our undoing. By 'seek' he asks us to *desire* this one thing above all else. We are to give the desire priority. There is no knowing when it will dawn upon us. For it to happen the ego has to be in abeyance, and in both mystical Christianity and in Buddhism, the transcendence of the conceptual world is, finally, always a gift. That is to say, it is not something we go after and find, but something which is given, something which is bestowed on us when we are ready for its reception. Christianity speaks of this as 'blessing' while Buddhism, especially Zen Buddhism, speaks of a 'ripening', like that of the apple ready to fall from the tree. When what is known as Jesus' 'kingdom' is understood, the rest of our lives will fall into place as he himself declares **(Mt. 6,33)**. We shall be properly and satisfactorily orientated to the rest of our life and also to others. In a word, we shall be 'integrated' as today's psychologists put it. This, too, is the meaning of being 'born again'.

Lin Chi concludes his admonitions by saying that when what he advocates finally dawns upon the seeker he or she will not have to 'believe' anymore since the whole thing will be as clear as day. Once having travelled a path, for example, we do not have to believe what a guide has told us; we know the way ourselves. Put the other way round: what you know you do not have to believe in and that, really, is all there is to the matter.

For the 'realists'

No doubt for many people reading this, the so-called mystical vision, is as remote as the possibility of life on another planet. On the other hand, our everyday life with which we are so familiar is in fact an expression of something which is not obvious to us and which we perhaps never suspect is there. The 'practical' individual experiences only the phenomenal expression of what, underlying, practical, everyday experience, we might call the Divine, or the Noumenal. All that which is derived from That-which-is-not, in other words, the existential proceeds from the Non-existential of which nothing can be said, but which, incredibly, can be nevertheless intuited by our 'normal' or everyday minds. That there is such a Mind behind the phenomena of our everyday life can be seen in all the things which we take so lightly for granted. Our bodies, for example, which we think we know so well function on a principle which has nothing whatsoever to do with our conceptual views of life. When we cut ourselves, the wound heals; when we eat, we digest what has been eaten; we breathe and are for the most part unconscious of the fact. Our heart pumps; our nerves react; our brain presents the exterior world to us and 'we' have nothing to do with all this, except on occasion to upset its function by unnatural habits of mind and body. Becoming aware, however, in a split second of egolessness or of what it is which is responsible for all this incredibly complicated yet concerted and coordinated activity is to awaken to ourselves and has no ecclesiastical overtones to it. The 'inward look' is just another wonder like all the activities alluded above and quite as real they are.

Theoretically, we need to realize that for 'That which is' there is also the counterpart 'that which is not'. That which exists must also have its corollary in non-existence. In this context we can say that we are all quite convinced that we exist. We tell ourselves that we can prove it by the effect we have on our environment, but we are not at all sure *who* is aware of his or her existence.

In this connection, a Taoist master, Hui, puts the matter in his own way:

> Perceiving the Buddhakaya means ceasing to perceive anything as existing or not existing…Existence is a term used in contradistinction to non-existence, while non-existence is used in opposition to existence. Unless one begins to accept the first concept as valid, the other cannot stand. Similarly, without the concept of non-existence, how can that of existence have any meaning? These two owe their being to mutual dependence and pertain to the realm of birth and death. It is just by avoiding such dual perceiving that we may come to behold the real Buddhakaya[7].

The realist refers always to the facts of our dualistic world. To do this he makes comparisons and draws logical conclusions which is, of course, extremely useful in managing our lives. What he generally does not appreciate, however, parallel with logical thought and ever present to the mind, is the faculty of insight.

In speaking of insight I am always moved to quote the experience of a child in this connection. Once again, it is an example taken from Raynor C. Johnson's book, *The Imprisoned Splendour* Because it is the experience of a child it lacks the depth and the wider significance of the adult in a similar way that a child's playing of a musical instrument may be technically faultless, but lack musical profundity. This is something which comes with later development of the mind and spirit, but the experience related here is nevertheless genuinely mystical.

> I must have been between five or six when this experience happened to me. It was a summer morning and the child I was had walked down through the orchard alone and come out on the brow of a sloping hill where there was grass and a wind blowing one tall tree reaching into immensities of blueness. Quite suddenly, after a moment of quietness there, earth and sky and tree and wind-blown grass and the child in the midst of them came alive together with a pulsating light of consciousness. There was a wild foxglove at the child's feet and a bee dozing about it, and to this day I can recall the swift inclusive awareness of each for the whole - I in them and they in me and all of us enclosed in a warm lucent bubble of livingness. I remember the child looking everywhere for the source of this happy wonder, and at last she questioned – 'God?' – because it was the only awesome word she knew. Deep inside, like the murmurous swinging of a bell, she heard the answer, 'God, God.' How long this ineffable moment lasted I never knew. It broke like a bubble at the sudden singing of a bird, and the wind blew and the world was the same as ever – only never quite the same. The experience so initiated has been the one abiding reality of my life,

unalterable except in the fullness and frequency of its occurrence.[8]

The author speaks of the 'inclusive awareness of each for the whole, I in them and they in me' which forcibly reminds us of Jesus' own words: 'I and my Father are one' (**Jn. 10, 30).**

The idea is also reflected in the reiteration of the phrase 'Son of Man' and in the phrase, '...the children of your Father which is in heaven' occurring in the New Testament, or, 'And are not two sparrows sold for a copper coin? And not one of them falls to the ground apart from your Father's will. But the very hairs of your head are all numbered' (**Mt. 10, 29–30).** Insight into the unity of life as it might be expressed today is at the heart of all religious experience and, in Christianity, man's relation to God, who is there thought of as a caring Father. This care is the central issue of both the Old and the New Testament. The very word, 'Father' naturally suggests a close relationship.

The common denominator

In the experience of insight illustrated above from various cultures of the world at different times in our human history, the understanding is always the same, although its description may vary. The Moslem will speak of Allah and naturally relate his understanding to his own frame of reference, the Christian will speak of God, the Hindu of Brahman and the Buddhist to the unitive experience of a long line of masters over the last 25 centuries. However, they are all in agreement about one thing and that is that they all acknowledge that the light of understanding floods the mind when the consciousness of 'I' has vanished. In that moment, then, there is no 'I see', but a 'seeing', not an 'I know', but a 'knowing'. There is, therefore, not two, but one. This is why Christian mystics have always referred to the experience as 'divine union'. Nonetheless, the term is one which conjures up the notion of extreme exclusiveness, of men or women, for example, shutting themselves up in cloisters or cells and sitting for months or even years in prayer. Added to this association is the thought of all kinds of penitential exercises ranging from a life of utter poverty bordering on starvation to all the repellent excesses of medieval self-immolation and self-castigation. Nothing could be further from the truth. Nothing in the life of Christ suggests that this is the means to a 'knowledge of God' or to 'self-knowledge' as we have come to call it. His teaching was in public, for the public, and his attitude throughout his ministry was that the love of God was available to every man and woman if they could believe this through his example. Buddhism, too, takes the view that austerities such as those alluded to above are 'vain and unprofitable'.

William Law (1686 - 1761), in speaking of salvation, says:

> In what does salvation consist? Not in the historic faith or knowledge of anything absent or distant, not in the variety of restraints, rules or methods of practising virtue, nor in any formality of opinion about faith or works, repentance, forgiveness of sins or justification and sanctification, nor in any truth or righteousness that you can have from yourself from the best of men and books, but solely and wholly from the life of God, or Christ of God, quickened and born again in you, in other words in the restoration and perfect union of the first twofold life in humanity.[9]

This is a very clear statement of the situation in Western, Christian terms and really says everything, but since we live in an only nominally Christian society, and because today we are fond of the logic and objectivity of the scientific view, we can also add the illustration of a modern author who sought to bring the insightful experience of 'being born again' to common terms. In doing so, he resorts to implacable logic to dissociate the insight as far as possible from its religious coloration. He takes logical implication to the point where the syllogism breaks down, and refers to the quoted excerpt below, *'Inconceivable for Thinking'* (III):[10]

The Space-Time subject-object phenomenal universe is a manifestation of mind, of which day and sleep dreaming are examples in a second degree. The result of this individualisation process, based on seriality, which all degrees of dreamers know as 'reality', has no objective resemblance to that which causes it to appear, because that which causes it to appear has no objective quality at all.

Therefore that is totally inaccessible to any form of objective cognition, let alone of description. The only words that can indicate it at all are This, Here, Now, and Am, and in a context which is entirely abstract.

...That wipes out everything objective and leaves an emptiness which represents fullness, total absence which represents total presence. Here the thinking (and not-thinking) process ends, and the absence itself of that is the Inconceivable.

Bringing this matter up to the present time and presenting it again in another way to the practically minded among us, we can say.

When I have looked at a jug I have supposed that eye-subject was looking at jug-object. But eye-subject is itself an object, and one object cannot be the subject of another object. Both eye-supposed-subject and the jug are objects of I-subject. But only when we realise that, in split mind, I-as-subject must always be itself an object while it also has its own supposed-object, do we understand that this constitutes an infinite regression, and that final transcendence is the understanding that I am not subject, for, since in reality there are no objects, there cannot be a subject.

No-objects and no-subject constitute impersonality, the resultant of the negation of each member of every pair of opposites, or No-Entity. Only whole mind can know this, and that is 'That I am'.[11]

Filling holes

And this, to round things off, is, once more, to 'be born again', since after the experience of 'looking into', the ego can never be in charge again. The state is one in which the experiencer is 'filled up' once and for all. It is to taste that water of which Jesus spoke while in conversation with the woman at the well **(Jn. 4)**. The existential human problem for which this is a solution has been satisfactorily summed up in a few words the author found penned on a scrap of paper which had been placed as a bookmark by someone staying in an ashram in India.

> Within you is a hole which you desperately try to fill. You stop up the hole with all kinds of satisfying things in order to feel good. Sometimes, if you can get enough of these things together, the hole is filled to the top and then you feel really happy for a time.
>
> But the hole is open at the bottom and the contents disappear bit by bit, so leaving you empty again and desperately looking for more to fill it up once more. There's only one thing you can do about this: You must throw yourself into the hole!

We will note that we have to do here with a situation in *this* life, not in any future life which we might imagine for ourselves. On the only occasion when Rabbi Jeshua speaks of the dead in answer to those who sought to know to whom a wife belonged after her several husbands had died, he said:

> He is not the God of the dead, but the God of the living. You are therefore greatly mistaken. **(Mk. 12,27)**

In another place he remarks: 'I have come that they may have life, and that they may have it more abundantly' **(Jn. 10,10)**. Here, he was not thinking of gratifying the senses or satisfying our worldly desires. He knew that these things were transient and are only a temporary task of 'hole-filling'. His 'more abundantly' signifies a wider horizon to our experience of life; he wishes his hearers to reach that point where they do not desire substitutes anymore. In this 'desirelessness' they *know* that which finally 'fills them up'. And they know that this erudition is 'not of this world' **(Jn. 8,31-3).**

In this connection, Jesus also speaks of a truth which makes one free:

> If you abide in my word, you are my disciples indeed. And you shall know the truth and the truth shall make you free. **(Jn. 8,31-32)**

Allowing ourselves to translate this sentence into modern idiomatic English again, it could read as follows:

> 'If you do as I ask, then you will really be my disciples,' or, simply: 'then you will understand things as I do.'

Since Rabbi Jeshua was very fond of direct, personal address which might have been closely related to Aramaic syntactical structure, or was a habit of speech in those times, or perhaps even a personal idiosyncrasy, he even goes as far as to say that 'unless you actually get inside me' you cannot understand what I mean. So he says,

> 'Whoever eats my flesh and drinks my blood has eternal life, I will raise him up at the last day.'

He goes on to stress the point:

> For my flesh is food indeed, and my blood is drink indeed./ He who eats my flesh and drinks my blood abides in me and I in him...This is the bread which came down from heaven – not as your fathers ate the manna, and are dead. He who eats this bread will live forever. **(Jn. 6, 55, 56 and 58)**

This was intractable stuff for those accompanying him. They considered it 'a hard saying' and complained about the terms used. Jesus justifies his position later, after hearing of their objections and says, 'It is the Spirit who gives life; the flesh profits nothing. The words that I speak to you are spirit and they are life.' And afterwards he adds by way of clarification, 'Therefore I have said to you that no one can come to me unless it has been granted to him by My Father.'

Quite clearly this has nothing to do with eating anybody. It may be that Jesus is making use of terms associated with religious animal sacrifice still employed in those days, but such an interpretation is less likely in view of the objections made to it by his followers. It has nothing to do either with 'transubstantiation' ritual of the Christian church. Jesus says quite distinctly that the words he speaks are 'spirit and life'. He means simply that if you can understand what he is talking about – and he is talking about the realisation of the self or 'everlasting life' – then that is equivalent to being on the same level as he is as far as apprehending his insight. He could have equally said: 'You will then know as I do, and you and I will be as one; there will be no difference at all in our understanding of things.'

The fact that one enlightened person understands another perfectly is a common acknowledgement in Buddhism and in other religions which know it as a phenomenon. Enlightened men and women also know who is not enlightened. This is definitely not to make any judgement of the latter, but merely to say that if a person has seen the spectacle of the Niagara Falls, let us say, he or she can share the knowledge with others who have been there and speak of the same details. If not, then the knowledge is only second hand.

Any other interpretation of the parable is indeed a 'hard saying' and also one of those bristling misinterpretations to which we have already alluded. Proof of the fact that Jesus was speaking of an intimate understanding which is 'nearer to us than the nose on our face' as Zen puts it is given elsewhere in religious literature. It is to be encountered in the writings of Meister Eckhart, for example, where the mystic speaks of 'his eye seeing with God's eye', and of God's eye seeing with his, and that the two are not different from each other. This oneness of vision is found in Zen Buddhism, too, as is shown in the commentary below.

Chao-chou's 'Mu' and its commentary

As we have seen, Chao-chou's answer to the enquirer as to whether there was the divine spark in the nature of a dog was a brusque 'No!' Thereafter the koan, 'Mu' (No!) was given to hundreds of thousands of seekers after the truth of their being. It was so effective that other, later great masters have commented on it. The following stems from Yün-mên (flourished 980-1052)

> Tell me, then, what is this blockade which Zen masters have set up (for seekers of truth)? It is exactly this 'Mu', that is the barrier. For this reason it is called the Gateless Gate. Those who can pass through (this barrier) will not only see Chao-chou clearly, but will go hand in hand with all the masters of the past and will see them face to face. You will be able to see with the same eyes that they see, and hear with same ears. Is that not a wonderful thing?

The commentator goes on to say, moreover, that to reach this end, everything we treasure as a mental concept must be abandoned. Every attachment must be thoroughly eradicated, even, he says, attachment to the Buddha who, if he gets in the way of our search, must be 'killed' with the sword of our endeavour. Total commitment to solving the *koan* (the search for God) is the absolute prerequisite for understanding. Jesus in the same context has this in mind when, turning to his disciples as the young man goes away to bury his father, says: 'No man, having put his hand to the plough, and looking back, is fit for the kingdom of God' **(Lk. 9, 62).**

Everlasting life

Two things will already be clear from the examples above that what Jesus meant by the term 'everlasting life' and the 'kingdom of God' are one and the same, and that both are a mental experience to be intuited and realised *in this life*, not in some inconceivable time and life after death. Since this intuition was the essential message of his teaching, it deserves further comment and illustration.

By 'everlasting' Jesus implies a 'life that cannot be destroyed'. Conversely, that which can be destroyed cannot last for ever. The term thus refers to That which sustains all life and which cannot be named or thought of as an object and can never die. It is pure Subjectivity as we have shown. Pure Subjectivity cannot be known as object, and yet it can nevertheless be understood by the human mind. It is, as we have said above, perhaps the greatest miracle of existence. This understanding may well have been known to other religions which have since ceded to those dominating the globe today. That is to say, intuitive understanding of our real nature is not the prerogative of any one group of people at any one time in history, but, on the contrary, that of all men at any time. Looked at rationally, we can see that it would be a very strange thing if this human intuitive faculty were reserved for the sole possession of Jews or Christians or Moslems or, for that matter, Buddhists. It is not so. The fact is that, in general, formal religious practice tends rather to obscure this inalienable truth of self realisation than promote it. There is among them all a fatal tendency which urges us to squander our precious time on the inessentials of formal observance and ritual, to concern ourselves primarily with the past, with what was said in days gone by and by whom, with the scripture of ordinance and command to support it all, and indeed with all the paraphernalia which constitutes the term 'religion'. None of them is concerned with the Now, either of this very minute of conscious existence, or of Jesus' Eternal Life, but quite the reverse: all of them preach their own fossilized theory which, apart from its ethical content, has largely proved to be useless during our human history in producing enlightened individuals and, tragically, continues to be wholly inadequate on all religious fronts as a means to promoting general spirituality.

On the other hand, the vision of Self-Nature, which is another description of 'Everlasting Life', will enable the perceiver to lead a much fuller life and at the same time be a useful blessing to his fellow men. So much has already been made clear. In conclusion, we might look at three examples given by Christ himself in order to discover what he means by the 'kingdom' and by 'everlasting life.'

Descriptions of the 'kingdom' and 'everlasting life'

Descriptions of the kingdom appear in **Matthew, 13** where many examples are given. These examples are rendered at different levels of understanding, a fact which the church has generally omitted to clarify during its history. The first in this gospel is that of The Sower and refers to distraction from the pursuit of the essential in life, that is, knowledge of God. The second (verse **24**) of the series is that of someone who plants a field with seed, but which is later spitefully scattered with weed by an enemy, and hence the 'tares' grow up with what he describes as the 'good seed'. This again is a warning to mankind of the distractions which surround us in life and which can put an end to our seeking for true understanding. Such distraction has always been with us in any age, but perhaps today it plays a more conspicuous role than in former times. He tells us that 'at the time of harvest', that is, at the time we die, the good and bad will be gathered up the bad cast into the oven to be burned and the good preserved. This does not mean that, at a final 'showdown' at some time in the nebulous future – a cherished belief common to all Christian denominations, despite its nebulousness – but, very practically and simply, our situation at death. It means that the good we have acquired will go on to be the basis of a new life and the 'tares', or that which has been useless in promoting our understanding of our true nature will be discharged as what the Buddha called 'unprofitable activity'. In other words, it will not be part of us, while the other, constructive part will be that element which we carry with us from one life to another until full realisation of ourselves is attained.

The third likeness **(Mt. 17, 20)**, this time on another level, suggests that enlightenment is like a mustard seed, indeed is the least of all seeds, but when it is grown it is greater than the herbs and becomes a tree so that the 'birds of the air come and nest in its branches.' Here, Jesus is referring to the phenomenon known as 'deepening' in Buddhism. It refers to the ever greater deepening of spiritual insight as time goes by. Sometimes this phenomenon is referred to in both Christianity and Buddhism as 'powers' following upon great enlightenment.

Returning for a moment to our stereogram or hologram picture we might, for example, come to notice more as we look into it. In the same way, some people come to see more and more the longer they look into deep water. It is the same with the mind. The deeper the enlightenment, the more is understood about the nature of our existence. This 'deepened awareness', as it is called, continues to grow in the enlightened person from 'kensho' (shallow understanding) to 'satori' (deep awakening). The depth of awakening may express itself in many ways, depending on the inner propensities of the person affected. It may manifest itself in the ability to heal, for example, as in the case of Christ, or it may be an ability to speak languages which have never been studied **(Acts 2, 4),** or the ability acquired by some samurai of being immune to attack, or it may be the power of bringing others quickly to enlightenment as in the case of many Indian sages, a notable recent case being that of Sri Ramana Maharshi in the last century, or the ability to do remarkable things such as understanding other people's private thoughts or desires **(Mt. 9,4)** or turning up in other places, often hundreds of miles away[12], most of which powers Jesus himself displays on occasion. We are told that the apostles and some of the disciples of Jesus were also endowed with these powers, both before and after Pentecost, **(12).** The fact is that once grasped by the intuitive mind, the knowledge of the Buddhist's 'other shore' and its potential, or what Jesus called the 'kingdom', increases to reveal many things formerly unsuspected by the receiver. What follows is an example of this 'growth' or deeper perception.

The example is taken from the enlightenment experience of a young Japanese girl who was a pupil of the late Zen master, Harada Roshi (died 1961). The full account is to be read in Philip Kapleau's book *The Three Pillars of Zen,* published some thirty years ago in the United States.[13]

Since she is confined at home by illness, the young woman writes to her teacher of the good news of her having attained *satori*. The excerpt here is considerably abbreviated but without misrepresenting the central issue. She says:

> Today for the first time I have attained great enlightenment. I am so overjoyed that all of me is dancing in spite of myself. No one but you can possibly understand such ecstasy... From the bottom of my heart I thank you and raise my hands in gassho(gesture of reverence and respect) to you. Buddhas and patriarchs haven't deceived me! The absolute truth of every word of the patriarchs and the sutras has appeared before my eyes with crystal clarity. Those who have only kensho do not know this state of unlimited freedom and profound peace. (My brackets)

Here, her Master makes the following comment:

> Now for the first time you have found the Way – fully realized your Mind. You have been delivered from delusion, which has no abiding root. Wonderful! Wonderful!

A day or so later she writes again to her master from her sickbed to announce:

> But now I have penetrated deeply and have acquired an unshakable aspiration to Buddhahood, it is clear to me that I can continue my spiritual discipline forever and in this way perfect my personality to its fullest, impelled by the Vow which rises naturally within me, to save all sentient beings.

To this the master says: 'I am overcome with tears.'

In the general comment to this exchange which took place in 1935, we read that this deepening usually takes between five and ten years, and is referred to in Buddhism as the 'wisdom of subtle and immaculate perception', or 'subsequently attained wisdom', and is the growth in wisdom referred to by Jesus. He touches again on this expansion of perception in a short reference immediately afterwards when he speaks of the kingdom of heaven as that which is 'like leaven, which a woman took and hid in three measures of meal till it was all leavened' **(Mt. 13,33).**

The next reference a little later is again on a different level. He speaks of the world as a 'field' in which the good seeds of wisdom are sown, 'the sons of the kingdom'. They represent the good in our world and that which is weed are the tares which come and choke the wisdom of man. Finally, there will be a time of reckoning when the wheat will be divided from the chaff. This will be the triumph of virtue when the 'righteous will shine forth as the sun in the kingdom of their Father. He that hath ears to hear, let him hear' **(Mt. 13,38-43).** The mood here is one of admonition with, perhaps, a tinge of prophecy. We do not know what kind of a 'multitude' he had before him, nor what their mood was on this occasion. We may not either assume that all that which appears in this chapter in Mathew happened serially. The difference in character between the parables and examples pointed out so far, together with those references which immediately follow this parable do not suggest a sequence. These things are brought to our attention in order to obviate the mistake made by his later interpreters that at this point we have grounds to instil fear into those who submit themselves to Christian teaching. Jesus' message to mankind was not education in fear, but, quite the contrary, instruction in how to love one another. It is difficult to imagine, for example, a man of his spiritual stature, together with his Father, enjoying the spectacle of people being thrown into the flames of damnation. Who would benefit from such iniquity? Would such a spectacle add one cubit to the honour of the Almighty? And what would be the point of this exhibition? The triumph of good over evil where the 'sons of the kingdom' have opportunity to gloat for an eternity over their less fortunate brethren? At the heart of such an interpretation is the stink of egotistic self-justification. Was this what Christ wished to convey? Despite the fact that the infamous Church which bears his name has, over the centuries, enjoined this view to consolidate its power and even resorted to its literal interpretation by actually burning people alive in various parts of Europe in the past, especially in Spain of the 15th and 16th centuries. Only a fanatical and barbarous minority could support such a view today. In the 21st century, by far the greater majority of people would dismiss such an attitude as repugnant, regardless of its source and this, to a degree, is a measure of our spiritual advancement.

What, then, did Jesus mean by his comparison? He meant quite simply that we should assess our priorities in this life while the going's good. After this life, the chances for rectifying things might not be so propitious. This is also the Buddhist view.

We should not forget as we read that Jesus' remarks always issue from that larger dimension of mind which we might refer to as the nirvanic. His every movement and his every utterance proceeds from that dimension. The world of nirvana was more, or just as, real to him as our mundane lives are to us. This fact should not be overlooked, and bears repetition. His warning to those who heard him on this occasion was that we should not allow ourselves to be overrun by what the strait-jacketed religionists of the 19th century referred to as 'the temptations of this wicked world', but which anyone with a little spiritual discrimination can recognize as those activities and attachments which do not lead directly to either enlightenment or long-lasting personal happiness. The Buddhist here speaks of those things which are part of the delusion of existence generally alluded to as *maya*.

How hard to break through
Is this, my maya
Made of the gunas
But he takes refuge in me only
Shall pass beyond maya
He and no other.

Lord Krishna is speaking here in the Bhagavad Gita and the sentiment is the same as that occurring in the New Testament in the parable of The Sower. He goes on:

Among those who are purified by good deeds, there are four kinds of men who worship me: the world-weary, the seeker for knowledge, the seeker for happiness and the man of spiritual discrimination. The man of discrimination is the highest of these.[14]

Maya is the realm of delusion, the state referred to above as that which captures our imagination and leads our minds astray like children watching a magician. As adults, we are enticed by its apparent promise of fulfilment, only to find sooner or later that these do not materialize. We are disappointed and so seek elsewhere and may spend a lifetime in such a search. These are the 'seekers for happiness' to which category most of us belong. In age we may well become 'world-weary' and our lives may even become bitter as a result. The moods of life (the *gunas,* or moods, referred in the stanza above) have left us frustrated and alone with our disappointment. In retrospect, the realisation that it was 'all for nothing', and that life itself will soon be at an end can be appalling. Hence the emotion in Jesus' utterance and the strength of his comparison.

Others may well spend their lives looking for that knowledge which will release them from the 'play of light and dark', those delusive forces which can be said to operate in creating the illusion we know as life. Their efforts may lead them to discover it in themselves through meditation, or it may not, but at least an effort has been made in the right direction. At death we will come to realise, Jesus asserts, that what we have spent our precious energy for has largely been in the pursuit of the evanescent and the unprofitable. We have missed the point of life and perhaps can only see at that moment where we have erred. However, in spite of this late recognition, the processes of life and death go on their inexorable way; we die and know not where or how we will be reborn. As the Japanese girl Yaeko above says shortly before her death a week or so later, we may spend aeons in other lives before we once more find the Way in human form which leads to liberation. So serious is our situation. It is in this sense that the 'tares' of his parable (like the 'chaff' of other comparisons) will be of no account then in our helplessness. Like chaff, it will be completely useless to us once we find ourselves after death in the process of transformation from one life to another. To deal with this situation, the sufferer desperately needs a source of energy and awareness derived from practice and accumulation in the living state. The great spiritual masters down the ages have drawn the attention of the living to the tragic condition of those who, at death, are quite powerless to determine their fate at this time. The poet, Shakespeare, dramatically renders this anticipation in his own words:

> Ay, but to die, and go we know not where
> To lie in cold obstruction and to rot;
> This sensible warm motion to become
> A kneaded clod;...
> To be imprison'd in the viewless winds,
> And blown with restless violence round about
> The pendant world;... Measure for Measure, Act III

This state of affairs is something Jesus constantly refers to, and indeed orientates his life to this last state, going as far as to prove later to those who followed him that it was possible to return to our waking life as a recognisable spiritual entity.

At **Mt. 13**, verse **44**, Rabbi Jeshua speaks again of the kingdom of heaven:

> Again, the kingdom of heaven is like a treasure hidden in a field, which a man found and hid; and for joy over it he goes and sells all that he has and buys that field.

Here again, the matter of setting priorities is alluded to and needs no further comment.

The wise and foolish virgins

The two other comparisons which follow this in the chapter, the merchant and his pearl, and the fishermen's dragnet with their catch of fish are similar in character to those dealt with above. A little earlier, however, at **Matthew 25, 1,** we come across the parable of the Wise and Foolish Virgins which also deserves commentary.

We are told that there are five wise and the five foolish virgins who are to attend a wedding. Five of them took oil for their lamps and the other half failed to do so. The bridegroom surprises them at midnight when they are already asleep with the result that those who had not taken the trouble to buy oil for their lights are embarrassed. In view of this situation, they seek to borrow oil from those who have some in their lamps, but are inhospitably persuaded to go and buy their own. While they are away on this errand, the bridegroom enters his chamber and we are told that the door is shut against them when they return to join in the celebrations.

To all intents and purposes, this appears to be an unpleasant story whose principal feature is a lack of compromise. If half the women's lamps were full, then a certain amount could have been shared by the others who were not so provident as to fill their lamps beforehand. We might safely assume that they knew each other well enough to offer such elementary assistance. This, however, is not so. They are told by the others to go out and buy oil in the middle of the night! A hard-hearted story with unlikely overtones, we say. In the first place, is it not extremely unusual for a man to marry in the early hours of the morning, and in the second to shut the door so resolutely against guests who, we can also assume, had the right to be there since they had been invited. The story, we feel is disenchanting, and we ask what this boorishness could mean.

Indifference

The meaning is simple. If a person shows no interest in this life in acquiring what we might call a 'spiritual perspective', how can he or she expect the benefits which derive from it? If we do not plant, how can we ever expect to harvest? Jesus refers to this issue elsewhere in another key, so to speak, when he proclaims that there will be many who come to him and say, 'Lord, Lord!' and he will turn them away, saying, 'Verily I say unto you, I know you not'**(Mt. 25,12)**.

The theme of indifference to God is referred to many times throughout the Gospels and it is clear from its faithful recording that it played a very important part in Jesus' ministry. Total indifference on the part of others to That which is at the core of our being could bring him to white heat. This is most clearly exhibited in the stunning parable occurring at **Mt. 22, 1-14** where, again speaking of the kingdom of heaven, he speaks of a king about to celebrate the wedding of his son and sends out servants to invite certain of his subjects to the wedding. However, there was no interest and so many stayed away. They 'made light of it and went their ways, one to his farm, and another to his business. The rest seized his servants, treated them spitefully, and killed them.' This made the king furious and he sent out his armies, revenged himself on the murderers and burned their city to the ground. This is probably a reference to the historical fate of Israel's prophets, a theme Jesus touches upon on a number of occasions in his clashes with the religious order of his day. The king then decides to invite others to the wedding and asked his servants to go into the 'highways' and gather 'all whom they found, both bad and good' in order to fill the wedding hall. One man, however, appears without a wedding garment, and upon being asked by the king why this is so, finds that the man cannot give him an answer. The king then orders this hapless individual to be bound hand and foot and cast into 'outer darkness' where there will be 'weeping and gnashing of teeth'. 'For many are called, but few are chosen,' Jesus concludes predictively.

The appearance of the man without a garment, that is to say, an individual who is there at the feast to 'get what he can out of it' and who cannot even formally acknowledge his host by wearing the garment appropriate to the occasion is an insult to royal generosity and is dealt with accordingly. This is what we might call 'active indifference' to God, a deliberate offence to the Power which sustains us in the world, and a wilful concern with that which is transient and worldly. It is a conscious choice, a premeditated denial of the love of God, an intentional snub. We may note here that Jesus refers in verse 5 to the preoccupations preferred in this case as alternatives by those asked to the wedding, the 'farm' and the 'business'. This kind of pan-faced insolence is most clearly shown in the example by those who cheerfully use the temple premises for trading purposes which incited the Master to rage **(Mt. 21,12 and Mk. 11, 15).**

Our mundane interests and our intense concern with self are for the most part at the centre of our lives. In general, Man has no time for an abstraction called God, although without the Unmanifest we speak of there would be nothing which could be manifested, including our precious selves. This unawareness often becomes an insensitiveness which is then no longer ignorance, but contemptuous disregard for the Source of things within us and, consequently, for others. It can be seen playing a role in every generation.

In illustration of this we could think perhaps of the early English capitalists who were quite content to grind the last ounce of work from their employees, allowing them none of the rights they accorded themselves of proper sleep and nourishment, relaxation, support when sick, pauses during work or even a commensurate wage for their labour compared with their own. How could such an individual qualify for greater spiritual development of any kind? Perhaps this is an extreme example, but if we look at ourselves today we can readily see that we do not have to behave like 19th century industrial dictators to be ineligible for spiritual illumination. All we need to do is to comply with what the advertisements are constantly telling us to do: have a good time; consume; buy; indulge the senses and the acquisitive instincts and, indirectly drain the earth of its resources. Or we can adopt the values we find implicit in some films and in much which is transmitted to us via TV. We can, if provoked, kill and maim if it suits our selfish desire, get on in the world at all costs, become rich if possible, or even powerful, make profit before any other consideration, exploit others and other living things, situations, materials and entertain the mind night and day, fill it with all the world's troubles, great and small, share the horror of every day's news and this will be enough to keep us from making any spiritual progress.

While it is true that in Jesus' time everyday life was on what we would now call a 'low profile' compared with the welter of distraction available to us today, there was nevertheless plenty of opportunity for attachment. There was attachment to tradition as we have seen and to political and social issues. In Jesus' retinue there were at least two people who were involved in political activity, Judas Iscariot, to judge from his name, wore a dagger (L. scari). This is a more likely translation, we suggest, than 'of the towns' in the Hebrew. Another carried a sword sharp enough sword to cut off the ear of a manservant at Jesus' arrest in the garden of Gethsemane **(Mk. 14,47),** and we read of 'Simon, also called Zelotes' in **Lk. 6, 15** and of the 'sons of thunder' at **Mk. 3, 17.** The evergreens of money, power and influence and personal wel -being were major preoccupations in those days, too, and are mentioned by Christ on a number of occasions throughout the Gospels. In laying up treasures of this kind, mental and material, it is very easy to deny ourselves the opportunity of growing up at all, let alone in self-knowledge. It is we who shut the door upon our spirituality, for either we provide a little oil for our spiritual growth or we do not, thus the severity of the parable.

False interpretations

The parable concludes with the words: 'Watch, therefore, for you know neither the day nor the hour in which the Son of Man is coming.'

This remark, appearing at the end of the parable, apparently clinches the interpretation the story has enjoyed for twenty centuries, that is, of interpreting the Son of Man as the bridegroom of the anecdote and mankind as those who sit and wait, prepared to enter the feast of God. In other words, humanity is waiting for Jesus to reappear to Man, which may occur at any time in history and in our lives. This is the traditional, ecclesiastical view. But the fact is that such a manifestation has not taken place even after two thousand years and that, in view of this, such an event is not very likely. As we grow in knowledge and power – and we certainly have done so in the last four to five hundred years – we are less likely to be taken in by such jejune ideas. The concept of an angry god that shall come to judge us at some predestined, human time in human history and condemn us for a life which, for most of humanity, is hazardous, difficult and short and, more frequently than not, fraught with hardship and suffering is an outrageous imposition. Moreover, how shall such a god adversely judge what, after all, is his own creation?

Those who can think at all will have long since asked themselves these questions and come to their own conclusions. Moreover, such a god is inconsistent with Jesus' attitude to his fellow man during his short ministry, which, for the most part, was characterized by kindness and understanding. He himself says that he is come not to judge **(Jn. 12,47; Lk. 6,37)**. He speaks of the forgiveness of enemies, shows tolerance **(Jn. 8,11)** forgives others, heals the sick, raises the dead, shows humour and compassion **(Mk. 6.4 and 9,37).** These attitudes ('for those who have seen me have seen the Father') **(Jn. 6, 64)** go evilly with the idea of a vengeful god calling the chosen few to everlasting joy and throwing the rest of humanity into everlasting fire. Only a monster, we say, could derive satisfaction from such activity. In addition to this, it is a massive contradiction of all that which we find in the New Testament in terms of Christ's dictates and behaviour and an offence to all those who can feel even in the slightest degree. This is the savage, primitive god of the totem pole and the human sacrifice.

In view of these few considerations, there are two lines of thought available to us for exploration in order to understand the parable and its implications. Either we accept the fantasy in spite of our knowledge and experience, or we assume that Jesus meant something else.

If the latter applies to us, then we may further reasonably assume that he had something concrete in mind as opposed to the fantasies above, something moreover which can be substantiated by other spiritual sources at other times which is the yardstick of our analysis in this essay. His remarks, when properly understood, all conform with other, universal spiritual knowledge. If this were not the case, we would be at liberty to dismiss the anecdote as having little or no value.

What does the remark about his coming mean? Did he mean, for example, 'Be vigilant, for you never know the time of death, when this shall come and pluck you away from the living.'? Perhaps. Although, to a better informed generation than that of the Middle Ages, this seems a poor substitute for advice on living our lives. Did this attitude which was so ardently believed in by that age all over Europe produce a better humanity, or more enlightened minority, or in the slightest anticipate Judgement Day? Looking back at those who practised such denial of life, we have to ask ourselves whether they were not wasting their time or killing life at its core.

If, however, Rabbi Jeshua, in citing the women of the parable of the Wise and Foolish Virgins, was speaking of *a state of mind* and not of some time after the death of the body, then his words again immediately assume unsuspected significance. In his admonition to 'watch', we realize that he could only be referring us to 'watch' the movements of our own minds or 'to stay alert' to its antics. What else would there be to 'watch' in this sense? He knew that if we do not remain conscious of what goes on in our minds, we have no control over our thoughts. And where there is no control, we easily fall under the influence of outer and inner stimuli (*maya*) and our minds become like vessels at sea without sail or rudder.

This fact is also known to Christians through the spiritual awareness brought about by the practice of prayer. The mind is sharpened to a point where the activities of daily life also come under the influence of a heightened awareness. Buddhism speaks of this as 'reining the mind', in Zen as 'taming the mad mind' and in the advanced states of meditation, of 'bringing about one-pointedness.'

> A meditator who is really determined to escape the round of births and deaths should realize that because of the ceaseless flow of his thoughts he is unable to put an end to samsara. If he really wishes to put an end to it, he must lay down all his feelings and thoughts again and again until he is entirely rid of them. (Zen Master, Han Shan, 1546-1623)

> All you need to remember are the following injunctions: First, learn how to be entirely unreceptive to sensations arising from external forms... Second, learn not to pay attention to any distinctions between this and that arising from your sensations, thus purging your bodies of useless discernments between one phenomenon and another. Third, take great care to avoid discriminating in terms of pleasant and unpleasant sensations...and fourth, avoid pondering things in your mind,

thereby purging your bodies of discriminatory cognition.
(Zen Master Huang Po, died 788)

This is the one type of awareness, the type which looks unflinchingly into the mind and refuses to be deflected by anything arising from within or without. All the four injunctions of the last quotation amount to one thing: look dispassionately at what is going on in the mind. In another place in the same book (p. 131), the master says, 'Do not permit the events of your daily lives to bind you, but never withdraw yourselves from them. Only by acting thus can you earn the title of "A Liberated One".'

Now this does not mean that we become zanies or automatons as might quickly be assumed by western minds which are immersed in the other extreme – over-stimulation – for most of the time. It simply means 'being on top' instead of in the subordinate position of being slaves to our thoughts and emotions. Zen is a radical method of achieving freedom, but a rapid one if practised properly. There are, however, other methods of being aware which harness what has been called 'heart power' or what we have referred to above as *bhakti*. A modern incarnation of the divine, in replying to a confused questioner, advocates the following:

(Questioner): 'Swami, can I even when I have no particular aim in life think of becoming one with God? I'm not really sure what this means.'

(Sri Bala): 'If you're without a goal, then decide now to always contemplate God's name. Say to yourself: 'I must never forget Him.'[15]

Thomas of Kempen, the 14th century recluse, speaks of watchfulness in the sense demonstrated above in his famous book, *The Imitation of Christ:*

Be watchful and diligent in the service of God; and often bethink thyself wherefore thou camest hither: and why thou hast left the world.'[16]

And again in this sense from quite another quarter:

> At all times, instant after instant, you should purify your minds, practise self-cultivation...perceive the Buddha within yourselves and bring about self-liberation. Hui Neng, Sixth Patriarch of Zen (born AD 638)

Without awareness there is the inevitable relapse into the associative thought-stream which takes us where it will. To be aware of what is going on in the mind is to realize a raised state of consciousness and so gain a degree of control over our reactions.

This, it is suggested, is much more akin to Jesus' meaning of being aware, of watching. It is not mere watching and waiting for death which would be foolish, but of being prepared for any event which confronts us in life, not only and exclusively the major situation of imminent death. The Church and Christians in general have always assumed that the kingdom of heaven is an after-life experience and so taken the parable of the Seed and the Tares to heart in this sense. So it is that this parable and others like it **(Mt. 13, 37–43)** have gained an advantage over other comparisons which Christ drew on the subject, either because they could not be satisfactorily aligned with the other parables or because they were not understood.

The 'Mustard Seed' parable, for example, occurring in Matthew and referred to above, which also pertains to the kingdom of heaven, apparently does not concern the after-death experience, but to life proper. Nor, for that matter, the parable following it depicting the woman and her leaven which occupies a place with the 'Mustard Seed' anecdote. The conjunction might be entirely a matter of coincidence, but it might also be a resort to counterbalancing descriptions of the kingdom of heaven to demonstrate that the kingdom relates to this life.

The parable of the Tares means that we should bend our minds to return to the Source by being aware of This in action within ourselves and not, on the other hand, being 'scattered abroad' by every thought and whim, every worldly distraction – in short by anything which is part of the illusion of samsara.

This is the essential meaning of 'integration' which we have referred to elsewhere. With regular, single-minded practice of awareness in this sense, general awareness is increased to the point where it becomes integrated into the personality. From that time on one is truly liberated and can act freely; one is no longer at the mercy of subconscious dictates. This process has been described as a drawing out of the last section of a 'mental telescope', an imagined three-stage structure where the first is the instinctive system common to all creatures, which responds to stimuli, feeds and excretes, reproduces, deteriorates and dies; the second is the structure of a mind capable of reacting in more complicated ways to the changing environment around it, from the very simple reaction to pain to the very complicated synapses in the human brain, and finally, the last segment which is the spiritual development of the human being as outlined above. In man's case, the first two have long been highly developed systems, whereas the third is still in a primitive state of development.

From time to time we come across Christian mystics who are also conscious of this larger state of awareness. Boethius, for example, adumbrates the lack of awareness of our true natures and, in speaking of ignorance, says:

In other living creatures ignorance of self is nature; in man it is vice.

Without awareness in this sense there is an inevitable falling back into the associative thought-stream which takes us where it will. To be aware of what is going on in the mind is to realize a raised state of consciousness and so gain a degree of control over our reactions. This is freedom indeed

The parable of the talents

The Gospel of St Matthew contains another parable in which Christ speaks of a man who travels into a far country, but before he does so he gives his servants money (the talents) to use wisely in his absence, 'each according to his own ability' **(Mt. 25, 14)**. This man of property entrusts three of his servants with a certain amount of money. The first receives five talents, the second two and the third only one. He then leaves on his journey. When he returns he is told by the first servant that he has earned a further five talents, making ten in all and the second also doubles the amount given to him, but the last who only received one talent, has nothing more than that given him originally. Although the man returns the money given to him, his lord is angry and complains that, had he given this to the bankers, he would have at least received interest on his sum. Summarily, he then commands that this one talent be confiscated and be given to the man that has made ten talents with the uncharitable observation that,

> For to everyone who has, more will be given, and he will have abundance; but from him who does not have, even what he has will be taken away./ And cast the unprofitable servant into outer darkness. / There will be weeping and gnashing of teeth. **(verses 29–30)**

Like other parables in Christ's repertoire, this, too, has a certain harshness, a hard, uncompromising core. Why, we ask ourselves, should the one 'unprofitable' servant be cast into 'outer darkness' where there will be 'weeping and gnashing of teeth?' Why such formidable punishment for a lack of commercial enterprise? Why the terrible anger of the master on his return, especially in view of the fact that the servant was honest enough to give back what had been entrusted to him? We will recall that he is rounded upon by the master of the house on his return and upbraided as 'wicked and lazy'. Lazy he might have been, and as he himself admits, he was afraid, but wicked? It is clear from the general tone of the parable that the issue is a pretty serious one, and reading it for the first time leaves us with the conviction that an injustice has been done. We have little understanding of the master's motives and our sympathies may well be with the servant.

The probable interpretation, it is suggested, is that, again, there is a skulking denial on our part of the divine within us and, as a consequence, a leaning for other, lesser substitutes during a lifetime. Since it requires effort to be aware of That which is not manifest to the senses and to remind ourselves of the fact that it is this which supports our life and everything else which is manifest to our understanding, we tend all too humanly to dismiss the idea and content ourselves with something – anything – which, of necessity, will be inferior.

We are glad to forget the former (to hide it in the ground) and grasp the latter for some kind of distraction – hence the word 'laziness' in the parable. Jesus, recognizing God in his own tradition as an entity with human attributes, accords Him angry disappointment at this situation. From the divine point of view, it is an example of contemptuous lack of recognition.

The Buddhist would say that there is no inclination on the part of an individual towards trying to recognize his own self-nature. As a consequence, the dispassionate laws of karmic cause and effect operate in any case to bring the individual back to birth at exactly that spiritual potential where he left it at death. He then has another chance, if he is lucky enough to be born as a human, to do something about it. But, the canon adds, there is also the danger of passing into a lower level than the human (i.e. of losing his talent altogether) and from there it may take aeons to break out into human potentiality again. Like Jesus, the advanced Buddhist regards this as a very serious situation and deeply regrettable if the cause of indifference is pure laziness. The possibility of losing our latent ability to become enlightened can take place on levels at which we are no longer in charge of the situation. These may include sudden death, or in situations where the early stages of self-cultivation are impossible, for example, in a country or community which is actively hostile to this line of thought and activity (in a former communist state, for example, or in a country which is either religiously intolerant or whose religion is incapable of embracing anything else but its own views) or in a situation where the hard work involved in survival might be so great as to preclude all other than this one activity and those of eating and sleeping. Lack of education (i.e. not coming into contact with people who may act as inspiration or even be guides towards spiritual understanding) can constitute a cause, physical or mental illness, accident – all of which may incapacitate us and, added to all these, the cares and the usual vicissitudes which assail human life to which Christ occasionally refers both in the parables and elsewhere **(Lk. 12,23 ff; Mk. 13,8),** Realising these things, part of his mission was therefore devoted to healing the sick. It is difficult when one is plagued by pain and incapacity to aspire to higher levels of consciousness.

Indeed, the possibility of our feet being placed on the road to self-realisation is in any case slim, and the much larger possibility or our slipping back into a state of nescience is always present until we have realised for ourselves what we are. Hence, the comparison of the 'broad way' which leads to destruction (of the potential) and the 'narrow path' **(Mt. 7,14)** which requires conscious cultivation of awareness as in the acquisition of any skill. Hence, without conscious attention, even the loss of that which might have provided a basis for further development can occur, like the seed which puts forth a tendril, but which later perishes for lack of nourishment.

To conclude, one other thing should be added here which justifies the wrath of the householder on his return. Jesus' deep enlightenment allows him a keen awareness of the seriousness of the circumstances. In Buddhism we speak of the great good fortune of being born human, since to be born human (among the many millions of other possibilities of coming into the world in other forms) allows us, the inheritors of human form, to step into the light of self-knowledge, whereas other forms do not afford their possessor that privilege. One thinks here of all other forms of terrestrial life, of (according to Buddhism), the denizens of hell, and those in what Christianity would refer to as purgatory, but also, surprisingly enough in that cosmology, those who enjoy (temporary) fulfilled joy in heaven. This state, however, denies them the inspiration to be wholly free of the samsaric system. Even so.

Violent death

In passing, it might be of interest to pause and consider the report of an individual who, in September, 1964, was involved in a serious motor accident in Switzerland. He was so badly injured that it was assumed at the time that he would not survive. His heart had stopped beating for nearly six minutes. He was nevertheless given resuscitation and miraculously returned to life.

The virtual death experience of those 5–6 minutes changed his outlook on life and death radically.

The author of the book recounting the experience had been brought up in a strict Catholic atmosphere and had naturally acquired the traditional view of that religion and that after death there would be a fearful reckoning. In the book he describes his new view of the world and says that he was surprised to learn that at that 'time of reckoning' the bad that had affected his life had fallen away like the 'chaff' of the parable and that only the good, the positive and happiness of life (the grain of Christ's parable) remained important.

> The second remarkable phenomenon was that according to this absolute standard of judgement those things which are judged as negative thoughts and deeds were completely extinguished in the judgement. The only things which were left to me were those scenes in which everyone involved was happy; where there was happiness not only in me personally,

but where harmony dominated in the whole of my environment and where all those taking part were positive towards what I had done.

I believe this to be a characteristic of God Himself, that is, total love: forgiveness through pure goodness and an infinite positiveness...we must free our consciousness once and for all from our karma and unite ourselves with Him ...and return to the unending Ocean which is God and there dissolve.[17]

We can assume that he speaks from direct experience when he maintains that...

Death does not involve a change of personality, since the personality is not bound to the mortality of the body. For the I-Consciousness only the means of understanding are changed and new dimensions are opened in the realm of non-material existence. (Ibid. p. 81)

The point about making every effort 'to put God at the centre of our lives' as the Christian would say is so very important that, if we can rely on the sequence of the narrative as correct, Jesus goes on to speak of an eventual Judgement Day where the 'sheep' will be on God's right hand and the 'goats' **(Mt. 25,33ff)** on the left and where the good shall 'inherit the kingdom prepared for you from the foundation of the world.' At that time He will ask whether compassion has been shown to others during a lifetime, to those others of our ken who hunger and thirst, to those who are poor (naked) and to those in prison, since these actions are the expressions of the divine in us. Whatever compassion is shown to them is also an acknowledgement of the Father for '...inasmuch as you did it to one of the least of my brethren, you did it to me.' Again, the rhetoric and the tone of this passage produce a clear and uncompromising message. It is a further illustration of the second great commandment, 'Thou shalt love thy neighbour as thyself.' How this is effected in daily life is illustrated in the parable of The Good Samaritan.

Buddhism enjoins this principle, seen as an inexorable process, and Buddhists vow to liberate 'all sentient beings' from the bondage of samsara, where compassion, tolerance and loving kindness are also an inseparable part of its teaching. Both before and after enlightenment, Buddhists are expected to act in a way which is conducive to the happiness and well-being of others, recognizing that we are all of the 'same substance' or, to put it another way, 'I' and 'the other' are both expressions of That which eternally IS.

There is only one small difference between Christian and Buddhist teaching here, and that is that after enlightenment, true compassion follows automatically; it is impossible to be enlightened about your own nature and then seek to harm others for an ego which is now seen quite clearly to no longer exist.

The question remains, however, exactly how to achieve the state of enlightenment. In this connection, even if Jesus was clear in stating the need for attaining the state, he was not as explicit as the Buddhist texts are. After all, there were only three years of Christian ministry in comparison with some forty in Buddhism. In the course of nearly half a century a lot more can be recorded by many more people and the recorded texts can be compared with one another in attempting to discover the truth which underlines them. Then, too, there is the individual experience of those who have come to enlightenment and who can give testimony themselves of its efficacy. Even in the Buddha's time there were many such enlightened masters who were able to lead others to the same state, among them the Buddha's contemporaries, Ananda, Sariputra and Subhuti. The socio-political ambience of the Buddha's time, moreover, and the locality in which he lived were also favourable to the reception and exchange of religious experience, whereas, as we have seen, this was not the case in Palestine two thousand years ago.

It is hoped that from all that has been quoted above that the illumination which Jeshua spoke of as the 'kingdom of heaven' is not an after-life abstraction, but a living reality. What happens after death is generally something over which we have no control but is, if we are to believe the attested information coming to us from those who have experienced 'clinical death' in recent times, closely associated with our thoughts and actions during life. Moreover, the kind of experience we have then is very largely determined by our general psychological level of aspiration during that life. As we have sown, so will we reap (**Gal. 6,7**). This is explicit not only in the gospel of Christianity, but also that of Buddhism in its teaching of karma. What is important, however, is not only the level of our ethical conduct towards the world we live in (not exclusively towards people, but also towards other living creatures, and even plants and inanimate objects) but, just as importantly, our level of aspiration for that which is neither sensual nor material. It has to do with our aspiration for illumination or with our desire to know something of the Self beyond the usual wants and attachments of samsaric life which clamour so insistently and incessantly for our attention. It is important because this is the one prerogative we can exercise to halt the process of rebirth.

> Two paths have existed since the world began, the bright and the dark. The one leads to a place of no return. The other back to this world of change and human birth.[18]

> At the hour of death, when a man leaves his body, he must depart with his consciousness absorbed in me. Thus, he will be united with me. Whatever he remembers before his departure will be realized by him thereafter. That which he has constantly dwelt on during his life is what he will go to. The ancestor worshippers will go to their ancestors; the deity worshippers will go to their deities and the worshippers of elemental powers and spirits will go to them. So, also, will my devotees come to me (.Ibid., The Yoga of Mysticism,)

The 'ground swell' of the parables

The current underlying the parables and that of Jesus' teaching in general is not guidance towards an 'after-life', to a 'resurrection' in another, heavenly world after death, I repeat, nor a recommendation of 'Christ as our Saviour' as intermediary between God and Man, nor the forgiveness of sin, nor a warning against the dangers of hell, nor even a promise of better times to come as one of an elect that shall sit on the right hand of God the Father Almighty for ever and ever when our 'sins' will be washed away in the 'blood of Christ.' It is none of these things. All this is, in any case, difficult to digest and, if we are honest with ourselves, we can recognize it as a doctrine which does violence to our common sense. What Jesus taught was simply and only a regulation of priorities. Rendered in modern terms, we can say: either we pursue all the world can offer us in terms of getting on in our careers, acquiring money and possessions, being successful, in promoting our comfort, satisfying our interests and desires and perhaps earning a name for ourselves into the bargain, or we relegate these things and ourselves to a second place in our lives. This is the message of the New Testament. For what, Jesus asks, shall it profit a man 'if he gain the whole world and loses his own soul. Or what will a man give in exchange for his soul?' **(Mt. 16,26).** Looking at the New Testament as a printer looks at copy, we can discover for ourselves that by far the greater part of the teaching in the Gospels is devoted to this either directly, as in the parables, or by inference than to any other.

The role of time in the Gospels

As with all life, time plays an ineradicable role. The sense of mission which, as we have seen, informs the Gospels like a tolling bell in the background is also an expression of the passing of time. In the course of life's business, especially when we are young, it is all too easy to overlook the passage of time when the intensity of our activities obscures the fact of its passing. This, too, is an aspect of *maya* or life's illusion. The Pharisees and their associates are a mirror unto ourselves in that they, like us, are conditioned by a certain pattern of values and behaviour. They, too, were anxious for recognition, content like children with the toys of wealth and influence **(Lk. 16,14)**, the acquisition of power and authority, all of which passes away with great rapidity and we with them. Thus the sobering truth of the nature of samsara. The moment we become attached to any of these things, we touch death, since all of them are bound up with time and our spiritual development is arrested. Everything which comes into being must pass; everything which lives must die and become something else. Even the stone monuments to great civilisations gradually but inevitably slip under the sand or are swallowed by the sea or throttled by jungle vegetation or are eroded by wind and rain. How much more is this true of our own ephemeral lives? This is beautifully summed up in a quatrain appearing in the *Rubaiyat of Omar Khayyam:*

> They say the Lion and Lizard keep
> The Courts where Jamshyd gloried and
> drank deep:
> And Bahram, that great hunter – the wild ass
> Stamps o'er his head, and he lies fast asleep.

Since nothing is permanent in samsara, nothing can be real in the sense we devoutly wish it to be. As we have seen, life is an illusion which dupes the majority of us. Very few of us are willing or enabled to recognize the illusion and so discover the truth behind it. 'For many are called, but few are chosen' (**Mt. 20, 16).** This ratio is so desperately tragic that those who have seen through the divine deception have only one interest at heart and that is to save others from the catastrophic effects of belief in it. Each time Jesus refers to his final hours it is as if this aspect of the passing of time were being emphasized and our minds drawn to life's evanescence.

It is as though he were saying: 'Time is passing very quickly. Be aware of what you are doing. Don't spend precious time chasing the baubles of this transient life! These are as nothing compared with a knowledge of God. If you do waste your time with the illusion of this life's treasures, you'll regret it!' There is urgency in his words, and as a consequence much of the New Testament carries this insistence, this sense of importunity. **(Lk. 16,14; Jn. 16.16–17: Mt. 3.2: Mk. 1,5; Lk.21,35** and elsewhere**)**.

The fact is that our egos (our identification with self) are blind to our own transience and Jesus knew this very well. To use Alan Watt's phrase, we have 'a specious and precarious sense of our own permanence', and it is our attachment to this idea which leads us astray or, as the Buddhist would put it, leads us 'to our identification and preoccupation with the illusion of *maya*.' The time illusion is part of our samsaric make-up. Rabbi Jeshua insists that we give up the idea of fulfilling our desires which will be gratified sometime in the future like those of the man in the parable **(Lk. 12, 18)** who desires to build bigger and bigger barns in the hope of greater harvests and instead concentrate on the Now of our existence. Once this has taken place, 'reintegration of the personality' has also taken place and the 'rest will be added unto you' **(Lk.12, 31).** In other words, life assumes a quality which is not distorted by our egoistic wishes. Everything which then comes our way, whether good or bad, even death itself, is seen and felt to be part of the great pageant of life which it is our privilege to experience and behold. Time is no longer felt as an imperative. From this vantage point and from this moment onwards, life is a deeply satisfying experience, not what it is for millions of us, a suffering twilight of unending, unappeased desire. The insight into our true nature is exactly like suddenly being in the possession of the answer to a racking problem. Before we know the answer we are frustrated by all kinds of false suggestions and unworkable substitutes. The answer to our minds seems to be sealed behind locked doors and the whole idea of solving it all may seem insuperable to us. However, when we have been told the answer or have worked out the problem for ourselves, how easy it all appears! That particular problem can never trouble us again.

As a modern illustration of this insight, the following conversation is recorded between a living Zen master and a young woman who attended a seven-day course of intensive meditation (*sesshin*) a few years ago. She is called into the master's room in the evening for *dokusan,* the daily interview with the teacher when meditators are required to give an account of their progress. She has been sitting for six hours in meditation and is tired. A moment or two of silence follows after she has settled herself on the cushion in front of him. Then he says: 'I see you are tired, but gather your resources together to sit for a little longer. Have you anything to say?'

For a long time there is no answer to his question, then: 'I feel as though I'm falling.' The master sits immobile, like one listening intently for a small sound. Hesitantly, the student continues. 'Yes, I'm falling; it's strange.' She does not move. A slight wind rustles the bushes which surround the temple building. Some of the branches gently brush against the large glass panes which form two walls of the room. Suddenly, the young woman exclaims: 'I think I know! Yes, I know!'

Master: 'Good, good, out with it!'

Student: 'There is no me. And the pain in my legs has gone…'

Master: 'Good, what else?' A long pause follows.

Student: 'I feel so light.' (half laughing) 'All the pain has gone. "Me" has gone… Oh, now I see!'

Master: (urgently) 'What do you see? *Who* sees?'

Student: 'There is only It. No me. I am free! I am happy. (tears come into her eyes) I see it all so clearly, what you've been saying in *teisho*[19] this week. It's as clear as anything! Why didn't I see it before?'

Master: 'I'm very happy for you. This is bodhi. Now you have passed through the "Gateless Gate"[20] of the old masters and understand what they understood. Before this day, the veils of delusion kept these things hidden from you, but now the veil has been lifted. That's all. Now you are truly free. Well done!'

Meister Eckhart, speaking from his own experience in the early 14th century, concludes:

As long as I am this or that, or have this or that, I am not all things and have not all things. Become pure till you neither are nor have either this or that; then you are omnipresent and, being neither this nor that, are all things.[21]

Getting there

He means that as long as we associate ourselves with this or that name or form we cannot be free of them. As long as I identify myself with this personality of mine (myself, whatever I think I am or others think I am) and as long as I have this idea or that piece of goods, I cannot realize that Oneness of being which is my birthright. I cannot stand on this side of the river and be on the other side at the same time, as the ancient Buddhists put it. If we want to enjoy the sun then we must wait for day, but if we want to see the stars, we must wait for night. To use an idiom, we cannot 'have our cake' (a worldly life) *and* 'eat it' (enjoy the benefits of spiritual insight or open eyes to the 'kingdom') or as Jesus himself acknowledged: 'You cannot serve God and mammon' **(Mt. 6, 24).** This is logical enough. It is not that we must live like hermits in order to see into the truth of ourselves or wear a hair shirt as John the Baptist is said to have done, nor do we necessarily need to go into a monastery for the rest of our lives or just give up everything in the literal sense and live like a clochard under a railway bridge. All that is needed is a change of viewpoint. We need not be 'of the world' as both Jews and Christians would put it or, as the Buddhist and Hindu would say, we need not be attached to life, not because it is evil as the former would avow, but, like the last, because it is to become attached to something which is illusory. What we have to do if we want to understand that which is eternal and which is also an integral part of ourselves is to 'become pure' as Meister Eckhart puts it. Of this the Zen Buddhist says, 'abandon attachment to all thought as it arises and concentrate on that which is there before anything stirs the mind.'

There will then come a moment when 'you neither are nor have this or that.' This is the portal of spiritual wisdom or, as Jesus would have put it, the gateway to the kingdom. Then we understand ourselves as part of the All, as a Oneness without division. It implies that we are no longer two (an ego split off from the real self) but one; it means that we are no longer double (which, incidentally, is etymologically associated with the word 'doubt'), but single (integrated). In the words of Taoism we have found the way to our real home. This 'home' is the realisation of the 'eternal' or 'everlasting life'. A few non-biblical examples, however, might help to put this into modern perspective.

> To realize the satori of Zen is to become one who is unhinderedly free, released from all chains, one who recognizes himself truly, being no longer attached to the forms of matter and spirit, one who faces the present world of existence and non-existence, life and death, good and evil, pro and con. The satori of Zen is not the satori of any particular act of a person, but the satori of the original self of a person regardless of who he is. It is not the satori of the visible and special phenomena, but the satori of the original, formless, undifferentiated, and nominal self.[22]

The Japanese word *satori* here is to be understood as the supreme insight into ourselves, with its accompanying understanding of our nature, together with the realization that we carry the Eternal around with us wherever we go and wherever we have been up till now, that it has always been with us and always will be so long as we live. Hence, the astonished exclamation on the part of the young woman above at not realizing this fact before. Understanding waits, so to speak, for our 'turning round' to realize it.

It is easy to think of a patient Father in this connection waiting for the return of those who have 'erred and strayed from Thy ways like lost sheep' or for the 'sheep' of the New Testament to return to the fold. This aspect of returning to our true selves is portrayed by Christ in the parable of the Prodigal Son. In turning away from the samsaric aspect of our lives, we can then discover the nirvanic. The samsaric life is all that we know of the world in all its varied pageantry and we know that it is constantly changing and passing away. Conversely, the nirvanic aspect is that which does not change. 'Since it is not born,' the Buddhists say, 'it cannot die.'

If it cannot die, it is eternal or 'everlasting' as Jesus put it. What this is can only be indirectly referred to as we have said, but now and again we discover someone who comes very near to making clear to the western mind what is actually at issue:

Ultimate and unconditioned 'reality' is negative and void. Let us be clear about this and express it in our occidental manner of speech, and try to see what exactly this idea of void is – for it is an idea like any other. The phenomenal, objective, relative world of sense impressions is an interpretation by divided and reasoning mind (which operates by a comparison of opposites) of noumenon, the absolute, subject, none of which (if you regard them as different in any way or as aspects of one whole) it is able directly to perceive. And the contrary, with which everything here in question is to be identified, is called Emptiness. As the Void it is the counterpart of Plenum, and all these qualities, the dharmas, treated as though they were 'things', are therefore elements in that plenitude. A void, however, is totally negative. If you think of Reality of Being, as you are taught to do, you are assuming something positive, and each of these positives is inevitably accompanied by its negative, which we have to term Non-reality and Non-being. It is this negative that is the Void or Emptiness and that negative implies its constituent plenum, so that this Void, being that which is not, is also that which appears to be, i.e. Non-manifestation manifested – which is the phenomenal and apparent universe or Samsara. This surely is the real message of these sutras – that our intuition must apprehend the negative reality of the Void in order to comprehend that its positive is Appearance, and that thus, and not the other way round, must they be seen if their identity is to be assimilated and not merely assumed… The 'real' nature of all manifestation is no nature, and of all ideas of 'reality' and of being – for all such are concepts or dharmas. They are directly negative or void, and only indirectly positive and relative.[23]

This is a way of putting the matter to minds which have become used to conceptual logic. It is not the way of Zen, since there one is expected to know first and reason later.

There is also some evidence in the Bible for supposing that Jesus had a closer group around him to whom he taught the principles of reaching understanding of the kingdom with more cogency and directness than by the aid of parables.[24] It may have been possible – although this is largely conjecture – that he brought a number of his disciples to a state of enlightenment by the sheer power of his personality, giving them the needed 'push' into understanding the nirvanic world as a number of Indian sages have done in the past and still do (notably in modern times, Swami Poonja of Lucknow), and as the Zen masters have done for centuries. How else can the power of the anonymous followers who went abroad before Pentecost to heal and preach the gospel in his name be accounted for? We are told that they took that knowledge with them which precedes the power to do into the towns and villages beyond Galilee. Their ability, in whatever degree, cannot be accounted for simply by the instructions we read of in **Mt. 10–42** and **Lk. 14,13ff.**

A more poetic way of describing the state of enlightenment – at least indirectly – is that given here by a modern master:

The Self is your Being
You have always been it: unfathomable Being
in which experiences and concepts come and go.
Your Self is that moment which neither comes nor goes.
It is the heart of the universe, Atman, Emptiness.

It is self-illuminating, for itself, by itself.
The Self is present within the breath itself.
You have no need to seek it. It is here.
You are That which you use in seeking.
You are what you are looking for! And That is all.
Only the Self is.[25]

Sri Poonja is urging his listeners here to attend for once to their inner beings, not to look outward as we are so used to doing every moment of our lives. When we look through our eyes at the world we see the world of objects; we are sensible of space relationships and the passage of time. All this and the reactive thought arising from their recognition is what we have chosen to call *samsara*. Looking inward we see nothing. That which looks cannot see itself. In Zen, there is the couplet:

The eye which sees cannot see itself;
The sword which cuts cannot cut itself.

Nirvana

This looking inward to perceive nothing – although it might not be recognized as such by beginners – *is nirvana*. This is enlightenment. Enlightenment must be there, otherwise there would be no samsara. Everything proceeds from Emptiness or, as the Christian and Hebrew would say, from God. It only needs a very short period of time to understand that which cuts across space and time in the dimension of mindful understanding. The potential to understand has been there all the time, although we are rarely, or never, conscious of it. This is why the author of the passage says that we need not seek (outside ourselves) for anything. It is here, that is to say, in this moment of time. Any other moment is either in the past or in the future. 'We', the conscious awareness of ourselves, our seeing and our hearing, our thinking and our feelings, proceed from that Mind. We are, so to speak, an extension of it. This 'extension' operates in the familiar world of relationships. For this reason we cannot possibly *seek* the source. That is, we cannot go out and *look* for any *thing*. The only means at our disposal is to retrace the 'extension' of our source and, in this case, go back to its origin. In practice, this means putting aside the past and the future, and concentrating on the *now*. Enlightenment cannot be anything else but now. Retracing this extension, as we have called it, back to the inarticulate source, which is the method of Zen, we come across Nothing, that is, the negation of relationship, non-being in the externalised sense.

Since there are no correlations to this state of understanding, all we can say is that we *are*. There is simply nothing else we can say. In the same way, Jesus says at **Jn. 8, 58**:

Most assuredly I say to you, before Abraham was I AM.

He means by this that, if we wish, we can be conscious of That which is there all the time and which sustains our being. In realising this state, we also ARE in exactly the same sense. There is no time relationship here at all. It is not a matter to be seen as a before-and-after relationship (the samsaric or dualistic view of life), but the *now* of what he refers to as 'everlasting life' (the nirvanic aspect of being). 'I AM' is the experience of enlightenment, here and now, the nirvanic state in which Jesus lived consciously all the time.

In connection with the teaching of Poonjaji above, it is interesting to see that he enjoins his students to turn back to themselves. Although Jesus did not ask his followers to look into themselves, he asked them instead to look at him and believe in him. This approach is not unusual either in Buddhism or other paths towards enlightenment. By watching a great master in all he does, the mind of the seeker can be brought to a state where it recognizes that Mind in the master which expresses itself through his actions. Since he lives (as Christ did) in that enlightened state of mind, all his words and actions proceed from the One Mind.

Many people have arrived at their own enlightenment in this way. A classic instance is given in the famous Zen anecdote below. It also indicates that among the great enlightened men in ancient China, not all lived in monasteries, but pursued a living in the normal way of things. In this way they were a light to many an 'ordinary' mortal who, as he went his way through life at some time encountered them. The following concerns one of these illumined individuals, here making his living as a boatman ferrying people across a river. He is in conversation with Shan-Hui, a would-be Zen man, but who as yet only possesses that proverbial slight knowledge which can sometimes be so dangerous.

> Boatman: 'At what monastery do you stay?'
> Shan-Hui: 'I stay at no monastery. The one I stay at no-one knows.' (Here he is trying to be clever, using Zen parlance to suggest that he lives in the state of No-being alluded to above. The Boatman is not put off by this, however, and pursues the point.)
> Boatman: 'What does it look like, the place that no one knows?'
> (Shan-Hui again uses his borrowed Zen plumage to impress his host as they set off across the river by saying): 'As far as sight extends, I see nothing comparable to it.'
> Boatman: (unimpressed) 'Where did you learn to say that?'
> Shan-Hui: 'It is beyond the reach of ears and eyes.' (This conundrum-like reply apes the erudition of someone already advanced in Zen who, in order to guide his aspiring pupils away from conceptual thinking, speaks in non-conceptual language, but the Boatman is still not convinced.) The boatman laughed heartily, saying: 'However fine your philosophy is, it serves you no better than the post to which the donkey is tied. When a line one thousand feet long is dropped into the pool, the intent is to sound the very depths of the abyss. Don't bite on the bait, but speak out, quick, quick!' When Shan-Hui was about to open his mouth, the boatman with his pole pushed him into the water, which made Shan-Hui abruptly realize satori.[26]

We can see from this that Shan-Hui was ripe for his ducking and the master, whom he took to be an ordinary ferryman, accurately judged his spiritual development at the time of his stepping into the boat.

On another occasion, Te-shan Hsuan-chien (780–865) declared, 'I'll give thirty blows to anyone who can say a word (about the meaning of Zen) and thirty to anyone who utters a word!'

He was approached by a young man in the audience. This young fellow was about to make a bow when, in a similar way to our other example above, the master struck him. The monk, who must have been a newcomer and unaccustomed to Te-shan's direct ways, protested warmly at such treatment: 'But I haven't even asked my question, why do you beat me?' The master put up his stick. 'Where do you come from?' he asked, 'I come from Kona,' the monk promptly replied. 'Even before you boarded the boat you deserved thirty blows,' the master retorted.

To some of us this treatment may well seem peremptory, even harsh, but its object is to rid us for a moment at least of our preconceived ideas and our habits of mind. In this example we are dealing with someone suffering under the latter. The monk comes forward as part of the ritual perhaps of asking the master a question or, alternatively, because he has some urgent spiritual problem on his mind and is hit before he can utter a word. His indignation at being hit is also a habit of mind and, seeing this, the master tersely utters his commentary on the man's development at that moment in time. For at that very moment our monk is not much more than a reactive 'machine', a mental robot, responding exactly as any reactive mind responds to external stimuli. In the worst degree it is to respond as the mob does, for example, at a lynching or, just a little less viciously, at a similar gathering of human beings, say, the crowd at a football match or our bull-baiting savages in the Spanish arena. Hence the swift condemnation, 'You deserved thirty blows before you boarded the boat!'

Our monk has two possibilities from then on: he can nurse his offended ego or he can see why the master chastised him. If he sees why, he can make progress or, if he is lucky, immediately see into his real nature in that very instant. From that moment on he will never again fall into the role of 'reactive' man.

How very important this is for our civilised advancement in the world today will be clear. It has indeed always been important, but in the past we have not always had the dubious advantage of being able to blow ourselves and our environment to bits while relishing our emotions.

Some people might object to the 'violence' Zen masters used on occasion, but, apart from the fact that serious violence was rare in ancient times, it tries with its slaps and pushes, its thwacks and prods, to make us aware of the fact that we are sound asleep for most of the time. We might add that in this state of spiritual sleep in which we are usually to be found, it is we who are the violent, reactive, aggressive, self-seeking animals, a fact amply demonstrated in our current lives and in our history. An occasional resort to a mild attack on our sleepy complacency in the best of interests is, therefore, justified to wake us up before it is too late. We, the seekers, are lucky in the extreme if, in this life, we can find someone in our acquaintance who can kick us out of our living dream. This someone must be a person who, like Christ, is immovably orientated to that other dimension of understanding. Christ referred to this dimension as his 'kingdom'. From this standpoint, he or she can judge our development and help us to understand something of 'Eternal Life' or 'That which exists before a thought is aroused,' be it ever so little in comparison. Time passes quickly. Every step towards fully awakened consciousness is a benefit to the possessor and to those around him. Many of us have come to realize this in our associations with enlightened people, both male and female.

From what is reported to us in the Gospels, Jesus was not only a teacher, but, since he lived in and, so to speak, 'out of' his 'kingdom', he was enabled to demonstrate the enlightened vision to those around him. As in the Buddhist outlook, his humanity arose from the recognition that we are all of 'the same substance'. It also accounts for the fact that Jesus could be at ease with 'sinners', wine-bibbers, prostitutes and tax gatherers and perhaps others regarded as socially disreputable by the Jewish society of his time. He knew they were all of the same human fabric. He knew only too well that as human beings we were all too prone to err. If this is the case, then we are to be forgiven, for 'I come not to save the righteous ... Those who are well have no need of a physician, but those who are sick. I did not come to call the righteous, but sinners, to repentance' **(Mk. 2,17)**. Sin, in this sense, does not appear to be the vicarious thing it was later expanded to be by his Church. 'Go and sin no more,' he advises the woman taken in adultery, and leaves it at that. And it should be noted that adultery was the only area of sinfulness which he gave more attention to during his ministry than anything else. In view of the horrifying, degrading death she had been prepared for, there is little doubt that the woman in question would have made off in the quickest time possible, no doubt considerably sobered by the experience.

We can see from what has been said in this chapter that Jesus, like the Zen masters of old, was anxious to clear the minds of those who came within his influence, that is to say, in the language of Zen, to 'turn them about'. This 'turning about' simply means to put them into contact with the wavelength of mind in the manner illustrated. He, like other spiritually advanced individuals, sometimes spoke of these matters as difficult. This occurs when, for example, he refers to those who are not worthy of freedom if they are not ready to follow him through every vicissitude, which meant at that time to risk the heresy of view other than that received by ancient Jewry. But, like others of his calibre, he sometimes said that the 'turning around' experience was 'easy' **(Mt. 11, 29–30)**. He knew then and we know today that this implies recognising the degree of spiritual advancement in those who came to him. In short, some are ready for the 'push' into the light of understanding (as was Shan Hui), while others may have to spend many years in the search for it. These are the facts of our spiritual existence.

The question now remains as to *how* we can recover our true spiritual identity.

---

[1] *Bhagavad Gita, The Song of God,* trans. Swami Prabhavananda and C. Isherwood, London, Phoenix House, 1956, p. 90.

[2] Ibid. p. 93.

[3] Bucke, R.M., *Cosmic Consciousness,* 14th ed., New York, E.P. Dutton, 1948, p. 358.

[4] Blofeld, John, ed., *The Zen Teaching of Huang Po, On the Transmission of Mind,* London, Buddhist Society, p. 116.

[5] Ibid. pp. 117-18 (my brackets).

[6] *Das Zen von Meister Rinzai* (Master Rinzai's Zen), ed. by, Sōtetsu Yūzen, Kristkeitz Verlag, Leimen, 1990, p. 45 (my translation).

[7] 'Buddhakaya' literally means "Body of the Buddha", i.e. the Essence of things, 'That Which Is' of the Hindu and the Quiddity of the Christian mystic. It is therefore a deep insight into the true nature of things understood in the deeper states of meditation or *samadhi.* For a modern, severely logical treatment of this in two short pages see, Wu Wei Wu, *Ask the Awakened* (see above), at (20), pp. 44-6.

[8] Ibid. p. 303.

[9] Law, William, *Selected Writings of William Law,* ed. by Hobhouse, S., London, 1939.

[10] Wei Wu Wei, *All Else is Bondage,* Hong Kong University Press, 1970, p. 3.

[11] Ibid, *Ask the Awakened* (See above at Chapter IV, 8) Section 5, p. 13).

[12] **Mt. 10, 6-10.** Here it is clear that the disciples sent out by Jesus could both heal the sick and 'cast out devils'.

[13] Kapleau, P. (See above at Chapter VI, 11), p. 277ff.

[14] Bhagavad Gita, p. 91.

[15] Quoted from a conversation contained in the book, Zimmermann, Klaudia, Verlag K. Zimmermann, Germany, Kandern, 1994, p. 112.

[16] Thomas à Kempis, *The Imitation of Christ*, ed. by C Bigg London, Methuen, 1954, p. 93.

[17] Von Jankovich, S. *Ich war klinisch Tot- Der Tod – Mein schönstes Erlebnis* (I was clinically dead – Death – my most pleasant experience), Drei Eichen Verlag, 1984.

[18] Ibid. *The Way of Eternal Brahman* and *The Yoga of Mysticism* respectively.

[19] 'Teisho' is a formal reading with commentary from Buddhist scriptures during a pause in formal meditation at a session.

[20] The 'Gateless Gate' is a Zen term for realisation or enlightenment. It is described as 'gateless' because there is no perceivable point of entry and yet there is clearly a barrier between seeing the truth and not seeing it.

[21] Meister Eckhart, *A Modern Translation,* ed. by R.B. Blakeney, New York, 1941.

[22] Blofeld, J. ed. (See above, VII, 4), Wun Chou Record.

[23] Wei Wu Wei (See above), No. 24, p. 52.

[24] **Mt. 13,** 16-17.

[25] Sri H.W.L. Poonja, *The Truth Is* (Poem: The Self), USA, Yudishtara Verlag, 1995. Appears as a German edition under the title, *Der Gesang des Seins* (The Song of Being), München, 1997.

[26] The account is taken from Suzuki, *The Doctrine of No-Mind,* London, Rider, 1958 (my brackets).

CHAPTER VIII

The means to understanding

Man that is honour, and understandeth not,
is like the beasts that perish.
Psalms: 49, 20

Q. *'How, then, does a man accomplish the comprehension of his own*
Mind?'
A. *'That which asked the question IS your own Mind.'* Huang Po

Humility

Although, strictly speaking, there are no direct means to 'attain' enlightenment, there are nevertheless some things which are necessary to observe in preparing the mind for its inception. These are like the soil into which a seed is planted. We can do nothing about the actual germination of the seed, but we can provide the best conditions for it to take place. As with the seed, actual insight into ourselves and creation, is an inherent capacity which can be stimulated by the recognition that we do not live alone and that without others we would neither have come into being, nor could we exist for very long.

Understanding this cultivates respect for others, an acknowledgement which is at the heart of both true Christianity and Buddhism, not to speak of it as a basic recognition in other religions. Humility has little to do with the practice of austerities, but very much to do with respect, not only for other human beings, but for all other living creatures, whatever their form, and even with respect for inanimate things. In this way, the ancient artists of China and Japan tell us, it is better to have deep respect for the brush and ink, the silk, the easel and the object of your attention, than to wear a hair shirt and live in a cave. Again, it is a matter of where the emphasis is placed. The first is to generate love and respect even for inanimate things, and so win humility by identifying the spirit with these things, while the second could be an identification with ego in overcoming self-imposed adversity. The first path is anyway easier and more natural. 'In order to really paint a bamboo well', these artists tell us, 'you have to become a bamboo.' In doing so, humility is automatically achieved and the door of perception is already opened.

The need for humility is reiterated in the Gospels and expressed in a number of ways at different times, so many times indeed that it is hard to overlook its congruity with the kingdom of heaven.

> And they brought young children to him, that he should touch them; and his disciples rebuked those that brought them. But when Jesus saw it, he was much displeased, and said unto them, Suffer the little children to come unto me, and forbid them not: for such is the kingdom of God. **Mk. 10–14**

The same incident is reported in **Luke** at chapter **18, 16–17.** In **Matthew 18,2ff,** the master goes even further and explicitly declares:

> And Jesus called a little child unto him, and set him in the midst of them, / And said, verily I say unto you, Except ye be converted, and become as little children, ye shall not enter

into the kingdom of heaven. / Whosoever therefore shall humble himself as this little child, the same is greatest in the kingdom of heaven.

We know today from our studies of child development that consciousness of 'I' as a separate entity is something acquired as the child grows older. Very small children have only a rudimentary knowledge of their presence as separate beings. Their ego, in other words, is undeveloped. It is clear from Christ's words here and elsewhere[1] that humility is profoundly connected with the realisation of the nature of the kingdom. We might say that the less developed the ego is, the nearer we are to that realisation. Conversely, the nearer we are to realisation, the less our egos interest us. We can go so far as to compare this process with the simplest of physical phenomena. If water is poured from one vessel into another, the first vessel will lose water in direct proportion to the gain of water in the second. Finally, there is no water in the first vessel, while the second is full. This might seem too facile an example, but it nevertheless represents the simple facts of the situation. Either we take the one path towards realisation where we certainly find reintegration and true happiness or we choose another path where the likelihood of not finding these is very great and the way precarious.

The first path suggests that there is something greater than ourselves which we can know and to which we can subscribe and which requires our maximum commitment, while the other assumes that we ourselves are masters of our fate and allows us to use our faculties to the full in order to gratify our desires. There really is nothing desperately moral or high-minded about all this, but simply – again – a choice of priorities.

'Why are you unhappy?' Wei Wu Wei inquires at the beginning of his book, *Ask the Awakened*, 'because 99.9 per cent of everything you think, and everything you do, is for yourself – and there isn't one.'

Jesus himself draws a very simple comparison as far as this is concerned. He says:

> No one can serve two masters, for either he will hate the one and love the other, or else he will hold to the one and despise the other. Ye cannot serve God and mammon. **Lk. 16,13**

And although he was speaking here specifically of riches (the covetousness of the Pharisees), he clearly points out there is a choice to be made. It is a choice between the aggrandisement of self (ego) or the pursuit of the divine.

Humility does not necessarily suggest a lifetime of self-denial. As hinted earlier, this may be suspect and conceal an ambition to succeed in overcoming worldly desire. It means, simply, 'non-desiring'. What is meant is shown here by an example from a source which is not at all biblical or even vaguely religious in origin, but is nevertheless a succinct example of the kind of humility alluded to above, humility which is not consciousness of itself.

Many years ago, an unofficial interview took place shortly after a celebrated concert with one of the world's greatest pianists. The details of this encounter are interesting and were roughly as follows:

> Q. 'Sir, can you tell me how you have developed your incredible technique…I mean how is it done?'
> A. 'To be perfectly honest with you, I don't know.' (General laughter). 'No, no, I'm being quite sincere; I'm not pulling your leg or anything. I just don't know.'

This time, instead of laughter, the remark brings a sudden, deep silence. Those present are nonplussed, but intensely interested in the possibility of some rational explanation. 'Can it be,' they ask themselves, 'that this internationally acclaimed master actually doesn't know what he's doing!'

As a help in overcoming the embarrassed pause, the pianist adds: 'I know only that to achieve what you kindly call 'incredible' takes a great deal of time and application. That I do know.

Q. But don't you have a special secret or a special way of going about things? I mean, what would you advise a student to do in order to reach out towards your own standard of playing?'
A. 'Practise.'

Again there is much laughter at this laconic, childlike, totally disarming reply. The young man asking the questions looks incredulously at the master. In his turn, the concert pianist gazes at the interviewer with a half-smile on his lips as though to say, 'I'm sorry I can't help you, but...' There is a longish pause.

The interviewer, himself a pianist, then murmurs something which reflects the feelings of the others present, so the master adds,

'Well I know that it must be something to do with synapses in the brain. That's clear. It's a matter of cultivating certain mechanical patterns in the brain and fingers, I suppose. I'm sure that it's quite complicated, neurologically speaking. It also has – at least in my case – something to do with a prior attitude of mind to the keyboard. I know what I can do and I do it.' (Appreciative noises from those listening). 'But I think this knowing you can do something comes from familiarity, from practice. Just how it's done, though, I don't know. I have no regular method or programme when I practise. I do what's necessary to be done. Some things are more difficult than others.' Another ripple of amused laughter at this utter simplicity. The interviewer decides to change his approach.

Q. 'When you give a concert, how do you feel? Is it a hair-raising experience for you as it is for many virtuosi?'

A. 'Well, yes, the first few minutes are awful I must admit. You wonder why you go in for this kind of thing!' (Laughter) 'But then there comes a state of mind after the first minutes or so where you forget all about the audience. There is then only the music; a kind of situation where there's 'no tomorrow' if you see what I mean. I just play on and when I come to the end, I stop and there they are, the members of the public, everybody clapping. Sometimes I have so forgotten all about them that their applause comes as a surprise! From now on I could play right through the night for them. When it's all over and the encores are done I go back to my dressing room and it all seems to have been a dream. At night on these occasions, shortly before I retire, I am often deeply moved by the sentiments contained in the music and very often think about the lives of the composers whose music I played in the evening.'

Q. 'Thank you for answering my question. I have just one more: You seem to enjoy playing immensely. Do you ever feel powerful at the keyboard, that is to say, when you play those amazing octaves and that huge, full tone you produce must give you a great sense of authority...'

A. 'Oh yes, but it's only for me. It's fun to get this machine to do things.' (meaning the piano). '.I'm not out to impress anybody. As soon as you start trying to impress, you lose your grip and make mistakes. Dreadful. At least that's what I think. Just play, that's all. Don't think of anything else, just play. Music flows; there's no one there to impress, no one playing, just the music.'[2]

This, it is suggested, is an example of true humility. The artist has erased his ego by sheer dint of practice, has submerged his ego with the music. No 'I' plays. Finally, there was nothing of himself left, only the music remains. The performer has forgotten himself. Like the artists in depicting bamboo in the earlier example, he had completely identified himself with what he was doing, and in this case had 'become' the music he was playing. Of this state of mind the ancients of the East say that the brush, the paint, paper and the artist are all one. They speak of the phenomenon of 'IT painting'. This is when the mind is like the unfilled vessel above. It is devoid of ego, but it is not a vacuum which remains, but a Fullness or a Potential which is inexhaustible.

As far as life is concerned, the more we forget ourselves, the happier we will be. This – again – means keeping an eye open to the demands of the ego which, when they arise, should not be put down with a heavy hand as the dictates of Satan, a remedy the Church fathers in every generation have suggested, but should be looked at in detachment. Detachment of this kind is a much more powerful weapon in curbing the ego and its desires than deliberate suppression. As has been known to the non-Semitic religions for several thousand years, namely Hinduism and Buddhism in particular, one cannot overcome mind with mind. To do such a thing is to finally distort its function and bring mental illness upon oneself. Passive but alert regard for what is going on within the mind, on the other hand, is to use a faculty lying outside the everyday, dualistic mechanics of mind. It is to employ detached awareness which is linked with the true Self. When we are aware in this way, we are cut off from its intellectual and emotional machinery. At this moment we are in charge of our lives and our thoughts, not the other way round. With a mind like this, we are not likely to put ourselves forward. It corresponds exactly then to the mind of the small child whose ego is either weak or non-existent. In that state we will be aware of the ego seeking an advantage, and be able to check it. Conversely, busy concern with ourselves automatically leads to a loss of the divine potential. Such concern is precisely like that of decanting one vessel into another as above, but this time reversing the process. Instead of leaving ourselves empty of ego, we fill ourselves with the delights of temporary gratification and so exhaust our potential. The matter is put just as simply in the biblical warning below, beginning with the description of a banal situation, and ending with a weighty antithesis.

> When thou art bidden of any man to a wedding, sit not down in the highest room; lest a more honourable man than thou be bidden of him./ And he that bade thee and him come and say to thee; Give this man place; and thou begin with shame to take the lowest room. / But when thou art bidden, go and sit down in the lowest room; that when he that bade thee cometh, he may say unto thee, Friend, go up higher: then shalt thou have worship in the presence of them that sit at meat with thee. / For whosoever exalteth himself shall be

abased; and he that humbleth himself shall be exalted. **(Lk. 14, 8–11)**

The need to possess a mind which is uninhibited by ego is expressed throughout Jesus' teaching and crops up again and again, touching a number of themes as parable or as an aside during his association with men. The emphasis he places on humility demonstrates his awareness of the basic spiritual law that where the mind is trammelled with ideas of self, there cannot be much room for self-development. In the Sermon on the Mount, he declares succinctly.

> Blessed are the poor in spirit,
> For theirs is the kingdom of heaven. **(Mt. 5, 3)**

Being 'poor in spirit' refers to the state of mind above where there is no sense of me' and 'mine', but only a receptive emptiness. 'Emptiness' here implies 'empty of ego or self' and the sentiment occurs twice in the so-called Beatitudes in Mathew.

> Blessed are the pure in heart
> For they shall see God **(Mt. 5, 8)**

The purity of heart is one erased of all thought of self. Clearly, it is a mind unencumbered by the affairs which concern most of us for most of the time. It is what Eastern adepts refer to as an 'unfettered mind', a mind not beset by the 'cares of this world' and at peace. Moreover, it is unfortunate if Jesus' loving testimony of this mind should have been converted into a narrow dogma of 'do's' and 'don'ts, interpreted as law and stricture, as something which has to be done. It is much more an observation, a declaration of truth, the enunciation of spiritual fact. True humility, as we have said, has little to do with 'acting in a humble manner'. There is no *conscious* self-effacement in it nor is there subservience. It is unaware of itself; it is the selfless unawareness with which small children are blessed.

In the adult it is well illustrated in the life and childlike spontaneity of the Japanese hermit monk, Ryukan (1758–1831), who once returned to his modest dwelling to find that the little he possessed had been stolen. At this moment he could say:

> The thief
> Left it behind
> The moon at the window!

This is to act from what Suzuki calls the Unconscious, that fundamental spring of being which exists before the concept-forming mind (with its attendant ego) has come into action. To live in this state as the Zen masters and other enlightened beings do, whatever their formal affinities may be, is to live in the kingdom of heaven.

While not all of us can be like Ryukan who, it is said, used to play hide and seek with the village children and became so engrossed in this activity that he carried on playing long after they had been packed off to bed, we can nevertheless try to return to an awareness of ourselves as human beings uncluttered by the attributes the world has accorded us since our childhood. We have nothing intrinsic to our nature which tells us: 'I am So-and-So; I belong to this or that community: I am an orthodox Jew; I am a Muslim, a Christian, a Buddhist; I am a doctor of law, a senator, a man of means; I own this and that, was educated here or there, am beloved by these and those; I do good works, am praised and acclaimed by this and that. I am a famous footballer, actor, philosopher, writer, politician, come from a long-standing distinguished family associated with the fortunes of the country for centuries and so on and so forth. All these things belong to the consciousness of ourselves which a small child does not yet possess. These appendages come later when we begin to compare ourselves with others, often substantially aided by the members of our family, our teachers and their teachers, and many, many others. The true man, Zen Buddhism claims, is the 'Man of No Title', the man who can say nothing of himself in these terms, has forgotten all he knew of such relationships, but who instead has realized himself. He has understood his true nature. We can take none of our worldly titles with us. All this drops from us at death. The recognition of ourselves, however, is precisely that which we take with us into the next dimension of consciousness we call death.

> Do not lay up for yourselves treasures on earth, where moth and rust destroy and where thieves break in and steal; / but lay up for yourselves treasures in heaven where neither moth nor rust destroys and where thieves do not break in and steal. / For where your treasure is. There your heart will be also. **(Mt. 6, 19–21)**

Chapters **5, 6** and **7** in the Book of **Matthew** are largely devoted to the cultivation of humility. Attitudes range, in order, from submission to persecution, forgiveness of those whom we think have wronged us, settling for compromise with an adversary, the stringent avoidance of evil (here to be interpreted as following the impulses of selfish concern), putting up with abuse (turning the cheek), learning to endure those who would seek to compel us to do things against our will, loving our enemies, not seeking personal advantage (For if you love those who love you, what reward have you?), not doing charitable deeds in public (for personal recognition), nor praying in public (parading oneself as virtuous), not making a great show of fasting (conceit). And after warning his hearers that they cannot serve God and mammon, he assures them that there is no need to worry about life unduly, saying...

> Take no thought for your life, what ye shall eat; neither for the body what ye shall put on/The life is more than meat, and the body is more than raiment. **(Lk. 12, 22–23)**

and continuing for the next nine verses to enlarge on the subject and bring it to a close which says in so many words, 'Let tomorrow look after itself' **(verses 26–34)**. During this advice, he says again **(v. 33)** that the most important thing is the need to adjust our priorities, cultivate the essential and leave the rest to God's care.

To our modern minds, and perhaps to the minds of those who listened to these recommendations two thousand years ago, such insouciance appears a little risky. There are mouths to feed and bills to pay, duties to fulfil for which we receive money, illness, the need to conform; there is the other's burden, the many problems of managing our lives, our relationships and so on.

Life cannot be simplified to leaving everything until the morrow, we protest. Some have even gone so far as to maintain that since Jesus had no family, it was easy for him to talk like this. But to aver such a thing is to nicely miss the point. It is not that we should ignore our responsibilities and live like 'children of the sun'; that is not what is meant. What is alluded to here is a state of mind which can stand back from whatever constitutes our duties and responsibilities in life. In this state of mental freedom (non-attachment) we can actually perform what we recognize as our obligations with greater efficiency. This is an extraordinary fact. All Zen teaching, for example, counters the desire to escape from life, from our responsibilities or our work with the admonition to neither make the latter the central object of our attention nor to neglect it. Huang Po, whom we have already encountered, has this to say here:

> On no account make a distinction between the Absolute and the sentient world...you must make no distinctions of any kind. ...Do not permit the events of your daily lives to bind you, but never withdraw yourselves from them.[3]

In the text from which this arises, Huang Po is insistent about not disassociating oneself from the tasks of a normal life and warns his followers not to distinguish between 'self' and 'other'.

It is a matter of 'sitting easy to life' and by this is the suggestion that by doing this we leave room for other considerations than those imposed upon us by our circumstances. This is what Jesus meant by 'losing our lives' (our attachments) to gain freedom of mind. Ideally, there should be a 'middle way' in leading our lives which might be described as a 'non-attached commitment', that is, of living our lives among the things of this world, but not being 'stuck' on any one aspect of it. In the state of enlightenment the same applies:

Before enlightenment, hewing wood and drawing water
After enlightenment, hewing wood and drawing water.

True humility, we can see from the above, is not to make a great show of 'giving up everything' nor even of demonstrating that we have 'withdrawn from the world', although there are some who can readily do this without making themselves suspect. It consists first of an intellectual recognition that egoistic thinking and activity is hollow, and second, in letting go of these things. It is an inner transformation. Moreover, we cannot all retire to a monastery to learn humility, for what would become of the world? But we can all experience a small transformation along these lines, and automatically the world would become a better place.

Taoism, which is associated with Zen inasmuch as there are elements in it which have been absorbed from Chinese tradition, speaks of the great Way (to enlightenment) as one 'without difficulty'. We could also refer to it as 'the Way of Humility'.

The perfect Way is without difficulty except that it avoids picking and choosing.

When picking and choosing is abandoned
Will everything be clearly understood.
Only a hair's breadth separates earth and heaven.
If you wish to know the truth, then do not concern
Yourself with right and wrong, this and that
For this is all a sickness of the mind.
Ancient Zen poem.

Jesus, too, speaks of his 'yoke' as being 'easy'. In **Matthew (11, 29–30)** he says:

> Take my yoke upon you, and learn of me; for I am meek and lowly In heart: and ye shall find rest unto your souls. For my yoke is easy and my burden light.

The 'picking and choosing' or 'discriminating between this and that' is the exercise of the ego. Here, it primarily refers to the desire for this and the dislike of that and not, generally speaking, to an intellectual choice where calculation and logic come into play to solve an everyday problem. We are essentially concerned here with our human emotions. Non-discrimination does not mean to live like a fool or to deliberately abandon the use of the intelligence. Rather, it is to live like 'God's fool' and not be predisposed to 'judge' in Christ's sense **(Mt. 7,1).** It is to give up our likes and dislikes. When we are thoroughly free of such distinctions whatever they may concern, then we are truly 'free' in Rabbi Jesus' sense and 'liberated' in the Buddhist sense. At the moment we arrive at true humility, at a point where all ego has evaporated, there is the Christian's 'Absolute', the Hindu's 'Divine Ground of Being' (Sanskrit: Prakriti), Buddhism's 'Nirvana', Zen Buddhism's 'Original Face', and the 'Dao' or Tao of Taoism.

This is what is meant by masters of Zen when they claim that there is 'only a hair's difference between heaven and earth.' It means that when the attenuation of ego is complete, insight into one's true nature and the liberation that goes with it will arise spontaneously. There is only this slight difference to adjustment in our way of looking at things to make an immense difference to our lives. Jesus refers to this (his understanding) as 'easy', and so it is when the conditions for insight have been fulfilled. It is then that we shall find 'rest unto your souls' because we will in that moment find freedom of mind. It is like bringing something into focus by the slight adjustment of a telescope or microscope. Before the regulation there is only a blur; after it, there is utter clarity. Even in this trivial instance there is often a feeling of satisfaction on our part when things are at last seen clearly. People in such a situation often say 'Ah, now I can see what you mean!' or some such expression. Exactly the same is true of the enlightenment experience. There are cries of joy and delight on suddenly being able to see clearly.

How?

What are the 'mechanics' of this process? A very simple illustration will suffice to make things clear. When the car has used up all the fuel, the car stops. So long as the car has only a drop or two of fuel in the tank it will continue to run (like our concept-seeking, pattern-making mind), but when there is total absence of fuel (i.e. when ego-centred thought runs out), there is then nothing which can power the vehicle forward and it comes to a halt (the mind then adopts a new tack, a standpoint of stillness wherein perception and understanding take over). The Buddha speaks of 'fire' in this connection. When the desires are thoroughly burned up, he says, then the mind is able to apprehend 'No-mind' – a state which is quite unsuspected by our usual mind-desire situation. The 'fire' (desire) is out, and this then is enlightenment, and the result of enlightenment is total freedom of thought and action.

All this implies that liberation is for every man and woman and that it is available to every individual in every moment. A divine intercessor or an intermediary on our behalf is not necessary, although a guide may be. In the last analysis we must come to realise the truth by ourselves and through ourselves. In the quotation above where Jesus says that we should learn from him, he means as in other places that he shows the way while we must find out for ourselves what is meant. The last act is our own realisation and no one can do that for us. Either we see, or we do not. No one can see for us. The interpreters of Christianity have from the time of St. Paul focussed their attention on the person of Christ so much that, ridiculously, the man and not the teaching have dominated. This, in Zen terms, is to 'look at the finger pointing to the moon' and not the moon, and is a grave mistake. Although it was his custom to speak in personal terms, referring to 'me' and 'I' during his teaching, Jesus certainly did not mean that we should make him the object of our religious concern. This would make him a substitute for God, and here there cannot be a substitute. There is only the One and Indivisible. After his blessing of the children in the Gospel of **St Mark** at **10.17,** we read of one who came running and, kneeling in front of Jesus, inquired what he should do to inherit eternal life. Before answering, Jesus asks, 'Why callest thou me good?' and insists that there is 'none good, but one, that is, God.' There is a tendency among us human beings to look for a leader. This is a basic instinct in most gregarious animals. The Jews of old time, sharing this human instinct, were looking for someone to lead them to freedom from the Roman yoke, but it is a great mistake to allow ourselves to be deflected from securing our own personal knowledge of the divine by submitting ourselves to prophets and masters. These are men like ourselves. They transmit what they have seen in various ways, but it stands to reason that they themselves are not the essence. Baso, an ancient Zen master, once turned on his monks with the advice: 'Don't go quoting scriptures and emulating the words and conduct of the ancients. Instead, get to know what they knew!' In the assumption that those who followed him would understand his message, Jesus says quite clearly:

> Believe me that I am in the Father and the Father in me: or else believe me for the very work's sake. Verily, verily I say unto you, he that believeth on me, the works that I do, shall he do also; and greater works than these shall he do because I go unto my Father. **(Jn. 14, 11–12)**

In order to make this crystal clear, since it is so important, we can simply translate this into modern English with a commentary. He says: 'Either believe that I have the divine in me, that we are one, or, (if you can't do that) believe me because I can work miracles and (have therefore demonstrated the power of God in me). I tell you in absolute truth (great emphasis) that if you believe me (i.e. understand what I understand), you will be able to do the same as I can and more. (I cannot be here much longer) because I am going to my Father' (to die and be reunited with him).

This state of affairs has not, unfortunately, come to pass among us human beings, despite the fact that great things have been achieved over the centuries by individuals who have transcended the ego by submitting themselves utterly to God (Bhakti), which is the same as saying that they have achieved the state of humility outlined above. What was asserted by Christ is quite true, astonishing though it might be to the ears of most of us. What he can do, we can do as well, provided we have tuned in to the Infinite or One Mind. That is the essence of the quotation. This, however, has nothing to do with Jesus' personality. Concentration on the personality as an intermediary between God and Man only gets in the way of discovering the truth for ourselves within ourselves.

Only when we have laid aside all these concepts, including the concept of a God (for our imaginations could never in any case conceive the Almighty), when we have put aside all our religious prejudices (that is, in any denominational sense which separates us from any other individual in the world), when we have really laid all this aside, then we can be said to have reached a state of true humility from which understanding then rises naturally to our consciousness.

Faith

Before we can experience the boundless sense of ease and something of that command over ourselves, our circumstances and our destiny which Jesus himself demonstrates so clearly, (*Ye shall be free indeed*) there must be the conviction that a 'wavelength of being' such as that alluded to in the many examples above is both possible and there for us to discover. To dismiss this religious experience as an impossibility or worse, to condemn the idea as so much esoteric nonsense is to land in that category of people whom Jesus described as those whose sin 'will not be forgiven them'. This means quite simply that such people are denied the 'eternal vision' from the very beginning because they deny it to themselves. Nothing could be more logical. If there are those who feel that there is a threat in the pronouncement, it is only to say that if we deny ourselves what is our birthright we can have no alternative but to accept the consequences. These are that we will be born again until we do find the religious insight, and that is a precarious business.

This doubt is the one great hindrance to 'breaking through' to realisation, so strong is the testimony of our eyes, our ears and our experience to the contrary. Our perception of the world we live in is ablaze with our thoughts, our prejudices, our rooted patterns of thinking, our desires and our attachments. The Buddha spoke of our ears and eyes, our sense of taste and smell and feeling as 'thieves' which rob us of true perception, that is to say, the senses are coupled with intense feelings and thoughts and it is these which deflect us from true insight.

To overcome this state of affairs, a good deal of faith is necessary, especially at the beginning of any endeavour to realize ourselves. 'Faith' here implies belief in something which is not within our experience and not present to the senses. Without faith, initial interest gained from books or from conversation with others quickly dries up like the seed of the parable falling on stony ground and we are denied the opportunity of a lifetime. It is relatively easy to find this inner assurance when we are in the company of a great master like Christ who, every day through his works, could prove the existence of a state of mind and power beyond the normal to those around him. It was common for him, for example, to ask those seeking his help whether they 'believed in him' before he performed miracles. At these times he was speaking of himself as the representative of his Father. This is his homely way of putting it. There is only the 'One'. This is what is referred to in Buddhism as the 'Buddha nature' which is within every creature, in Man and all other sentient life.

While Christianity requires faith of its followers from the outset, traditional Buddhism acquires it by rigorous logic, that is to say, faith is adopted *after*[4] Buddhist argument has exhausted all other possibilities. It is not, therefore, to arrive at yet another concept like a detective or a philosopher, but to realize the end of concepts. As in the state of true Christian faith, there is no more thought, no more doubt, but only a state of mind untroubled by either. It is into this state of mind that a healing breaks forth in the Christian devotee or, in the case of Buddhism, enlightenment takes place as we have seen.

At a lower level than that required for enlightenment we can see a similar process taking place in hypnotism. In hypnosis, the mind is brought to quiescence by a doctor or a dentist or by some other qualified person and a suggestion is injected into this tranquillised state of mind. Sometimes this is accompanied by the most dramatic results. The very fact, for example, that extensive surgery can be conducted under its influence is proof enough of the power of the mind and, equally, of the existence of another 'wavelength' of mind than that which we recognize as normal.

Most of us human beings only come into contact with a state of mind which has abandoned every concept and persuasion perhaps once in a lifetime, if at all, after childhood. Some of us may become re-acquainted with it from our later reading. This fact is very clearly revealed to us by Jesus' own testimony, his manner of address, his utter conviction in all he said in his replies to his questioners, his commitment to the sick and needy, especially in his astonishment at the witlessness of others, his references to his Father as an intimate experience (in contrast to the usual deference) and the sudden outbursts of irritation at the blindness of those around him, flaring up from time to time into anger and castigation.[5]

As far as his 'own testimony' concerned, Jesus speaks of himself as the 'true vine' and the 'true way' **(Jn. 15.1 and 14.6)** and to men as 'wise' if they follow his words, for they are like those who build their houses on a solid foundation **(Mt. 7, 24–27)**. In Mark's gospel, we learn that when the scribes came down from Jerusalem they accused him of casting out demons in the name of Beelzebub **(3,23–27)** to which he parries with: 'How can Satan cast out Satan?' In **Luke, (7,24–26)** he asks, addressing himself to the multitude – almost, we could easily imagine, with a touch of sarcasm or at least gentle irony – 'But what did you go out to see? A prophet? Yes, I say to you, and more than a prophet' and goes on to cite **Isaiah (40,3)** as confirmation of his presence among them. These quotations merely to cite a few from a great number of utterances which recall his mission to the Jews.

Rabbi Jeshua's manner also demonstrates very clearly that he acts from depths of such absolute conviction that he can take the liberty of overturning the tables of the money-changers in the temple and, as Mark observes:

> He would not allow anyone to carry wares through the temple, at the same time declaring that 'Is it not written, "My house shall be called a house of prayer for all nations?" But you have made it a den of thieves.' **(Mk. 11,16)**

It is not very difficult for us to imagine the consternation provoked among the merchants at the temple on this occasion. It is quite likely that the presence of God in the temple was the last of their considerations at the time. Again, it was only his popularity with the people which prevented Jesus at that moment from getting into serious trouble with religious authority for such conduct, Mark notes in conclusion to describing this incident. What I wish to point out is that Jesus was apparently oblivious of what consequences his action might have in other quarters. For him, it was only the insult to God which counted and this had to be righted there and then.

In the same gospel, at **(9,19)** there is another incident which illustrates by his manner the fact that Jesus was working from a possession of knowledge and power with which those around him were not familiar, not, in this case even his disciples. He voices his exasperation when someone in the crowd announces that they had appealed for help from one of his followers and found that he could not assist his mentally handicapped child. 'O faithless generation,' he cries, 'how long shall I be with you? How long shall I bear with you? Bring him to me.' In this case the scene affords a sudden, very vivid, endearing insight into Jesus' personality.

In another place, we are given a further chance to see Jesus as the wise and loving individual he was when, for some reason known best to himself, he turns away Legion, who had begged to be allowed to follow him with the gentle words, 'Return to your own house, and tell what great things God has done for you.' **(Lk. 8,39)** He does not say 'what I have done for you', but instead 'what God has done for you', which demonstrates again that he felt himself to be the instrument of God. In this case God has worked through him to bring about a remarkable transformation in a madman.

There is a similar warmth in the words addressed to the woman 'having an issue of blood' in chapter **8** in **Mark's** gospel: 'Daughter, be of good cheer, your faith has made you well. Go in peace.' Those familiar with this incident in his ministry will recall that the woman had not declared her presence in the throng and that the gentle words addressed to her when she was brought forward by one or two in the crowd were very likely prompted by her fearfulness. It seems pretty clear that the last thing she wanted was that the intimate details of her indisposition be exposed to all ears, which was quite natural. What must be stressed, however, is that she had put herself into touch with his 'wavelength' by her faith and that Jeshua had recognised this immediately since, as we have already pointed out, he lived in this dimension as well as in the normal world. When Jesus twice asked 'Who touched Me?'

(Lk. 8,45) in this connection, Peter and those around him point out that since there was such a press of people, the question is an unreasonable one. It is very common for 'ordinary' people to make the mistake they did and two examples, here one ancient and one modern, illustrate the point from, so to speak, the 'normal' end of the mind's spectrum,.

Geese overhead

The first is that of a master and follower out for a walk together in ancient China when wild geese pass over their heads. 'What are they?' the master asked (as though he had not realized what kind of birds they were). 'Geese, master,' the student observed correctly. 'Where are they flying to?' the master then pursued. 'They have flown away, sir,' the student returned, whereupon the master gave the lad's nose such a violent tweak that the lad cried out in pain. 'Flown away,' the master roared, 'How the devil could they have flown away when they have been here since time immemorial?' On hearing this, it is said that the young man's back ran with sweat and he saw into the nature of things. What Baso, his master, wanted to say by this gesture was that, a though the phenomenal geese may well have passed overhead, there was That which animates them and which is omn present and eternal. The boy, Hyjakuju, was only living in the ordinary, familiar world of time-space and, up to the point of speaking, had no inkling of that other 'wavelength' as we have described it so far, and which interacts with the normal. Baso, however, lived in both worlds and because of that could see the deficiency in his pupil.

Where do you live?

So that we should not assume that the insight we speak of is something only related to the past, the next illustration occurred about eight or nine years ago and is the report of an interview between a truth-seeker, and the great Dharma Teacher, Dai Poep Sa Nim, a Korean woman master who today has her headquarters in Paris. It should perhaps be added that Dai Poep Sa Nim is a very attractive person physically, and her manner is friendly and engaging. For this reason it was easy for the male in this interview to be led into the error of thinking that he was enjoying a pleasant conversation with a beautiful woman, and that there was nothing much out of the ordinary behind the words uttered. The interview is given verbatim here and affords an insight into the two worlds we speak of during what appears to be a simple exchange of formalities. We shall refer to the two as D and X respectively.

D. 'So you're back in Paris again. Do you like the city?'

X. 'Oh, yes, very nice. I always feel at home in Paris.'

D. 'Really? Yes, it is a nice town I must admit. Rather expensive though.'

At this point X, agreeing, makes a humorous comment on the price of things by way of polite conversation, when D cuts him short.

'Where do you come from?' she asks suddenly. X answers the question politely.

'Where's that?' Dae Poep Sa Nim asks. The student goes on to explain carefully where he lives while D looks bored. Seeing this, the student stops abruptly. The two look at each other.

D. 'You are boring me.'

X. 'I'm sorry.'

D. 'For goodness sake, man, I asked you where you come from and you come out with all this tripe!' Here, the student looks quite dumbfounded.

D: 'And now you look like a fool into the bargain. Goodness me, I only asked you a simple question. What's the matter with you? Let's try, again. Where do you come from?'

The student does not know now what to say or do and feels stupid. Dae Poep Sa Nim waits a moment longer and then rings the small handbell at her side which is the signal for him to rise, bow and depart. As he goes out, she repeats the address he has given her with a comical mixture of amusement and derision.

What the master in this case wanted to hear was not geography, but *where* the student felt himself to be at the moment of asking. What, precisely, was his home, his here and now, his mental state *at that very moment.* Put in the terms above, she wanted to know on what mental 'wavelength' he was; whether he had perceived her wavelength and could talk to her in those terms or whether he was still bound to the 'rails' of routine thinking. It turned out that he, like Hyakuju above, was still in the familiar, dualistic world. As a Zen teacher, Dae Poep Sa Nim exhibited considerable patience on this occasion. It was different in ancient times when such spiritual obtuseness was rewarded with a smart thwack from the *kyasaku.*[6]

On one occasion (**Lk. 9,55**), we are told that Jesus and his disciples were not well received at a certain place in Samaria, whereupon James and John turned to Jesus to ask whether they should not 'command fire to come down from heaven and consume them, just as Elijah did?' This is a very clear example of their own poorly developed spiritual condition and shows that at that moment at least they are still securely bound by parochial prejudice and seized by the desire for revenge. Jesus rebukes them by telling them in so many words that they are not aware of themselves (not awake in the sense suggested in the last example) and that the whole idea of His coming is not to destroy men's lives but to 'save them', that is, bring them to realisation.

Another incident in the Gospels, again at **Luke (12, 23ff,),** is the famous recommendation to consider the 'lilies of the field'. The likeness is generally understood in the spirit suggested at verse 25 where the Master says 'And which of you by worrying can add one cubit to his stature?' In other words, as an injunction not to worry about what we should eat or wear or do, not to concern ourselves too much with worldly affairs. Its message is in absolute antithesis to today's modern world. Nowadays people acknowledge such advice – if they read it at all – as a pretty cornucopia which cannot be taken seriously. Jesus would not have wanted us to give up our lives with the result that we end up as beggars. This would be foolishness. What he wanted to draw our attention to was our own selves, our minds and our thoughts. Nothing could be more central to our lives, for example, than our own attitude of mind. It is from this bent of mind of ours that all our actions follow. Paradoxical though it will certainly seem, the activities we need to undertake in order to sustain our lives will be better done if they proceed from a state of 'having given up all attachment to them' than from a state which rigidly focuses on their successful issue.

Faith exemplified

Rabbi Jeshua's remarks about shouldering life easily are at once a reminder of God's immanence in us all and a reflection of his own state of mind.

This state of mind is manifested in the long reply to the Jewish priestly order who had complained of Jesus' healing in the temple on the Sabbath **(Jn. 5,17–47)** where thirty verses are devoted to an explanation of his relationship with the Father and his mission in life. Here again, he speaks of everlasting life in the sense we have described it above **(verse 24** and also at verse **39)**. Moreover, it is clear from this passage how easily he could be mistaken for a dreamer or someone not quite right in the head, especially in its personalisation of an intimate relationship with God, My Father has been working until now, and I have been working, **(v. 17)** its overtones of imminent judgement and its open censure **(verses 22 and**

38ff) as well as the parallel with Moses (**v. 46)** as someone who had written of him long before his appearance on earth. All the allusions, however, support the assertion above that Jesus felt himself one with what he calls his 'Father' and what Zen Buddhism would refer to simply as the 'One'

All this was very hard to digest for the normal, rigidly conditioned priesthood of his time and, let us be honest with ourselves, would have been a lot to take in for people of any epoch, even today where there is far more tolerance of the eccentric and the extraordinary than, say, even fifty years ago. At the same time it shows very clearly how deeply involved the speaker was with his conviction.

The same self-assurance can be seen in **John. 8,23,** where Jesus explicitly condemns those around him: 'You are from beneath; I am from above. You are of this world; I am not of this world.' The conviction persists right up to the last meal with his disciples when he says that he will not drink wine until the day he drinks it with his friends in 'My Father's kingdom.' **(Mt. 26,29)** and especially at **Mt. 26,54** where he declares categorically: '...hereafter you will see the Son of man sitting at the right hand of the Power, and coming on the clouds of heaven.'

We also see this state of mind reflected in the replies to those with whom he comes into contact, in answer to his disciples at **Mt. 15,16** where everything is as clear as day to him, but dark to those who enquire into the meaning of his parables. Similarly at **Mk. 4,13** where he says (perhaps in surprise) 'Do you not understand this parable? How then will you understand all the parables?' A better translation here might have been 'any' instead of 'all' to make better sense in modern English. A few verses further on in this chapter **(v. 40)** it is very easy to see from the disciples' point of view that their friend lives in a different world from theirs. They are astonished beyond words to find that the wind has been stilled and the sea calmed. 'Why are you so fearful,' Jesus asks, as though it were the most natural thing in the world to control the elements, 'How is it that you have no faith?'

If we are ready to accept Mark's record of this event as a true, unadulterated recollection of what actually happened in word, spirit and sequence, then Jesus' ingenuous assumption that his friends were of the same mind as he is as revealing as the story is astonishing.

Faith as a function of non-attachment

Most Christian commentators promote faith as the need to believe in those who apparently do not yet possesses the virtue. They understand faith as it is defined by the dictionary as (1) 'unquestioning belief that does not require proof or evidence, (2) unquestioning belief in God, religious tenets etc.[7]' While unswerving faith in this sense (bhakti) is an undoubted means to religious insight, it is not the only one, as they would have us believe. The fact is that faith of this type, humility and non-attachment all play a role in producing the understanding Jesus was eager to impress upon his hearers. If, in other words, we can act from a mind that is not attached in the sense outlined in an earlier chapter, this already implies a recognition of something which is beyond attachment. The following illustrations taken from the New Testament illustrate this conviction.

> Ye have heard that it hath been said, An eye for an eye, and a tooth for a tooth; but I say unto you, That ye resist not evil; but whosoever shall smite thee on thy right cheek, turn to him the other also. And if any man will sue thee at law, and take away thy coat, let him have thy cloak also. And whosoever shall compel thee to go a mile, go with him twain. (**Mt. 5, 41.**)

> Give to him that asketh thee, and from him that would borrow from thee, turn not *thou away*. (**Mt. 5, 42**)

Both these admonitions not to be attached apply not only to the things which we possess, but to the mental habit of *stereotyped reaction*. In both cases this kind of reaction implies that we are about to lose something when solicited. Either we are about to lose what we own or we are about to lose face. Both quotations are an exhortation to humility and non-attachment, but underlying that conduct which can act freely in the way suggested is a higher plane of understanding and this is based on faith.

The practice of non-attachment increases faith, here understood as belief before proof that there is a higher consciousness can be demonstrated. By habitually practising non-attachment, a metamorphosis slowly takes place in the mind which paves the way to a mental state which is ready to receive that higher understanding we speak of. This is why in all religious orders, novitiates are enjoined to live humbly and simply, to rein in the appetites, to make the least demands on the environment, to appreciate not only the use, but also acknowledge the presence of everything, even such simple objects as the bowl from which they eat and the cushion on which they sit to meditate.

Once the desire for things, for entertainment, unnecessary bodily comforts, distraction and I-related activities have been reduced to a minimum, the ground is automatically prepared for a state of mind from which they have been weaned, for a mind which, now it has been cleared of these considerations, can begin to apprehend a plane of being which may be quite unsuspected, but into which enlightenment can strike. Examples of this have already been given. Sometimes, however, the mind can be cleared in an instant and faith in a new way of looking at things be established.

It is said that the Japanese Zen master, Bankei Eitaku (1622–1693) was adept at bringing people to an abrupt appraisal of their state of mind where, for perhaps seconds only, the mind was emptied of its usual preoccupations. Two cases are cited here which afterwards resulted in the person concerned changing his mind from a preoccupation with material things to a mind open to receiving instruction in matters of the spirit.

Bankei was in the habit of holding meditation sessions which lasted several days at a time and which may have been the precursor to the modern 'sesshin'. People from all walks of life were invited to these and were expected to undergo an austere regimen of regular meditation interspersed by commentaries on the essence of realisation. The number of those attending varied from half a dozen to thirty or more.

On one of these occasions, a young person was caught in the act of stealing, and this fact was immediately reported to the master with the request that the person be sent home forthwith.

However, to the community's consternation, the master did nothing about the matter. A day or so later, this same thief was exposed again, and again the issue was reported to Bankei. But once more, nothing was done. The thief was not even reprimanded, much less sent packing.

In view of this, those attending debated with each other and decided to present Bankei with an ultimatum: either he would dismiss the thief or they would all leave the next day. In the evening, Bankei called his meditators together and declared that if this was so, they would be obliged to leave. 'If you wish, you may go somewhere else, but I intend to keep this one thief here. You all know what is right and wrong, but this young fellow doesn't, so who will teach him what *is* right if I don't?' At this, the young thief stepped forward from the assembly with tears streaming over his face. From that moment on, he had not the slightest interest in stealing. He had looked profoundly into himself and from then on his desire for the collection of material vanished, to be replaced by an opened mind. The creation of such a mind, we should note, could not have been accomplished by any form of punishment.[8]

The next example is a case of one awakened to himself by explanation. It is the case of a layman who had probably been meditating alone for years without much hope of quietening his mind sufficiently to bring about satori. It is very probable that he lacked the faith necessary to overcome subconscious objections to the possibility of ever understanding He says:

'I don't doubt that in the No-mind state there are no deluded thoughts. Nevertheless, I can't get over my own need to think. I just can't stay in a state of thoughtlessness.'

Now, this is a real problem. We can safely assume that the man had been trying for a long time to reach a state of calm where no thoughts, deluded or not, could enter his mind. On the one hand, he had faith enough to believe that there was such as a state of No-mind, but on the other, he is here near to capitulation. This is an obstacle encountered by a great many students of Zen. Indeed, one could almost consider this stage as one necessary to overcome before illumination can take place in the mind. Bankei, knowing very well what the frustration was, having experienced it himself as a younger man, has this to say in reply:

'When you were born into this world, you were nothing other than the Unborn Spirit. It was only when you began to grow up that you began to see and hear things which others in their delusions did and so adopted their delusions as your own, and that's why you find yourself in your present state (a faithless state of being). In all those years you accepted all this stuff and embodied it piece for piece into your own nature (conditioning) until there was no room for anything else and now this is the thanks you receive for it! But you can be sure of one thing: none of these deluded thoughts were inborn. They have all been acquired. When you come to realise the Unborn (the One), all these other thoughts will vanish immediately.

It's like the case of a drinker who is now suffering from the effects of alcohol and for the sake of remaining alive he has to give up the habit. But he can't give it up just like that. The desire remains and creeps up on him the moment an opportunity to drink offers itself. However, our man, let us say, is determined not to drink anymore and ruin his health.

He knows that if he keeps up this spirit of determination he will one day be free from its influence and so preserve his health. With deluded thoughts it's the same: if you just continue to look at these thoughts as they arise and not to be affected by them in any way, you will find that eventually they will be dissolved in the Unborn.'[9]

Faith without object

There is a difference here between that which is generally understood by us in the West as 'faith', which is usually construed as 'belief *in*' something or somebody. We say, for example, that we believe in the 'holy Church of God' or in 'Jesus Christ, the Son of God' or in God Himself; we believe in someone's abilities or that we believe (in the fact that) 'everything will be all right in the end'. In the type of faith illustrated above, however, there is no object. Faith is seen as a state of mind where the mind is gradually emptied of its contents by an act of will. The drinker does not allow his mind to be disturbed by the thought of drink. He does not suppress the thought or the temptation, but simply looks at the thought arising in the mind with impassivity and non-attachment. To suppress the temptation would be to aggravate his condition and in the worst case drive him mad, a situation where 'the last state of that man is worst than the first.' Exactly the same method is prescribed for the meditator above. This is 'faith without object', a state upheld by the will and concentrated on what arises in the mind. The important thing to bear in mind here is that this kind of faith is not intent on *achieving* anything. It is that state of mind which Zen describes as having 'no abiding place'. In other words, it is not distracted hither and thither by intercepting thoughts. It is a state of absolute equilibrium from which, when deepened, anything can take place. It is that supreme reservoir of imperturbable mind where 'not a thought arises', but where its possessor is in sole command of every situation. It is from this undifferentiated

Mind that those phenomena we call 'miracles' take their issue. It is clear from what we read from the course of Jesus' travels throughout Galilee and elsewhere that he had uninhibited access to this mind which Bankei describes as the 'Unborn' or the 'Unmanifested' or which we can call 'That which has no form.'

Jesus regretted its absence in others, reprimanding those around him for their lack of faith, but perhaps not realising on these occasions that the condition of 'non-discriminative mind' ('faith' in this sense) is something which has generally to be earned with hard work rather than being an immediate realisation, which is rather the exception than the rule.

What 'undifferentiated Mind' means in action is illustrated by a famous story from Japanese literature, involving a young man who was desirous to learn the art of swordsmanship. In seeking for a master of the art he was told of the existence of an old man who lived by himself in the hills of north eastern Japan who, it was said, had been invincible in his time, but no one knew these days whether he was still alive. Convinced that he could learn something from this man, the boy set off on a hazardous journey into the mountains to find him. After several days of discomfort and deprivation on the way, he at last came across an old man living in a remote valley from which the smoke from a solitary fire betrayed his whereabouts. Discovering his dwelling at last, the lad greeted the warrior with respect and then asked him whether he would be willing to instruct him for a day or so in the art of swordsmanship. The old man proved to be open and friendly, saying at once that he would be glad to instruct him, and that the lessons could begin the next day.

The next day came and went. And the next and so on until a week or two had passed and the lad was given no formal instruction. In disappointment and frustration, the young man again addressed himself to his mentor and said that so far nothing had happened in the way of instruction and he would be glad if lessons could get started. The old man readily agreed, showing the same friendly enthusiasm as before, at which the boy thought that it was possible after all that the old one was no longer quite right in the head. However, not many hours had passed after this interview when the boy was struck heavily with a stout stick from behind while gathering firewood. He turned in his pain to see that it was his companion who had hit him so hard. Through tear-filled eyes he watched the latter running away chuckling to himself with glee as he did so. Nothing was said about the incident at their mutual evening meal later, and it seemed that the old man had recovered his equanimity. The lad viewed this behaviour with suspicion and was put on his guard. A day or two later, suddenly and as if out of the blue, the old man appeared before him again with a heavy stick in his hand and rained a number of blows on the lad's back before the latter could even take note of the situation. A few seconds later, and after taking cover, the young man was amazed at the alacrity with which his aged companion took to his heels. These acts of sudden, unanticipated violence continued to take place and sometimes occurred several times a day, although not every day. Sometimes they were followed then by an unaccountable lull in activity, so that the boy gradually developed both a sense of insecurity and an acute awareness of imminent attack. Assaults during the night were also frequent, which only intensified this awareness. One day when the lad had been hit particularly hard so that he could no longer lift an arm to defend himself, he took the master to task later and told him that he was going too far.

To this, the master looked up from chopping wood and asked sarcastically whether his apprentice would prefer ripe fruit to be thrown at him. The lad understood the significance of this remark.

The weeks passed into months and eventually the boy learned how to defend himself to an extent and even parry the blows which had formerly knocked the wind out him or so injured him that he was unable to do more than limp away as fast as he could from his assailant. From now on, regardless of wherever he went or whatever he did, he carried a heavy stick himself and kept it within reach when he was busy doing other things. Summer and winter came and went. Three years passed. With time the lad had learned to be ever on the alert and was finally in a position not only to parry the blows with which the old man sought to fell him, but also to rally for a counter-attack. However, the old man was always too quick for him, and astonishingly agile and very strong for his age. One day, however, the young man saw a chance for revenge for all the bruises and humiliations he had received. On returning from the small herb garden they cultivated together, he found the ancient samurai bending over the fire, engrossed in watching some vegetables simmering in the frying pan. He had the lid of the pan in his right hand ready to replace it and with the other he turned the vegetables with a wooden spoon. The lad crept up on his tutor and in a flash, brought his stick down upon the old man's head with all the force he could muster. But before the stick could even touch his pate, the master intercepted the blow with the lid. The stick failed to land on his head, but instead glanced off the lid harmlessly to one side. All this took place within a fraction of a second and without the old man even turning to face his attacker or indeed even ceasing to stir the vegetables in the pan! This was when the young man saw into the implacable mind of the true swordsman.

Later, we assume, the apprentice swordsman was able himself to acquire that state of mind which in the swordsman neither desires to win against an opponent nor shuns death, but which is above both these. Its possessor acts from the same springs of mind which cause rivers to flow, the trees to leaf and the earth itself to maintain its orbit. The huge significance of this is stated concisely and emphatically by Master Jeshua on a number of occasions.

> If thou canst believe, all things are possible to him that believeth. **Mk. 9,23**

Then came the disciples to Jesus apart, and said; Why could we not cast him out? And Jesus said unto them, Because of your unbelief: for verily I say unto you; If you have faith as a grain of mustard seed, ye shall say unto this mountain, Remove hence to yonder place; and it shall remove; and nothing shall be impossible to you. **(Mt. 17, 19–20)**

...Have faith in God.
For verily I say unto you That whosoever shall say unto this mountain, Be thou removed, and be thou cast into the sea; and shall not doubt in his heart, but shall believe that those things which he saith shall come to pass; he shall have whatsoever he saith. **Mk. 11, 22–23**

This is neither so difficult to understand nor so unlikely as we are inclined to assume when we first hear it. The situation is something akin to the innocence of the child who brings a bucket of sea water to the beach from the ocean and declares it has the 'sea' in its little vessel. Strictly speaking, there is nothing false in the child's announcement. What it has in its bucket is identical with the sea, the only difference being one of dimension.

Clearly, the example above is not what might be expected as an illustration of faith in the usual sense we use the word, but more one of extreme alertness. However, attention is drawn again to the dictionary's use of the word 'unquestioning'. Here lies the key to understanding an 'equilibrium of mind'. In both states, that of alertness or keen attention to the world around us and the unquestioning condition of total belief, there is nothing in the mind which disturbs its equilibrium, no intrusive ideas, good or bad, no discursive thinking, no discrimination between one thing and another, no emotion, no inspiration, no past and no future; there is only a calm but intense awareness of what is going on, a registration of the now of each moment which passes. Or, to put it another way, the mind is free of everything but that of which it is immediately aware.

Christian believers will say that there must be an object of faith. They will declare that if someone is dreadfully ill, for example, that person will need an object such as his or her conception of God to help them through to health again. In such a situation it would perhaps be a personal visualization of Jesus Christ matched with the firm belief that a cure will take place as a result of that combination. This is certainly true as the thousands of proven cases of actual cures in the face of medical resignation or abandonment have demonstrated for many centuries. Notwithstanding, the actual healing process takes place when both subject (the patient) and object (the divine symbol) are completely forgotten. We have already seen this in reference to the Japanese woman on her way to an island in the Pacific, but an even nearer example occurred a few years ago in the case of a woman living not far from the city of Heilbronn in Baden-Württemberg, Germany. It is interesting because it affected a woman who was finally helplessly unconscious. The details are as follows.

The woman was a pious Catholic who, when she was about forty-five, discovered that she had multiple sclerosis. The disease advanced rapidly and within a year or two she was totally paralysed. Prior to this she had always entertained a firm belief that she would one day recover so that she could 'go about the Lord's business' as she called her work of helping others. She was quite convinced of this, but the disease soon overtook her to a degree that prevented her henceforth from taking an active part in any devotions or performing work of any kind. Finally, she fell into a stupor where she was more dead than alive. During the progress of the disease, her nearest relatives did everything in their power to maintain her consciousness, and even as she inexorably receded into this death-like condition, they bestowed the most tender care upon her. Finally, as it was clear that her end was approaching, they decided as a very last measure to take her to the French city of Lourdes in the hope of a cure. A special train was fitted out to deal with the very sick and handicapped patients on this occasion and she, together with her relatives and a few close friends were then transported the several hundred miles to France.

The small party of relatives and friends were there for several days before it was her turn to be passed through the waters. The day at last arrived when the woman was then totally immersed for a few seconds. When she was taken up prior to drying the body, she opened her eyes for the first time in several months, and a little later announced that she would like to sit up in bed. Doctors examined her condition in the days which followed with the pronouncement that she was fully cured. She needed only rest and recuperation after so many years of being confined to her bed. A few months ago, this same woman celebrated her eightieth birthday after having worked in orders for the last thirty years in the service of others.

The interesting thing in this case is that she was completely unconscious when she entered the waters. She was neither in a position to hope for healing nor to entertain fears that she might not have sufficient faith for a cure. One could say with truth that she had abandoned everything, but that the will and unshakeable faith were still at work within her subconscious mind.

The rest of her life's concerns had been totally given up, leaving the mind empty. It was into this 'emptiness' that the curative spirit could enter. At the point when this actually happened, there was no subject to be cured and no object acting as curative power. There was, as the Buddhists say, only Mind.

These three, humility, non-attachment and faith, work together as one in providing the right 'soil constituents', so to speak, for enlightenment to flourish. Although we can isolate them as here in an appreciation of their function, they are not really separate from one another.

To use another simile, it is rather like riding a bicycle for the first time. At first, there is much concentration on maintaining balance and then the need to combine this with steering and pedalling, but after a shorter or longer time, we are enabled to do all three together and finally to cycle without thinking about these things at all. So it is with the spiritual life. Of the greatest importance is the cultivation of non-attachment, created and sustained by awareness or mindfulness. As with the cycle in the example, the main thing here is the energy of propulsion, without which steering and balance are ineffective.

Obstacles to enlightenment

To bring things to a conclusion and so complete these observations on enlightenment, it is necessary at least to outline the hindrances to a life of inner freedom and happiness. Bringing them to notice helps those seeking the truth to place matters in perspective. Some of these hindrances to self-development come from the outside, others from the inside. Some are mentioned in what has been handed to us in the form we know as the New Testament, some are not. This does not imply therefore that Jesus was unaware of them since they may have been alluded to during his ministry, but have not been recorded.

The first and greatest of these stumbling blocks is the concept-ridden mind, and has already been dealt with in detail. Suffice it only to say that if there is anything which comes out clearly in the Gospels as a whole it is the freedom of mind which Jesus himself demonstrates throughout them. The one thing which was an anathema to him was the habit of binding the spirit to word and law within a tradition, and he opposed it bitterly on every occasion he found himself confronted with it, using the language of castigation, violent condemnation, humiliation and sarcasm **(Mt. 23,13–19; Lk. 5,21–23; Mk. 7,6 and elsewhere)**. Not only did he take every opportunity to revile the mind-binders of his day, but, practical individual that he was, he lived out that freedom of mind among the people of his time. Although very much a part of the Jewish tradition, he was not bound by it. He recognized much of it for what it is and was, that is, an attempt to bind the living spirit to the splints of written precept. All religious traditions suffer from the weight of this imposition, some more than others. Since the point of spiritual development is mental freedom and not bondage, all tradition is a potential hazard to liberation and has to be transcended.

We might regard tradition as an external danger, while the internal danger is that of concept-forming habit which, in turn, leads to cemented personal opinions. These, too, have to be abandoned in the interests of gaining personal integrity. Very often, these can be exposed by the conscious, meditative mind as mere bulwarks set up against possible injury to a tender ego or as a bastion to our inner security. In both cases they represent resistance to change and adaptation. Their eradication can only be achieved by deliberate apperception repeated many times. Generally speaking, this is more difficult to do than the giving up of a hidebound tradition. Jesus gave no clear guidance as to their elimination, merely implying their presence in human kind by his conduct and attitudes. In Buddhism, on the other hand, hardened attitudes of mind and the reflexive behaviour attached to them are treated in detail.

One of these attitudes is scepticism, here referring to an inward dismissal of the fact of any spirituality or anything greater than the self. In Buddhism it is referred to as 'doubt' or entertaining 'wrong opinions'. This may be merely opinion or it may have its expression in leading a sensual, self-orientated life, all of which we have alluded so far. As we have seen, this is castigated by Jeshua as the one sin which is not forgiven. Buddhism, too, refers to this mind-set as a considerable obstacle to advancement.

The others are the opposite poles of the same phenomenon. They are sloth and idleness on the one hand, implied in the Christian tradition in the parable of The Sower where the seed falls on stony, arid ground where the seed dries up, and on the other by excessive worry and concern about the welfare of self which is well illustrated by reference to the 'lilies of the field' touched upon above.

Finally, there is a last hindrance to spiritual advancement contained in the submission to ill-will which is quite clearly referred to in the 'Lord's Prayer' as the need to forgive, and implied in the 'Sermon on the Mount' where the antidote to ill-will, the peacemakers, are blessed. It is a recurring theme in the New Testament as is found notably at **Mt. 5,39: Mt. 5.44: Lk.6, 35; Lk. 6,29** and elsewhere.

The concept of sin

If we address ourselves to the facts of four Gospels we will find that sin does not figure as a major preoccupation in them. According to the reports we have of his pronouncements, Jesus' prime concern throughout his ministry was that we should not spend our lives attending to our shortcomings, but that as human beings, we should not allow anything to interfere with our love of God and man, neither law nor the habits of tradition, neither our social nor racial prejudices, nor even our religious precepts. All sin is eclipsed by these two loves. Where there is wholehearted devotion to these two precepts (bhakti) there can be no room for sin. The idea of sin then is simply irrelevant. If we are fully occupied with an appreciation of God as expressed in His world we will not be likely to go out and do harm to our neighbour. We would not be likely to steal from him or covet his wife, and be even less inclined to murder him.

Especially in the last thousand years of its existence, the Church has made the profound mistake of concentrating on the aspect of sin to the detriment of the true message of the New Testament, which is that God is waiting to be discovered in us all. All we have to do to find the happiness we yearn for is to turn in His direction. Sin, then, diminishes in proportion to our endeavour like the darkness which recedes before the dawn. These are the good tidings of the New Testament, not the prospect of hell and eternal damnation. Almost every page of the Gospels offers palpable proof of these tidings, explicitly in the teaching, and implicitly in the values and conduct of the teacher.

The ecclesiastical emphasis on sin at the expense of faith and love over two millennia is a perversion of truth which, in retrospect, can be assessed as a crime against humanity, a felony largely committed in the interests of the preservation of clerical power, and accounting for myriads of perverted lives. One thinks here not only of those hapless mortals who at some time or other fell foul of the perverse notions of heresy and the like, but also of the millions whose lives were, and still are, psychologically mutilated by an exaggerated awareness of their alleged sinfulness. In the past, the Church was ever ready to murder those who erred and strayed from her ways. Especially was this true in the Middle Ages, where today we are staggered at the cruelty and hard-heartedness involved in punishing so-called 'sinners'.

Interestingly enough, if there was one thing which put Rabbi Jeshua off balance and which sometimes provoked him to white heat, it was the cavilling, heartless, legal lovelessness of the priestly establishment of his own day. These were the people who would rather acquiesce in the incredible savagery of a stoning, for example, since this was 'according to the law', than allow the compassionate (not to mention intelligent) understanding of an issue they judged as a crime. For them (as now in some countries where stoning is permitted) such bestiality was an excuse to inflate the ego of the judge and his accomplices as well as to give the mob a palpable target for its own self-hate. The callous 'clause-and-paragraph men' who thought so much of themselves were those for whom the Nazarene had the greatest contempt and for whom, moreover, he reserved his hardest words. The whole of chapter **23** in the Book of **Matthew**, for example, is for thirty-nine verses devoted to a round condemnation of the values and attitudes of the scribes and Pharisees, interspersed with expletives such as 'Fools and blind!' (verses **17** and **19**) and at verses **13, 23** and **27** with the added warning 'Woe to you. But woe to you, scribes and Pharisees, hypocrites!'

At verse **13** he declares that these '…have shut up the kingdom of heaven against men; for you neither go in yourselves, nor do you allow those who are entering to go in.'

In passing, this is particularly interesting in that it is clear evidence that Jesus was not speaking of a geographical kingdom to be experienced after death, but a realisation in this life.

At verse **23** he tells those around him, an assembly which we may assume to have been made up of the common people with a sprinkling of those being directly addressed in this way. He says of them that they have attended to the petty things of the law, but '…have neglected the weightier matters of the law: justice and mercy and faith.' Here, he is almost certainly using the word 'justice' to imply judgement which is fair and honest, not the mindless application of the law which, in its severity, assumes its executors to be sinless and therefore morally above other men. 'For they bind heavy burdens, hard to bear, and lay them on men's shoulders, but they themselves will not move them with one of their fingers'(**Mt. 23, 4.**).

A little later, at verse **15**, he even goes as far as to imply that the scribes and Pharisees are the 'sons of hell'. Nor does he stop there in his obloquy, but goes on to tell them that their self-exaltation, hypocrisy and foolishness has contributed to the murder of the prophets of old. Here, he is of course referring to a state of mind common to his hearers, not to this one group of clerics. On another occasion, Jesus is particularly fulminatory, indeed abusive: 'Fill up, then, the measure of your father's guilt. Serpents, brood of vipers! How can you escape the condemnation of hell!' Hard-heartedness and hypocrisy stink in his nostrils, and thus the explicitness of the language **(Mk. 10, 2–5ff)**.

Pride and conceit, hypocrisy, insincerity, usury and exploitation, all of which are mentioned in the Gospels as the habits and attitudes of the priestly caste in his day were likely to incense the Galilean to such a degree that he sometimes lost control of himself. There was the occasion occurring in St Luke's gospel, for example, which is hardly, if ever, referred to from the pulpit. It is the passage occurring at **Lk. 11, 38–40** and what follows:

> And when he spoke a certain Pharisee asked Him to dine with him. So he went in and sat down to eat. When the Pharisee saw it, he marvelled that He had not first washed before dinner. Then the Lord said to him, 'Now you Pharisees make the outside of the cup and dish clean, but your inward part is full of greed and wickedness. Foolish one! Did not He who made the outside make the inside also?

Then he is reported as pursuing the matter as follows:

> Woe to you Pharisees! For you love the best seats in the synagogues and greetings in the market places. Woe to you scribes and Pharisees, hypocrites! For you are graves which are not seen, and the men who walk over them are not aware of them.

If, again, we are at liberty to accept what follows in the chapter quoted as the truly reported sequence of events, Jesus then proceeds to rebuke his host and others present in no uncertain tones **(Lk. 11, 42ff)** and worse, to even extend his condemnations at this highly inappropriate moment to every Pharisee.

A moment or two later, the lawyers, who apparently are also present, object to this tirade by pointing out that this rebuff is indirectly aimed at them as well. In reply, Christ rounds on these, too, accusing them, among other things, of shameful exploitation, of being the descendants of murderers, and in spirit as the accomplices to the murder of the prophets of old.

This is very strong stuff, particularly in the circumstances, and quite naturally arouses intense indignation. The upshot is a first-class row with 'vehement' **(11.53)** remonstration. Apparently, emotions ran so high at this moment that in the meantime '…an innumerable multitude of people gathered together so that they trampled on one another' **(12,1).** To make matters even worse, Jesus, assured of his personal safety by the presence of the crowd, continues to vilify the tribe of Pharisees from this safe vantage point. Not a very pleasant picture, the less so since it appears to be without provocation, or at least none is mentioned in Luke's account, and the need to wash one's hands before eating in those days being a perfectly reasonable request.

Although the instigation of such a scene in such circumstances (as an invited guest) was tactless and inopportune on Jesus' part, it was supposed to draw our attention to the pettifogging abidance by the letter of the law, pharasaical hypocrisy, the swanking enjoyment of rank and title, the abuse of privilege and the shameless exploitation of those less privileged, all of which is typically human behaviour which turns up again in exactly the same spirit, if in a different garb, centuries later in medieval Christianity. And not only there. All human history exhibits this pattern of behaviour, and it can be seen as hard at work today as in the ancient world. It is, we know, simply a matter of power and the corruption of power. But while it is all very well to sit back and observe, like Lord Acton, that 'power corrupts and absolute power corrupts absolutely', the question remains: *Why* do human beings act like this?

The answer, Buddhists believe, is that our egos are blind to our own transience. To use Alan Watts' phrase, we have a 'specious and precarious sense of our own permanence.' It is our attachment to this idea which leads us astray. Contemplation of our certain passing, on the other hand, deals a great blow to the ego.

Sin as the expression of ego

Ego, orientation to self and the inflation of self is the one great obstacle to illumination and, incidentally, to our personal happiness. As well as from that briefly outlined above, we can see from other passages throughout the Gospels that the Master was keen on exposing egoistical behaviour, knowing that the ego is at the root of all crime and therefore of all antisocial activity. Murder, theft, rape, usury and exploitation, the abuse of authority, injury to others (and to other creatures), lying, cheating, covetousness, cruelty in all its forms, maligning others and all the forms of denial which refute That within us and within others – all of them are expressions of ego. Withdraw the sense of self-justification from them and they no longer exist. Expose the ego and the sin as well as the need to atone for it disappears. The idea of redemption, too, disappears like removing a stone in a shoe. When the stone is no longer there, the pain vanishes. Despite the fact that this was clear to Jesus in his critical attention to ego in the men of authority around him, he does not give us guidance about laying the axe to the root of the matter. Instead, he appeals to our better nature and asks us to be forgiving as God Himself is forgiving. If we forgive others their misdeeds (in an act of humility and, therefore, ego-less), He will forgive us. Although he himself does not punish anyone during the course of the New Testament, since, as he says, he is come not to judge humanity, but to free mankind, he nevertheless still thinks in the terms of his fathers, that is, of punishment and reward **(Mt. 6,1–6; Mt. 6,23; Mk. 9,41; and Lk. 6,23)**. These, though not part of his conduct during his ministry, were nevertheless subconsciously absorbed by those who came after him and acted out on their own plane of mental development. Hence the cruelty which was later to accompany the growth of the Church to a world power which in no way set it apart from the heathen beyond its precincts. Indeed, the undisputed conviction that crime or sin was to be followed by an equal degree of punishment did not receive serious review until the late nineteenth century.

With Buddhism it was different. Ego-inflation or self-aggrandisement was recognised from the beginning as a path leading to ruin and dealt with by demonstrating the non-existence of ego as entity.

What this means precisely is well illustrated in the following event related either as fact or legend some seven or eight hundred years ago in the Spain of the Moors. The same truth which it embodies has found its way into other cultures, and whether it actually occurred or not is unimportant compared with insight it affords into the workings of our minds.

One day the caliph had withdrawn from the heat of the day into an ante-chamber away from the mainstream of palace life, there to take time off to read and rest. He had not been there very long before he heard a noise. Curious to know what was the cause, he retired into the deep shadow which another part of the room afforded and waited. A woman appeared and, after looking around surreptitiously, made for a finely-wrought vase which stood on a pedestal in the room. She grasped the vase, enfolded it in her robe and was about to make off when the caliph stepped from the shadows and demanded what she was doing. The thief was so surprised that folds of the gown fell apart to reveal a man holding tightly to the vase.

'What do you want in here?' the caliph asked, but the thief was so surprised that he could hardly say a word. 'Is it the vase you want?' he asked rhetorically. The thief could only nod and held on tight to the vase.

'Then take the thing,' the caliph commanded, 'it's yours!' The thief turned on his heel to flee when the caliph called after him, 'What do you say when something is given to you?' The thief, suddenly aware of his manners, said, 'Thank you,' standing there in mid flight for the exit. 'And take off that silly robe you're wearing; you look a fool,' the caliph added with a smile. The thief did as he was told and was gone in the wink of an eye, leaving the robe where he had stood.

Needless to say, he didn't get far and was soon apprehended by the court guard and thrown into a dungeon to await trial and execution the next day.

A large crowd had gathered together in their eagerness to watch an execution in one of the palace courtyards devoted to the dispensation of justice. Several of the caliph's officers were there, the grand judge, the vizier and other dignitaries awaiting the appearance of the caliph himself who was always invited to attend these functions and who, with a wave of his hand, could pronounce over life and death.

On his arrival and having seated himself with due dignity on the throne of justice provided for the occasion, the prisoner was brought forward to receive the charges against him. He was thrown to the ground before the judge and the others at the bench where he trembled from head to foot in his irons. The officer then proceeded to read aloud the charges brought against him: 'You are hereby condemned for (1) for trespassing on property belonging to His Infinite Majesty, the Caliph of Spain, and (2) with breaking and entering the private quarters of His Majesty and there removing and stealing a precious vase belonging to our esteemed Lord (may Allah give him long life over us), and (3)...' But before the officer of the law could go on, the caliph raised his ringed hand for the proceedings to stop. Rising, he then said, 'Loose him from his chains! I gave him the vase you mention. It's his to do with whatever he likes.' A murmur of astonishment and disappointment ran through the assembled crowd. 'Moreover, he thanked me for it,' the caliph added, 'Therefore, let him go. He is a free man!' The caliph then withdrew to his chambers without another word. As for the accused, he was given the vase and ordered to clear off. The crowd parted to allow him access to the castle gate and freedom, angered and frustrated at not being allowed to be entertained with an execution, or an amputated limb at the least.

A few days later, the man appeared again at the palace gate with the request for an audience with the caliph. After much administrative ado, but perhaps because he still had the vase in his arm, his request was finally granted. The caliph received him in his private quarters with a smile and bade him be seated in his presence.

'No woman's robe, then, today?' he enquired, to which the thief replied by throwing himself to the ground, 'Sire, you are indeed the wise and compassionate ruler men say you are! I thank you most humbly for sparing my life and bring your vase back to you with my most abject apologies!'

'Would you care for some tea?' the caliph replied with a smile, and he clapped his hands for tea to be brought. 'I see that you are no longer attached to the vase,' he added, 'Is that right?'

'No, Sire, it is yours,' said the thief in a small voice.

'Then neither am I', said the caliph, 'so just leave it to stand there, and let us enjoy our tea.'

The beauty of this tale will not be lost on us, for sure, but the anecdote is more than a tale showing royal magnanimity in the matter of forgiveness. It just as clearly displays our egoistic attachment to things. The thief is egoistically attached to an object, the officers to their task of pompously seeing justice done, and the mob to its bloodlust. Only the caliph is truly free and, in the last scene, the thief himself. We can well imagine that now he realises his folly in being attached to a thing and that, more than the caliph's generosity of spirit, he prizes the freedom he has gained from no longer being the slave of his ego. At this moment, the ego ceases to exist, for it has been dealt a death-blow. This is the point.

The desire to cultivate ill-will or to harm others in some way, either physically or mentally, is rooted in our egos. In this way, some of us, albeit unconsciously, see these actions as a means of self-expression, of manifesting the reality of ego, of establishing ourselves in the world or simply as a means of freeing ourselves from the situation in which all of us find our personalities entangled. Generally speaking, we are not aware of what is going on within us when this rooted desire gives way to expression. This is the reason why the majority of individuals, when asked why they have committed a crime, for example, cannot give an adequate answer. The reason, it is suggested, has been well summed up by Richard de Martino in modern psychological terms as follows in describing the ego as trapped within itself. He sees it as a

> ...subject-object contradiction... Its being objectless and subjectless is a negativity of total bondage and obstruction in which subject and object in their contradictory, dualistic polarity impede and impound one another in one constricted, helpless clog.[10]

This is the situation before enlightenment, where our natural instincts and energies are either bound or perverted by some social structure, some belief of some habitual pattern of behaviour or, if we are lucky, where these energies can be sublimated in the exercise of an art say, or a sport or some other activity where we can express ourselves adequately. However, for the great mass of humanity, these are generally subverted or distorted. This, in turn, renders us either frustrated with life, unhappy or disappointed or, in so many cases, twists us into mental – and all too often –even physical cripples. De Martino continues:

> When, however this root core (having been narrowed down by our attention to the koan or some such procedure), bursting, uproots and turns upon itself, then the ego truly dies and the 'great death' (Buddhist term) which is at once the great birth of 'great awakening' .[11] (My brackets)

This, he adds a line or two later, is its resolution and fulfilment: 'In dying to itself as ego, it is born and awakens to its Self as Self.'[12]

Looking at it in this way, we realise that we are all faced with the same problem, and all of us seek our own ways to solve it. For this reason, none of us can be the judge of another.

So much was clear to Jesus, too. Despite his altercations with the orthodoxy of his acquaintance, he says quite clearly: 'Ye judge after the flesh; I judge no man' **(Jn. 8,15)** '...for I came not to judge the world, but to save the world'. **(Jn. 12,47)** 'Judge not that ye be not judged.' (**Mt. 7, 1**; and **Lk. 6,37)** and hinting that judgement is, in any case, an egotistical affair, he says in the same book at **Lk. 5, 30** ...I judge: and my judgement is just, because I seek not my own will...'

Redemption

If an individual solution to the problem above leads some of us to antisocial behaviour, others may not presume to resolve that problem by seeking to compensate for a wrong done by committing another (punishment), but by addressing ourselves to the kernel of the problem, the ego, which means in effect releasing the criminal (the individual) from his inner incarceration and getting him to face up to his own ego. In addition, it means re-routing the suppressed energies implied in that imprisonment into more creative channels. Much progress in this direction has already been achieved in the area of criminal psychology today and that is greatly to our credit, but it is time now to draw everyone's attention to his own mental make-up which includes this problem and resolve the situation shown above by making it an integral and essential part of child education. In other words, it is time that we applied the techniques of spiritual liberation to the normal psyche, that is to say, *before* it breaks out into crime or turns its energies to self-mutilation in one form or another. Liberation from the clamours of the small self so that we may 'walk under the sky as free men and women' mindful of our true selves is at the very centre of Buddhism. It is also the deeper meaning of the Christian term 'Redemption'. The core of redemption, too, is not the 'forgiveness of sins', not that primarily, but the joy of knowing that we are free at last (redeemed) from the insistent ego which is finally seen for what it is – a non-entity.

The Lord's Prayer

When we think of ego in this connection, we are not thinking of simple conceit, a ridiculous pride in knowledge, say, or good looks or some other relatively harmless prowess, but of the harmful variety of blind, egotistic behaviour which seeks its own advantage to the detriment and suffering of others, of thinking and conduct which is entirely attached to the idea of self or ego. Inherent in what has become known to us as The Lord's Prayer is the foil to self. The older form of the prayer is given here for aesthetic reasons:

> Our Father which art in heaven. Hallowed be thy Name. Thy kingdom come, Thy will be done, on earth as it is in heaven. Give us this day our daily bread and forgive us our trespasses as we forgive all those that have trespassed against us. And lead us not into temptation, but deliver us from evil. For Thine is the kingdom, the power and the glory, for ever and ever. Amen. **(Lk. 11, 2–5)**

The very first word is not 'My' but 'Our', suggesting that God is common to all; 'our' is something shared, a bond. The author could have chosen a vocative form 'O Father!' or 'Thou, Father, who are etc...', but prefers instead the mutuality of 'Our'. The use of the word 'Father' is a similar term of embracement and at the same time suggests associations such as respect, awareness of superior knowledge and capability, strength, protection, guidance, thoughtful kindness, wisdom, security, reliability and so forth. The Father of the Universe is therefore omnipotent and omniscient, but not cold and aloof. Behind the biblical figure of the 'Father' is also the love He has for us his creatures, in the same way as an earthly father loves his children. Implicit in the word 'Father' is also the conviction that a father knows what is best for his children. He knows from wider experience what is harmful and what is beneficial for them, and loving care is at the centre of his dealing with them. All of this in turn directly involves humility on our part. Similarly, 'Hallowed be thy Name' is an expression of the deepest reverence. The 'inner room', so to speak, of the mind quietens in recognition of something much greater than the desiring 'busy-ness' of the everyday mind. For those who sit in meditation, for example, it is recognised as the second stage of recollection, that of moving into ego-less quiescence and of bringing the ceaseless activity of our everyday mind to a halt. Nothing could be more free from ego than these words and this state of mind.

'Thy kingdom come...' is an extension of the quiescent mind which has now been attained either in prayer or meditation. The phrases can be understood as 'Let Thy kingdom come...' or 'May it be that Thy kingdom come...' Alternatively, we could say 'Let it be that the kingdom of heaven be known.' The kingdom, as understood in what has been outlined above, is a state of mind, so-called 'cosmic consciousness'. It is the Bodhisattva's vow never to rest until every 'sentient being has been saved', in other words, until he or she has come to enlightenment or experienced cosmic consciousness. The inference is that the world is not enlightened, but, on the contrary, dominated by selfish desire. If there were more generalised enlightenment, there would be less evil (sin) in the world. Enlightenment is the 'light' which Jesus speaks of in contrast to 'those who walk in darkness'. Seen in this way, 'Let there be more light in the world' would be an alternative translation.

'Thy will be done' is similar to 'Let your wisdom prevail' (i.e. 'not mine') and is at the same time a declaration of submission – the opposite of self-interested demand. It is a petition to God for that state of mind which has given up self, a substitution of God's will for our own. It is a listening to, or an *awareness* of, 'the still, small voice', the act of being 'still and know that I am God'. It is, in short, a declaration of total humility.

'...in earth as it is in heaven' simply means 'in this life of ours' which, although it might appear to be quite cut off from the perception of 'cosmic consciousness' or enlightenment as illustrated above, is nevertheless contiguous with that possibility in every moment.

If this is difficult to grasp at first, we can imagine a straight line for a moment which runs from point A to point B. We can think of this as our life conceived lineally. Most of us, as we proceed along the line from birth to death, are concerned with what has gone before or what lies ahead. Past and future are our correlates, so to speak. Memory affords us the opportunity to recall the past, and the older we become, the more we tend to be preoccupied with our larger pasts than with our dwindling futures. There are a great many people, too, who are more concerned with the past than with the moment in which they live. The past appears to them more enjoyable because it is unassailable. It is a safe haven into which neither the present nor the future can intrude. On the other hand, and incidentally in our modern materialistic world of acquisition and sense satisfaction, the future has almost become a substitute for life itself. All business, for example, is linked to it in terms of 'expansion' and 'development' and, since we live in such a world, our education and our development as human beings is closely associated with what we envisage as 'the future'. The more intensively we live in the 'future' with regard to realising our aims, the quicker life appears to pass. But what of the present? In the West we usually imagine the 'present' as a hair's breadth, an infinitesimally short interval 'existing' between one moment and another. Theoretically, this interval separates past and future. We can even go so far as to imagine that, because the interval is so infinitely small, it cannot have meaning since, as soon as the past is over, the future is already here. In this way, we think of the infinite future 'coming' from somewhere and passing without interruption into the past.

Because modern human beings have a strongly developed sense of the passage of time, we punctuate our individual and collective lives with time intervals and refer to these as past and future. This is all very well and very useful of course in arranging our lives, but we forget that during the course of transition from future into past there is an awareness of present which is able to give these concepts meaning. Looked at in another way, we can say that if there were no present, there would be no past nor future, only duration.

However, the present is more than a mere theoretical point of orientation separating what we imagine to be real past and future. Using our geometric example again, we could imagine the present to be like a line drawn at right angles to the A-B line in the direction, say, of C. As we progress along A-B, C inexorably accompanies that movement in another spatial dimension, like a shadow which faithfully follows every action. C is consciousness and also that dimension of higher consciousness which we have discussed above, the 'Kingdom of Heaven' of Christianity, the *Paramâtman* of Hinduism, the Emptiness or *Śunyata* of Buddhism. That is why the mystics of every age and every religion have spoken of 'transcending time'. In this state (the 'heaven' of the Lord's Prayer) past and future are seen as theoretical ideas like the lines of longitude and latitude on a globe, useful for practical purposes, but entirely fictitious. The reality, they say, is the *now* of this moment. Whether Moslem, Buddhist, Hindu or Christian, they all maintain that this 'Now' is eternal. It is the 'everlasting life' of Jesus' pronouncements **(see Mt. 19,16; Jn. 3,15, 17,3, etc)**.

Johann Gottfried Herder expresses this very well in his *Amor und Psyche*:

> Here on earth our life is but a dream
> And we, like playing shadows over waves,
> Come and go, measuring our sluggish steps

In terms of Time and Space, and all the time -
Though we know it not – we abide in life eternal.[13]

Jesus' plea in the prayer, is that we mortals may live as much in that eternal moment (which in any case accompanies us throughout our lives) as we do in our everyday lives, our 'normal' wavelength. It means that we should be aware of this 'now' which travels with us along the samsaric 'straight line' with all its vicissitudes. It entails being aware of ourselves in every moment, for awareness is our link with the nirvanic and the eternal, with that which Jesus calls 'heaven'.

Give us this day our daily bread and forgive us our trespasses
as we forgive all those that have trespassed against us.

Jesus has mentioned elsewhere **(Lk. 7,47; Jn. 20,27)** that we should forgive one another. Not to forgive is to harbour resentment and the desire for revenge, both of which can be immediately recognised as highly egotistical in character. Egoism, as we have seen, blocks rapport with the divine, (Buddhism's No-mind) and so the creative energy which is love or compassion cannot flow. This restricts our development like a plant which is entangled with weed. Forgiveness, on the other hand, recognises our own weaknesses and so deflates our ideas of self, allowing that which is not ego to enter the mind. To humbly eat the daily bread which comes to us through the labour of many hands, having forgiven everyone, accepting and forgiving ourselves as well as others, alert to the moment, respectful and attentive of others' needs in the community, all this plays an important role in Zen training, and, no less in the best of Christian religious communities.

'And lead us not into temptation, but deliver us from evil.'

This line reveals the speaker as thoroughly conversant with what the Buddhist recognises as *samsara*. In this view the world is a very dangerous place; it admits that anything can happen to us at any time. Death and disease, change and decay are our constant companions. It is wisdom borne out by our own lives and in those of others around us. But there are other lurking dangers than the circumstantial ones of death and disease. There are the ego-centred tendencies within ourselves (temptations) which can also destroy our earthly lives or, after it, throw us into hell. Among these are, as we are aware, an inordinate desire for wealth or power without the responsibilities which their possession involves, the tendency to exploit in order to fulfil selfish desire, whatever forms this may take or indeed anything which bolsters the ego at the expense of the environment, human and other, but also other byways like the addiction to alcohol and drugs, which, while not in themselves criminal activities, nevertheless lead us away from the goal of liberation. The biblical word 'temptation' also implies the tendency to commit sin in the sense suggested above, in falling away from God towards ourselves.

In Buddhism, the emphasis is not on curbing the tendency to sin. It does not dwell on the symptom, but strikes at the cause: the ego.

Added to internal deviations from the Way are the karmic destinies of others which may collide with our own. Very simple examples of these are the destinies of nations where young men were pressed into the army in days gone by, a millionfold tragedy, succinctly expressed by William Blake:

> And the hapless soldier's sigh
> Runs in blood down palace walls,
> **Songs of Experience, 'London', V.III**

Or we may think of the fate of men, women and children caught up in the mortal coils of mass persecution in any age, or simply of a collective disaster like drought or famine, earthquake, volcanic eruption or contagious disease. The line of the prayer could therefore be rendered as: *'Let us not fall prey to the destructive tendencies in ourselves and deliver us from the forces of karmic accident.'*

'For Thine is the kingdom, the power and the glory for ever and ever. Amen.'

This is a return in spirit to the first two lines of the prayer and rounds it off. It is the recognition that God is the kingdom, that He is all powerful and that this power is immanent at all times, now and for ever. It is the one thing which never changes. In Buddhist terms it is the That which is always present, and which is 'neither born nor dies.'

The Lord's Prayer is a *bhakti* prayer of submission to the guidance of divine will. The Buddhist approach is different only inasmuch as it subscribes to the *vichara* method which invites us to be aware of that which is going on in the mind from moment to moment. To look inward and be aware in this way is to be in control. In this state of mind, one is not 'led into temptation'. For the true Christian believer this would mean that the 'divine will' is done at once if the practitioner is already in that state of consciousness from which he can survey the operations of karma. He is in that moment without thought (and, therefore, desire) and is free to determine his own fate. He is independent of the dictates of ego (and, therefore, free of sin) since he discerns their true nature and also sees clearly how ego arises. His state of mind at this stage is exactly that of the Buddhist.

The diagram – and other ways of saying the same thing

As we have said, the letters A and B of the diagram indicate a lifespan. The important thing to grasp is that the line C, perpendicular to AB is intimately connected with the lifespan line. The nirvanic line, C, touches AB at all points. The point of contact is conscious awareness. The individual consciousness, the person, passing along the line A>B from birth to death experiences life, samsara, but, as he does so, may not at all be aware of C, which follows every step of the way. He can, like millions of his kind, pass through the whole cycle of his existence and is never even for a moment aware of the other dimension.

If, on the other hand, there is an awareness of C, the experiencer will notice as in the examples above that there is no time and no space. Time and space disappear. Where there is space and time there are events and, consequently, the experience we have referred to as samsara. Where mental movement along the line ceases for some reason or other, the point of nirvanic entry is made possible. Then there is only stillness (*Śunyata,* Emptiness, nirvanic insight). People experiencing this state, C, refer to the feeling of 'time standing still'.

Entry into this nirvanic state is achieved by constantly returning to stillness, by quietly meditating. This means nothing more than bringing the mind back to its original state before thoughts arise. Parallel with this is the practice of intense awareness in daily life.

We can proceed a step further in this theory by suggesting that the line A-B is generally limiting. Following what T.S. Eliot once referred to as the world moving 'In appetency, on its metalled ways of time past and time future,'[14] in which we may think of our life as the 'tramlines' of our desires, we can think of our life, therefore, as restricted to these two dimensions. This restriction results in frustration: our past is irrecoverable and our future is full of unfulfilled desire. However, at every and any point along the way, we can stop the passage and move at right angles to the samsaric line. This not only happens dramatically as in moments of inspiration and visions of truth, but may occur in a more modest form when we push back the veils of our prejudice for a moment or transcend our habitual patterns of thought. It can happen, let us say, on hearing great music or on experiencing other forms of art which move us from our habitual way of looking at the world into another, deeper experience of its and our own potential. It can happen in a lecture hall when our minds are stretched to embrace other aspects of our existence which were hitherto unsuspected, and it can happen when we witness the exemplary behaviour of another person. We can gain entry into deeper awareness by contact with children, as many a poet has recorded, or simply by fully experiencing our natural surroundings. The important point here is that we have moved, be it ever so little.

From earlier considerations, we know that we can continue to move in the other direction until a general, deeper perception takes place and eventually learn to stay in the dimension while living out our everyday lives, moving, as we have noted above, on two levels.

We can now see from the diagram that there is nothing strange about this. It is simply to be detached for a shorter or longer interval from the AB condition and its strict, dualistic relationships which affect every conceivable aspect of our lives on that level. In illustration of this, we can assert that where there is light there must also be dark, where there is pain, joy; where there is beauty, also ugliness, love, hate, assertion, resistance, and so on without end. Detachment is liberation from this state of affairs. At first, our entry might be of short duration, but the more often we seek the 'stillness' as it is so often called, the more likely we are to reach a state where we do not wholly lose the feeling of being there even in the many activities of daily life. A permanent abode is granted only to the very few at this stage in our human development, and is for those who seek that sanctuary before anything else which worldly existence may offer. It also accounts for the declarations of those who have reached this state that they are 'not of this world' **(Jn. 18,36),** or may sometimes describe people as 'possessing divine power' and so on. When the few among us say this, they mean that they inhabit the world of nirvana, as all men (potentially) are capable of doing if they exert themselves sufficiently. Below are examples, ancient and modern, in illustration of what has been said so far:

When Time stops the universe disappears

It is here all the time precisely because it is beyond the reach of time; and it cannot be held because time is intermittent.
It is present in every now-moment between the tick-tock of serial manifestation via which it functions indirectly
We know it eternally. It is the background not only of thought … but of every act of living.
That is why it is pure function, and what pure Function is.
From: *Wei Wu Wei,* All Else is Bondage[15]

It is too clear and so it is hard to see.
A dunce once searched for a fire with a lighted lantern.
Had he known what fire was,
He could have cooked his rice much sooner.
Zen Master Mumon (1184–1260)

And again (Genesis):

I move,
Space becomes (as a result of my movement),
Time is born (as a measure of my movement in space),
I have objects (because I have become the subject of space and time),
Dualism is established,
The Universe appears,
I identify myself with my objects (and there are illusory egos),
I suffer illusorily (and suffering becomes universal).
Wei Wu Wei,* All Else is Bondage *(XVII) p. 20**[16]**

Wei Wu Wei's arguments are always intended to take us away from our entrenched standpoints and turn us in the direction of self-knowledge. His tone is crisp and clear, unambiguous and uncompromising, and it has something of the manner of the ancient Zen masters in its forthrightness. Krishnamurti, on the other hand, in his book *Freedom from the Known*, speaks of inner freedom in a manner which is more conversational, but nevertheless underlines the same point that we have discussed above:

> Most of us, inwardly, are never alone...You are never alone because you are full of all the memories, all the conditioning, all the mutterings of yesterday; your mind is never clear of the rubbish it has accumulated. To be alone you must die to the past. When you are alone, totally alone, not belonging to any family, any nation, any culture, any particular continent, there is that sense of being an outsider. The man who is completely alone in this way is innocent and it is this innocence that frees the mind from sorrow. We carry about with us the burden of what thousands of people have said and memories of all our misfortunes. To abandon all that totally is to be alone, and the mind that is alone is not only innocent but young – not in time or age, but young, innocent, alive at whatever age – and only such a mind can see that which is truth and that which is not measurable by words.[17]

The word 'alone' here signifies what we have described as stillness, the approach to non-conceptuality, non-dualism or nirvana as suggested in the diagram illustration. It has nothing to do with loneliness, but with self-sufficiency. From this state of being, a person can practise true compassion. The author refers to the weight of the past which sullies the present and pleads for its abandonment in order to regain the first innocence of childhood and the glimpse of eternity which accompanies being 'alone'. Such people are able, like children, to enjoy nirvanic perception while in samsara.

Of this, William Blake sings:

He who binds himself to a joy
Does the winged life destroy;
But he who kisses the joy as it flies,
Lives in eternity's sunrise.
'Eternity', from: Poems from *Rossetti* (1793)

This is the life of Zen, or indeed the life of anyone who has understood the meaning of their existence, regardless of their affiliations. The modern sage, Maharshi Mahesh Yogi, commenting on the Bhagavad Gita,[18] puts it all very clearly:

> A man who has attained cosmic consciousness is always established in the Self, even while engaged in activity. This state of consciousness is the mature state of Sanyasa, a state of complete non-attachment of the Self with activity, even while activity continues in the relative field of life. Such complete non-attachment is not possible unless the mind is established in eternal contentment. The constant practice of gaining Yoga, or Union with divine consciousness, brings the mind to the state which gives eternal contentment, thereby establishing a natural state of Sanyasa or renunciation.[19]

'If you want to understand Zen,' said Ying-An one day to a group of devotees, just be mindless, wherever you are, twenty-four hours a day, until you spontaneously merge with the Way. This is what an ancient worthy called, 'The mind not touching things, the steps not falling anywhere.' The word 'mindless' here means not allowing the mind to dwell on concepts or emotions or become attached to anything. It implies simply accepting things as they are when they come and not resisting the unpleasant or embracing the pleasant. It does not mean either stoical indifference as some might immediately infer. Stoicism is a different kettle of fish. Stoicism is to use the mind to quell the mind. It is stalwart acceptance of fact both pleasant and unpleasant, the habitual suppression of feeling which infers using the will to control them. This is not the 'mindless' state of Zen. This 'mindlessness' has something of the Taoistic principle of 'letting things happen', of not interfering, of allowing things to come into being as fruit ripens or as a tree bends before the wind and water seeks low ground. Nor has it anything to do with an attitude which might be described as 'anti-intellectual' or 'bovine stupidity'. On the contrary, when the mind is allowed to function naturally without the interference of the busy intellect, its intelligence potential increases, as can be seen in the case of those using Zen techniques in the study of the martial arts. It is all a matter of 'flow' rather than 'push'. Eventually, says Ying, you will acquire that super consciousness which characterises the sage. This is to merge into the Way (Tao). By 'not touching', the older master means that the mind is not allowed to be caught up or involved in its usual habits of association and emotional connivance with thoughts arising.

Projection from the state of AB above into that of C can be induced in all sorts of ways so that one can say that any circumstances can be spontaneously used or sometimes deliberately contrived by a master to effect the transition.

There were occasions when the old masters simply turned their backs on questioners at a point during their brief conversations. They knew then that such an action could effect the desired result. On other occasions they would utter a loud cry, wordlessly raise their eyebrows or resort to an uncharacteristic gesture, or simply remain silent. At other times they might seize the questioner or administer a slap or a cuff or say something offensive. Some of these methods have already been illustrated. Whatever method was used, the idea is always to stop the thought process. Some masters like Lin Chi (Jap. Rinzai) were almost always roughly persuasive while others like Huang Po and Bankei were quieter but no less acutely aware of the state of mind of the questioner before them. The following brief interview demonstrates the method of stopping the thought process by suddenly throwing the questioner back upon his own resources. I have taken the liberty of rendering the original into modern idiomatic, conversational English in order to give it relevance to life today.

A monk: 'I was so pleased to learn from what your reverence said to us yesterday evening about everyone being born with the Buddha-nature. What I can't understand, though, is that if we all have this Buddha-nature, deluded thoughts shouldn't arise in the first place.'

Bankei: 'At the very moment you said this, what kind of delusion was there?'[20]

There is no doubt that Bankei could have answered this earnest question in a more discursive way, but instead he immediately seizes on the essential issue of the monk's state of mind, the elation experienced by the master's words the previous evening and the scrap of doubt still left in the questioner's mind which he uses to propel the monk into another direction than that of conceptualisation.

A state of being prepared

Many people will ask how it is with those who have no master at hand to help them to realisation. The answer to this is that if the desire to know ourselves is great enough we shall be led in the direction of a solution. There is nothing mysterious about this. People who have difficulties of any kind are led towards an answer to their problems by the mind, whether these problems are spiritual or mundane. It is a recognised psychological law that every thought, which assumes a clear image in our minds and which is backed by desire, strives for fulfilment. In both instances, the spiritual and the mundane, the mind must first be emptied of all prejudice (pre-judgement) in anticipation of an answer. Hence the ancient Indian maxim 'When the student is ripe, the master will appear,' is a fact of experience. The master may well be an actual person, but very often guidance can be in the form of material put in our way from which we can learn or it may be the words of a friend or simply a sight or sound. An ancient poem sums up the experience of being precipitated into *satori* like this:

Mount Lu
In misty rain; the river Chë runs high.
When I had never been there, how I longed to see it!
Then I went and soon returned, it was nothing special after all:
Mount Lu in misty rain; the river Chë runs high.

There are other records of men and women at the point of realisation who have been awakened by the cracking of a twig, the call of a bird, or on seeing the full moon or smelling damp earth, recognition of the coming of spring and so on and so forth. There is truly no end to the immediate causes of *satori*.

The Sermon on the Mount

Jesus lists some of the factors conducive to enlightenment in his short commentary which we know as the Sermon on the Mount **(Mt. 5,1–11):**

Blessed are the poor in spirit.

Being 'poor in spirit' does not refer to any form of spiritlessness, but instead refers to the state of mind already described as striving to understand that which is not attainable to the intellect. It is that absolute humility which immediately precedes enlightenment.

For theirs is the kingdom of Heaven.

Those who can find this state of mind in themselves will live in what Jesus describes as the kingdom of Heaven.

Blessed are they that mourn. For they shall be comforted.

The word 'mourn' has not received the attention it deserves in theological commentary. In English, the word is immediately associated with death and the reactions of those who have lost someone they love, hence the grief and sorrow arising from this situation. In the Lutheran translation of this sentence, however, we find the words 'Leid tragenden', i.e. 'sufferers'. In German, it can, but must not necessarily be associated with the specific instance of death. The line could, therefore, be rendered: *'Blessed are those who suffer (or who must suffer), for they shall be comforted.'* This slight adjustment throws a great deal of light onto the meaning of the utterance. The pronouncement, like the others which belong to it, is at the same time a promise. It is a message of hope to those who for some reason experience suffering. Using the reference above, it is a reiteration of the existence of C as an alternative to the AB progression. That is a prosaic way of putting it perhaps, but the really important thing here is that the declaration has been made. It carries the great tidings of the Buddha who said in so many words: we are not bound to suffer; there is a way out. This is of the greatest significance.

We could imagine a life which offers us no salvation from suffering. Our lives could quite easily resemble the various hells ably portrayed by the existentialist writers in this century. But this is not so.

Each line of the beatitudes is prefixed by the word *'Blessed'* and, coming first in the sentence, it conveys a certain emphasis. How, in this instance, we ask ourselves, can those who suffer be blessed? It is because suffering is very often a means of bringing us to our senses, that is to say, to an appreciation of values which we may not have considered before. Illness, for example, very often brings us humility and an awareness of others' suffering. Frequently, it makes us aware of the brevity of life so that we come to ask ourselves what meaning it has. The experience is one which moves us into other areas of understanding and perhaps into an entirely changed attitude towards life.

Blessed are the meek, for they shall inherit the earth.

Many commentators equate this with the first beatitude, but it does say 'the earth' and not the 'kingdom'. At first, it seems to be a blatant contradiction to what we know about the world, since there it is certainly not the meek who rule, but the rich and the powerful, then as now, although in many places not so barbarously as they once did. The word 'meek' suggests a lack of arrogance, in short, the prerequisite for entry into the kingdom of Heaven. To put it prosaically: that humility or emptiness of mind which allows us to discern our real natures will assure us a place in the kingdom.

It has nothing to do with 'taking things sitting down', but 'taking things as they come'. It means not putting our busy minds in the way of the flow of things as they happen. To intrigue, for example, in order to gain personal advantage is to interfere with the flow; any criminal activity (and all criminal activity is antisocial) is to personally interfere with the natural flow of life in order to gain advantage over others or for oneself. To accept the natural 'fallout' of experience without seeking personal benefit is to live, as the Chinese say, 'with the Tao' and not against it. The trial of Jesus is a good, though tragic, illustration of 'allowing things to happen' in this sense. In the circumstances Jesus found himself, he could well have employed his powers to side-step the issue as his detractors suggested **(Lk. 23,35)**, but instead he accepted his destiny. It is interesting to note, too, that had he resorted to any means, human or superhuman, to disentangle himself from the fate which awaited him, his credibility would have been utterly destroyed for posterity and we would know no more of his fate than that of the malefactors who were executed with him.

Imperturbability

An example of 'allowing things to happen', of 'meekness' in the Taoist sense outlined, is given by the account of an ancient Zen master, who was accused by a girl in the village of being the father of her baby. This of course was a scandalous situation for such a dignitary and caused a great stir in the community, but when he was informed of his trespass he just said: 'Well now, fancy that!' Accordingly, the baby was brought to the monastery and someone was found to look after its needs for several months; an atmosphere of outrage among the monks as can well be imagined.

After a few months, however, and as the baby began to grow, the mother began to miss the child. Investigations were made and the real father was finally exposed as a young fellow in the village who was now charged with the responsibility for his offspring. All this was accompanied by much shame and embarrassment on the part of the two young people, so that eventually they appeared before the master to express their remorse for what they had done and to offer an apology.

'Well, well, fancy that!' said the master in reply to their tearful explanations, and handed the baby over to them. The baby found a proper home and rightful parents and the religious community learned a lesson in meekness.

'For they shall inherit the earth' therefore means that in the acceptance of samsara's vicariousness, the weak are its master. This explains the use of the word 'earth' (the samsaric aspect) rather than the 'kingdom of Heaven' (the nirvanic aspect). The first and the third beatitudes, therefore, are not synonymous with one another.

Blessed are those who hunger and thirst for righteousness, For they shall be filled.

The word 'righteousness' presents a problem. If we are to understand it as 'just and moral behaviour' or 'moral rectitude', then it is simply and only a pronouncement on the good life, a word of promise to all those who do not kill, lie, steal or commit adultery. We might think of it as meaning that the moralists shall have their day at the last, and God shall be justified of his elect.

The words 'hunger and thirst' suggest a very strong desire, and if we associate this desire with the devout wish for a moral environment, here presumably based on the Hebrew interpretation of what is socially acceptable and what is not (to which, we recall, death by stoning also belongs), then it looks very much like a fundamentalist standpoint. Christ's ministry, however, could also be described as a campaign against bigotry and fundamentalism. His utterance could be interpreted but also weakened to 'Blessed are they who yearn for a better world, for that is to come,' thereby ignoring the fact that the verb 'filled' in the second part of the sentence is the complement of hungering and thirsting. What, then, does 'righteousness' mean?

It means, I suggest, the path which leads to God. It necessarily embodies moral conduct, since without it we cannot tread the path. The words 'hunger and thirst' mean whole-hearted commitment to God. The reward of such dedication is that fulfilment which each of us desires.

The word 'God', however, is freighted with all kinds of uncomfortable personal and all too human overtones which have come down to us via the Old Testament as well as interpretations of the divine imposed on us by the Church. If we can clear our minds of this ecclesiastical ballast and think of 'God' as the opening of our minds to greater, hitherto unsuspected vistas of understanding and, moreover, to an understanding which liberates us from our meddling, restless, smaller selves which are always yearning for satisfaction, then the phrase automatically assumes greater significance. In this sense, then, we can render the words into modern English as: 'Happy indeed are those who persist in their search for God, for they will certainly be rewarded.'

Illustrations of what this means in practice is given below in instances of advice to aspirants by three masters living at different times over the last 700 years or so. The first is that given by Chinese Ch'an (Zen) master Kao Feng (1238–1295):

> If we train in self-cultivation, we should strive like a prisoner condemned to death and awaiting execution in a jail. It happens that one evening the jailer has a few drinks, gets drunk and falls into a heavy sleep. Taking advantage of this unique chance, the prisoner rids himself of the *cangue*[21] and fetters and escapes under cover of darkness. The place is infested with tigers and poisonous snakes, but he runs away without paying attention to them. Why is this possible? Because his keenness is to escape at all costs. If we develop the same mind in our self-cultivation, we are bound to succeed.[22] [23]

In another place, Kao says that if we really give ourselves up wholly to the pursuit of satori 'with unbroken continuity' and are not successful, he will be content to descend to the deepest and hottest hells for his deceitful words.

The next example is from the discourses of Han Shan (1546–1623).

> Ch'an training consists solely of concentration on that which is (self-existent) before your mind is disturbed by a thought, and if you exert yourself unremittingly, self-realisation is bound to follow very quickly.[24]

In another place during this discourse he says:

> A student determined to escape from the wheel of birth and death, should know that, because of the unceasing flow of his thoughts, he is unable to put an end to samsara. If he now wishes to stop it, he should lay down all his feelings and

passions, and lay them down again and again until he is rid of them all.[25]

This may seem unusual to the Western view of things, but it simply means total commitment to the aim of answering the question: Is there any God? or What does it all mean? or, in Christian terms, devoting oneself to God in all things at all times.

Attentive awareness of this kind is like the eventual boiling of water in the kettle when it is held long enough over a source of heat.

The next example, a modern one, is the advice given by Master Hsu Yun (1840–1959):

> At all times and in all places this doubt should be looked into unremittingly, like an ever-flowing stream, without giving rise to a second thought... when the state of purity and emptiness appears... one should arouse the doubt to be immediately followed by one's awareness and contemplation of this state. Awareness of this state is freedom from illusion; this is wisdom.

The 'doubt' Hsu Yun refers to in this passage is the 'hunger and thirst' of needing to know. In Zen practice it is the cultivation of a feeling of insecurity similar to worry and uncertainty which eventually promotes a constant return of the attention to the basic question (Chin. hua t'ou) 'What?' or 'Who?' In the West we would say: 'What is it all about? What is the meaning of life?' In this case the question is reduced to the one word, *Who?* or *What?* and reinforced by the feeling of doubt to become an all-embracing, all-consuming question which fills the hours of the day until the solution breaks in upon one.

Blessed are the merciful, for they shall obtain mercy.

Here, Jesus is referring to the simple samsaric laws of cause and effect, of which most people are aware. Buddhism (and certainly Christ himself) is cognizant of the fact that these laws not only apply to this life but also to other lives in the future. So it is that anyone who practises mercilessness in this life may appear to get away with it, as many tyrants appear to have done in history, but this is, in fact, an illusion. Inexorably, the law of cause and effect will come into action sooner or later so that a balance is achieved. Conversely, those who practice compassion and forgiveness will find the same at the hands of others in this life or in a reincarnation.

Blessed are the pure in heart, for they shall see God.

This corresponds to **Matthew 5, 3**, and those who are 'poor in spirit'. Purity of heart does not refer exclusively to 'the good life', which has for so long been assumed in this connection, although the 'good life', the moral life, is certainly an invariable prerequisite, but it means acquiring that state of mind alluded to above, where all discursive thought is abandoned for a single-minded concentration on what Zen calls the One. To relieve the reader of an all too frequent reference to Buddhism and to Zen in particular, the next example comes from Islam.

> Abu Sayed said: 'All the hundred and twenty-four thousand prophets were sent to preach one word. They bade the people say, 'Allah,' and devote themselves to Him. Those who heard this word by the ear alone let it go out by the other ear; but those who heard it with their souls imprinted it on their souls and repeated it until it penetrated their hearts and souls and their whole beings became this word; they were released from the sound of the letters. Having understood the spiritual meaning of this word, they became so absorbed in it that they were no more conscious of their own non-existence.'[26]

It will be seen at once how similar this is to the repetition of the Zen *koan* or the Indian *mantra* in producing single-minded absorption and from there (by implication) to the sight of God of which Jesus speaks. Again, the only difference between the two expressions of religious devotion is in approach: the one is concerned with impersonal Mind, while the other is the bhakti concentration on the person of God through the repetition of His name.

Blessed are the peacemakers, for they shall be called sons of God.

For centuries, this has been acknowledged as the worthy pursuit of arbitrating between contending parties, of pouring oil on the waves of human dissension, thereby producing a more harmonious environment and, by implication, a more harmonious world. Honourable and needful though this certainly is, it subtly misses the point. We are quite willing to accept the idea that a loving God would wish everyone to live in peace with his neighbour so that in this way we mortals reflect His own love towards us. In addition, the interpretation appears to be strengthened by Jesus' own exhortations to 'love your enemies, do good to them that persecute you and despitefully use you' to 'turn the other cheek' and in general to be in line with the second commandment.

There is, however, another interpretation which is equally, if not more, persuasive. The word 'peace' (here, the Hebrew, *shalom*) is rooted in the idea of health, completeness, integration and can be compared with our own word 'whole', from which the word of greeting 'hail' (hale, healthy, whole) is also derived. Thus, the archaic 'Hail to thee!' originally meant 'Goodness or health (or wholesomeness) to thee!' As an opening to human contact it is a peaceful approach signifying 'I mean well' and expressed as 'I wish you well.' The same is true of its use in the Semitic and Hebrew languages. If we apply this idea to the biblical saying, then, it assumes a different aspect. 'Blessed are those who promote wholeness...' By 'wholeness' is meant 'integration, wholeness of mind' in the sense described and illustrated in all the examples given above. It means that those are truly blessed who can transmit the message of integrative seeing to others who walk in darkness. They spread light and liberation, and so in this sense they are the 'sons of God' or the 'children of God', since they are directly affiliated to the light of understanding. Inasmuch as their work promotes this understanding and breeds respect for all living beings and the world in general, animate and inanimate, it is blessed indeed.

Blessed are those who are persecuted for righteousness' sake, for theirs is the kingdom of Heaven.

This is the logical extension of the verse above. Because men in general did not seek the light in Christ's day anymore than they do now, but are content in the main with the fetters of their social conditioning and their instinctive reactions, the task of those leading them towards liberation from these has never been an easy one. Frequently enough, it has been a downright dangerous undertaking. Not only the example of Christ, but also that of Socrates some five hundred years before his advent is a clear example of what can happen to those who champion advance in human consciousness. Although it is characteristic of Jesus to harp on the string of persecution, it remains a fact even today that with the *bhakti* religions, such as Judaism, Islam and orthodox Catholicism, there is great resistance to the idea of revision, despite the fact that their ancient structures no longer fit in anymore with the circumstances of modern life.[27] However, in the case of all three, anyone bent on bringing about a change of attitude which emphasises that freedom of mind spoken of in this essay at the expense of traditional observance would certainly meet with intense opposition aimed at removing him from circulation. And this, ironically enough, despite the fact that all three have sprung from the same recognition of truth. This is because each declares and imposes, while Buddhism does not and is here the one exception. Like scientific investigation, it posits an issue, examines the facts which surround it and draws conclusions.

The Buddhist argument moves from complication to simplicity, from bondage to liberation, from samsara to nirvana, not the other way round. That is to say, in its teaching it does not begin with the illumined state experienced by someone else and from that develop a religious system, but, on the contrary, begins with the state in which we find ourselves and moves from there towards personal illumination. The Buddha's own illumined experience is used as a comparison to measure our own progress.

The desire to persecute those who do not share our beliefs, for example, arises from the will to vindicate ourselves. The will to vindicate ourselves in turn stems from a lack of personal integration and a state of insecurity. All this can ultimately be traced to a state of not being sure about things, about our relationship to God and our fellow man.

Buddhism would assert that it is a basic ignorance of our inner world, the mind, and, consequently, an ignorance of our true interrelationship with the outer world, and, particularly, of our kinship with others. Its declared aim is to dispel this primordial ignorance. If, in doing so, those who are illumined (strictly speaking, they can subscribe to any religion) are persecuted, they are especially to be honoured (blessed) because this proves that they are of the kingdom of Heaven. To put the matter another way, we could say:

'People who are persecuted for bringing light to others (or putting them on the right way towards enlightenment or a knowledge of God) are to be (especially) honoured, for they are the true possessors of an enlightened mind.'

Rabbi Jeshua suggests that those who know the truth about the relationship above are not concerned about what happens to the body during persecution since they dwell in another state of mind which is beyond suffering in any form, mental or physical. It does *not* mean that those who are persecuted for spreading the gospel are blessed and can enjoy the kingdom of God in an after life (as a reward), although this interpretation in its simplicity has suited the Church for many centuries. In the first place, the state of mind Jesus refers to as the 'kingdom of Heaven' is now, not later, and in the second, no one is blessed for being persecuted. But to be beyond persecution, to rise above it in a way given in the examples below is to be truly blessed. Thus, Hugh Latimer, the translator of the Bible into English, could say to his companion at the stake:

> Be of good comfort, Master Ridley, and play the man. We shall this day light such a candle by God's grace in England as (I trust) shall never be put out. AD 1570

Sir Thomas More could joke about his condition prior to being beheaded:

> I pray you, Lieutenant, see me safe up, and my coming down let me shift for myself.
> **(uttered on mounting the scaffold in the year 1535)**

Or in the case of the 17th century samurai who, while he was being hacked to death by his enemies, could quote from an old poem on the beauty and evanescence of cherry blossom. Or of the priest, Kolbe, who in a moment of true enlightenment in Auschwitz, stepped forward to offer his own life for that of a fellow prisoner who had been condemned to death. Or in the case of the Chinese sage and Buddhist whom a pack of Red Guards discovered in the mountain recesses of northern China. They escorted him to the valley where they were intent upon exposing and humiliating him before the people. During the descent, he sang and laughed and talked to them of the teaching which transcends life and death. But they scorned the old fellow and laughed at him, telling him he was an old fool. 'Ah, I see you don't believe me,' he said at last, 'What a pity!' So saying, he continued to sing and chant from the sutras, but when the party reached the bottom of the mountain, the guards had only a corpse to show for their trouble. And the many tens of thousands of other cases in every culture and every age where a glimpse of the kingdom of Heaven has enabled individuals to transcend themselves.

---

[1] There are any amount of references in the New Testament which refer to the need to humble oneself, to take the lower seat at the rich man's feast, to be like little children, to whom the kingdom of God and heaven is accessible, that the kingdom of heaven is of the nature of a child's unconscious simplicity, and that to enter the kingdom we must be like them and that the "first shall be last and the last first" and so on.

[2] The interview referred to took place in the early fifties and is a more or less verbatim report of what was exchanged between about a dozen music lovers who talked to the pianist after a performance at the De Montfort Hall, Leicester. The pianist has since died, as have many of those who were present, and so no specific references can be made or permission sought to print names. The interview nevertheless took place in the lounge of the hotel at which the pianist was staying.

[3] Blofeld, J. *The Zen Teaching of Huang Po*, (The Wan Ling Record), p.130 and 131.

[4] There is no doubt that faith or 'belief before knowledge' plays a part in Buddhism, too. There must be an acceptance, for example, of the fact that one *can* be enlightened with effort. Sometimes, even after effort without the blessing of enlightenment, there is need for faith to continue the effort.

[5] Jesus expresses irritation and occasionally loses his temper at the following points: **Lk. 11, 43-47; Mt. 21, 13; Mt. 23, 14-19; Mt. 16,8; Mt. 23,29-33; Mt. 17,17.**

[6] The 'kyasaku' is a flat stick, about 80 cms in length, used to give meditators (usually on request) a short, sharp formal slap to prevent their falling asleep.

[7] See *Dictionary of Contemporary English,* Langenscheidt-Longman, 1995, p. 490, section 2, 'Religion'.

[8] Taken from Bankei's Dialogues with his pupils, of which there are very many. The story also occurs in English in the book, Wilson-Ross, Nancy, *The World of Zen*, New York, Random House, 1960. p. 79.

[9] Occurring in Waddell, Norman, ed., *The Unborn* (Die Zen-Lehre vom Ungeborenen), München, Otto Wilhelm Barth Verlag, 1984, p. 130.

[10] Quotation taken from Fromm, E., D.T. Suzuki, and R. de Martino *Zen Buddhism and Psychoanalysis.*London: George Allen and Unwin, 1960, p.166.

[11] See Fromm et al.

[12] See Fromm et al, p. 166-167.

[13] The original German runs: Ein Traum ist unser Leben hier/Auf Erden hier./Wie Schatten auf den Wogen schweben/Und schwinden wir/Und messen unsere trägen Tritte/Nach Raum und Zeit – und sind (und wissen's nicht)/In Mitte der Ewigkeit.

[14] The line is taken from T.S. Eliot's poem, *Four Quartets,* 'Burnt Norton' III, in *Collected Poems, 1909-1962,* London, Faber & Faber, 1963, p.193.

[15] Wei Wu Wei, *Ask the Awakened* (See above at Chapter IV, 8). Section 8, p. 251.

[16] Wei Wu Wei, *All Else is Bondage* (See Chapter VII, 10 above), xvii, p. 20.

[17] Krishnamurti, J., *Freedom From the Known*, London, Victor Gollancz, 1969, p. 69.

[18] Maharishi Mahesh Yogi, one of the great spiritual masters of our time, took up residence in Hertenstein, Switzerland, for a time and taught from there for several years.

[19] Maharishi, Mahesh Yogi, *On the Bhagavad Gita A New Translation and Commentary,Chapters 1-6,* Penguin Books, 1971, verse 23, p. 288-9.

[20] Waddell, N. (See above), p. 131.

[21] A heavy wooden collar put round the neck of petty criminals in ancient china.

[22] By 'self-cultivation' in this context is meant the deepening of meditation which will eventually lead to enlightenment. This requires discipline of one kind or another (either willed self-awareness during the activities of the day or the discipline to sit and meditate each day). Hence the idea of 'cultivation'.

[23] Luk, Charles, *The Secrets of Chinese Meditation,* London, Rider, 1964, p. 58, Master Kao-Feng's commentary, (b).

[24] Ibid. p. 56 and

[25] Ibid. 50 to 51 respectively.

[26] Taken from Huxley, Aldous, *The Perennial Philosophy,* London, Chatto & Windus, 1972, p. 319.

[27] Since 'God is never found at the end of an argument,' as the Hindus say, it is probably impossible to enter into a dialogue with

these religions in the hope to meet on common ground, despite the fact that this may well exist. It is highly unlikely that there will be any agreement which could bring fruit in terms of a new viewpoint. The best humanity can hope for is the exercise of strict mutual tolerance of each other's opinions and, in the meantime, produce enlightened men and women who have no religious allegiance in the formal sense. This has so far worked very well in India where Hindus, Moslems and Christians have revered and sought the help of the same individual. The work of both Sai Babas is an example of this kind of universalism, tolerance, love and cooperation.

CHAPTER IX

'By their fruits shall ye know them.' (Mt. 7 20)

A time may come when the local heritages of the different
historic nations, civilizations and religions will have coalesced
into a common heritage of the whole human family.
Arnold Toynbee[1]

Looking back on two thousand years of Christianity, what shall
we say? What fruits has it borne? Until its ecclesiastical wings
were clipped by a general consensus of political opinion in the
northern and western states of Europe during the 18th century
and later by the advance of science in the nineteenth century,
we can say with truth that most of it is a horror story without
compare in the history of man. This is the larger perspective
gained from our position at the beginning of the 21st century
and a view which is corroborated by historical fact. Such a
view does not deny of course that this dark history has been lit
here and there by enlightened individuals, nor does it dismiss
the good that has been done by hundreds of thousands of
people calling themselves Christians during that time, both as
individuals and as collective units. Nor can one overlook the
great works of art which the Christian ideal has inspired.

Added to this, such a view does not ignore the great spirituality of the few, recorded and unrecorded, who were able to transcend the social, religious and political bondages of their time. Reviewing the phenomenon as a whole over this long period, we can see that, for better or for worse, the Christian Church has been compounded with our political and social development in a agonizing growth towards the humanitarian principles we enjoy today. At best during this time, its ethical aspirations have certainly been something of a foil to the barbarism which, even now, is still just beneath the surface of our civilisation,[2] and at worst its myth has been an oppressive stumbling block to scientific endeavour in the past and, until quite recently, the freedom of the human spirit in general. By 'freedom', here is meant the freedom to think without encumbrance, to recognize and to acquiesce in truths which may not at all conform with what the Church, or any representative ecclesiastical or religious body might imagine or proclaim to be truth, and, moreover, to avail ourselves of the choice to act freely in accordance with that freedom. Christianity as embodied by the Church, and the Catholic Church in particular, is and always has been quite firmly closed to modification of its beliefs even in the light of demonstrable fact.[3] Many people familiar with Church history could not have resisted an ironic smile when, after an attempt on the Pope's life some years ago, he was rushed to hospital for an emergency operation. Had it been left to the Catholic Church in the past to finally decide upon the issue of anatomy and physiology, there would be no surgery and little effective medicine today, since for a very long time after Michelangelo's illicit nocturnal visits to mortuaries in order to study the human body, anatomy was forbidden as 'a desecration of God's temple.'

For centuries, scientific thought has clashed with pre-conceived Christian convictions, with 'belief', demonstrable knowledge with superstitious fiction but, little by little, biblical legend has been forced to give way to rational, defensible fact, and today, this erosive process is accelerating rapidly. The Christian Church is beginning to topple under the weight of ever more widely disseminated scientific knowledge and historical fact. Today, anyone can read for themselves of the long procession of popes at large in the Vatican down the ages, many of whom for the first 1400 years of Church history were outright rogues by any standards, others profligates of the worst kind, intriguers, warmongers and whoremongers, murderers and decadents almost beyond description. That the Church's history is one drenched in the blood of innocent men and women who have dared to question its authority is something anyone can confirm and condemn by their reading. Universally proven facts such as these and others can no longer be ignored, and inasmuch as it has committed these crimes, whether these lie in the past or not, underlines the fact that the Church has failed universally to fulfil its purpose and, much more important, has failed to understand and practise the teachings of the New Testament. Arnold Toynbee[4], in speaking of this matter in his essay *Essence and Non-Essentials in Religion,* has the following to say on the subject.

> The true purpose of a higher religion is to radiate the spiritual counsels and truths that are its essence into as many souls as it can reach, in order that each of these souls may be enabled thereby to fulfil the true end of Man. Man's true end is to glorify God and to enjoy Him for ever: and, if the ecclesiastical authorities were to make this true purpose of their religion the paramount consideration in the determination of their policy, they would be constantly re-tuning their unvarying essential message to different wavelengths in order to make it audible to different audiences. Instead, they are apt to make the preservation of their church their paramount aim; and this consideration tempts them to insist that their religious heritage must be treated as an indivisible whole, in which the accidental accretions are to be accepted as being not less sacrosanct than the essence itself. They are moved to take this line by two fears. They are afraid of distressing and alienating the weaker brethren, and they are afraid that, if once they admit that any element in the heritage

> is local and temporary and therefore discardable, they may
> find themselves unable to draw a line or make a stand
> anywhere, till the very essence of the religion will have been
> surrendered.
>
> Such a policy is not only wrong; It is also bad psychology
> and bad statesmanship. It is bad psychology because it implies
> that the essence of the religion which the ecclesiastical
> authorities are seeking to safeguard has not the power to hold
> hearts and minds if it is stripped bare of accidental accretions
> and of institutional wrappings. The badness of the
> statesmanship has been demonstrated repeatedly by the event.

Although this is certainly correct, its appraisal is mild. The fact
is that the Church from the beginning has mistaken the non-
essential for the essential. This failure to perceive and act upon
essentials is akin to a woman who falls in love with the
psychologist who is treating her for a mental illness. The
psychologist and not the disease then becomes the most
important focus of interest. Or we can think of a man, Christ,
who comes to tell the citizenry of a town that fire has broken
out in a building. Instead of attending to the fire in all haste,
the public turns out first to interrogate the man. Finding that
his tidings do not correspond with their own ignorance (not
having detected a fire themselves), they then proceed to
murder him for bringing bad news!

In the first instance, the Church has fallen in love with the
personality of Christ and for two thousand years has
concentrated on the man and not the essential message which
was to enable men and women to perceive what is behind the
illusion we call existence in the terms described above. The
man Jesus has been presented to the world by this organisation
as the man, even today, who knows everything, a man for all
seasons, omniscient and omnipotent, the centre of the life of
the Church and the centre of our own lives, the answer to
every question, a saviour and redeemer, an intermediary
between God and Man, the man, we must never forget, who
was condemned and murdered by a miscarriage of the law, yet
who died to fulfil an ancient prophecy and for the rest of

humankind in perpetuity. He died 'that we may live'; his 'precious blood was spilled for us' we are told, and yet all this has nothing whatever to do with his urgent message to men everywhere: viz. that time is short for the realisation of ourselves, that God dwells within us whatever our station in life, that if we fail to appreciate these things we will surely suffer, and that, of equal importance, our attitude to others should be one of love and forbearance at all times. In the second instance, we can see that the fire in the city is important, not the man bringing the news. All the rest is secondary. But it is this 'rest', the crucifixion, the resurrection, the intense preoccupation with sin, the attachment to an extremely vague interpretation of the life hereafter, an obsessed concern with the individual parables and actions of Jesus' life as a focus of attention, instead of searching for the Mind behind all this. All the other matters are secondary, and include the rigid, uncompromising, unthinking, even imbecile attachment to ancient Hebrew fictions. In retrospect, this marginal preoccupation with adventitious matters constitutes a serious aberration from the original teaching. Moreover, it has long since reduced the Church to a sclerotic, religiously incompetent wreck, that is to say, using the word 'religion' in the context of what has been said above, so that today there is hardly any real life in it which is not purely administrative. Belief and dogma, precept and prescription, living in the past and hoping for a future have, for almost two millennia, become substitutes for life itself. Once again, all of this is a graphic example of what we have referred to throughout as the habit of 'looking at the finger instead of at the moon', and in this case of elevating the teacher above that which was taught, and of substituting man-made, dualistic concepts for true religious experience of Unity.

Two modern examples of the 'sclerosis' and imbecility referred to may suffice to illustrate the point.

The present pope and his associates are set against all kinds of contraception and that in a man-made world which, by its increasing numbers, is visibly eroding its own environment. If world population increases at the present rate, catastrophe is imminent. All the world can see the facts, but the Church still sleeps with the idea that the seed of Abraham shall populate the world **(Gen. 1,28),** for the God of Abraham saw that it was good several thousand years ago and he cannot be denied. This kind of conviction and its moral enforcement on millions of people is patently criminal in today's world. Here, a biblical fiction collides with the real world to become a pernicious threat to our very existence.

Another example of ecclesiastical obduracy appeared in March, 1998, reflected in the form of belated regret for the failure of the Vatican to do more in the early forties to protect Jews in Europe from wholesale extermination at the hands of a raving lunatic. This acknowledgement was all very well, proper and necessary after such a long time, but it is important in this connection to recall the fact that the regard for Jewry which obtains today is not the result of the Church realising the enormity of the crimes committed against Jews during the last war, but the reaction of a public which is better informed. We have become more acutely aware of our human criminal potential. In the forties of the last century, however, it is quite likely that Pope Pius XII entertained the common view among the Catholics of his time that the Jews were responsible for the death of Christ, stupid and primitive though this conviction is, and because of this 'belief' he was not so committed to saving their lives as he might well have been had the potential victims been Christians. Again, it was a matter of a reprehensible superstition being confounded with reality. Had he been flexible, he could have abandoned this absurd view and called upon the catholic world to rally against Hitler's madness – and a pope has this power and authority – then the 'Führer' would almost certainly have been dissuaded from his intentions with the result that millions of people would have been saved from ignominy and destruction.

This is not to suggest that Pope Pius XII deliberately refused to do what might have been possible for him. There is evidence to show that he was truly concerned for the plight of the Jews at the time. What he can be criticised for, however, is that he was asleep to the possibility of a change of direction, of doing something quite outside the context of administrative procedure and ecclesiastical protocol. Had he been truly awake to life as his Master was, he would not have hesitated to exert himself to correct the situation. Here was a situation perfectly parallel to that of the Good Samaritan on a international scale, and in retrospect, Pius' blindness and ineptitude, bigotry, partiality or whatever it was which prevented him from taking forthright action was to set him with the Pharisees and others who crossed to the other side of the road to avoid embarrassment.

But so it is when we are in bondage to an idea which has been shared by generations of others and is still believed, even when it no longer has the slightest relevance any more to our lives.

The taming of elephants

The phenomenon of conditioned blindness can be compared with the taming of elephants. While the animal is still small it is caught and tied to a stake by a stout rope. It is then trained by the mahout to do certain jobs, but above all to react to commands in this position for several months, during which it grows in strength and eventually becomes quite familiar with its tasks and the orders which go with these. Later, it is put to work. It becomes attached to its master, for that is its nature, and grows in stature and obedience until it serves human beings as a very useful beast of burden. At night after its work is done, this huge animal is loosely tied to a stick by a piece of light cord. Now, if it wished, it could escape at any time by simply walking away, but the bonds of conditioned habit are stronger than cords of any kind.

Instead of training the minds of those in its care in the acquisition of freedom of mind, the Church has always fallen back on the old soporifics of a better afterlife (of which practically nothing is known) and resorted to what it calls the saving blood of Christ, which was ostensibly spilled for posterity two thousand years ago, so that those who believe such an odd idea may be guaranteed this life after death, about which we know nothing. Clustered around this central concept is all the emotional uproar about Jesus' death and the intensely morbid concentration on the events which led up to it, so that it is small wonder that the cross has become Christianity's gruesome symbol, instead of one signifying the good tidings of a freed consciousness. Practically all the rest of the Church's teaching is an equally morbid concern with sin (especially is this so in the Catholic Church) which, as we have tried to demonstrate, is certainly not the message of the New Testament. This can be very simply ascertained by comparing the number of references to sin in the New Testament, with those which refer to the love of God and the love of one's neighbour, to faith, the need to wake up to life, and to be unattached to the world. With the aid of a computer, this can be assessed within a few seconds. The result is a revelation. More than that, this simple statistic can be regarded as a lethal blow to the Church's teaching for almost two thousand years! Applying the same statistical yardstick, the Christian believer can estimate in the same indisputable way how much space is given over in the Gospels to accounting for Jesus' loving activities, which were the living, practical demonstration of what he had realised in his heart, with those passages in it concerned with sin and punishment. The word 'punishment', for example, occurs only once in all the four gospels.[5]

From comparisons such as these, we can very easily deduce the fact that the reality of the *life* of Jesus was a living demonstration of the truths set out above, not his death. It was

340

proof of that Mind which is in us all. The Resurrection is the triumph of this Mind over matter and Jesus' last reminder to his followers of its existence. This is the essence of his teaching, and the simple, incontestable fact is that he did not preach sin and atonement, but love for God and man **(Jn. 15,17)**.

That the Church has concentrated on sin for nearly two thousand years of its existence is the one great blatant misrepresentation of which it is guilty. It is a disfigurement of the Word, which has placed an intolerable burden on the Christian community (and, therefore, on Western man) since its inception. As we have seen, sin, so-called, is antisocial ego-attachment and, as such, a sign of personal inadequacy; it is seeking gratification in things outside the mind *at the expense of others* with the unconscious intention of gaining a sense of wholeness and stability. In the short or long run it can be seen by the wise man to be unprofitable since it does not lead to the desired result (i.e. stability and wholeness). The better way to deal with our 'un-wholeness', therefore, is to take the direction of what biblical writers refer to as 'righteousness' which, while it certainly has to do with right conduct, has mainly to do with attaining greater consciousness and, at best, enlightenment, however shallow. Light is light, and darkness is darkness. Concentration on sin and its 'atonement', whatever performances this may entail, is like replying to someone who asks us the way to a particular place by telling them what paths to avoid. While such guidance may be of some assistance it is more likely to be confusing. The answer to the sinner's plight is Jesus' good news, not sin writ large.

> What is the good news? That true life, eternal life, has been found – it is not something promised, it is already here, it is within you: as life lived in love, in love without subtraction or exclusion, without distance.

> In the whole psychology of the 'Gospel' the concept of guilt and punishment is lacking: also the concept of reward. 'Sin' – any distance that separates God and man – is abolished:

precisely this is the 'good news'. Blessedness is not promised, is not tied to any conditions: it is the only reality. The deep instinct for how one would have to live in order to feel oneself 'in heaven', (i.e. to feel whole and adequate) to feel 'eternal' while in every other condition one certainly does not feel oneself 'in heaven': this alone is the psychological reality of 'redemption' – a new way of living, not a new belief.
Friedrich Nietzsche, *The Antichristian* (my brackets)

Does this not sum the matter up once and for all? As to the other factor so beloved by the Church, that of life after death or the kingdom to come, this has been very well crystallised by Brother Steindl-Rast in Stephen Mitchell's book, *The Gospel According to Jesus:*

Jesus could very well have made both these statements in close juxtaposition: the kingdom of God is coming and at the same time it has come. By 'the kingdom of God' Jesus meant 'God's saving power made manifest.' Thus, the kingdom has come wherever that manifestation takes place – in our hearts, in our relationships, wherever we are given the strength to overcome alienation. (By alienation I mean being cut off from others and from our true Self, and I use it as the exact equivalent of sin, anything that cuts our wholeness asunder.) There is a parallel here to Buddhists striving for enlightenment while at the same time affirming that each of us is enlightened from the beginning. On the social level, the kingdom has come with every Bodhisattva ('enlightenment-being,' the archetype of compassion); but the Bodhisattva is at the same time the one who for eons and eons awaits what Christians would call the ultimate coming of the kingdom …It is quite true that the kingdom of God both has come and is coming; but this 'is coming' is in the present, not the future.[6]

The question arising in the mind after considering the gospel from the point of view above and from what has gone before is: what have these things to do with a catechism of do's and don'ts, the unhealthy contemplation of a man's death on a cross, with instilling the fear of hell into the minds of millions of people, with the primary preoccupation of sin and death, with the idea of devil and demons, with a gloating and wallowing in the trial and torture of this individual, and with an alien social and religious culture? The answer is: precious little.

A comparison

At the expense perhaps of a drop in dignity but not in accuracy, there is a close parallel here on the psychological level between the acceptance of our religious tradition and that of the much more recent acceptance of Hollywood tradition. The concept of the cowboy in that tradition, for example, as it has been ingrained in the minds of people in the West over the last sixty years or so, is something familiar to everyone. Although the comparison may appear trivial in comparison with matters religious, the mechanics of the process of conditioning are exactly the same. So, too, is the resulting conviction arising from the process. In our so-called 'Westerns', the frequent repetition of bar and shoot-out scenes, the violent fist-in-the-face encounters, saloon break-ups, posses of good men or bad men on horseback racing over desert land either in the interests of pursuing justice or escaping with loads of bullion freshly looted from the local bank are all well established visual clichés accompanied by the tacit assumption (suggestion) in the minds of millions of people all over the world that all this is historical fact. Precisely because the impact of these ideas is visual and because they were projected upon the mind at one time in a warm, comfortable place such as a cinema, for example, where outside stimuli are reduced to a minimum, the hypno-suggestive effect is very powerful. So universal and powerful were these effects that many of the values projected or implicit in films like these have had a profound influence on the American people. The historical fact, however, is that nothing of the kind projected on screens throughout the world ever happened. The bare facts of cowboy existence, the real 'Wild West', has such a low profile compared with what Hollywood has made of it that we would probably not even be able to recognize it if it were shown on the screen for us to review. Life for the average cattleman, for example, was hard, rough and dirty with long hours of physically demanding work. Frequently, it was also lonely work and often enough frustrating for lack of variety. It could well have been that this frustration led to relations deteriorating between the ranchmen from time to time, but the idea gained from Hollywood that one could just pull out a handgun and shoot someone during a quarrel is entirely fictitious. The gun was only used to kill sick or prowling animals and, very occasionally, cattlemen were obliged to return the fire of attacking Indians. Apart from this, life and working conditions were much the same as they are today on large ranches.

On comparing the two conditioning processes we see in the one example, that of the cowboy tradition, that it is a spontaneous and random process acquired by watching films, in the second, that of religious education, it is consistent and consciously directed. We make our first acquaintance with it very early in life. Then there is the fact that this indoctrination takes place for the most part in the sacrosanct atmosphere of a church or its precincts and that it is carried out by an authority with a long tradition to which, in most cases, our parents belong. Add to this the weight of millions of people in the past having given their contribution to the same belief and then the regular attendance of a church service or mass where music and intonation play a further powerful part in deepening the conviction and we have a very powerful conditioning force. By the time we reach early youth, the conditioning is complete and so deeply rooted in our minds that it is very difficult indeed to modify our thinking, still less to abandon the mental structure altogether. It may be difficult, but it is possible. Whether it is possible or not to see things differently is up to us, not to any capacity outside ourselves.

344

The possibility to act independently and consciously was very clearly demonstrated in Europe a few years ago in the case of a collective rise in conscious awareness. Prior to 1989, Eastern Germany, the former GDR, was such a tightly organised network of fear and oppression that it was once described by a journalist as 'the biggest prison in the world'. So firmly was the country in the grip of its rulers that, had someone maintained in the sixties or seventies, for example, that a bloodless revolution would take place before the end of the century in the German Democratic Republic, he would have been laughed out of countenance. But the fact is that just this came to pass. A similar development took place in South Africa. Both these examples demonstrate that we are able to a large degree to determine our own destiny. As far as the Church is concerned, what is desperately required is a new viewpoint, a deeper insight into the teaching which will provide the energy to raise the consciousness of its members. For this, more enlightened human beings are needed within its ranks. This enlightenment, this awakening to oneself need not be the great enlightenment of a master. That cannot perhaps be expected, but any distance taken in the direction of self-knowledge as outlined above would increase the quality of Christian consciousness – to the immense benefit of the Church.

We need to sit down and liberate our minds of all the accrued superstructure of centuries. To arrive at the same understanding as Jesus we do not need any of it: neither pope, nor curia, nor Vatican, nor bishop, nor priest, nor church, nor service, nor mass, nor theological debate, nor book, nor ritual, nor catechism, nor rule, nor regulation, nor any intermediary whatsoever. All that is needed is a humble, vacant but receptive mind and, if we wish, a question: What did he mean by 'the kingdom of Heaven'? Only stillness and an open mind is necessary to penetrate the meaning of this phrase. How near indeed were the ancients to Zen in advocating us to 'Be still and know that I am God' **(Psalm 46,10).**

Non-conceptual stillness *is* the kingdom. But it must be realised and there are no short cuts for the ambitious. Here the ancients were both precise and correct: 'For God is spirit and they that worship Him must worship Him in spirit and in truth.' **(Jn. 4,24).** The 'spirit' is the stillness, and 'truth' sincerity.[7]

Some larger implications

For many believers all this may well sound outrageously heretical and be quite unacceptable. If this is so, we might ask ourselves how it is that the organisation which has always been so quick to censure and to counter any diversion from the norm has also failed so miserably in producing a better world. And how is it that where it has failed, secular organisation has largely succeeded, and not only in the material sector. The flood of information coming to the minds of this generation is so great that a degree of raised consciousness is the inevitable consequence. In the course of its reception, the information has to be processed in some way or other, however simply, and this in its turn promotes the faculty of discrimination and, therefore, judgement. All of it means that those who respond to the information stimulus, and most of us do eventually come to judge the issues placed before them. Christianity, formal or otherwise, is no exception. Whereas in times past the Church was immune to criticism, today it is under fire. Because it has failed to remain a force in the lives of the vast majority of people, we could be perfectly justified in abandoning it altogether. Many people have already taken that step. On the other hand, although to opt out is our inalienable right today, this would not diminish the validity of a great truth. Nor is it a help in a world of deteriorating morals. We are not speaking here of anything to do with sex, but of a disregard for 'the other' in the so-called countries of the 'first world'. This disregard includes all 'subconscious' activities (low-minded ego-bolstering) such as low-minded greed which expresses itself everywhere in our overblown capitalist society, low-minded robbery, whether permissive or official, and the exploitation which this entails, low-minded violence, actual and virtual, committed and implied, low-minded destruction of the natural environment, the destruction of other forms of life and resources for human consumption, which is another expression of low-minded violence and, in some countries, low-minded political and social persecution (which always embraces the low-minded containment and abuse of power) and, finally, almost everywhere, the low-minded refusal to cultivate the ideal of fairer distribution of wealth. There is a greater need than ever today to create and sustain a living ethic based not on the conduct of one man who lived 2000 years ago, but on the recognition of a living ideal of mental health. The world we live in today has nothing to do with messianic prophecy; such an idea is an embarrassment to our intelligence and a hindrance to clear thinking. What is needed is an ethical code lit by insight and supported by rational inference. That is to say, we do not entertain evil (antisocial or egocentric) thoughts, for example, because some 'Big Brother' will punish us for it in this life or in the next, but because it is bad for our own development. If, for example, we lie and steal and intrigue (bear false witness), do physical and mental harm to others, then we shall not feel better in life in the long run, but worse. We will not add to our spiritual stature. We lose our integrity and our happiness, and our self-respect, and this is not worth any substitution we may find in the outside world. This is the Buddhist view, plain and unencumbered by other considerations.

Education and a rational attitude to religion

Rationality and religion, as many people assume, are not diametrically opposed to one another. The ideal of mental health, in the sense outlined above, is something which could be taught in schools, for example, and, moreover, occupy a place at the top of the curriculum. Encouragement in mutual appreciation and understanding is something else which could appear as an item on the agenda of early schooling. In this, the young people who are to be the later generation of adults would be introduced at an early age to apprehend the fact that we all 'proceed from the One' as Buddhists say, and as such, each of us is worthy of what the Christian calls 'love'. This would be a means of giving children a sense of personal worth and social identity which is so essential to our spiritual development, not to mention the stability of our society. The introduction of this item alone would contribute enormously to the reduction of crime, for example. Until recently, the truth of mutual respect for one another could be seen in Asian countries before the concepts of 'competition' and self-assertion were introduced from the West. It was a 'living example' of social harmony, especially in the countries under the influence of Buddhist thinking, and was one of the most precious expressions of its teaching in modern life.

Those pupils in such a school who showed an early propensity for intelligent awareness could, in addition to communicating with and assisting those who are not at their level of understanding, would be trained much later in that awareness of themselves which leads to enlightenment from which point, if the enlightenment is deep enough, they would go on to become a positive asset to everyone around them. If, further, this procedure were allowed to flourish in an environment based on a scientific approach to what at the moment we call 'religion', that is to say, an approach which is shorn of those cultural and historical attributes which get in the way of our understanding, we could for once actualise the essential message of love and tolerance. Instead of the spirit of competition, exploitation and violence we have today, we could eventually come a lot nearer to Pestalozzi's hope of salvation for humanity.

The 'scientific' or 'rational' approach to religion would require us to establish the basic principles on which all the traditional religions are founded, namely, an awareness of Mind and the practice of care and respect for one another. It would concentrate on the development of our acquaintance with Mind to produce more and more people to fulfil Nature's purpose which, apparently, is to bring us all one day to spiritual maturity. Again, it is a matter of helping ourselves. Either we help ourselves or we remain the subconscious creatures we are at the moment. Either we become aware of the need for this and act upon it or we allow ourselves to be acted upon and so be managed by the sub-conscious elements in our societies.

We can see quite clearly in Nazism and Stalinism how these elements have affected humanity in the recent past. These two, and the horrors which accompanied them are not just two historical abstractions which we can now sit back and comfortably review in a time of peace. The minds which produced them and upheld them were there before they came into being and are with us now. This is a fact all of us must awake to and deal with immediately. To put it another way, we can say that the two systems were and still are a measure of our general spiritual development. Our several religions and their legends have done little or nothing to relieve humanity of this terrifying presence among us. Most of man's religions are primarily concerned about their own narcissistic exclusiveness or, alternatively, strive to impose their will on others, so leaving little or no room at all for an interchange of ideas, much less for an adjustment and adaptation to the modern world that this might bring in its wake. The stark stupidity and incongruence of our inflexibility in this regard was graphically illustrated some time ago in the German weekly magazine, *Der Spiegel*[8], which showed the photo of a pious young Jew reading from his book of prayer together with others of his persuasion at a religious meeting in Hebron. Strapped to his side he wears a modern machine gun.

The orthodox Jew, the Baptist, the Protestant, the Catholic, the Muslim and the Hindu may well find all this heretical and quite unacceptable, but the time is fast approaching when our individual religious myths and traditions will have to make large concessions to reality. Since a clash of cultures of the type envisaged by some thinkers today could probably embroil the world in an Armageddon, religious re-education must be regulated to demonstrable reality and not to myth, cant and unsubstantiated 'belief'. In short, and if we are to survive, it must be rationalized along lines which have characterized other scientific and social revolutions towards human advancement.

Evidence of increased consciousness in the political arena and in society

The last 100 years have already witnessed immense modifications in our society, not only in the obvious advances made in science and technology, but also in outlook, mental changes which, along with developments in science, have, like them, both increased and accelerated over the last fifty years to constitute a painless revolution in attitudes and thinking. These new attitudes have affected the way we dress, the way we entertain ourselves, our working conditions and our attitudes to work itself, our relation to sex, to the role of women in society, our attitudes to the body, our eating habits, even the length of lives has changed. This process of enfranchisement, of widening our horizons will almost certainly continue if we are permitted freedom from catastrophe. It is possible that in the next 100 years at the outside, scientific enquiry will have progressed to the point where, having solved many of the problems associated with preserving good health as well as our social well-being that scientific endeavours will be made to discover our true nature. This, as Toynbee suspects, will have produced a *modus vivendi* common to all men on the lines of peaceful coexistence and mutual understanding, and that this *modus vivendi* will also include not only mutual tolerance, but proper understanding of our religious instincts.

Religious exclusiveness is already under duress and in those countries enjoying western-type democracy gradually beginning to pale into insignificance. The time is ripe for us to recognise our common humanity whatever our private religious practices may be. That which unites us all is the common denominator of our humanity together with the mind in us all which is capable of development towards higher consciousness. Because we are growing closer together with every year that passes, we can never return to the provincial thinking which, by way of example, marked the European political stage in the last century, a situation where each nation was convinced that its own culture was the best – with appalling consequences.

A Utopian dream? I think not. Proof can be seen in modern Europe where the recognition that we are first of all men and only secondly believers or non-believers Frenchmen and Poles, Belgians and Dutchmen, Britons and Spaniards has already been realised. Where at one time only internecine struggle existed, we have a remarkable, peaceful coexistence. The very fact that it is impossible today to imagine a war breaking out between, say, Britain and France, Germany and Poland or Spain and Portugal is in itself a considerable advance in public consciousness and at the same time a growth in the process of true civilisation (that is, not merely material, but also mental) undreamed of by our forebears. The vision of the European state has already been fulfilled in the minds of the majority of people living on the European continent; the rest is formality. It was the ideal cherished by a few politically enlightened individuals after the horror of wholesale war over fifty years ago and has now become a reality. It represents another post-war wonder, not, this time in the field of economics or technology, but in politics and in the thinking of the common people. We might pause to consider for a moment that this small advance in consciousness has affected several million people.

Other viewpoints are emerging, too, which reflect a growth in consciousness. One of them is active in putting an end to despotism, a political disease which has plagued humanity for thousands of years. Gradually, politicians are waking up to the realisation that the dictator and the tyrant no longer have a place in the field of human administration, and there are even moves to remove them from office in another country while not actually being at war with that country.[9]

Better communications between countries has led to an informed populace which is now better able to resist tyrannical ambitions. Dictators cannot arise where there is general political awareness. Added to this has been the recent setting up of an independent commission for the trial of war criminals at The Hague, Holland. The idea of committing the leader of another country to stand independent trial is something which would have been inconceivable at the beginning of the last century, and represents another changed attitude to our social order. The bloodless revolutions of East Germany and South Africa as well as the peaceful collapse of communism in Russia are veritable triumphs for increased awareness in the political field, not to mention the gradual, if painful, emergence at last of China from its Maoist legacy.

Even in military circles today, despite the horrors of weapons of mass destruction, there is a new wave of consciousness infiltrating the minds of those who have to do with such operations. The old order of the day of conquest, rapine, plunder and murder of the civilian population, annexation, colonialisation, subjection, deportation, and exploitation has given way to targeted attack on military positions with an eye to limiting the number of civilian causalities, and with the desire to aid the civilian community when necessary during and after hostilities, to the deliberate reduction of risk to soldiers and to compensation for loss of life and limb, and, moreover, to a general unwillingness to enter war at any time unless this is urgently necessary. These are attitudes which are entirely new and represent a revolution in our thinking where military activity is concerned. The idea of war as a game of conquest and self-aggrandisement for the few has totally fallen out of fashion, as have the wars of exploitive aggression leading to imperialism and enslavement. When we compare all these items to the general attitudes of those in power during the 17th, 18th and 19th centuries as well as the first part of the 20th century, it can be seen at once that all of them are examples of more humane and therefore more advanced thinking. It represents conscious advancement, albeit in an area of human activity which can generally be regarded as subconscious and harmful.

Increased awareness can also be seen in the realisation current among millions of human beings that something must be done to curb wastefulness and protect the environment of which we are a part and from which we derive our being. As yet, however, there is no general appreciation of the fact that we, too, are creation, but only that 'the environment' is different from ourselves, an object which can be exploited or not according to our egotistical human way of thinking. However, in the light of what is happening in this area, it is likely that there will be a change of focus in the near future.

There is also growing alertness to commercial criminality and potential crime, for example, ranging all the way from petty corruption connected with the distribution of town council jobs to particular contractors and nepotism in local government to the arraignment of international oil concerns for their irresponsibility in matters of pollution. In Europe and the USA there is a general awareness among leaders there that peace must be maintained wherever this is at all possible, although, despite this, the arms racket continues to be a major source of income for their governments. This could be described as a darker, subconscious area of human thinking and action.

Another vulnerable area is the phenomenon described by some as the 'glass human being' which has come about as the result of the revolution in communications and which, in the hands of a subconscious individual like a Hitler, a Stalin or a Mao, could lead to totalitarianism with the lid off. World domination by monsters like these (and their henchmen) still remains a threat to our spiritual development as much today as yesterday. Among the most powerful antidotes to this possibility is the promotion of democracy, the raising of general consciousness, together with the production of enlightened people who can continue the movement towards a less violent, less egocentric and less exploitive world. For there is no doubt that the quality of life has increased for millions of human beings compared with that of, say, a hundred years ago, and certainly that of two hundred years ago. At the moment, the distribution of that quality of life is still primitive and unjust, but the trend towards extending better material conditions to more and more human beings is clearly visible.

There is no doubt either that the mental horizons of people living in our times, even among the most humble of us, are wholly different from those who lived, say, in Mozart's time, not to speak of those who lived two thousand years ago. In general and in the West at least, they are more self-confident, better dressed, better fed, better cared for in health matters, better informed on all fronts of existence, have a choice of profession, have personal rights and also rights which protect their livelihood and their safety while at work. Especially the younger generation today have freedom of movement and freedom to choose whom they marry and by whom they have children; they are free from banditry and arbitrary justice, either from groups of individuals or from the state. They are free from religious obligation and have long since been free from ecclesiastical oppression. They are free to educate their children how and where they wish, free to buy and sell and trade and manufacture, free to pursue their own interests and associate with others to form groups sharing those interests and indeed much else. Many or all of these liberties were impossible in many countries during the nineteenth century, let alone before that time. In addition to these freedoms which are gradually spreading to many other parts of the world where, formerly, such privileges were much more restricted or even non-existent, both personal initiative and intelligence quotients are on the increase. All this is very positive, and all of it has taken place without the intervention of any formal religion. It has had nothing to do with its anachronistic codes and dictates and has not arisen from any religious zeal to change the world for the better. It nevertheless reflects a 'religious' development viewed in the light of what is essential religion in the sense discussed above. It is an expression of raised consciousness and as such is a benefit to everyone.

Not peace but a sword

It has long been asserted that while the world may change, human nature does not change much and it may well be true that certain instinctive features in us have persisted through the millennia up to now. However, it is both a fact of experience and a historical fact that enlightenment also brings about changes in this respect, changes which have a profound impact on the character. Proof of an awakened state, together with its consequences on human character can be seen occurring as long ago for example as the accounts given in the Acts of the Apostles. We recall the little cowed community of followers, all of whom, except for Peter, bolted to safety when Jesus was arraigned before Caiaphas and Pilate, but whose members later, after the experience of Pentecost, became what Zen Buddhists call 'golden-haired lions', that is, fearless, enlightened people.[10] Whether these changes take place to enrich our personal lives and, as a consequence, enrich those around us depends not on science in which we have an almost childlike faith, but on our own efforts, our own conscious will to change from subconscious to conscious men and women. To do this we have to take the imperative of Rabbi Jeshua literally and 'Watch!' **(Mk. 13,37)** and when he reminded his hearers that he was not come to bring peace, but a sword **(Mt.10,34),** he did not mean dissension, much less war, but that his mission was to *wake people up* from their lethargy, their pathetic dependence on tradition and on 'that which is written', their natural inclination to kill and maim in the name of that tradition and generally to behave either like sheep on the one hand or rabid, mindless dogs rather than men on the other.

How needful this awakening to our selves is and how relevant the message still is can be seen on the streets of Israel and Palestine, in Jakarta, in Afghanistan, in Iran and in the two states of Ireland. Here, to mention merely a handful, we can see quite clearly what it means to fall foul of religious conviction, to be more involved in the coils of tradition than in rising above our lower natures. In the activities of fanatical religionists of whatever persuasion we can see subconscious man at work, the animal from which we have evolved. At such moments of unthinking violence we are not one whit better than the animals we condescend to think of as lower than we are, and our religious credentials are not worth the paper they are written on. What, then, can we do about the situation?

Thinking twice

We can think twice. We can think again about the value of our religious convictions. The horrors of our religious past and of the present must force those of us who can think at all to reconsider our situation. At the very moment we think twice about a thing we are awake. We are alive. We are conscious. In this state we can take decisions free of the hindrance of preconceived notions. We can step out into a new dimension as one steps out from a fetid cellar into the fresh air outside. We can see, as Epicurus saw over 2300 years ago, that we need not be chained to a God-bound tradition, for our God will, from any point of view, always be too great for our powers of conception.

Epicurus gives us something to think about – to think twice about – when he says in speaking of the evil in the world:

> Either God wants to conquer evil and can't, or he can conquer it, but doesn't want to, or he can't and doesn't want to, or he can and wants to. If he wants to and can't, then he is weak, and this cannot be. If he can and doesn't want to, then he is mean, which is also alien to him. If he doesn't want to and can't, then he is both mean and weak, and therefore not God. But if he wants to and can, which is seemly for God, where does evil come from, and why doesn't he take it away?

This is the knot by which all the religions of Semitic origin find themselves trussed, and, seen from their point of view, it is hard to sidestep Epicurus' logic. The solution to the problem he poses is not to concern ourselves with a 'God-out-there' or what we imagine to be His representative. What we have to do, and the only thing we can do in the long run, is to attend to the Light within us, and this begins with awareness. We must disencumber ourselves from the past and start to live in the Now of Eternity. This is easy inasmuch as we are already in it (although we may not be aware of the fact), and difficult inasmuch we want to take our egos with us into the eternal present and that we find, doesn't work. This is why we feel frustrated. Once our egos have been abandoned, together with all our concepts of good and bad, we find ourselves wonderfully free, alive as never before, and, just as important, in charge of our lives. The idea of sin and evil as conceived in the quotation above and in the minds of theologians and others dissolves like snow in the heat of the thaw. We are then the masters of ourselves and of our lives, whatever our particular fate in samsaric existence may have in store for us.

A 17th century samurai describes the necessary state of mind we should possess as he stands with his sword poised at the frontier of life and death. We should call to mind here that he speaks from direct, practical experience, not theory.

> The mind of the warrior should be no different than his everyday mind, whether engaged in battle or in everyday activities. See to it that your mind is open (calm and alert) whether in daily life or in combat, neither distracted nor unnecessarily tense. Your mind should be unattached (and should rest) in a state of imperturbability. This state must not, however, for a moment be allowed to take over so that one sinks into (a state where) one is off guard. If your body is at rest, make sure that your mind is alert. If the body is actively engaged, don't allow the mind to be disturbed, and never let the body be influenced by your mind (be influenced by excited emotions, say of anger or a desire for revenge).

> Don't be put off [so that your spirit sinks] but at the same time don't get involved with what is going on. (My brackets)[11]

This is the mind we need for the future, not only in promoting our own personal mental health and development, but in facing the challenges which lie immediately before us. It is also the mind which, when employed in meditation, will lead us directly to enlightenment. Its secret is that we should not be distracted by anything. Finally, the ego dies from starvation and with it the problem of evil. Only the light and comfort of the spirit is left which some will call God.

It is said that Jesus once made a remarkable comparison which may well not have been understood until today in the light of new possibilities of interpretation. It comes not from the four, ecclesiastically permitted historians of Jesus' ministry, but from the Gospel according to St. Thomas. It is remarkable in that it fits in perfectly with Buddhist teaching and, incidentally, especially with Zen meditation. It runs as follows:

> Jesus said: 'The kingdom of the Father is like a woman who carries a pitcher a long way which is full of flour. The handle of the pitcher broke and the flour streamed out behind her as she went along. But she did not notice what was happening.

When she arrived home and placed the pitcher on the floor, she discovered it was empty.'

It is suggested that the running flour in the parable is what Jesus would describe as the Word of God which, like the imagined perpendicular lines suggested as an aid to understanding above, runs parallel with our lives in every moment, although we might never be aware of it. The tragedy is that when we arrive home (at the end of life) we realise that which we have lost, but at the same time see that the 'Now' of our lives is charged with the possibility of its realisation in every minute.

The Buddha, too, gave his word to his followers that liberation was possible in this life and urged them to strive mightily to break the bonds of samsara.

'Get ye across this sticky mire (samsara); let not the moment pass…for they shall mourn whose Moment is past.'[12]

The future

Scientific endeavour has shaped the age we currently live in and will continue to strongly influence the future. This influence has a marked practicality about it. The attitude is based on the concept of functionality which poses the critical question, 'Does it work?' and 'How can we increase efficiency?' Its concern is for success and performance and therefore with objective phenomena: it is not concerned with values, subjective understanding or with self-assessment.

The danger inherent in this attitude is that everything can be sacrificed on the altar of success, performance and profit. Everything can become, and much has already become, a 'commodity'. The consequences of this can be very clearly seen today in action in the way science and commercialism are at work in agriculture, the pharmaceutical industry, research for military purposes, medicine, the acquisition of land for building projects, the fishing and forestry industries, the exploitation of men and women for profit, environmental destruction and pollution to mention just a few of the more serious delinquencies which have issued from a mindless preoccupation with self-interest. The consequences of this busy thoughtlessness have already been recently expressed in terrorist activity, and it is time for those who are awake to other values than mere money-making to help widen our horizons to embrace an active respect for men and women, for all the creatures which share our existence and for the environment in which we live. For this, we need people who are enlightened, people who have been mentally reintegrated on the principles outlined above – in other words, people who know the nature of the human mind and the samsaric structure on which it is based, and who can act upon this knowledge for the benefit of others, not people, on the other hand, who are mere 'believers', whose role in our human history has so far been a very dubious one.

Our future is fraught with a terrible potential unless there are those among us to question our motives and incentives. The possibility today, for a tyrant to gain the upper hand in any economically powerful country using current resources of information and manipulation, for example, could make Hitler's Gestapo and Stalin's network of oppression look like a tea party in comparison. The nightmarish aspirations of modern medicine realised to the tune of 800 million animal lives each year is already a proven statistic. There is no effective organisation to counter this outrage. And what of so-called 'Globalisation'? Will this mean wholesale commercialisation, the consolidation and polarisation of economic power to a few organisations as is the accelerating trend today? Will it mean monopolisation, together with the levelling and standardisation of values, the substitution of training for what was once recognised as education, the creation of a universal consumer society and the attrition of democracy? Or will it be realised as a serious attempt to bring prosperity and equality to millions of our fellow men? Again, success or failure to make headway as true human beings will depend on us. Our destiny is not written in the stars, but in our own minds.

As we stand on threshold of the 21st century, there are three possibilities open to us: either we go forward at Nature's pace whose time might allow us to annihilate ourselves in one way or another long before we have reached the goal of universal enlightenment, or we regress to barbarity as we did only half a century ago, or we can go forward consciously into the future with our eyes and minds wide open. So far in our religious history, all but a few have been content with the heritage of legend as ritual, tradition and 'belief', but the good news underlying them all is that all of us can aspire to full enlightenment and many of us can achieve it. The enlightenment of the few may be great, that of others less, but that matters little in the long run. Not all plant life in the human garden is made up of great trees; there are shrubs and shy flowers which also contribute to its colour and variety, but all of them turn to the sun. The need for Man to 'turn to the sun' is the essential message both of Buddhism and the New Testament.

---

[1] Toynbee, Arnold, *An Historian's Approach to Religion,* London, Oxford University Press, 1957, p. 266-7.

[2] Here, we need not only confine our attention to recent regressions in south eastern Europe, but also in the Middle East where, despite the ethical qualities preached by both sides, there is resort to the ancient, subhuman ideas of an eye for an eye and a tooth for a tooth.' Barbarism is rife, too, in the exploitive activities of some western nations, in the waste of raw materials, in the politics of expansion at the cost of the environment, human and natural, in the policies of deforestation, in the meat, tobacco, arms and pharmaceutical industries, the conscious disregard of the spread of poverty which our economic convictions produce, genetic technology, Islamic, Protestant and Catholic terrorism (in Ireland) which has held sway in that country for the last thirty years, the prevalence and tolerance of an international mafia and the general decline in the appreciation for the dignity of human life reflected in much of what passes for our 'entertainment'.

[3] One immediately thinks of this pope's aversion to contraception generally and of the dark, ulterior motive behind this policy in the interest of producing more Catholics in the world, but, perhaps just as important, the steadfast unwillingness on the part of its leaders firstly, to admit to much more of its evil past (and therefore to much which is fallacious), and secondly, to reconsider whether its doctrines withstand unprejudiced scientific examination in the light of what we know about ourselves and our world today.

[4] Ibid.

[5] Mt. 25, 46. 'And these[the sinners on God's left hand] will go away into everlasting punishment, but the righteous into eternal life.' Although it only occurs once, it has played a long, hateful role in the history of Christianity. That mankind should endure 'everlasting punishment' of eternal fire after an average life of (in the best case) barely seventy years is for us today an offence to our intelligence, whether it comes from the mouth of Christ or not. Moreover, recent research into post-mortem experience, in as far as it goes, has nothing of this character. In a word, the claim is an outrageous one. Here, Jesus falls into one of his exclamatory moods, reminiscent of the declaimers of the Old Testament where more passion than sense is revealed.

[6] Mitchell, Stephen, *The Gospel According to Jesus,* London, Rider, 1991, p. 73ff.

[7] This has a very important connotation for the seekers of truth, for the interesting thing is that we cannot deceive the higher Self within us. There are no short cuts to enlightenment or, as the Christian would put it, a 'knowledge of God'. We have to be utterly sincere in our efforts to reach this state and be prepared to give up everything to do so. This is the burden of the words 'truth' and 'spirit'.

[8] *Der Spiegel*, No. 41, 8th October, 2001, p. 163.

[9] It could well be that the example of Slobodan Milosović is the first of many. The concept of bringing criminal heads of state to trial can be regarded as a step forward in international consciousness.

[10] The reference to a 'golden-haired lion' in Zen is to the fearlessness and independence of mind which accompanies enlightenment.

[11] Miyamoto Musashi, *The Book of Five Rings,* New York, Bantam Books, 1992, p. 36-7.

[12] Dammapada – *Sayings of the Buddha.*

APPENDIX

It was six men of Indestan,
To learning much inclined,
Who went to see the elephant
(Though all of them were blind),
But each by observation
Might satisfy his mind.

The first approached the elephant,
And happening to fall
Against his broad and sturdy side,
At once began to bawl:
'God bless me but the elephant
Is very like a wall.'

The second, feeling of the tusk
Cried 'Ho! What have we here
So very round and smooth and sharp,
To me 'tis mighty clear
This wonder of the elephant
Is very like a spear.'

The third approached the elephant,
And happening to take
The squirming trunk within his hand
Thus boldly go and spake:
'I see' quoth he, 'the elephant
Is very like a snake.'

The fourth reached out his eager hand,
And felt above the knee:

'What most this wondrous beast is like
Is mighty plain,' quoth he.
''Tis clear enough the elephant
Is very like a tree.'

The fifth, who chanced to touch the ear,
Said, 'Ay, the blindest man
Can tell what this resembles most;
Deny the fact who can,
This marvel of an elephant
Is very like a fan.'

The sixth no sooner had begun
About the beast to grope,
Then, seizing on the swinging tail
That fell within his scope,
'I see' quoth he, 'the elephant
Is very like a rope.'

And so these men of Indestan
Disputed loud and long,
Each in his own opinion
Exceeding stiff and strong,
Though each was partly in the right
And all were in the wrong.

John G Saxe

BIBLIOGRAPHY

Books referred to in this work

Baigent, M. & Leigh, R., *The Dead Sea Scro'ls Deception,* London, Jonathan Cape, 1991.

Balsekar, Ramesh S., *A Duet of One,* Los Angeles, Advaita Press, 1989.

Berger, Klaus, *Wer War Jesus Wirklich?* Stuttgart, Quell Verlag, 1995.

Bhagwan Rajneesh, The Autobiography of a Spiritually Incorrect Mystic, New York, St. Martins Press, 2000.

Blofeld, John, *Wun Chou Record.*

Blyth, R.H., *Zen in English Literature & in Oriental Classics,* Tokyo, Hokuseido Press, 1942.

Buchan, John, *Memory Hold the Door,* London Hodder & Stoughton, 1940.

Bucke, R.M., *Cosmic Consciousness,* 14th ed., New York, E.P. Dutton, 1948

Capra, Fritjof, *The Turning Point, The Tao of Physics,* USA, Simon & Schuster, 1982

De Rosa, Peter, *The Great Myth,* London, 1991.

Dietl-Zeiner, Johannes, *Das Kastrierte Evangelium, Die Falsch Übersetzte Bibel und die Wiederentdeckung der Lust,* Ariston Verlag, 1996.

Eckhart, Meister, ed. R.B. Blakeney, New York, 1941

Eliot, T.S. *Collected Poems 1909–1962,* London, Faber & Faber, 1963.

Fromm, Erich & D.T. Suzuki, *Zen Buddhism & Psychoanalysis,* London, George Allen & Unwin, 1960.

Goddard, Dwight, *A Buddhist Bible,* Boston Boston, Beacon Press, 1970.

Gruber & Kersten, *The Original Jesus*, Shaftsbury, Element Books, 1995.

Huxley, Aldous, *The Perennial Philosophy,* London, Chatto & Windus, 1972.

Jankovich, von S., *Ich War Klinisch Tot – Der Tod – Mein Schönstes Erlebnis,* München, Drei Eichen Verlag, 1984.

Johnson, Raynor. C., *The Imprisoned Splendour,* London, Hodder & Stoughton, 1958.

Johnson, Raynor C., *Watcher on the Hills*, London, Hodder & Stoughton, 1959.

Kapleau, Philip, *The Three Pillars of Zen,* New York, Harper & Row, 1966.

Kempis, Thomas à, *The Imitation of Christ,* ed. by C. Bigg, London, Methuen, 1954.

Krishnamurti, J., *Freedom From the Known,* London, Victor Gollancz, 1969.

Lapide, Pincus, *Has the Bible Been Properly Translated?* Germany, Gütersloher Verlagshaus, 1992.

Lapide, Pincus, *Flüchtlingskind,* München, 1980.

Law, William, *Selected Writings of William Law,* (ed. by Hobhouse), London, 1939.

Luk, Charles, *The Secrets if Chinese Meditation,* London, Rider, 1964.

Maharshi Mahesh Yogi, *On the Bhagavad Gita, A New Translation & Commentary,* London, Penguin Books, 1971.

Milgram, S, *Obedience to Authority,* New York, 1974.

Mitchell, Stephen, *The Gospel According to Jesus,* London, Rider, 1991.

Musashi, Miyamoto, *The Book of Five Rings,* New York, Bantam Books, 1992.

Obermeier, Siegfried, *Starb Jesus in Kaschmir?* Holzminden, Volker Hennig Verlag, 1994.

Payne & Bendit, *The Psychic Sense,* London, Faber & Faber, 1943.

Po, Huang, *The Zen Teaching of Huang Po, On the Transmission of Mind,* ed. by John Blofeld, London, Buddhist Society Publications, 1958.

Poonja, H.W.L., *The Truth Is,* USA, Yudishtara Verlag, 1995.

Poonja, *The Song of Being,* München, Sphynx Weisheit, 1997.

Poonja, *Wake and Roar,* Pacific Centre Press, 1993.

Ranke-Heinemann, Uta, *Nein und Amen, Anleitung zum Glaubenszweifel,* Hamburg, 1992.

Rees, Laurence, *The Nazis – A Warning from History,* London, BBC Books, 1997.

Rinzai, Zen Master, *Das Zen von Meister Rinzai,* ed. by Yuzen Sōtetsu, Germany, Kristkeitz Verlag, 1990.

Rops-Daniel, Henri, *La vie quotidienne en Palestine en temps du Jesus,* Paris, Librarie Hachette, 1986.

Saxe, John, *The Six Blind Men of Indostan* (see appendix).

Schwabe, H., *Was ist Wahrheit, Die Historische Jesus,* Frankfurt, Main, 1998.

Suzuki, D.T. *The Doctrine of No-Mind,* London, Rider, 1958.

Suzuki, D.T., *Zen and Japanese Culture,* Bollingen Series, LXIV, New York, Pantheon Books, 1959.

Suzuki, D.T. *The Essentials of Zen Buddhism,* London, Rider, 1962.

Toynbee, Arnold, *An Historian's Approach to Religion,* London, Oxford University Press, 1957.

Waddell, Norman, *Die Zen-Lehre des Ungeborenen,* München, Otto Wilhelm Barth Verlag, 1984.

Watts, Alan, *The Way of Zen,* New York, Pantheon Books, 1957.

Weddig, Fricke, *Der Fall Jesus - Eine Juristische Beweisführung,* Hamburg, Rasch & Rohring, 1995.

Wilson, Ian, *Jesus – The Evidence,* London, Weidenfeld & Nicholson, 1984.

Wilson-Ross, Nancy, *The World of Zen*, New York, Random House, 1960.

Worm, Alfred, *Vom Menschensohn zum Judenstern,* Wien, Va Bene Verlag, 1993.

Wu Wei Wu (pseudonym) *Ask the Awakened,* London, Routledge & Kegon Paul, 1963.

Wu Wei Wu, *All Else is Bondage,* Hong Kong University Press, 1970.

Zimmermann, Klaudia, Verlag Kandern, K. Zimmermann, 1994.

Standard religious works referred to in the essay

Der Ochs und Sein Hirte, (Ten Oxherding Pictures with Commentary), Pfullingen, Neske Verlag, Germany, 1988.

Dictionary of Classical Literatures & Antiquities, ed. by H.T. Peck, New York, Cooper Square, 1965.

Dictionary of Contemporary English, München, Langenscheidt-Longman, 1995.

The Holy Bible, New King James Version, Thomas Nelson, 1994.

The Babylonian Talmud, ed. by Reinhold Mayer, München, Goldmann Verlag, 1963.

The Bhagavad Gita, trans. by Swami Prabhavananda & C.Isherwood, London, Phoenix House, 1956.

The Dammapada, translated from the Pali original and edited by Juan Mascaró.

Recommended further reading

Adams, Robert, *Silence of the Heart,* USA, Acropolis Books, 1997.

Armstrong, Karin, *A History of God,* London, William Heinemann, 1993.

Augstein, Rudolf, *Jesus, Menschensohn,* München, dtv Verlag, 2001.

Bhagwan Rajneesh, *Autobiography of A Spiritually Incorrect Mystic,* New York, St. Martins Press, 2000.

Borg, Marcus, editor, *Jesus und Buddha,* Berkeley, Ulysses Press, 1997.

Brück, Michael von & Lai Whalen, *Buddhismus & Christentum,* München, Beck Verlag, 1997.

Dalai Lama of Tibet, *The Opening of the Wisdom Eye,* Wheaton, Theosophical Publications, 1966.

Dalai Lama, *The Good Heart,* Massachusetts, Wisdom Publication, 1996.

Denzler, George, *2000 Jahre Christliche Sexualmoral, Die Verbotene Lust,* München, Piper Verlag, 1997.

Deschner, Karlheinz, *Kriminalgeschichte des Christentums, 3 vols,* Hamburg, Rowohlt Verlag, 1986.

Dollinger, Hans, ed., *Das Schwarzbuch der Weltgeschichte, 5000 Jahre der Mensch des Menschen Feind,* Frechen, Komet Verlagsgesellschaft, 1998.

Dürckheim, Karlfried, Graf von, *Japan und die Kultur der Stille,* Weilheim, Barth Verlag, 1971.

Foster, Paul C., *Beckett and Zen,* Massachusetts, Wisdom Publications, 1989.

Gyatso, Geshe Kelsang, *Introduction to Buddhism,* Tharpa, 1992.

Gyatso, Geshe Kelsang, *The Joyful Path of Good Fortune,* London, Tharpa, 1990.

Held, Robert, *Inquisition, Folterwerkzeugen vom Mittelalter bis zum Industriealter,* (Spanish/German bilingual edition), Baar, Swan, 1985.

Herrigel, Eugen, *The Method of Zen*, London, Routledge & Kegon Paul, 1960.

Herrigel, Eugen, *Zen in the Art of Archery,* London, Routledge & Kegon Paul, 1953.

Herrmann, Horst, *Sex & Folter in der Kirche,* München, Orbis Verlag, 1998.

Hetzel, Harald, *Buddha Gautama's Letzte Interview in der Hölle,* Ireland, Wassermann, 1995.

Howard, B.A., *The Proper Study of Mankind,* London, Ginn, 1946.

Hroch, Miroslav & Anna Skybová, *Die Inquisition im Zeitalter der Gegenreformation,* Stuttgart, Kohlhammer Verlag, 1985.

Huxley, *Ends and Means,* London, Chatto & Windus, 1937.

Kersten, H. & E.A. Gruber, *Das Jesus Komplott, Die Wahrheit über das ‚Turiner Grabtuch',* München, Wilhelm Heyne Verlag, 1992.

Kurz, Robert, ed. *Das Schwarzbuch des Kapitalismus,* Frankfurt, Eichborn Verlag, 1999.

Leggett, Trevor, compiled by *A First Zen Reader,* Vermont, Charles E. Tuttle, 1960.

Leong, Kenneth S., *The Zen Teachings of Jesus,* New York, Crossroad, 1995.

Lucille, Francis, *Eternity Now,* Middletown California, Truespeech Productions, 2001.

Luk, Charles, *Ch'an and Zen Teaching, 3 vols,* London, Rider, 1962.

Miles, Jack, *God, A Biography,* New York, Alfred A. Knopf, 1995.

Passalecq, George & Bernard Suchecky, *L'encyclique cachée de Pie XI. Une Occasion manquée de L'Église face à l'antisémitisme,* Paris, La Découverte, 1995.

Ronsac, Charles, editor *Le livre noir de communisme,* Paris, Robert Laffont, 1997.

Rosa, Peter D., *Vicars of Christ,* Bantam Press, 1988.

Roth, C., *The Spanish Inquisition*, London, Robert Hale, 1937.

Sanders, E.P. *The Historical Figure of Jesus,* London, Penguin, 1993.

Suzuki, D.T., *Essays in Zen Buddhism, 3 vols,* London, Rider, 1958.

Thich Nhat Hanh, *For A Future to be Possible,* London, Shambala, 1987.

Toller, Eckhart, *The Power of Now,* New World Library, California, Novato, 1999.

Uli Weyland, *Strafsache Vatican,* Essen, Bettendorfsche Verlagsanstalt, 1994.

Wienpahl, Paul, *Zen Diary,* New York, Harper & Row, 1970.

Wilson-Ross, Nancy, *Three Way of Asian Wisdom,* New York, Simon & Schuster, 1966.

Wolf, Hans-Jürgen, *Sünde der Kirche,* Hamburg, Nikol Verlagsgesellschaft, 1995.

Yallop, David A., *In God's Name,* Poetic Products, 1984.

Zimmer, Heinrich, *The Philosophies of India,* USA, Princeton University Press, 1951.

INDEX